AINDRA
Kirtan Revolution

AINDRA
Kirtan Revolution

KALACHANDJI DAS

INWORD
PUBLISHERS

Copyright © 2022 Carl Herzig (Kalachandji das)
All rights reserved.

For further contact:
Yadav Jani (Yadavendra Das)
aindra.biography@gmail.com

ISBN 978-0-9995419-1-3

Published in the United States by
Inword Publishers
Gainesville, FL
www.InwordPublishers.com

Book design and layout by Eight Eyes
eighteyes.com

Genre: Biography & Autobiography / Religious

CONTENTS

Preface   vii

Part One: America   1
Part Two: Vrindavan   89
Part Three: The Heart   349

Epilogue   409
About the Author   419

PREFACE

A personality like Aindra Prabhu cannot be described in one book. Meditative and explosive, serious and comic, shy and outrageous, simple and complex; a dedicated and expert musician, scholar, pujari, *kīrtanīya* (kirtan leader), teacher, and disciple, Aindra was a composite of diverse, even contradictory qualities—and often misunderstood. But he was always intense. And not merely different, but unique—seeming to be not of this world or bound by it.

Whatever one's view of Aindra's ideas, his potency can't be denied, and even today he remains a leader on the front line of Sri Chaitanya Mahaprabhu's *sankīrtana* movement, his kirtans touching hearts and transforming lives around the world, continuing to attract people to and support them in Krishna consciousness.

Many contributors helped produce this volume. Akincana Krishna das and a team of devotees conducted hundreds of hours of interviews; Vraja Kishor das drafted an early version; and Yadavendra das coordinated the project. Multiple readers offered comments, corrections, and suggestions or otherwise participated in the years-long effort.

Contained herein are stories told from the range of perspectives by individuals who interacted with Aindra Prabhu at different stages of his life. It is far from exhaustive and makes no claim to be the sole, definitive version. There are many, many inspiring and instructive stories about Aindra not included, and readers are encouraged to share their own experiences and views of his life, teachings, and influence.

Likewise, a great cast of characters played roles in Aindra's story.

Some may seem more prominent in this book because they are more extensively quoted, but as many as are mentioned in this account, even more are not—and among them some of Aindra's closest associates. Requests to not be included have been honored; other omissions are without intention. But none diminish any of those devotees' importance or contribution to Aindra's—and Srila Prabhupada's—mission.

After Aindra's departure, one senior devotee reflected, "In order to understand Aindra Prabhu, first you have to love him." It is my hope that this volume will help readers get to know Aindra as a person and as a devotee—to come to love him—and gain a clearer vision of him as an exemplar of dedication to chanting the Holy Names in kirtan and *japa*, maintaining one's spiritual vows, following the instructions of and remaining faithful to the spiritual master, reading books by Srila Prabhupada and the Vaishnava acharyas, serving Srila Prabhupada's Society, and reestablishing the practice of *hari-nāma-saṅkīrtana*.

In service to and for the pleasure of the Vaishnavas, I beg the reader's forgiveness for any errors or offenses and humbly offer this volume at the feet of Sri Sri Radha-Shyamasundar, who daily cast Their munificent gaze and bestow Their blessings on the dedicated participants in Krishna-Balaram Mandir's—Aindra's—24-hour kirtan.

Kalachandji das (Carl Herzig)
May 15, 2021

PART ONE

America

CHAPTER ONE

"Hey," Julie called as she walked in, "you're into spiritual things. Well, get a load of *this*!"

Eddie was sitting on the floor, his long red hair draped around him. Julie tossed a paperback into his lap.

It was 1972, December. Eddie was only nineteen, but he'd been reading spiritual books, like Ram Dass's *Be Here Now*, for a few years, searching, he said, for "truth."

On the book's cover was a painting of a beautiful, blue-skinned youth bejeweled and garlanded with flowers, standing waist-deep in an ocean beneath a cowl of hooded cobras, four arms aloft holding a conch shell, a lotus flower, a mace, and, encircling a raised finger, what looked like a ring of pure energy. Ornate lettering spelled out the title, *Śrī Īśopaniṣad*, and below was the author's name: His Divine Grace A.C. Bhaktivedanta Swami Prabhupada.

Eddie knew where Julie must have gotten it. "The Hare Krishnas were all over," he later remembered. "You ran into them wherever you went." He'd met the Krishna devotees a couple years before, singing and dancing out on the streets of downtown Washington D.C., and they had given him another paperback, *Beyond Birth and Death*, with a macabre cover image of a skull with a lotus flower growing out of its eye socket. He'd been intrigued but hadn't gotten very far into it. "I was taken aback when I read in the first paragraph that we are not these bodies," he later remembered. "And Prabhupada said that it was 'easier said than done,' harder to realize than it sounded. So I shelved it and didn't read any more ... it was just too heavy for me to deal with at the time."

He had met the devotees again that fall, at a demonstration against the Vietnam War. Playing gigs in local bars and clubs, he'd developed a reputation as an emerging electric guitarist, and the band with whom he played lead guitar, Monolith, had recently opened for the popular rock group Iron Butterfly and had been invited to perform.

"He'd been more into acoustic strumming, more as an accompaniment to sing by," one bandmate described. "But there was a transformation when Eddie got behind that '56 Torino-red, white-pick-guard, triple-pickup Stratocaster. It was a sweetheart, and the sound he got out of that guitar was amazing. He was a rare talent. He would go into a trance, get in that zone. We had to make a recording so that he could hear himself, out of that consciousness. And then he started playing with sound on sound, having, like, a communion with his own playing—yearning for perfection."

After their set, a friend had told Eddie that the devotees were in the crowd. "You should check them out," she'd said. "It's your kind of thing." And he had followed her along a trail of incense that led to a circle of devotees playing hand cymbals and two-headed drums, singing their mantra.

One of them, a young woman in a sari, had handed him a magazine and a packet of incense, and he'd given her all the money in his pocket: twenty-five cents. He'd thumbed through the magazine and giggled at a photo of the devotees' unusual-looking guru. But when a devotee had explained their belief that God was a musician, a flute player, he'd been impressed.

At seventeen, Eddie hadn't been able to absorb everything, but in the two years since, he had begun to take the idea of karma more seriously and had adopted a vegetarian diet. To cut what he had understood to be his bad karma to a minimum, he'd reduced his diet to just a few figs a day. Normally, his brother John described, he was "muscular, stout, chubby at times," but he'd become gaunt, almost emaciated.

❧ ❧ ❧

Over the next week, Eddie worked his way through the *Īśopaniṣad*. The book was full of unfamiliar vocabulary and complex philosophy, and he pored over the text for hours at a sitting. "I started reading with the *Īśopaniṣad* in my right hand and a dictionary in my left," he described. "Prabhupada's English seemed very high to me; mine had been reduced to vulgar street English. It took me a whole week to finish, because I was really going through it carefully, trying to absorb and understand it clearly." And little by little, looking up words on almost every page, he began to make sense of the concepts.

"The Supreme Absolute Truth is personal," he read. The idea drew him in. He'd heard of Brahman and Paramatma, the all-pervading formless Absolute and the omnipresent Supersoul who resided in everyone's heart; now he saw that both were facets of an original, supreme *person*: Bhagavan.

He also understood that the Absolute was beyond the grasp of the human mind. But as he read, he learned that the Supreme Person could reveal Himself through bhakti, a yoga practiced mainly by chanting and hearing about Krishna, the Supreme Personality of Godhead.

By the time he finished the slim volume, he was convinced. In the back he found a black-and-white photo of Swami Prabhupada gazing upon him with calm but piercing, all-knowing eyes. He was attracted to the swami but "actually afraid of him, because I realized that I had met my true spiritual master. I didn't read the About the Author section, because I was afraid of him. I didn't want to know more about the author, because I knew that if I found out too much about him, I would have to surrender to him. My head was on the floor and I was just crying and crying, because I knew the jig was up"—it was time.

He couldn't stop thinking about what he had read. And he wanted more: the *Bhagavad-gita*, which Swami Prabhupada kept mentioning. A friend gave him a paperback edition of the *Gita*, from Penguin, but its text wasn't as clear as the commentary in the *Īśopaniṣad*. He wanted to read the swami's presentation, the *Bhagavad-gītā As It Is*.

He figured the best place to get a copy would be the D.C. Krishna temple, but he never seemed to get there. One Sunday, a friend invited him to come along to a "Love Feast," but he was busy and couldn't go.

Eddie's long bright-red hair was a big part of who he was—"the most precious thing I had," he said. "I was very attached to it." He'd been letting it grow for years and wouldn't let even Julie cut it. But he was so upset that he couldn't attend the temple feast that he pulled out a pair of scissors, chopped off a fistful of locks, wrapped them in a brown paper bag, and handed the package to his friend. "When you get to the temple," he said, "ask them to offer this to Krishna as my sacrifice."

❧ ❧ ❧

Eddie and Julie had met in high school and been together since 1969, when, as sixteen-year-olds, they'd hitchhiked the three hundred miles from Maryland to the Woodstock music festival in upstate New York. They had performed together at local festivals, she singing and he on guitar, but their act hadn't survived Eddie's drive for musical perfection.

Julie was a tattoo artist; Eddie worked at a nearby wool factory for a while, then as a carney on the amusement midways of traveling carnivals. Once in a while he would get a paying music gig, one time hiring on to accompany burlesque dancers in a roadshow. But most of their income came from selling their arts and crafts at fairs around D.C.—Julie embroidered jeans, and Eddie did leather work and macramé.

One day around the end of March, the two went into D.C. to check the bulletin board at a music workshop downtown, near Dupont Circle, to see if there were any listings of work for musicians. There was nothing available, but on the way home they stopped at an Indian grocery store, where an empty rack of Spiritual Sky incense caught Eddie's eye. It reminded him of the lotus-flower incense he'd gotten from devotees at the anti-war march and gave him an idea.

Eddie convinced his friends to drive him to nearby Q Street—2015 Northwest: the D.C. Hare Krishna temple. The temple was in a tall, narrow brick building in a tight-packed row of tall, narrow brick buildings, with a half-exposed basement, two stories, and an attic. You could drive right past it without noticing.

He and his friends parked in front and just sat there, staring at the door. "Everyone else was too afraid to come in with me," Eddie recalled. "They were afraid they would have to surrender to something, and nobody wanted that."

But he felt like he was being pulled by some kind of physical attraction. So he got out of the car, walked up to the front entrance, and rang the bell.

After a minute, a young man with a shaved head and in orange robes came to the door. "Hare Krishna," he said. "Can I help you?"

Flustered, Eddie forgot his reason for coming. "Can I have some incense?" he blurted out. "It's all sold out at the store."

"I'll go get some," the devotee said. "Please, wait here."

When the door shut, Eddie berated himself for not asking for what he really wanted: a *Bhagavad-gita*.

Then it opened again, and out came the devotee. "We don't have any incense left," he said, "but maybe you'll be interested in this—the *Bhagavad-gita*."

Eddie was shocked and thrilled. How had the devotee known what he'd wanted? It must have been some kind of divine arrangement.

When the devotee asked for a donation, Eddie gave him two of the three dollars in his pocket (the other was for gas to get home).

The devotee handed him an extra-long necklace of wooden beads. "Here," he said. "Chant the Hare Krishna mantra on these—'Hare Krishna, Hare Krishna, Krishna Krishna, Hare Hare/ Hare Rama, Hare Rama, Rama Rama, Hare Hare.' One mantra on each bead." He took the beads in his right hand and showed Eddie how to hold them. "When you've chanted on all the beads except the big one, that's one round. We chant sixteen rounds every day. Absorb yourself in the sound of the mantra."

"Do you think I could ... well, come in and take a look around?" Eddie asked.

The devotee took one look at Eddie's broad, unguarded smile and opened the door wide. "Of course," he said. "Welcome!"

Inside, Eddie was left to wander around. At one end of a big front room, on what seemed to be an altar, was a painting of five figures singing and dancing and playing drums, hand cymbals, and brass horns. Peering into the kitchen and across, through a closed window, he saw birds, chipmunks, and squirrels all perched on the outside sill, as if waiting for something. A young woman dressed in a sari came in and walked toward them, carrying something in her cupped hands. When she opened the window, the animals didn't scurry away. "Haribol, spirit-souls," she called out, and tossed them a handful of crumbs and scraps. "Do you want some *prasādam*?"

Wow! Eddie thought. *She called them spirit-souls! That's how she sees them!* He'd read about that. "We are not these different bodies," he remembered, "male, female, human, and animal; we are spirit-souls."

"Excuse me," he said.

The woman turned with a smile. "Hare Krishna!"

"Hare Krishna," he said. "Um ... do you think it might be possible for me to come and, well, stay with you guys—just for a few days, to see if you are really, you know, living what it says in your books ... and to learn how I could do that, too?"

"Sure!" she said. "Why not?"

"She kind of blew me away," he later remembered. "I thought it was like a closed club or something and hard to get into." But there didn't seem to be any restrictions.

"Sure," she repeated. "How about tomorrow?"

Tomorrow?! Move into the temple *tomorrow*? Eddie suddenly became aware of how tightly bound he was to his life. "I was tsunamied with the realization of how attached I was, of how many of my attachments I'd have to give up in order to actually accomplish her suggestion of coming and staying in the temple the next day."

He thought of all his possessions—amps, guitars, his cat. He'd have to separate from friends ... maybe even Julie. "My cat is pregnant," he said. "I can't just leave her."

"Don't worry," she assured him. "You can offer a bowl of milk to Krishna by chanting the Hare Krishna mantra over it, and then if you feed it to her, she'll be born as a human being in her next life."

Eddie returned to the car in a daze, unable to speak or even think about anything other than how he had to join the temple the next day: *tomorrow*.

First he had to figure out what to do with all his belongings. "I didn't understand that I could engage things in Krishna's service," he said in retrospect, "and I didn't want to be hassled by having to sell all this stuff. I just wanted to get out of the material world and join the Hare Krishna movement. My friends were thinking I was totally mad."

Some of them had already seen the beginnings of a transformation. "He didn't just jump off into it," one described. "It developed over the period of a few months. He was a free spirit, never just took something by rote. He would analyze the philosophy and make sure it applied to his life practically. He was no unthinking zealot. He was definitely inspired, and he went right to it, but with a certain degree of ... 'digestion.'

"But he was interested, and he was happy about where he was headed. Several things were coming to an end at once. The band had disbanded, and he was still with Julie, but you could tell it was near the end of their relationship. It was one of those jump-off points, and he jumped off—jumped off one thing, jumped onto something else."

There was only one way Eddie could do it: he had to give everything away. Knocking on door after door, he would hold out a guitar or small amplifier and say, "Here ... it's yours."

They would hesitate.

He would insist: "*Take it!*"

"But that's your favorite guitar!" the friend would say. "It's a vintage—"

"I know, I know," he'd interrupt. "It's my favorite—the vintage Strat my father gave me. Take it; it's yours!"

"Like a madman," he recounted, "I started giving it all away to anyone and everyone—my guitars, my amps, whatever I had. I was just giving away everything."

Julie thought Eddie's visit to the temple had driven him over the edge. Ever since she had brought him that book, he'd been obsessed. They had discussed the philosophy many times, but now she saw that he was serious.

"I have to go back to Godhead," he said. "I'm finished trying to enjoy the material world."

She knew what that meant: he was going to move into the temple and never come back. She fell at his feet, clasped his ankles, and burst into tears. "Not now!" she said. "Not yet!"

"We have to go back to Godhead ... so why *not* now?" He had hoped she might join him.

"Don't go! I'm not ready yet! I'm not finished enjoying; I'm not finished enjoying *you*!"

Eddie looked at her on the floor, but instead of Julie, he saw a hungry tigress eyeing him as if he were a slab of meat, keeping her paws on her prey.

"She didn't realize it," he said years later, "but at that moment she was manifesting the most horrible form of the material energy."

He and Julie had been together for three years, but they didn't have any children and weren't legally married, and he felt like their relationship had become what Swami Prabhupada called "mutually beneficial exploitation." He felt repulsed—not by Julie, but by all of material life. "If you're not ready to go back to Godhead with me," he said, "I'll have to go without you." And he stepped out of her grasp, packed some things into a duffel bag, picked up his cat, and headed out the door.

CHAPTER TWO

EDDIE GAVE AWAY every one of his instruments and all his musical equipment and brought the cat out to his countryside childhood home: Father's Farm.

Eddie had been born Edward Franklin Striker on March 12, 1953, in Arlington, Virginia. He was the third of five children—a girl and four boys: Carlyn, the oldest; Chris; Eddie; Graham, who had special needs and to whom Eddie was especially kind; and John—all except John with flaming red hair (Eddie was expelled from school for wearing his too long). The kids' mom and dad, Diane and Art, grew fruits and vegetables, kept animals, and raised their children in a 1960s back-to-nature alternative lifestyle in a log cabin that, with Eddie and Chris's help, they had built themselves in the secluded hills of rural Haymarket, Virginia. The nearest neighbors were a mile away.

"It was hippiedom," Eddie later described. He shared a room with

Chris, which, in the style of the times, he first painted black and then covered with iridescent Day-Glo red and green swirls and images of a solar system and stars, a rising sun, and fantastical creatures racing through the cosmos.

Art grew high-THC strains of marijuana, paid for, he said, by the C.I.A. There was always pot around, and other drugs, and drinking, and the farm was the regular site of big, blowout parties. Art wasn't Eddie's biological father, but he was all of the kids' dad—a musician, collector, amateur historian, and hot-tempered self-educated radical philosopher, quick to argue and hard to get along with. As Eddie got older, he and Art were often at odds, even, as one friend described, "at each other's throats."

Art and Diane were both creative artists with a love for crafts and music. He built and played several string instruments, and she played the Autoharp. "Music was rich in the family," John remembered. "The whole household revolved around music." Once or twice a week they held songfests at the cabin, inviting local friends and musicians to come to sing and play together.

As Art became more difficult and he and Diane got into more conflict, Eddie, wanting to bring the family closer, had the idea for them all to write music together. "One of our favorite things to do," Diane later told John and Carlyn, "was for the whole family to get together and sing folk music. Your daddy would play the guitar."

As for religion, Eddie recalled, "My father was a Lutheran, and for the first few years of my life, we would go to church," where Art, Diane, Chris, and he would sing and play holy music. "My mother was a Roman Catholic, but she didn't appreciate that it was so hard to get answers, like when she would ask the nuns questions and they would say, 'Don't ask these kinds of questions or you'll go to hell.' So she more or less defected."

When Eddie was five, Art put a five-string banjo in his hands and taught him to play in the traditional clawhammer style. Next he gave him a "git-fiddle," a guitar, and showed him how to play bluegrass—traditional folk music from the Appalachian region with roots in English, Scottish, and Irish ballads and dance tunes—which Eddie later credited as "my roots, early influences." And before long, the whole family was performing as a group, playing at festivals and other bluegrass events, sometimes with the renowned guitarist and banjo player Lester Flatt and Earl Scruggs and their band, the Foggy Mountain Boys.

From their elementary grades on, Chris and Eddie performed at school talent shows and assemblies, Eddie singing and on guitar and Chris singing harmony—featuring folk songs by the left-wing singer-songwriter Woody Guthrie. They played at regional competitions and over time began to do shows at fairs and other gatherings, passing a hat for contributions. "Good money for those days," Diane remembered.

From his early teens, Eddie was an innovator, experimenting with mixing different styles, sounds, and instruments. Once, he took the top section of Carlyn's alto saxophone, the sound of which—saxophones generally—he never much liked, and attached it to his flute, which he'd played in the high-school orchestra. He built speakers out of television consoles and constructed other musical equipment. "He had a really, really good construction logic," one bandmate described, "and he learned quickly."

Eddie joined a family friend's acid-rock band, playing Jimi Hendrix–inspired electric lead guitar. "He was also an excellent flautist," John recalled. "Musically, he pretty much excelled at anything he pursued."

※ ※ ※

The family cabin sat at the foot of the wooded Bull Run Mountains—part of the Blue Ridge chain of the Appalachian range—where thousands of soldiers had died during the Civil War. Virginia had been a Confederate state, and Union troops had set fire to the town of Haymarket, burning all but three houses and the church to the ground.

The kids all had experiences with ethereal spirits, whose presence even visitors could perceive, and the family would stand at the kitchen window and gaze out on the ghosts of soldiers riding through the woods on their horses. As John described it, "The area was alive with shadows of the past."

Eddie sometimes played with ghosts in the hills, letting them try to possess his body and then kicking them out. And, as he told and others in the family confirmed, he learned astral projection, by which he could witness distant events. "He was," said John, "very connected to the universal energy, the creation force."

"He was picking up on the *anima loci*, the natural spirits who lived there," Diane agreed. "And in his strong spiritual connection to the land, he was picking up on the people who had been there before, on the All Creator and the fact that we were all one."

As a child, Eddie wanted to be a Native American, and for one birthday his parents got him a kit to make a traditional headdress, which he and Diane constructed with turkey feathers they'd dyed red. "I told him that he had to have Indian parents to actually be an Indian," she remembered, "and he was so mad at me because I wasn't one."

The woods were a sacred place for Eddie, and he and his siblings would follow animal trails up into the hills. When he learned flute, he would wander through the trees playing as the family's goats followed behind.

"One day, I was tromping through the woods," Carlyn remembered, "and I could hear what sounded like a bird, a wood thrush, but it wasn't a bird; it was a flute sounding like a bird. And sure enough, there was Eddie sitting on a log with his flute, and I could hear lots of wood thrushes singing, and he was playing their songs back to them. There must have been at least a dozen singing all around him. Sometimes they'd go into a counterpoint thing, the wood thrushes taking part of his song. It was so unbelievably beautiful. I just stopped and watched and listened."

The whole family hunted and fished for food, and Eddie was an excellent shot, but he loved animals. The family had lots of them—cats, dogs, ducks, geese, guinea pigs, horses, goats, and a donkey—and raised Collies, Pekingese, chickens, and ponies. Eddie's first pet was a drake he'd named Suzy. Through the 4H Club, a youth group organized by the U.S. Department of Agriculture, he bred Nubian goats, showing them and winning prizes at county fairs—even first place with his favorite: Wondergirl.

He would get extremely upset whenever he found a cricket or grasshopper with an injured leg, and when one day Diane accidentally stepped on an ant, he was mortified and decided he would become a bug doctor and learn how to put splints on insects' broken limbs.

But he was also full of humor—the family mischief-maker—and his siblings never knew what he might do next. Once, still a young child, he found a mason jar full of cash his parents had been saving to buy a car, taken it into the bathroom, and flushed the bills down the toilet one by one, fascinated by how they looked swirling down. By the time his parents found him, three quarters of their savings were gone.

When Eddie got a wild idea, he would get what his family called "the gleam" in his eyes and pronounce, "Ah, I got a good one!" Early one April Fool's Day, when Art was sleeping in and the kids couldn't get him out of bed to take them to the store, Eddie rushed into the bedroom shouting, "Daddy, Daddy, there's a big hole in your guitar!"

"Daddy bolted out of bed," Carlyn remembered, "charged into the living room, and grabbed his Martin. 'I don't see a hole,' he said. And there was Eddie, a huge grin spread across his face."

"April Fools!" he'd called out, laughing. It was just the guitar's sound hole. But at least he'd gotten Art out of bed.

※ ※ ※

Now, in 1973, Eddie was returning to the farm, carrying what little remained from his renunciation giveaway: his cat, a couple sets of clothes, the chanting beads he'd been gifted at the temple, and a few books: Srila Prabhupada's *Bhagavad-gītā*, the *Īśopaniṣad*, and a dictionary.

His parents had broken up. Diane was living in another town in Virginia; Art had spiraled into a sinkhole of depression, drinking, and drugs.

Looking back, Chris and John agreed, even though Eddie had what John called a "jubilant spirit" and they all enjoyed, in Chris's words, "spikes of relative pleasure—and we did love going out exploring and communing with nature and playing music together—it hadn't been a particularly happy childhood for any of us."

"We were living with our father's despondency," John remembered of the days of separation. "His anger, his alcoholism—his hell. It was a destructive environment. Eddie had escaped, gotten out. And it wasn't just an escape; it was also a cleansing of all the negative stuff that was happening. He was going through a cleansing process."

But now Eddie was asking if he could stay a few days to think about his life. "I was trying to figure out how I could move into the temple in just one day," he recalled, "and I couldn't do that. But I wanted to move in that direction. So, I decided I would stay at my father's farm for a while and start reading the *Bhagavad-gita*.

"The importance of chanting was emerging, too, because in the *Gita* Prabhupada would refer again and again to the *mahā-mantra*. And then there was the instruction that I should try to chant sixteen rounds."

He was still smoking pot, even as he read and chanted, "but contradiction or not," he said, "it was all having a very serious impact on me."

When it was time to feed his cat, he filled a bowl with milk and, remembering what the devotee at the temple had told him, held the bowl to his heart, closed his eyes, and intoned, "Haaaaareeeeee Kriiiiiiiishnaaaaaa."

For the next few days, Eddie sat at the kitchen table reading and trying to chant. In the *Gita's* introduction he read, "*Bhagavad-gītā* is best understood by a person who has qualities similar to Arjuna's. That is to say he must be a devotee in a direct relationship with the Lord."

It made sense, he thought. Arjuna understood what Krishna was saying, so if he wanted to understand the *Gita*, he too had to develop a direct relationship with Krishna. And Prabhupada was suggesting that he could.

He was especially struck by Prabhupada's list of the five different types of relationships one could have with Krishna. One could be a devotee "in a passive state ... in an active state ... as a friend ... as a parent ... as a conjugal lover."

He reached for his dictionary and looked up the word *conjugal*: "Of or relating to the married state or to married persons and their relations. For example: Newlyweds in a rapturous state of conjugal happiness." He could hardly believe it: Prabhupada seemed to be telling him that he could attain a direct romantic spiritual relationship with the Supreme Personality of Godhead. He wondered how a man could be inspired to develop a conjugal relationship with Krishna. But the *Gita* was clear: "We are not these bodies." His current body was male, but that wasn't his real "self," his true spiritual identity.

He kept reading: "Every living being, out of the many, many billions and trillions of living beings, has a particular relationship with the Lord eternally. That is called *svarūpa*. By the process of devotional service, one can revive that *svarūpa*, and that stage is called *svarūpa-siddhi*—perfection of one's constitutional position." That was his goal, he realized, what he wanted to achieve. And he wanted to achieve it in this lifetime.

Prabhupada explained that the way to realize one's constitutional position was to chant the Hare Krishna mantra, what he called the *mahā-mantra*, the great mantra.

Eddie decided to give it a try. "I was used to chanting Om in relation to other spiritual groups," he said, "so I was thinking that this mantra was also similarly chanted, long and drawn out."

He crossed his legs in a lotus yoga position, grasped the first bead next to the big one that marked the beginning and end of the loop, closed his eyes, and with a deep breath began chanting:

"Haaaaaaaaaaareeeeeeeeeeee Kriiiiiiiiiiiiiiiishnaaaaaaaaaaaaaaaaaaaa."

Another breath, then:

"Hareeeeeeeeeeeeeeeeeeeeee Kriiiiiiiiiiiiiiiiiiiiiishnaaaaaa."

After ten minutes, he felt tired and opened his eyes. Looking down at his beads, he saw that there were still nearly a hundred left to finish one round. How could the devotees do *sixteen* rounds every day? It seemed impossible. *How do they do it?* he wondered.

❦ ❦ ❦

One early morning, when Eddie felt ready to take another step toward surrender, he left the farm and hitchhiked the sixty miles to Georgetown, where he had seen the devotees chanting on the streets.

He just wandered around until he heard the faint but unmistakable clinking of hand cymbals. He ran toward the sound and as he got closer heard the booming of drums and began to make out a dozen young voices singing the *mahā-mantra*. When he turned a corner, he saw a group of devotees dancing away from him, down the street.

One of them, Laksmivan das, saw Eddie running toward them, "like an elf fresh out of the forest," long red hair streaming behind him, a loose shirt flowing over a pair of shorts, and Eddie's round, rosy, boyish face lit up by a wide smile. As he caught up with the devotees, one of his sandals slipped off, but he just kept going with one shoe, chanting with the group.

"Your shoe fell off," one of the devotees, Padma-malini dasi, told him.

"That's okay," he said. "I might lose you. I'm staying with you guys."

For the next week, Eddie hitchhiked into Georgetown every morning to join the devotees' *saṅkīrtana* party and stayed with them all day and into the night, chanting Hare Krishna and handing out copies of their *Back to Godhead* magazine. And over the next few weeks, he became more and more involved and brought books, posters, and chanting beads home for his siblings, shared what he was learning with his friends, and introduced both groups to the devotees.

"He was always expressing a kind of awe," Laksmivan remembered. "I would tell him some basic point of Krishna consciousness, and he would look at me with the most earnest expression. His mouth would open wide and he'd nod slowly and say, 'Ohhhhhh!' He was just absorbing everything—in retrospect, very seriously."

At night Eddie would follow the devotees back to the temple, drink hot milk with them, and listen to them read aloud about Krishna from a book with His name. Then he'd hitchhike back to the farm, getting in around midnight.

"He was happy," John recounted, "joyous and blissful. He had the bliss of the spirit within him, and he showed that."

With his long hair, however, Eddie felt out of place among the devotees—all of the men had shaved heads. "A week later," he recounted, "I was begging to be allowed to shave up."

"Well," one devotee answered, "a shaved head is really for people who live in the temple, chant sixteen rounds every day, and follow the four regulative principles."

"They wanted to make sure I was going to follow," he remembered, "that I wasn't going to shave up and then go smoke dope or something." In fact, he had brought a bag of pot with him, "just in case." So, he climbed out the fourth-story ashram window onto the fire escape and emptied his bag into the wind.

As for his long hair, the devotees offered an alternative to shaving. "For now, why don't you just tie it back in a braid?" one suggested. "Then it won't fly around all over the place." So, he began to go out with the *saṅkīrtana* party wearing a red braid that hung down past his waist.

On Sundays, the street chanting ended a few hours early so the devotees could prepare for a feast at the temple. When they returned on Eddie's first Sunday out, some devotees were already in the temple room, holding beads in their hands and murmuring the *mahā-mantra* to themselves.

So, that's how they do it! he thought.

As more devotees and guests sat down, the kirtan began, and after a while, the lead singer stood up and demonstrated a dance he called the Swami Step, and everyone joined in. Then one of the devotees spoke about the *Bhagavad-gita* and answered questions. That was followed by another kirtan, louder and more lively than the first, with everyone in the crowd, Eddie included, dancing with abandon. When the kirtan came to a close, the dancers collapsed to the floor and then, after repeating a few short prayers, sat in long rows. Two or three of the devotees walked down the line, serving out food from metal buckets. And before he knew it, Eddie, who had hardly been eating, found himself seated before a plate piled high with exotic preparations.

At first he just picked at the food. When the devotee who had been feeding the squirrels and birds on his first visit asked why he wasn't having more, he explained, "If I understand karma right, it's sinful to kill things just to eat. So, I try to eat as little as possible."

She smiled and said, "That's nice. But in the *Bhagavad-gita* Krishna says that those who eat only food they offer to him in sacrifice are freed from all karma. That's why we eat only *prasādam*, spiritualized food. It's been offered to Krishna, so it has no karma."

Eddie surrendered himself to the concept, and to the mountain of food in front of him: rice, a vegetable curry, cauliflower pakoras, and "the most incredible strawberry halava ever." When he finished, he was offered more, and then again, and before the night was over, he'd had five plates of the *prasādam*, including twenty of the thin, crispy papadam wafers, "poppers."

He was one of the last people still sitting, munching the last bits of a popper, when a devotee came up to him and asked, "How would you like to do some devotional service?"

"Sure!" he replied. "I'd love to!" *Who wouldn't?* he thought. The idea sounded attractive, almost exotic.

"Great!" the devotee said. "Let's clean up."

Eddie figured they were mopping the floor so the temple room could be closed up, but when he and the devotee were done cleaning, everyone came back for another kirtan. The singing and dancing went on for another two hours, alternately building and retreating, then getting faster and louder. Eddie lost all sense of himself in the waves of the mantra. Krishna's name was so sweet, so engaging. "My eyes were closed the whole time, and I was just dancing and dancing and dancing ... It was so ecstatic and blissful.

"When the kirtan ended, I opened my eyes, and everything was so vibrant and amazing. The whole world was surcharged with spiritual nature." Then he became aware of a sharp pain: the soles of his feet throbbing, blistered.

❦ ❦ ❦

Late one Saturday night back at the farm, Eddie sat at the kitchen table, reading the *Gita*. "Daddy," he called out, "you gotta hear this! It's incredible!"

Art looked at him skeptically. "What is it?"

Eddie read a few sentences aloud, then looked up to see his father's reaction.

"Don't give me that swami stuff," Art said. "You don't know this, but I read *Bhagavad-gita* before you were even born."

Art had read Swami Vivekananda's version in college. The book had presented a Mayavada, impersonalist, perspective, and "didn't do much good for him," Eddie remembered. "He was still into every sinful activity imaginable."

Next, Eddie's attention shifted to chanting on his beads. Now that he had a clearer idea of how to use them, he wanted to give sixteen rounds another shot. It was the night before Easter, past ten, when he closed his eyes and began.

"I was completely mesmerized. I was really impressed, amazed, because when I opened my eyes, it was already daylight. Time had passed without me knowing it. It was a dramatic experience for me. I felt like I'd gained a profound experience of what it meant to surrender to the instructions of the spiritual master, to complete the minimum of sixteen rounds.... So at that point I made my decision that it was time for me to join the temple."

"Tomorrow" had finally come.

CHAPTER THREE

"I'VE MADE MY decision," Eddie told his father. "I'm going to join the temple." When a familiar combative look came over Art's face, Eddie added, "Maybe just for a week or two, to see if they are really living the philosophy they talk about in their books."

Art didn't like the idea, and they argued back and forth, but Eddie's mind was made up. "Well, look," Art said finally. "I'm not going to have you leave by hitchhiking. I'll drive you there."

Along the way, they reviewed the pros and cons of the decision. "Son," Art said, "Don't you think you might be limiting yourself by entering into monastic life?"

"Externally, it may appear that I'm limiting myself," Eddie said, "but if that can get me to the door to the *un*limited, wouldn't that be worth it?"

Art seemed satisfied with the response. Self-discipline, he knew, did facilitate personal growth. At least Eddie wasn't blindly rushing in.

That night Eddie slept in the temple's men's ashram, a big room on the third story with just enough space for twenty or so devotees to lie in a row on the floor. Just as he was on the verge of sleep, "as I entered into that twilight zone between waking and dreaming state," he had a vision: "Suddenly I was surrounded by angelic, saintly, even godly entities. I couldn't understand who they were or where they were from—they didn't seem to be Western devotees; they were brilliant, effulgent, and godly beings, and they were challenging me, forcibly convincing me with argument after argument, telling me again and again that this was the chance I was going to get in this lifetime—my chance to enter the spiritual world. They were saying, 'You must stay, you must stay.' They were surrounding me and telling me in unison, 'You must stay, you must stay, you must stay and never leave.' "

Eddie felt sure that what he had experienced wasn't a dream, and he understood that this was his best opportunity for making spiritual advancement. "It was very vivid," he later reflected, "and I was solidly convinced. Because of that experience, I decided the next morning that I would never leave this Krishna consciousness movement. They had convinced me that I'd made mistakes in previous lifetimes and that that was why I had been born in this lifetime—and that I must stay, that this was the chance I was going to get to go home back home, back to Godhead."

That day, Eddie made what less than a week before would have been his ultimate sacrifice: he had the devotees shave off his flaming red hair, leaving a long ponytail in the back—a Vaishnava *śikhā*, like a flag waving atop a temple.

"Boy, your *śikhā* is a whopper!" one of the devotees exclaimed. "We have to cut it at least in half."

"And that," he said with a laugh years later, "was the beginning of the end of my *śikhā*! I felt liberated from my preconceptions of myself." Later he had a dream in which Srila Prabhupada told him, "At least you cut off all that hair for me." "It was very powerful," he said, "and I appreciated it. At least I had done that devotional service in my life."

CHAPTER THREE 23

Eddie woke up with the other devotees well before dawn every morning to attend *maṅgala-ārati*, the day's first program. There were a couple dozen other residents, and together they would chant the *mahā-mantra* and dance as the altar's picture of five dancing divinities—the Pancha Tattva—received a traditional offering of incense, fire, water, cloth, and flowers. After kirtan, he would join the others in chanting sixteen rounds on his beads—*japa*—in the temple room, "greet" the Deities in another *ārati*, and then attend the morning class: a reading, lecture, and discussion of a verse from the sacred text *Srimad-Bhāgavatam*.

After class, a few devotees would start preparing breakfast while the rest—nineteen or twenty—went out onto the streets, playing hand cymbals and drums and chanting the *mahā-mantra*. They would chant their way along six city blocks, reaching the main business district in time to greet the rush-hour crowd. Once the morning rush had died down, they would turn around and chant their way back to the temple. They'd get back by nine or so, have breakfast, and be out on the streets chanting again within the hour. With packed lunches, they would stay out all day, taking turns chanting and handing out *Back to Godheads* in Georgetown or on the Mall, the area between the Washington Monument and the Capitol building, which attracted crowds of tourists. They'd stay out for fourteen hours, not returning to the temple until nine or ten at night. Then they'd have hot milk while listening to a reading of pastimes from the *Kṛṣṇa* book and after that, go to sleep. Eddie loved the regimen, which he found "blissful but exhausting. It was all about kirtan—performing *hari-nāma-saṅkīrtana* and distributing books and passing out feast invitation cards side by side with the *saṅkīrtana* party. It was great!"

On one of Eddie's first mornings out, a devotee handed him a mridanga and invited him to lead the chanting. "Okay," he said, accepting the drum, "but how do you play it?" The devotee showed him a simple beat. "And that," he remembered, "was the only beat I knew."

❧ ❧ ❧

One night at the end of his first week, Eddie had another vision. "Practically everyone was asleep," he recalled. "My eyes were open; I wasn't sleeping or dreaming, but neither was I directly awake. Then, suddenly, I heard an amazing sound coming from a distance. It was indiscernible but extremely captivating—incredible, otherworldly. It was unlike anything I'd ever heard—an other-dimensional sound, not from here, completely transcendental. It was getting louder and louder, like it was coming closer.

"At first, the source of the sound was not visible, but then I saw it, as if it was coming out of a painting. There was no painting, only a wall, but it was like how a painting uses dimensions to give a sense of distance and foreground—like a beautiful painting coming to life in multi-dimensions right in front of me.

"It was unclear at first, but as it got closer, I could see that it was definitely some kind of stampede—a stampede of cowherd boys and cows and calves. Krishna and Balaram were there, and they were all coming toward me out of the wall, from beyond the wall—through the wall, so to speak. It was on a different dimensional platform, not confined by this physical realm. It was coming from the spiritual dimension.

"I could hear the sound of thousands of feet pattering, and ankle bells jingling on all the cowherd boys, and the thumping of hooves of thousands of cows, and buffalo horns blowing—all kinds of totally blissful, joyful sounds of merrymaking. Boys and cows and all kinds of beings were running and playing and laughing. I heard Krishna playing His flute, and the cowherd boys were playing theirs. Krishna and Balaram were running ahead, and all the cowherd boys—thousands of them—were racing behind Them, trying to catch Them, running along joyfully.

"The sound was so blissful, and as it came closer, this blissful nature had a more and more direct effect on my consciousness—the experience of *ānanda* upon hearing the sound was increasing and increasing in my heart.

"They seemed to be on a platform four or five feet above the floor I was lying on. It was as if they were walking on glass: I could see the bottoms of their feet as they rushed toward me. Krishna and Balaram and thousands of cowherd boys came from a distance, stampeding over me, and then Krishna was looking down on me with a beautiful smile, playing His flute and looking at me with enchanting eyes. He was glancing down at me from that dimension, down through the glass, and making eye contact with me, with an incredibly compassionate expression. He was just overwhelming me with attraction, inviting me to join them with His glance: 'Don't you just want to be with Me?'

"I could hear His flute clearly, really hear it, and I was listening to what He was playing. The sound was so incredible; my hair was standing on end, and as they rushed over me, it became uproarious and tumultuously sweet. They were all laughing, bursting with joy and chasing after Krishna. It was so much fun, incredible fun, and I was seeing, experiencing it all. Krishna looked at me in such a sweet and loving way. The *ānanda* experience of their influence totally overwhelmed me. And then I fell unconscious.

"All I remember from afterwards is that I woke up the next morning wanting to tell somebody about my vision but was afraid that they would think I was crazy. But the experience convinced me that Krishna was a reality and that this movement was for real. It wasn't that Srila Prabhupada was taking us for a ride and we would end up at the end of life realizing that when you're dead you're dead. It had been only one week, but the experience made me fully convinced of the power and potency of the Hare Krishna movement—that there really *was* a Krishna, that it wasn't just a mythological story."

It was a formative experience for Aindra, and a memory he held close to his heart for the rest of his life and often recounted to others in emotional detail, tears flowing from his eyes, as he preached about the importance of remaining under the protective umbrella of Srila Prabhupada's Society.

CHAPTER FOUR

DAMODARA DAS, THE D.C. temple president, could see that Eddie was a natural—a classic brahmachari "brimming with enthusiasm and always willing to do more. It was as if there had never been any life for him except being a devotee of Krishna. He just drank it in."

Sometimes when Eddie was doing kirtan with devotees on the streets, he would play flute. "I had played flute in my high-school orchestra," he remembered, "so when I came to the movement and joined the *hari-nāma-saṅkīrtana* party, I used to bring it along and play. I played during my first Sunday feast, but I was into jazz flute and my playing was a little jazzy, so it didn't exactly fit; plus, I was overdoing it a little bit, and it was driving my temple president crazy. After about the third time, he took me aside and told me, "Bhakta Ed, maybe it would be better if you just played kartals and mridanga for a while and joined in the chanting—purify yourself so you get a chance to hear Krishna's flute. Then you'll know what spiritual flute playing is really about. Besides, you can't play the flute and chant Hare Krishna at the same time."

Eddie didn't tell Damodara that he had already heard Krishna's flute in his vision, but Damodara's last point made sense, so Eddie put his flute aside and tried to concentrate on chanting.

❦ ❦ ❦

Devotees sometimes performed dramas at the Sunday feasts. But when Ananga Manjari, who was directing one about Krishna's avatar Ramachandra, approached Eddie and asked if he'd play a role, he shyly declined.

"At least take a very small role," she suggested.

"Like what?" he asked.

"Well," she said, "I need a few villagers, citizens of Ayodhya. Why not be one of them?"

It took some convincing, but finally he agreed; he would be in a crowd begging Rama not to leave His home city.

He had just one line: "Rats will overrun the city!" But he was so shy that during rehearsals he could barely be heard. Again and again, Ananga Manjari had to encourage him to speak louder and with more confidence.

In contrast, Eddie had no hesitation about kirtan, and he was frequently called upon to lead the chanting, especially during *maṅgala-ārati*. He obviously had musical talent, and he also had an ability to make the kirtan enthusiastic without becoming too loud or too disturbing to the next-door neighbors, who lived just on the other side of the temple-room wall.

❦ ❦ ❦

ISKCON already had many centers, and with thousands of devotees throughout America and Europe, Srila Prabhupada could not always be directly involved in each temple's affairs. So it wasn't uncommon for him to acknowledge his acceptance of new disciples by mail, sending their spiritual names and directing the local temple leaders to perform the initiation ceremonies.

On January 16, 1974, Prabhupada wrote to Damodara:

I have accepted as my disciples those devotees recommended by you, and their spiritual names are as follows:

Edward Striker, Aindra dasa
Neil Kallmyer, Nilambara dasa
James Machuga, Jagara dasa
Pamela Machuga, Padma-malini devi dasi

Now instruct them very seriously about their responsibilities. To promise to follow the four prohibitive rules and to daily chant sixteen rounds means they cannot deviate. You can hold a fire yajña and inform them that in promising before the Deity and before the spiritual master, one cannot later break the rules without being punished, just as in the law court one is held for perjury. If we simply follow these instructions however, spiritual life becomes very simple and we can go back to Krsna in the spiritual world at the end of this life, which is the success of the human life. You may send their beads for chanting to Kirtanananda Maharaja.

Shortly thereafter, Srila Prabhupada granted Aindra second, brahmana, initiation, conveying the Gaudiya Vaishnava Gayatri mantras to him via cassette recording. By then, Aindra was the most senior brahmachari in the temple, which had moved from Q Street to a prestigious location in nearby Potomac, Maryland.

As Amara das, a new bhakta at the time, described, "Aindra immediately struck me as a humble devotee of Lord Krishna and serious disciple of Srila Prabhupada. He offered me many important instructions on the various details of Krishna consciousness, and whenever I did anything wrong, he would immediately correct me. Initially it was somewhat annoying—there were so many new things to learn, and he was quite particular about his kirtans, and everything had to be just right—but he was so humble and serious about it, requesting me with folded hands to do everything correctly and properly. He was very serious about devotional service. If for any reason you forgot or failed to execute an instruction, he would become very stern. All the brahmacharis were on their toes when Aindra Prabhu was in the ashram!"

❦ ❦ ❦

Now that Aindra had received brahmana initiation, he could serve the Deities directly on the altar as a pujari. He had always been primarily a *saṅkīrtana* devotee, so at first he was a bit reluctant, but the authorities encouraged him. "One day," Amara recalled, "Aindra stayed back to perform his first *ārati*—the noon *ārati*. He took it extremely seriously, studying all the different mantras, items to be offered, and other details. He was quite nervous about it and especially afraid of making any offense toward the presiding temple Deities, Sri Sri Radha-Madana-mohana.

"When the curtains opened, he was really nerve-wracked! You could see him shaking as he struggled to remember all the details involved in offering the *ārati* properly. He took it so seriously! Later on, we joked about how that first *ārati*, which should have lasted about twenty-five minutes, had taken him over forty-five! But that's how careful he was about worshipping his beloved Lordships and executing everything properly for Them."

Aindra dressed the temple Deities in the morning before going out, usually returning around noon to serve Them lunch and offer *ārati*. In the half hour or so in between, he would meditate on his newly received Gayatri mantras.

Whenever he had a few minutes, he would work on learning how to play the harmonium. He would hover over it, pump the bellows tentatively with his left hand, and stumble around the keyboard with his right index finger, figuring out the melodies for devotional songs and prayers.

❦ ❦ ❦

A new devotee farm project was being developed in nearby Delaplane, Virginia, and one day the following spring, Aindra, who was in the area distributing books, decided to stop for a visit. There were only three devotees living on the farm, and when Aindra arrived, only Amara, who had been sent there to serve, and one other, Aghari das, were present. "We showed him our cows and took him around the farm," Amara recounted, "and then Aindra had the idea to take a cow-dung bath. We had also been curious about doing it, since according to Vedic science, taking a bath in pure, fresh cow dung is very purifying and cleansing. Aghari collected the fresh dung straight from the cow so that it never touched the ground, and all three of us stripped down to our underwear and rubbed it all over our bodies, faces, and *sikhas*. Aindra even rinsed his mouth out with the dung, though neither Aghari nor I went quite that far. Aindra was always the most extreme and dedicated among us."

※ ※ ※

One of the attendees at Aindra's second initiation had been Visnujana Swami, the founder and leader of the Radha-Damodara Traveling Sankirtan Party—brahmacharis who crossed America in vans and renovated Greyhound buses chanting and distributing books. Devotees described how he chanted like he was crying for Krishna, totally absorbed in the Holy Name. He had an "intense spiritual charisma," and his kirtans were attracting and inspiring devotees and bringing them to ecstatic devotional heights.

"Visnujana Maharaja came through with his Radha-Damodara bus and changed my life," Aindra remembered. "I love Visnujana Maharaja. He was one of my greatest heroes."

The Radha-Damodara Party had passed through D.C. several times, and Visnujana knew Aindra as a temple pujari. "He was making a serious push to get me to come and be Radha-Damodara's pujari," Aindra remembered. "But at the time, I was deep into a vanity of thinking I was one of Srila Prabhupada's frontline book distributors, and I had done that for quite some time and wanted to continue.

"I had heard that being a pujari on one of the buses meant that I would have to wake the Deities in the morning, bathe and dress Them, do seven *āratis*, prepare at least three fruit offerings, and then dress the Deities again and put Them to rest at night. It was quite a plateful, and I was thinking, *How will I be able to continue with my book distribution in my effort to serve that aspect of Srila Prabhupada's mission?*"

"Yes, Maharaja," he finally said, "I want to ... but is it going to interfere with my book distribution?"

"Aindra Prabhu," Visnujana said, "never say you want to do

something if you don't mean it. Because if you say you want to do something and you're not actually doing it, it means you don't really want to do it. If you really wanted to do it, you'd be doing it!"

"I really appreciated that," Aindra would say years later. "I thought it was a remarkable, intelligent reply. It had an impact on me and stuck with me for the rest of my life. I thought that was great—never say you want to do something unless you are really willing to do it. Not 'Oh, yeah, well, I want to go back to Godhead, *but* … what about my various material attachments, my various egoisms, my egocentrism, my inability to recognize the need to get all the help I can get?' "

CHAPTER FIVE

In 1976 ISKCON D.C. moved to Potomac, Maryland. Damodara had resigned from his position as temple president, and in an effort to help the devotees maintain their vows and to keep their behavior with each other at a high standard, the new president, Brisakapi das, was implementing a policy that everyone living in the temple should be married, a householder, in the grihastha, family, ashrama.

"Aindra Prabhu," he said, "You need a wife."

"I already *had* a wife, prabhu," Aindra replied—Julie had been like a wife to him. "I renounced her to become a devotee, and it wasn't pretty. I'm not going through any of that again. I've renounced marriage and embraced the renounced order."

"I think you really need a wife," Brisakapi repeated.

"Look," Aindra maintained, "I know what you're up to. You're trying to get all the brahmacharis married. Well, I'm *already* married!"

"I've got eleven wives," he said, referring to the five incoming and five outgoing senses, led by their queen, the mind, "and all of them are completely out of control. What am I going to do with *another* one? Prabhu, I'm just not grihastha material, period. So, back off."

At the end of class one morning Aindra raised his hand and when called on asked the speaker, Ananga Manjari dasi, "How does one stay renounced in the grihastha ashrama?" He had given up everything—Julie, his music, his possessions—to join the temple, but now he was in a standoff with the temple president about pairing up with someone again.

"The grihastha ashrama is like going to a feast on a fast day," Ananga Manjari answered. "If you are fasting, why go to the feast?"

Aindra took the answer to heart and through the years frequently repeated it to others, especially to brahmacharis in regard to associating with women and getting married. If one intended to remain renounced, he understood, one had to avoid situations that might disrupt one's renunciation; if one wanted to maintain one's vows, one had to avoid situations that might lead to breaking them. And that required commitment and strong determination.

Neither Aindra nor Brisakapi would relent about Aindra getting married, but Aindra came up with a solution. "You want everyone here to be married," he said, "but I don't want to get married. So I'll leave. I'll go join Visnujana Swami's Radha-Damodara Party."

Brisakapi agreed to Aindra's proposal but asked him to stay and take care of the temple Deities until the rest of the devotees returned from Mayapur, India, where they had gone for the annual Gaura-purnima festival. Aindra hadn't sold enough books to qualify for the trip.

Aindra contacted Visnujana Swami, who was also in Mayapur for the festival. "I told him that I wanted to join the Radha-Damodara Party after the devotees at the temple came back from Mayapur. Unfortunately, news soon came back from Mayapur that Maharaja had left us."

Visnujana had disappeared. No one knew what had happened to him, but the understanding was that he had left his body, and he was never seen again. "I was so disappointed, for many reasons," Aindra remembered, "but especially because this meant that his *hari-nāma-saṅkīrtana* program would more or less collapse. And it did ... the focus shifted away from *hari-nāma-saṅkīrtana*."

CHAPTER FIVE

"The Hare Krishna movement will never be the same without Visnujana Swami," Aindra lamented. "And," he added years later, "it never has been."

Nearby, the president of the Baltimore temple had become embroiled in scandal, and the temple suddenly found itself without resident devotees or anyone to care for its Gaura-Nitai Deities.

Aindra volunteered to help and moved there until a more permanent solution could be worked out. For about six months he was the temple's only resident, every day waking up Gaura-Nitai in the morning, dressing Them, performing *āratis*, and cooking and serving Their meals. If he ever found himself with a few minutes to spare, he would practice kirtan melodies on the harmonium.

One day, a devotee living nearby showed up at the temple carrying two small brass Gaura-Nitai Deities. "I got Them for my son," the man explained, "but he doesn't worship Them anymore. So I want to give Them to you." And he placed Them in Aindra's hands.

Aindra turned the Deities around and around, studying Them carefully. "Where did you get Them?" he asked.

"They're Srila Prabhupada's 'Hare Krishna Dolls,' " the man explained. Prabhupada had wanted to distribute small Gaura-Nitai Deities as "Hare Krishna Dolls," or "Lucky Dolls."

"I don't know how to repay you," said Aindra, overwhelmed with appreciation. And he worshipped those Deities every day for the rest of his life.

❦ ❦ ❦

As the emergency in Baltimore subsided, Aindra had to figure out what to do next. If he returned to D.C., the temple president would insist he get married. If he stayed in Baltimore, he would have little opportunity to preach. So later that year he joined the Radha-Damodara Traveling Sankirtan Party, which after Visnujana Swami's departure had shifted its focus to book distribution.

When Aindra had joined the D.C. temple, the devotees' main activity had been chanting on the streets while distributing books and magazines. They had done fourteen hours of public kirtan every day. But now devotees were spending less time chanting and more time distributing.

Aindra heard reports of how pleased Srila Prabhupada was by

how many books were going out. "Go on increasing books, and go on increasing my pleasure," Prabhupada had written Giriraj das Brahmacari. He had inherited the emphasis from his own spiritual master, Srila Bhaktisiddhanta Sarasvati, who had specifically requested him to print books. Srila Bhaktisiddhanta had reasoned that if a printing press published books celebrating the name, form, qualities, and pastimes of Krishna, it would function like a mridanga, supporting kirtan. But whereas the sound of an ordinary mridanga traveled only a short distance, the printed word could travel around the world—a *bṛhat*, great, mridanga.

Devotees were distributing books in record numbers, and Prabhupada was appreciating their service. In Richmond, Virginia, later in Minnesota, and then Chicago, Aindra was distributing twenty books and up to four hundred *Back to Godheads* daily. It seemed to him like a good output, but it wasn't much compared with other Radha-Damodara devotees, who were selling dozens of books. To some of the bus leaders, Aindra seemed too shy, too sensitive, and too pensive to be successful.

Even though Aindra did not distribute as many books as the others, the bus-party devotees respected his sincere devotional attitude. Dravinaksa das knew him as "an unassuming, quiet, humble book distributor who never put himself in front but humbly did his service without looking for recognition."

At the end of each day, especially during big pushes like the annual Christmas marathon, devotees would assemble to hear the *saṅkīrtana* scores, an account of books distributed and money collected, counted in "*lakṣmī* points." For Aindra, it could be a humbling experience, since there were quotas that devotees were expected to meet, and he didn't usually meet them.

One evening when the bus leader announced the scores, some devotees had collected over two hundred points, some over three hundred, and one or two over four. Each time a score was announced, everyone cheered.

As the devotees' names were called, Aindra became increasingly nervous. Finally, he heard his own name. Then silence.

"What's this?" the leader asked. "*Twenty dollars?* Is this a mistake?"

Aindra stood up. "No," he said, "it's not."

"It must be," the leader countered. "You went out all day long, during the Christmas season, and all you collected was twenty dollars?"

Aindra nodded.

"That's ridiculous!"

Aindra just stood there, trying to look the devotee in the eye. "Well," he tried to explain, "I guess I had trouble with my mind."

" 'Trouble with your *mind*?' "

"Yeah," he offered. "I guess I wasn't so determined."

"You weren't so *determined*?"

"Well," he said. "I was having difficulty ... and ... so ... I sat down and read." No one said a word; no one moved. "I guess I was just in maya."

The leader walked right up to Aindra and slapped him across the face. "Get out of maya!" he ordered.

Afterwards, another of the temple devotees came over to Aindra to offer support. "I hope you can overlook what happened," he said. "That's not the right way to inspire someone."

Aindra just looked down. "It's okay, prabhu. It didn't hurt that much. Krishna is correcting me."

He was soon transferred to another bus, then another. After a while, he felt like he was playing musical buses, like the game of musical chairs—changing every few months.

Each bus had several satellite vans, each van with a leader and two men going from one town to the next. Since he was one of the less successful collectors, Aindra usually served as pujari for the Deities of whatever bus he was on—the service he had previously declined.

⚜ ⚜ ⚜

The devotees on each of the Radha-Damodara buses collected thousands of dollars every day, and almost all of it went toward publishing Prabhupada's books. Little was reserved for the devotees, so they had to find other ways to support themselves and keep up a reasonable standard of Deity worship.

To get flowers, they would drive around looking for cemeteries. Everything should be used in Krishna's service, they reasoned, and the departed souls would benefit if the flowers were offered to Krishna on their behalf.

In Louisville, Kentucky, Aindra found a big cemetery fenced in by a wall and across the street from a forty-story condominium. He strolled through it during the day, memorizing the locations of the best flowers and various landmarks so he could find them later, in the dark. Then, in the dead of night, he returned to "do my *saṅkīrtana*."

"Around two o'clock in the morning, I drove up, parked the van in the condominium parking lot, walked across the street, and jumped over the wall into the cemetery. I had a flashlight but could only bleep it on and off quickly. The cemetery was spooky, totally dark, so I bleeped the light around a few times to get my bearings and find my landmarks. I would move from one landmark to the next, bleeping the flashlight on for a second to find the next, until I got to the flowers I was looking for.

"I would come back to the fence with huge bunches of flowers—wreaths and wreaths of them—and dump them over the fence. Then I'd go get more, dump them over the fence, and go get more, and then I would climb over the fence and put them all into the van.

"But someone up in the condominium was watching my flashlight bleep on and off, thinking it was a grave robbery. So, this time when I climbed over the fence and had just finished putting the last flowers into the van, suddenly there were sirens, and twelve squad cars were right on top of me. And then policemen got out of the cars with their guns drawn and pointed at me, shouting, 'Put your hands on the van and don't move!'

"I thought, *Uh-oh! Boy, am I in trouble!* The policemen came over and shined their flashlights into the van, but all they saw was flowers. One of them came over to me and said, 'Son, just what exactly are you doing out here?'

" 'Well, gee whiz, officer!' I said in my best down-home style. 'Our church is kinda poor, and we don't have the money for flowers to decorate our altar. I didn't think the dead folks would mind too much if we took their flowers and offered them to God.'

"And as soon as I said that, the head officer, the sheriff, just broke out laughing, and then his men followed suit, laughing and laughing and crying their eyes out. The sheriff put away his gun, and then the rest put away theirs, and he said, 'Son, you take some advice from me: you get yourself in that van, get on down the road, and don't never come back.' "

CHAPTER SIX

IN JULY OF '76 the Radha-Damodara Party converged on D.C. for the 200th anniversary of American independence. Srila Prabhupada was there, and though Aindra had been His Divine Grace's initiated disciple for three years, he had never seen his guru maharaja in person.

At first he was surprised by Prabhupada's small stature: "I had this conception that he was a monolithic entity, a singularly huge entity, a giant personality, because his voice was booming and deeply resonant, and he sounded like the absolute truth coming through the ages—a giant representative of the Supreme Personality of Godhead. So, I was feeling very reverential, 'respectfully distant' and all these things. Then when I met Srila Prabhupada for the first time, I was totally shocked. His physique was so small in comparison with the picture I'd had in my mind. It seemed like such a contrast—the profundity of his writing, the power of his recorded voice, and his exalted position had inspired awe, made him seem superhuman."

Aindra wanted to stay as close to Prabhupada as possible, and whenever he could, he would join him on his morning walks, walking near Prabhupada but just behind him.

Each morning, after his walk, Prabhupada would stop briefly at his quarters and then proceed to the temple, accompanied by devotees, to greet the Deities. One day, while the devotees were waiting for Prabhupada to come out his door, someone strapped a mridanga around Aindra's neck and told him to lead the kirtan. And just at that moment, Prabhupada came out.

Aindra suddenly found himself walking just a few feet from his guru maharaja. "I wasn't a mridanga player, really," he remembered. "I wasn't that good then (and I'm still not that good now), but I was doing the best I could, playing in my simple way, like how Akincana Krsnadas Maharaja would play, chanting Hare Krishna from the heart, which is my natural way of chanting."

"I was walking side by side with Srila Prabhupada, just a foot and a half away from him, right by his side, very happily chanting away at the top of my lungs and banging on the mridanga. And he turned to me and sang along—'Hare Krishna, Hare Krishna ...' I was only a step away, maybe a foot and a half from him, happily chanting, happy to be walking right beside him, chanting with him, and able to hear him chant Hare Krishna, too.

"And then he just turned to me; cocked his head back a little in his typical, regal Srila Prabhupada way, tilting his head in that Bengali fashion; looked down at me, even though I was a little taller than him; gave me a very positive glance of approval; and said just one word, which remains with me as my only hope: '*Jaya!*' It was the only word he ever said to me in my whole Krishna-conscious life, but that one word carried so much inspiration and potency. How did I get a *Jaya!* out of Srila Prabhupada? It was simple: I was performing *hari-nāma-saṅkīrtana*.

"When Prabhupada said '*Jaya!*' I took that as a great inspiration, because he was saying *Jaya!* in relation to my chanting, to my performing *saṅkīrtana*. *Jaya* means victory, so I could understand that Prabhupada was pleased with my meager attempt to chant Hare Krishna and do kirtan. I got lifelong inspiration from that to try to perfect my chanting of the Holy Names. I might not be doing anything else that gets a *Jaya!* out of Srila Prabhupada, but at least that much I did.

"And that's been my whole idea ever since. It was not just *Jaya!* to me; it was *Jaya!* to my endeavor to do *saṅkīrtana*, to sing the Holy Name, Hare Krishna, for the rest of my life."

❦ ❦ ❦

Usually when Srila Prabhupada was nearby, Aindra, like most of the devotees, was out distributing books. But one night a *mahā-harināma*, a big public kirtan, was scheduled in downtown Georgetown. It would be like the kirtans he had experienced when he'd first met the devotees; he couldn't miss it.

But his van leader wouldn't allow him to go. "Isn't there any way?" Aindra pleaded. "For old time's sake? For the inspiration it will infuse into my book distribution?"

The van leader told him that there was no higher service, nothing more important, than distributing Prabhupada's books. Prabhupada had been clear about its primacy. "Regarding *saṅkīrtana* and book distribution," he had written Tamal Krishna das in 1974, "both should go on, but book distribution is more important. It is *bṛhat-kīrtana*."

It couldn't be interrupted for anything, the van leader insisted, not even kirtan.

But on this occasion, Aindra pointed out, both could happen: if he stopped just an hour earlier than usual, he could still get to Georgetown before the kirtan ended.

The van leader reacted as if Aindra's response were an act of disobedience. "I am your authority," he asserted. "And I am saying that you are going to distribute your spiritual master's books, not going out for *hari-nāma*. If you go to the kirtan, you'll be going against the orders of your authority; you'll be engaged in *vikarma*, sinful action against the injunction of Vedic authority." He himself, the van leader claimed, was the representative of Srila Prabhupada, who was the representative of all the acharyas in the *guru-paramparā*, the disciplic succession, who represented all the Vedas.

I should be humble, Aindra thought. But when did humble become stupid? He had read all of Srila Prabhupada's books and given years of his life to distributing them, and he knew both their importance and the importance of surrendering to the guidance of one's guru. He just thought the van leader was misapplying Prabhupada's instructions. Chanting was the sine qua non, the necessary condition, the essence, of one's devotional life. And Prabhupada had spoken to him directly, affirming his dedication to kirtan—"*Jaya!*" But now the van leader, Aindra's most immediate authority, was holding him back.

"It was at this point," Aindra recalled, "that I started to think, *This is all a lot of BS*. On one side, Srila Prabhupada was saying '*Jaya!*' because of my performance of *hari-nāma-saṅkīrtana*, and practically the same day the van leader was telling me that if I joined the *hari-nāma-saṅkīrtana* party, I was doing *vikarma*! *I may not get the* mahā *plate for distributing the most books*, I thought, *but at least I can get a* Jaya! *out of Srila Prabhupada!*

"I began having differences with certain managerial points of view. I continued to respect all of these people as devotees, but my point of view started to change drastically. We had a difference of opinion— big time."

There was no question that Prabhupada relished positive reports of book sales. And yes, he had directed that "if there is any occasion of necessity ... we may assign everyone for distributing our literatures; there is no loss for that." But he had also, in the very next sentence, stipulated, "But it is always better if there are also some devotees chanting loudly on the street."

The day after writing to Tamal Krishna, Prabhupada, having read in the D.C. devotees' weekly *saṅkīrtana* newsletter that they were going out to chant on the streets all day, had written to Srutadeva das that book distribution was "the best kirtan," "better than chanting," but followed, "Of course chanting should not stop." And just a year after writing to Tamal Krishna about *bṛhat-kīrtana*, he had written to him, "To manage a sankirtana party nicely is more precious than all other activities. That is the verdict of the *Bhagavad-gita* and the mission of Lord Sri Caitanya Mahaprabhu."

Sadhana provided the power for preaching, Aindra understood. "Books are the basis,"

Prabhupada had stated, but "purity is the force." Purity arose from sadhana, and its essence was attentive chanting of the Hare Krishna *mahā-mantra*.

"Prabhupada's program, especially in the beginning, was based on *nāma-saṅkīrtana*," Aindra later stated. "He never advocated that book distribution should be to the nearly total exclusion of *nāma-saṅkīrtana* ... that one had to take precedence over the other."

"It is this sankirtana which is the life and soul of our movement," Srila Prabhupada had written Srutadeva. "Sankirtana and book distribution should go on together side by side [in "parallel lines," he wrote to Govinda dasi]. I am always glad when these activities are increasing and my pleasure is always increasing."

"The idea of *bṛhat-kīrtana* seems to indicate that book distribution takes precedence over *nāma-saṅkīrtana*," Aindra continued, "but you have to carefully understand the whole meaning. Book distribution is *bṛhat-kīrtana* in the sense that the words in a book have greater audibility; they can reach a larger audience....

"*Nāma-japa* gives us the power and purity to be able to propagate Krishna consciousness in a real way. Similarly, *nāma-saṅkīrtana* may seem to have a more limited range of effect than the distribution of a book, but the truth is that *nāma-saṅkīrtana* empowers individuals to change the world.... It is the *yuga-dharma*.

"Yes, we agree that book distribution is our number-one business. But why? Because it promotes the *yuga-dharma*, *nāma-saṅkīrtana*. We have to continue performing *nāma-saṅkīrtana* while distributing books about it, or else the people reading the books will see no living example of what they are reading and have no opportunity to participate in it."

In another talk, Aindra reiterated, "Why did Srila Prabhupada stress book distribution? Because book distribution is for the purpose of philosophically convincing others to join Lord Chaitanya's *saṅkīrtana* party."

That's how he had been attracted: "I came to the movement because of having been convinced philosophically by reading one of Srila Prabhupada's books, the *Īśopaniṣad*. That's what actually brought me to the point of surrender—reading that book—because it talked about *saṅkīrtana* and the *Bhagavad-gītā* talked about *saṅkīrtana*, about chanting Hare Krishna, performing the *yajña*. The practical application of the knowledge in the books was there in our daily performances of *nāma-saṅkīrtana* in the streets."

Devotees, Aindra felt, were heeding only part of Prabhupada's directive, and public chanting was being marginalized, sometimes disregarded altogether. It was difficult to combat or even question what was happening, and he was concerned that devotees might lose faith in the fundamental principle that purification came from sadhana and that the most effective sadhana was to chant the Hare Krishna *mahā-mantra*. Without the purity born from *nāma-saṅkīrtana*, books would not *remain* the basis. "Book distribution is Srila Prabhupada's heart and soul," he acknowledged. "And *nāma-saṅkīrtana* is the heart and soul of transcendental book distribution."

Improving ISKCON's purity by increasing the amount of time devotees spent chanting seemed to be the most effective way to solidify the basis of book distribution and empower the efficacy of preaching. But when Aindra expressed his conviction, he often got a negative response. "Go out on *harināma*?" he was questioned. "That's impractical, *prabhu*. An army runs on its belly. And we are preachers. We have to be ambitious for spreading Srila Prabhupada's message, not just chant Hare Krishna like *bābājīs*."

He longed for a time when every temple would have dozens of devotees going out on the sidewalks daily to chant from morning until night, distributing Prabhupada's writings alongside the chanting party, just as they had when he had first joined.

❧ ❧ ❧

Two weeks later, Srila Prabhupada was in New York City for the city's first Ratha-yatra. Aindra and his group followed, but without a moment to spare. "We were doing pretty well, distributing a lot of books," he said, "so my *saṅkīrtana* leader didn't want to stop and leave for New York. I had to keep telling him, 'Come on! We have to leave a little bit earlier so we can arrive alive and be alert for Prabhupada's lecture in the morning.'

" 'No, no!' he said. 'We will be able to understand Prabhupada's lecture if we put out extra effort to sacrifice for his pleasure. *Bhaktyā mām abhijānāti*—you can only understand the words of the pure devotee by bhakti, so let's show our extra bhakti and stay out 'til a million o'clock distributing books.'

"Finally, at nine or ten that night, I convinced him we should leave."

It was a seven-hour drive from Richmond into Manhattan, and

Aindra's van rolled up to the temple at around four, just before the temple's morning program. "After *maṅgala-ārati* there was a *japa* period," he remembered, "but Prabhupada was going on his morning walk, so we all jumped into vans, chanting our *japa* as we raced through red lights to catch up with him."

At eight, Prabhupada sat down on the *vyāsāsana* to lecture. The temple was packed full with hundreds of devotees, so Aindra slid into the back. He was relieved to have made it in time, but as the lecture began, his eyelids started to feel heavy. "About one minute into the lecture I started to doze off," he recalled. "I was totally exhausted. I started dreaming. In the dream I couldn't see Prabhupada in front of me, but I was hearing every word, listening carefully."

"The dog is also thinking like that: 'I am this body,' " Prabhupada lectured. "So, where is the difference? The dog thinks, 'I am this body'; I think, 'I am Indian.' So, where is the difference between the dog and me? There is no difference. Simply by dressing nicely? But if you dress a dog very nicely, does it mean that he becomes a human being? A dressed dog, that's all. Dog dancing. So shastra says that if one is still in the bodily concept of life, then he's no better than an animal."

Aindra drifted off to the sound of Prabhupada's voice, dreaming that he was listening to a recording. "Then I woke up and remembered I was in a class with Srila Prabhupada right there. But a realization dawned on me that there was no difference between my being in the class physically and my hearing Prabhupada's cassettes. That gave me more inspiration to listen to them."

The next morning, Prabhupada again sat again on the *vyāsāsana*, but this time Aindra was better rested and managed to find a closer place to sit. Before the lecture began, however, devotees brought Prabhupada a big platter of cookies adorned with roses, and devotees stampeded past Aindra, eager to get a cookie from Prabhupada's hand.

Aindra worked his way through the tide of bodies, swept sometimes closer to Prabhupada, sometimes further away. "Soon I was standing right in front of Prabhupada with my hand practically in his lap. My finger was practically touching the plate. I was stretching out my hand, thinking, 'C'mon, Srila Prabhupada ...'

"The whole time, devotees were getting their cookies and leaving. My hand was right there in the middle, right on his lap. He would put a cookie in one person's hand, then that hand would leave and a new hand would come in. He would put a cookie in that hand, then it would leave and a new one would come in. There were a lot of devotees, so he was passing them out pretty quickly—a cookie here, a cookie there; one hand, another hand; new hand, new hand, new hand; cookie, cookie, cookie ...

"I was, like, 'C'mon, Srila Prabhupada.'

"The plate finished. A devotee took it away and a new plate came, but Prabhupada was doing the same thing again: a cookie here, a cookie there ... and he kept crossing over my hand. It became obvious to me that he was intentionally avoiding me.

"My hand was there, like, 'C'mon, Srila Prabhupada!' The plate was down to twenty cookies, then ten, then nine ... eight ... I'm thinking, 'Oh no! C'mon, Srila Prabhupada. Come on, Srila Prabhupada!'

"Seven cookies ... six, five, four, three, two, one ... 'Oh! Srila Prabhupada!'

"He gave the last cookie away. He didn't give me any."

Why is Prabhupada ignoring me? Aindra wondered. *Am I too puffed up, thinking myself one of the big, important book distributors? Is he doing this to humble me?*

The whole time, Prabhupada had been grinning, but now he started chuckling outright. Reaching to the edge of the empty platter, he picked up a rose and with a playful smile, chuckling, flicked it right at Aindra's face. "Everyone else was 'getting the mercy,' but it was like he was playing a special game with me. Srila Prabhupada was joking with me! So, I was thinking, *Wow, fantastic! At least I'm good for a laugh; at least I'm good for a joke.*

"There was this misconception of Srila Prabhupada being like an unapproachable giant. I had that misconception. I never understood the personal side of Srila Prabhupada, until I saw him playing this game with me."

༺ ༺ ༺

Srila Prabhupada had arrived in New York in 1965 and struggled through many hardships to spread the philosophy of the *Bhagavad-gita*. Now, just a decade later, the chanting of Hare Krishna resounded off the skyscrapers of what he had called "the most important street in the world," as thousands of devotees marched down Fifth Avenue

CHAPTER SIX   47

in the Ratha-yatra, chanting, dancing, and pulling huge festooned chariots of Jagannath, Baladeva, and Subhadra.

Aindra was in ecstasy. In the midst of one of the largest Vaishnava celebrations ever held in the West, with twenty thousand plates of *prasādam* served and devotees singing and dancing through the streets of Manhattan, he felt that there was still hope for the American *saṅkīrtana* movement.

After the festival, however, he had to go back to work, traveling through the Mid- and Southwest with two other devotees in a van attached to one of the Radha-Damodara buses. They tried to wake up early and keep a temple-like program of kirtan, *japa*, and *Bhāgavatam* class, but their schedule was irregular. For breakfast they ate mostly bulk handouts of government surplus: peanuts, cream cheese, peanut butter, and lettuce. Sometimes Aindra would mix honey with condensed milk and add dates and nuts and cheese—a "sweet bomb." "Sometimes in the morning I would have cookies or sweet rice. My maya was Philadelphia cream cheese and Oreo cookies." Then each devotee would be dropped off on a street corner or in a parking lot for the rest of the day to distribute books to passersby.

In the evening they would get picked up and taken to a motel room, or the van would stop for the night in a parking lot, where the three devotees would read from the *Kṛṣṇa* book and drink hot milk before going to sleep—just like in the D.C. temple when Aindra had joined.

❧ ❧ ❧

Srila Prabhupada departed this earthly realm in November of 1977. By that time, *hari-nāma-saṅkīrtana*—chanting in the streets—had already diminished, and devotees were mainly distributing his books. "But after Srila Prabhupada left," Aindra remembered, "all over the Society there was a great decline in and neglect of the primary process given to us by Sri Chaitanya Mahaprabhu in the matter of the congregational chanting of the Holy Names.

"When Srila Prabhupada was physically present, in D.C. we used to go out for *saṅkīrtana* fourteen hours a day, chanting and dancing and distributing *Back to Godhead* magazines and a publication called the *Saṅkīrtana Newsletter*, which focused on our distribution of books. We would send Prabhupada a weekly report, and one week, in reply, he wrote that he had received our newsletter and was 'very pleased to hear about the results of your *saṅkīrtana* and book distribution.'

" 'Actually,' Prabhupāda wrote, 'this Kṛṣṇa consciousness movement is based on *saṅkīrtana*, the congregational chanting of the names of Kṛṣṇa. I started this movement by sitting under a tree at Tompkins Square Park and performing *saṅkīrtana*.' In conclusion, he wrote, 'Therefore I want that this *saṅkīrtana* and book distribution go on side by side.' "

That had always been the idea, Aindra knew—to chant the Holy Names in public while distributing books, for each activity to support the other. "But after Śrīla Prabhupāda departed, in the middle of our religious fervor to double and redouble book distribution, we never actually got refocused on the principle of *saṅkīrtana* and book distribution being performed side by side, and then book distribution turned into *not*-book distribution."

In a massive funding drive, devotees were sent out without books to simply collect money and sell other items. "*Saṅkīrtana* came to mean painting-*saṅkīrtana*, carved-candle-*saṅkīrtana*, sticker-*saṅkīrtana*, musical-Christmas-card *saṅkīrtana*, bargain-bin-*karmī*-record-album-*saṅkīrtana*. Everyone was going out 'on the pick.' It came to mean anything and everything except what *saṅkīrtana* literally meant: congregational chanting of the Holy Name. Just pick it to the bone and bring it back home to fill the big black hole—with the crisis of mismanagement, the big black hole, never filling.... We weren't even telling people about Krishna, wouldn't even say the words *Hare Krishna*, because we didn't want to implicate the movement in what we were doing.

"All over the world, except maybe in Russia, book distribution came to a virtual standstill. Hardly anyone was going out—only a few determined stalwarts—and trying to get anyone to go out on *hari-nāma-saṅkīrtana* was like pulling teeth. And, practically speaking, on account of the dwindling of some devotees' faith in the Holy Name, faith in the instructions of the spiritual master also weakened."

The movement, Aindra felt, had turned in the wrong direction. "In my heart of hearts, I saw a need to at least try to push back in the other direction—to try in my small little way to augment a consciousness of the need to perform *hari-nāma-saṅkīrtana* in our Society."

CHAPTER SEVEN

By 1979, the Radha-Damodara buses and vans had scattered, and Aindra moved to the Chicago temple. Again he tried to introduce daily *hari-nāma-saṅkīrtana*, but he wasn't surprised when the temple president told him that chanting didn't pay the bills and sent him out to collect.

For the next six months, he and his *saṅkīrtana* partner—one aged around twenty but wearing a grey wig, the other (Aindra) in a bright red wig, looking like he lived in his car—went door to door selling imitative paintings imported by the roll from Hong Kong and roved sidewalks and parking lots, soliciting donations in exchange for rock-and-roll albums discarded by record stores and radio stations.

Finally he couldn't take it anymore. *This isn't devotional service*, he saw. *It's just crap, and I'm never doing it again.* "At that point," he later described, "I said to myself, *The buck stops here.*

This is where Aindra das starts redirecting his energies toward hari-nāma-saṅkīrtana.

"What I saw was devotees losing their inspiration in Krishna consciousness due to not gaining a taste for congregational chanting of the Holy Name, because the congregational chanting was so much de-emphasized in our movement. Devotees weren't doing it, and because they weren't doing it, they weren't getting the experience that was meant to be the basis of their realized *vijñāna*, their realized faith in the process of *saṅkīrtana-yajña*, the *yuga-dharma*."

Soon thereafter, there was an upheaval at the Chicago temple, and many of the devotees, including Aindra, left. Aindra joined Ganapati Swami and his traveling *saṅkīrtana* party on their preaching program at the University of Wisconsin, in Madison, and other colleges. Maharaja was visiting the schools with a half dozen men, setting up small festivals on campus lawns, chanting, preaching, and distributing books. Aindra liked the program and respected Ganapati Swami, but the devotees were still taking turns going out on the road with paintings and records.

One morning Maharaja noticed that Aindra had taken out a small box, which opened into a small altar for his brass Gaura-Nitai Deities, and was worshipping the Deities. He took Aindra aside and told him that it was better if devotees didn't have their own personal Deities, since worshipping Them could distance the devotees from the Deities in the temple. The discussion ended with Maharaja confiscating Aindra's Deities and the altar-box.

Aindra felt helpless. He was dealing with a sannyasi, someone he admired, and he had loved playing mridanga and chanting with Maharaja's group. But he was upset. For a few days, he tried worshipping his Deities with *mānasa-pūjā*, imagining the elaborate process in his mind, but it wasn't the same. He was torn. He thought he had finally found a chanting program into which he could put his heart, but he couldn't give up his Gaura-Nitai.

Nor did he find Maharaja's arguments against keeping personal Deities compelling or applicable to his situation. He had moved from one temple to another, and as soon as he had become attached to the Deities in one place, circumstances had taken him away to another. Worshipping his Gaura-Nitai had been one of the only constants in his devotional life.

I just have to stand by my beliefs, he decided. *I have to have the integrity to act according to my own realizations.* And so that night, without a word to anyone, he found his confiscated Deity box, grabbed his few things, walked out to the road, stuck out his thumb, and hitchhiked back to Chicago.

❧ ❧ ❧

The Chicago temple accepted Aindra back as pujari for their Jagannath Deities. For the rest of the year and through the next, he did his morning and evening pujari service and dedicated the rest of his time to chanting on the street. He tried to get more devotees to participate, but despite his efforts to impress on them the primary importance of *hari-nāma-saṅkīrtana*, some just saw him, as one devotee put it, "as a big baby with a bad temper—always whining, complaining, and demanding that people see things his way."

He lived in the nook of a hallway leading to a bathroom, which he had transformed into a small room with stalks of bamboo, and used whatever hours or minutes he could to create new clothes and accessories for the Deities. "Some mornings on my way to the shower, I'd find Aindra asleep on the stairs leading up to the altar," Sarvopama das remembered. "He might still have had a pair of scissors in one hand and a piece of cloth in the other. Or he might have been arranging some jewelry in a special way. He was so dedicated to the Deities that he would literally fall asleep while doing some final service for Them long after everyone else had taken rest."

Aindra performed his Deity worship with personal care. After all, he realized, he wasn't dealing with a statue; he was dressing and worshipping Krishna Himself. He would sometimes retire the Jagannath Deities for the night by picking Them up, cradling Them in his arms, and rocking Them to sleep while singing the *mahā-mantra* like a lullaby.

And he would weep when he was with Them—and also while reading Prabhupada's books, discussing Krishna, and singing in kirtan. "We didn't realize what a great soul he was," Sarvopama later commented. "Some of us, mistaking his genuine earnestness and sincerity for mundane sentimentalism, even called him 'Cryindra.' "

❧ ❧ ❧

One morning Aindra told Sarvopama, "Prabhu, you *have* to do Deity worship!"

"I don't *have to* do anything," Sarvopama replied, slinging a backpack full of books over his shoulder. "I'm on my way out to distribute Prabhupada's books at the airport."

The next morning, Aindra again made the same declaration, and Sarvopama again resisted.

Finally, the third time, Sarvopama relented. "Okay," he said, "what do you want me to do?"

Aindra taught him how to bathe and dress the small Deities of Radha and Krishna. "He started me with the small Radha-Krishna Deities," Sarvopama remembered, "and I did that service regularly for the next fifteen years.

"When in 2007 I arrived in Vrindavan, I immediately fell at his feet and thanked him for saving my life. Crouched at his feet and looking up at him almost thirty years later with tears of gratitude in my eyes, I explained how those Radha-Krishna Deities had protected me—how, while other godbrothers spun off in different directions, the service he had given me provided a kind of shelter and protection."

❦ ❦ ❦

During wintertime in the Windy City, the Chicago temple got really cold. And yet, even with devotees bringing back collections, the temple still didn't have heat. Neither the altar nor the ashram was heated, and the frigid Chicago winter was hard to bear. The only working heater was in the temple president's room.

Aindra was upset. How could a temple authority let Krishna and Krishna's devotees freeze while he kept warm? When he complained, however, the temple authorities turned it all back on him. "Who should we blame for this difficult situation?" one asked. "Ourselves. Krishna fulfills all desires. You wouldn't be in this situation if you didn't desire it."

The advice infuriated Aindra; it absolved guilt and halted progress. And it motivated him to move on. "All right, then," he replied, "I'll change my desire. I desire to take your leave."

But where could he go next? Would another temple be any different? Everyone was collecting instead of doing *saṅkīrtana*, and the word of the institutional authorities was absolute. To speak against one, as he had found out in D.C., could be considered treasonous. A "zonal-acharya" system was being enforced throughout ISKCON, with some of the Society's gurus, each of whom had exclusive dominion over a geographic zone, demanding lavish personal worship. Devotees could be initiated only by their zone's guru, and putting their full faith in him, many were told—worshipping him—was the only way they could receive Srila Prabhupada's mercy.

"Hare Krishna," Aindra said aloud. Suddenly he felt safe: sheltered and secure. The Holy Name, he realized, was his only shelter. Anything could happen. He could live anywhere. It didn't matter; he would always have Krishna in the form of His Holy Name.

He thought of Vrindavan. Prabhupada had cited Sri Chaitanya's description of the spiritual Vrindavan, Radha and Krishna's eternal abode: "The trees of that land are all desire trees: you can have anything you want from any tree. The land is made of touchstone and the water is nectar. In that land all speech is song, all walking is dancing, and the constant companion is the flute. Everything is self-illuminated, just like the sun and moon in this material world. The human form of life is meant for understanding this transcendental land of Vṛndāvana, and one who is fortunate should cultivate knowledge of Vṛndāvana and its residents.... An expansion of that Vṛndāvana is present on this earth, and superior devotees worship the earthly Vṛndāvana as nondifferent from the supreme abode."

And in his introduction to *Śrīmad-Bhāgavatam*, Prabhupada had written, "Vṛndāvana-dhāma is nondifferent from the Lord because the name, fame, form and place where the Lord manifests Himself are all identical with the Lord as absolute knowledge. Therefore Vṛndāvana-dhāma is as worshipable as the Lord." Quoting Rupa Goswami in *The Nectar of Devotion*, he had stated that " 'attainment of transcendental loving devotional service to the Lord is the goal of life, and it can be achieved very easily for one who lives in Mathurā-maṇḍala [the district of Vrindavan] even for a few seconds.... Certainly Mathurā will deliver the desires of the devotees, who simply aspire to be engaged in the devotional service of the Lord.' In the Vedic literature it is also stated, 'How wonderful it is that simply by residing in Mathurā even for one day, one can achieve a transcendental loving attitude toward the Supreme Personality of Godhead! This land of Mathurā must be more glorious than Vaikuṇṭha-dhāma, the kingdom of God!' " And further, in his *Sri Upadesamrita*, Rupa Goswami explains that Vrindavan is superior to Mathura because that is where Krishna performed His *rasa-lila* pastimes.

❧ ❧ ❧

Importantly, Vrindavan had also been Srila Prabhupada's residence, where at the Radha-Damodar temple, which he had called the center of the spiritual world, he had begun his life work of translating and commenting on *Śrīmad-Bhāgavatam*.

In his eight years as a devotee, Aindra had never been to India. Book distributors were sent to Vrindavan for spiritual inspiration, but only if they sold enough books. And he didn't. Besides, he was a *pujari*, and he hadn't wanted to give up his Deity worship. But now things were different, and he decided to go.

"Finally, finally, after eight or nine years," he later remembered, "I was going to go to Vrindavan! For one reason or another, either because I didn't do my book distribution quota or because I had to take care of the Deities, I was never able to go. But now, finally, there was nothing stopping me."

❧ ❧ ❧

Aindra walked out of the Chicago temple with a box of books tucked under one arm and a duffle bag hanging from a shoulder. At the nearest main street he stuck his thumb out to the passing cars and hitchhiked yet again, headed east.

He sold books along the way, and by the time he got to Detroit, he had earned enough money for bus fare to D.C., where he stayed just long enough to see his family and sell whatever of his old belongings were left after he had given everything else away.

His visit with his father didn't go well. Art was upset with Aindra for selling vintage firearms that Art had given him, and they had a big argument. The two had been at odds for years, and selling the guns was the last straw. Art, drinking heavily and deep into his own demons, lashed out at what he saw as his son's rejection, going so far as to formally disown him.

Aindra's visit with his mother, who by then had remarried, went much better. "He was radiant," she recalled. "He had brought some cookies with him, and he gave one to the dog and said it would be reincarnated as a human being."

"We had a nice philosophical discussion," her new husband, a longtime family friend, said, "and I came away feeling that his experience had created in him a sense of realism that we hadn't seen before—the shine that had been replaced by a 'patina.' But it was a realism that was in harmony with where he wanted to be, from seeing for himself what did and what didn't work.

"And he was more universally minded when discussing and translating processes and concepts that were important to him but not to people who were coming from other points of view. He handled other people's criticism extremely gracefully and never got into a defensive posture. He had achieved this wonderful, neutral grace of acceptance of the lives going on around him, without reacting to them. He had mastered that reactive nature within himself."

Aindra also visited his youngest brother, John. "I had been only nine or ten," John remembered of previous times when Aindra had visited after joining the devotees, "but he had brought me the *Bhagavad-gita* and other writings, and these beautiful posters. My walls were covered with his Krishna posters, and my bookshelf was full of his books. Several times, he brought his drum and cymbals, and we would play together and chant. He was already a spiritual leader, even then, because he made me aware of other things beyond the agnostic way we were raised and opened me up to my own spiritual path."

Now on his own, with a job and steady income, and seeing that his brother was on the right path for him, John gave a donation for Aindra's upcoming trip. "He was on his way to India," John said. "That was his calling."

CHAPTER EIGHT

FROM D.C., AINDRA continued to New York. The temple on West 55th Street had recently been sold, and the Deities, Sri Sri Radha-Govinda, who had originally been installed in the Henry Street temple in Brooklyn after Their arrival from Jaipur in 1972 and moved to Manhattan three years later, had moved again, a few blocks southeast, to a small building on 7th Avenue.

Aindra served as a pujari for Radha-Govinda for a few months, but as soon as he had raised the funds for airfare, he was on a flight to India. From Kolkata, he took a public bus the eighty miles to Mayapur, ISKCON's international headquarters and the birthplace of Sri Chaitanya Mahaprabhu, the founder of the *saṅkīrtana* movement. And a few days later, from nearby Navadvip, he boarded an overnight train to Mathura and took a rickshaw the rest of the way to Vrindavan.

When Aindra arrived, Raman Reti, the outlying area of Vrindavan that housed ISKCON's Krishna-Balaram temple, was still relatively undeveloped. "From the roof of the guesthouse one could see trees and grass everywhere," Madhurya-lila dasi later remembered. There were groves of mangoes, and herds of nilgai, Asian antelope, roamed the flower fields and mango groves. "We could see all the way to the Yamuna, and it was common to see and hear peacocks and green parrots in the nearby forests. The Vrindavan *parikramā* path was soft, silky sand. Everyone would say 'Radhe, Radhe!' There weren't any shops in front of the temple gate, and only tongas and rikshaws were on the main road. It was hard to make even local calls, what to speak of international calls. And there were not many devotees living there, so we got to know everyone and formed close relationships, even with visiting devotees from all over the world."

The temple itself was even more beautiful than Aindra had imagined. The black-and-white marble floor glistened under rows of arches, and a dark tamal tree spread an umbrella of leaves over the courtyard. The Radha-Krishna Deities, Sri Sri Radha-Shyamasundar, were flanked by the *gopīs* Lalita and Visakha, and Radharani seemed to blush with love for Her Shyam.

Still, Aindra felt, something seemed wrong. A recording of Prabhupada's kirtan played from speakers mounted atop the temple's three towers. Why was there a recording? he wondered. Where was Prabhupada's 24-hour kirtan?

"I'm here!" he announced to a devotee. "Where do I sign in?"

The temple president welcomed Aindra and informed him of the standard policy, established by Srila Prabhupada. "You can stay here for three days," he said. "After that, you have to do service or rent a room in the guesthouse."

When Aindra asked what had happened to the 24-hour kirtan, he was told that it had lasted only a year or so before fading away, three years before.

"But Prabhupada wanted 24-hour kirtan in Vrindavan," he said. And Vrindavan was the spiritual heart of ISKCON. If kirtan could die out there, was there any hope for its resurgence anywhere in the movement?

"Prabhupada wanted many things," the temple president told him—planetariums, varnashrama, cow protection, new temples, book distribution, feeding the poor ...

But what was most important? Aindra asked himself. Preaching. And what was preaching? Giving Krishna consciousness, love of God, to others. And no one could give something they didn't have. To actually preach, one had to become Krishna conscious. And the primary means of achieving that in the Age of Kali was *kṛṣṇa-nāma-saṅkīrtana*. What, then, could be a higher preaching priority than kirtan? What could be more important?

Aindra joined the pujari department and for a few months served Sri Sri Krishna-Balaram, the temple's presiding Deities, on the center altar. He spent most of his eight free hours each day in the temple room chanting and playing mridanga. In time, his daily eight-hour kirtans started to gain support from local *vraja-vāsīs* and pilgrims, but sometimes not as much from the temple devotees. Aindra wanted the kirtans to be "vigorous," and though eventually the temple book distributors saw that when the kirtan was more ecstatic visitors bought more books, at first some complained that it was too loud and interfered with their preaching. "What kind of kirtan is that?" they questioned. "We want to play something nice that attracts people."

Sitting one night on his trunk, which he had chained to a railing of the roof of the *gurukula* building next door to the temple, where he was staying, he read a new book, *Preaching is the Essence*, a compilation of quotes from Prabhupada on the subject of preaching.

Inspired by Srila Prabhupada's words and disappointed by the state of the temple's kirtan program, Aindra decided to return to America, where, following Prabhupada's example, he could preach to Westerners. But how? *How about a traveling roadshow?* he wondered—like what Visnujana Swami had done with the Radha-Damodara Party? After all, he was a musician and he knew how to bring a show on the road, having traveled with carnivals when he was younger.

"I knew about how they constructed the sideshows," he remembered. "They'd pack them into a tractor-trailer, and then they would open the side and a false front would come out." He would outfit a box truck with side-doors that opened all the way, build a facade, and transform the truck into a moving temple. He could drive it to fairs and public events, open it up, do *hari-nāma-saṅkīrtana*, and then fold everything up and drive to the next city—a *saṅkīrtana* festival on wheels!

CHAPTER NINE

AINDRA RETURNED TO America in the spring of 1981 with his vision of a traveling temple, Sri Sri Gaura-Nitai, and two new additions to his altar: brass *mūrtis* of Srila Prabhupada and Srila Bhaktisiddhanta Sarasvati. When the New York temple president, Tosan Krishna das, asked what service he would do, Aindra replied, "I want to help the temple get back its street *harināma*."

"And how would you do that?" Tosan Krishna asked, starting to like this fiery young man.

"I want to set up a stage outside the public library on Fifth Avenue," Aindra explained, "with a real sound system, flags, banners … and big paintings!"

Now, here's a man with spirit! Tosan Krishna thought. *A little rough on the outside, but with a heart of gold.* He agreed to the plan and brought Aindra in as a pujari.

On a typical morning, Aindra would finish his service on the altar, tuck a rolled-up carpet under one arm, sling a mridanga over a shoulder, and head out to chant. Sometimes Rasatala das would help, sometimes Kurma Rupa das, who was serving as a bhakta leader. Most days, Aindra would venture out alone, towing a handcart of equipment: a small portable amp with a microphone, stand, and cables; a few posters mounted on cardboard or light plywood; and some books and magazines. He would roll out the carpet at Rockefeller Plaza; Times Square; or Bryant Park, just behind the library; set up the equipment; put the books on display; and then sit down, mridanga in his lap, and chant until evening. Now and then, one or two devotees would join him.

At first he was constantly on the lookout for the police. "Show's over buddy," they'd order. "You can't perform amplified music in public without a permit."

He saw that he needed to start playing ball with the police instead of hiding from them. Tosan Krishna helped him figure out how to get the right permits, and every morning, Aindra would go to the police station of the precinct where he wanted to chant and get the twenty-dollar permit. He became a regular customer at the station and a familiar sight on the streets, now able to set up and stay in one place, using a folding table as a low stage. Sometimes the police would stop, but only to listen.

Aindra became known as a tough character, even for New York—a maverick with a strong personality and a penchant for shastra. He would scrutinize devotees' classes and ask pointed questions. "What you're saying doesn't sound right, prabhu," he would challenge. "Where does this idea come from? What is the reference?" And he would keep pressing the issue until the speaker either provided a satisfactory answer or admitted to not having an authoritative source. But that could drag on for hours, which was annoying to many of the devotees, who had to get started with their day.

His kirtan wasn't popular with everyone, either. His voice was still developing, and some devotees found it displeasing. And although he stayed with traditional melodies, he played them in a way that many people couldn't follow or just didn't like. Sometimes when he was leading, devotees would leave, or refuse to play instruments or sing along.

"His kirtans were very intricate, complex," one devotee remembered. "He used Indian ragas and changed the rhythm—sometimes slow, sometimes fast. Some devotees would complain and ask him to make it more simple, but he didn't listen to them. He didn't care; he never changed. He didn't try to please the crowd; he wanted to please his Deities."

"He was very concerned about the melodies," Kurma Rupa recalled. " 'Is this a bona fide melody?' he would ask. It was hard to tell what 'bona fide' meant, but those were the only melodies he wanted to chant—traditional Gaudiya Vaishnava tunes, tunes in our line."

Aindra wanted people to pay more attention to chanting—to be alert, on their toes, unsure what would happen next. When someone once suggested that it was like he was pulling the listener's ear and that by pulling their ear to be more attentive he gained their attention to the Holy Name, Aindra snapped his fingers and said, "You've got it; you've understood me." Then, when he got people's attention, he would switch gears, speed up. He didn't mind if his kirtan struck some as confusing or difficult to follow. They would just have to exert a little more effort.

A lot happened in the New York devotee community over the next couple of years: Tosan Krishna relocated to Vrindavan; Bhavananda Goswami and Ramesvara Swami were appointed co-Governing Body Commissioners (GBCs) for New York; the Seventh Avenue temple was sold; and in November 1982 Sri Sri Radha-Govinda moved to a big new temple in Brooklyn, on Schermerhorn Street, not far from Their original home on Henry Street.

Aindra continued to focus his attention on the streets, going out daily on *saṅkīrtana*. He would encourage guests at the temple to join him, and gradually a few of them began going out to chant with him at least somewhat regularly.

❦ ❦ ❦

Renunciation, described in *Śrī Caitanya-caritāmṛta* as "the basic principle sustaining the lives of Śrī Caitanya Mahāprabhu's devotees," had been a central feature of Aindra's spiritual practice since even before he had met the devotees. But in New York he began to adopt further austerities to promote his spiritual progress. Observing authorized *vratas* like Ekadasi "has a lot to do with learning sense control," he said. "And the purpose of our learning sense control is that we can control lust, because as long as lust is prominent, there is very little chance for its antithesis—*prema*—to manifest. It's very unlikely.

"Just like the example of the prostitute who was converted by Haridas Thakur. She was told to distribute all her valuables to brahmanas and Vaishnavas and then come and sit in her *kuṭīr* to chant three lakhs of *nāma* before Tulasi Maharani. But she was also advised to eat frugally. It is described that by eating frugally, like a bird, she became thin and her senses became weak, and thereby she was able to gain control over her senses. When she gained control over her senses, only thereafter *prema* manifested in her person."

As cited in the *Hari-bhakti-vilāsa*, "One who passes the Cāturmāsya season without observing religious vows, austerities and chanting of *japa*, such a fool, although living, should be considered to be a dead man." Forty-two austerities and observances are prescribed, and Srila Prabhupada states in *Śrī Caitanya-caritāmṛta* that "Cāturmāsya should be observed by all sections of the population. It does not matter whether one is a *gṛhastha* or a *sannyāsī*. The observance is obligatory for all *āśramas*. The real purpose behind the vow taken during these four months is to minimize the quantity of sense gratification."

Aindra and a few other friends decided to observe the Cāturmāsya *vrata*. "Our program," Chaturatma das remembered, "was to sleep on the floor, rise early, chant extra rounds, and sing kirtan and read shastra in the temple daily. We didn't shave or cut our hair, drank water only once every six hours, and ate only once a day [directly off the floor, without plates or utensils or even our hands]—just a simple *kichari* cooked without oil, salt, or any spices. There are dozens of rules, and we followed almost all of them." Only he and Aindra ended up the four-month period still maintaining their vows.

❦ ❦ ❦

While working on constructing the temple altar one day (he helped build the decorative gate), Aindra noticed a short flight of stairs in the back, leading up to a door that opened to a small, dilapidated loft. He showed it to his friend Ramabhadra das, the head pujari, and said, "This is where you should live, Ram."

"You think so?" Ramabhadra asked.

"Yeah," Aindra confirmed. "You should be close to Radha-Govinda."

"But it's a mess," Ramabhadra said.

Aindra smiled. "I'll fix it up!" He cleared out the loft, cleaned it, installed lighting, painted the concrete floor, and finished the walls and ceiling with a stucco that he painted a brownish saffron, explaining, "Psychologists say this is the most relaxing color." He created a shelf in a window bay and even furnished the room with a captain's bed, a bed and dresser in one.

Aindra himself had moved into the brahmachari ashram, but, wanting more seclusion, he set up his quarters in a large closet in a back corner of the temple's basement. It was dark, poorly ventilated, and leaked in the rain, but at least it was private. A thin mat and bed were his only furnishings; the rest of the space was filled with paraphernalia for *harināma*: instruments, musical equipment, decorations, and a four-track Tascam tape recorder.

He also started doing kirtan in the temple—in the dining hall when devotees were honoring *prasādam* and in the temple room after *śayana-ārati*, while the Deities were being put to bed. "Aindra is getting very good with the harmonium," commented Vaiyasaki das, a renowned ISKCON *kīrtanīya*.

❦ ❦ ❦

When in New York, Bhavananda das Goswami, as co-GBC, liked to meet with each of the local preachers to see how their projects were going, and Aindra looked forward to his interview. It was the spring of 1983, two years since he had gotten the inspiration on the Vrindavan rooftop for a mobile kirtan temple. He had heard a rumor that Bhavananda was considering a plan to turn the unused part of the temple basement into a recreational area, and if that was true, he thought, there might be money available.

The meeting began smoothly. Then Bhavananda asked, "Is there anything I can do to help you expand your project?"

Aindra spoke right up: "Yes! I need a truck!"

"A *truck*?" Bhavananda asked.

"Yes. I want to turn it into a temple and drive it to important spots in the city to perform *hari-nāma-saṅkīrtana*. I know exactly how to do it; I just need money to buy the truck and the materials."

"How much do you need?"

"The truck will be about seventeen thousand dollars, and I'll need to travel to buy materials to make it look like an authentic temple ... and a sound system ... and instruments ... Altogether, about twenty-five thousand."

Bhavananda laughed aloud. Here was a young man with ambition. "I'm not going to just give you all that money," he said, "but I'll give you the down-payment for the truck and loan you the rest if you commit to repay at eight hundred dollars a month."

Aindra flushed with excitement. It might really happen.

CHAPTER TEN

AINDRA WENT RIGHT to work. The traveling temple would feature the kind of ornate arches he had seen in the Dallas temple and at New Vrindavan, with embroidered cloth like what had been used in the first San Francisco Ratha-yatra. He could get amplification, mirrors, lighting, and even molds for the arches in America, but he needed to go to India to get cloth and musical instruments—mridangas and a harmonium.

Aindra's 1983 trip took him mainly to Jagannath Puri and Bhubaneswar, where he stayed with Gaura Govinda Swami, who was developing a Krishna-conscious center in the jungle outside town. Gaura Govinda asked if Aindra would chant at a program, and when he did, the locals were impressed to see a Westerner do kirtan with so much fidelity to the essential Gaudiya spirit. On his side, Aindra was impressed with Maharaja, whom he came to see as a *mahābhāgavata*, a pure devotee.

In Pipli, a town outside Bhubaneswar, he bought cloth, canopies, and umbrellas. But he thought he might have trouble getting all his luggage through Indian customs without an export tax or bribe.

In Delhi he met a Bengali man who was an ISKCON donor and a high-ranking customs official at the airport. Aindra described his situation, and the man offered to get him through all the checkpoints without fees. He had only one condition: "Please bless us by visiting our home, doing kirtan, and taking *prasādam*."

When Aindra arrived at the man's house, he was met at the door by a dog. *Oh no*, he thought. *They're feeding this dog some kind of fish or meat. They probably aren't strict vegetarians. Prabhupada said we should be reluctant to accept even water from anyone who isn't chanting sixteen rounds a day and following the regulative principles. Am I really going to accept food from them?*

After the kirtan, the man offered Aindra *prasādam*.

Aindra declined.

The man was upset. "If a sadhu is our guest and we don't feed him, we will be cursed!" he said. "Please accept *prasādam*."

Knowing the significance of the point in Indian culture, Aindra relented. "Okay," he said. "I will take fruit."

By the time they were done eating, it was getting late, and the man insisted that Aindra spend the night.

Since joining the movement ten years before, Aindra had spent every night in an ISKCON temple, an ISKCON bus or van, or a room paid for by ISKCON funds. Under the circumstances, he agreed to stay over, but only outside in the yard. So the family brought out an Indian wood-and-hemp-rope cot, and Aindra slept under the stars.

Almost as soon as Aindra fell asleep, Srila Prabhupada appeared to him in a dream. "What are you doing?" Prabhupada asked. He seemed disappointed.

"O Prabhupada!" Aindra replied. "I am collecting materials to build a *hari-nāma-saṅkīrtana* festival on wheels!"

Then, in his dream, Aindra had a realization—*Book distribution is Prabhupada's heart and soul, and I've abandoned it!* He fell into tears, feeling like a disappointment to his spiritual master.

"Even to this day, when I remember it my heart becomes agitated," Aindra recalled, "because even in a dream it struck me that I was explaining to Srila Prabhupada that I was doing something

CHAPTER TEN 69

other than what I had been doing for years.... And as I was telling him about my enthusiasm for augmenting *hari-nāma-saṅkīrtana*, it suddenly dawned on me that I was focusing on something other than the number-one, most important, solid work. We come and go, but the books will remain. My recordings are also going out around the world, but they are dependent on electricity. But even if it ends one day, God has given us sunlight for one purpose—so that with it we can see into the *śāstra-cakṣu* by reading the literature left by our predecessor acharyas.

"When I realized what I was telling Srila Prabhupada, I immediately started crying and crying and crying. I was weeping on Prabhupada's shoulder; he held me to his chest, and I was weeping on his shoulder. He was patting my head and saying, 'It's okay—you are doing it very nicely. Don't worry, it's okay.'

"But I was so unhappy hearing myself saying to Srila Prabhupada that I was no longer distributing his books ... because book distribution is my life and soul, and it still is my life and soul even though I have not been doing it for many years.

"And at that moment, I had a wonderful experience: Srila Prabhupada was no longer a monolithic unapproachable giant; he was my older brother. It dawned on me that Radha and Krishna are our everything and that my guru is my older best friend, my older brother. And from that time on, by appearing in that dream and behaving with me in that way, he established within my heart that my guru is my best friend."

❦ ❦ ❦

Aindra returned to New York with instruments, paraphernalia, and material for the truck, empowered to complete his project. And in December, under the name of ISKCON-New York, he purchased a box truck fitted with a Ford Econoline engine. He turned the unused half of the temple basement into a workshop (Bhavananda's plan for a rec area had never manifest) and labored through the winter nights converting the truck into a temple.

"Why are you wasting so much time on this crazy idea?" devotees asked.

"This is what I was born to do," he replied, confident that he was fulfilling Srila Prabhupada's desires.

There was a lot of work, and it took months. By spring, Bhavananda and Ramesvara had run out of patience and gave Aindra a deadline: "By lunch next Wednesday your truck is either finished or it's *finished*."

Aindra had completed the decorations and basic structure. On the outside, the vehicle appeared to be just a basic white truck, but the two side doors opened to an ornate temple room, with golden pillars supporting North-Indian-style arches constructed with polyurethane, backdropped by red curtains reaching down to a black-and-white checkered floor. The ceiling was draped with beautiful Indian cloth and held a pair of crystal chandeliers. It looked just like an Indian temple, but on wheels.

He had assembled six decorative panels for the truck's exterior—three beneath the doors, hiding the truck's wheels and undercarriage with images of golden lotus petals, and three above them, each weighing a hundred pounds, ornamented with golden peacocks and lotus whorls.

But there was still work to be done. One design problem was how one man alone could erect the upper panels. Aindra was working on a plan to join them and hoist them by cable with a jack, then climb onto the roof and lower the arches into place, but he didn't know if he could finish setting it all up before the rapidly approaching deadline.

Devotees would occasionally stop by to watch Aindra's progress, but most of his help came from outside. When a Venezuelan man who was a regular guest at the temple saw the truck parked by the front door, surrounded by the decorated panels and cloth, he asked what it was.

"It's a temple," Aindra explained. "I have a deadline to meet, and I'm way behind schedule. Will you help?" The man did.

Frank, a Black Vietnam veteran who lived in a homeless shelter a block away, also lent a hand, and with their assistance, Aindra worked through the Tuesday night before the deadline, went straight to *maṅgala-ārati*, then worshipped his Deities and took a nap.

A bit before lunch the next day, he went out to the truck to meet Ramesvara and Bhavananda, who had come with an entourage of assistants and disciples to evaluate the result of twenty-seven thousand dollars and four months of work.

When Aindra opened the doors, the group was impressed. But

when he lugged out the heavy panels, they became skeptical. As he tried to hoist the top three arches into place, a jack malfunctioned and the panels crashed to the ground. Fortunately, there was no serious damage and no one was hurt, but it was a close call that showed that the design still needed further thought.

"You've got one more day to figure it out," the swamis told Aindra as they left.

That afternoon, the Venezuelan man returned and saw Aindra and Frank still working on the truck. "What happened?" he asked.

"It was a disaster," Aindra replied. "The arches fell, and I nearly got myself killed."

The trio spent another night trying to solve the problem. Finally, they purchased an electric winch and installed it on the truck's roof. It hoisted the arches reliably, and the next day the truck passed the test with flying colors. Ramesvara and Bhavananda were satisfied, Aindra was ecstatic, and the traveling temple was ready to roll.

CHAPTER ELEVEN

WITH THE MOBILE temple ready, Aindra took his Deities from Their shelf in Ramabhadra's room and installed Them on Their new altar with a full *abhiṣeka* ceremony. And from that point on, he basically lived with Them—sleeping on a mat in one corner of the truck.

"He was married to that truck," Rama Raya remembered. "But not many devotees would participate. At best, it was something devotees would go to if they had nothing else to do. He was like a lone soldier."

"I started going out every day for no less than eight hours a day, rain or shine, with or without anybody—I didn't care," Aindra recounted. "If no one was willing to come out, then Gaura-halleluiah anyway! That was fine. There were days when many devotees came out to help and days when there was next to no one."

Frank stayed on as Aindra's assistant and played kartals in the kirtan. Then one day, miraculously, out of the blue, he received an inheritance: a collection of Indian musical instruments. He gave them to Aindra, and they became the small group's kirtan staples.

The Venezuelan man remained as well, going out with Aindra almost every day, and was soon initiated as Subala das. He was a musician with a background in Latin bass guitar, so he was thrilled when Aindra handed him what looked like a big fretless bass—a tambura—and gave him a few basic instructions on how to play.

And so the kirtan began. "His singing wasn't as amazing as it became later," Subala commented, "but it was very intense. He would absorb himself in it and move his head from side to side, projecting."

"His voice wasn't as beautiful back then," Rama Raya agreed. "Not as melodic, not as refined." But he already had his trademark intensity. "He would crouch behind the harmonium, absorbed in chanting, shaking his head from side to side, crying out the *mahā-mantra* as if his life depended on it."

Subala tried applying his Latin bass techniques to syncopate the rhythm of the tambura strings, but as soon as he did, Aindra turned to him and said, "What the hell are you doing?"

"You don't have to talk to me like that!" Subala objected. He stood up, about to walk off, but Aindra settled him back down and explained the tambura's musical role: to lay down a steady, harmonic drone as an essential but almost subconscious reference point for the main melody.

The crew grew to five regulars, Subala and Frank joined by Kaunteya on mridanga, and Carlos, a temple guest from Brazil, on kartals.

Early every morning, before rush hour began, the white truck would pull up to a sidewalk and Aindra, in saffron robes, would emerge from the driver's door and fill the parking meter with coins. The two side doors would swing open, clouds of incense would billow out while exotic Indian *shenai* ragas resounded from a Peavy sound-system, and a small crowd would gather during the half-hour set-up.

The kirtan would begin slowly, gather intensity, and continue full force for the next eight to twelve hours. Morning commuters would pause their rush to see and hear the exotic sights and sounds on their way to work, and when they came out for lunch at midday they would find the truck still there, the kirtan still going. And in the evening, as they returned home from the day's work, Aindra and the other devotees would *still* be there, chanting with even more enthusiasm.

Aindra's presentation attracted occasional hecklers, but he wasn't disturbed. A good heckler would attract a nice crowd, especially when Aindra stopped to refute their challenges one-on-one, and he had the advantage of not only transcendental knowledge but also a microphone.

Sometimes he would stop chanting to speak with an onlooker or give a short talk. "The dog is running on four legs," he told one passerby. "And the so-called civilized human being runs on four wheels. What's the difference? I say there's no difference! Unless human beings cultivate spiritual consciousness, they are no different than dogs!"

He invited people to chant and always gave *prasādam* to those who gathered—something from the morning offering, or fruits and nuts. When there were leftovers from a Sunday feast, he gave out full plates.

Within a week, Aindra's kirtan temple made the second page of the *Daily News*. The coverage was positive—rare at a time when much of the media portrayed ISKCON as a cult—and included a photo of Aindra and his kirtan crew chanting.

As Garbhodaksayi Vishnu das, who had become a devotee after seeing and hearing Aindra in the truck, remembered, "He would go into any community—Harlem, or downtown Brooklyn (when it was still a seedy place)—and open it up. It would blow people's minds when the incense bellowed out. It's hard to impress people in New York, but they would stop in the street with their mouths wide open. It was a regular truck, but then he'd open it up and ... Bam! Vrindavan!"

"I thought it was the most amazing thing," Bhurijana Prabhu later admired. "It looked like the spiritual world was transposed into New York; it was so incredible. I hadn't understood that he was such an artist.... It was one of the most amazing things I have ever seen."

"He was an advanced devotee," noted Garbhodaksayi Vishnu. "He wasn't in any clique, and he was friendly to everyone; he didn't have friends or enemies. As an African American, I was impressed that he had no concept of race in his mind. You could feel it.

"He might just walk up to you and tell you something he had

found funny and then walk away. He was a people person and very intelligent, street wise, and politically astute and aware of what was going on in the real world. I told him about my issues trying to give up marijuana. He told me, 'I had a quarter pound of pot when I first joined the temple, and I just threw it out the window.' He was so senior and advanced, but you could talk to him about real issues and struggles like that.

"He was so jolly and happy, and so into chanting. It wasn't just emotional; he was also deeply philosophical—an amazing combo. His singing was full of joy; it was so moving to hear him sing. He had so much devotion, shakti, and charisma. He'd lead the kirtan most of the time, but he'd have other people lead, too. If you were with him, at some point he'd have you at the microphone.

"It was such a blissful experience. People would go out with him and want to get shaved up that same day. He seemed to have an endless energy to chant. At least twenty people joined the temple from his program, and at least forty became congregation members."

Even with the success of the mobile-temple preaching, however, Aindra still had a hard time getting devotees to come along. So one morning, to attract their attention, while everyone was sitting at breakfast he danced into the room chanting and playing mridanga, looking even more disheveled and unkempt than usual, accompanied by two devotees dressed as comical bungling bhaktas, right down to their bright, mismatching socks. As Aindra banged out a simple beat on a mridanga, the three of them danced and chanted the *mahā-mantra* with exaggerated accents: "Hahray Kreeeeshnaaaaaaaaa, Hahray Kreeeeshnaaaaaaaa ..."

Then an attaché-case-carrying businessman, played by Lokamangala das, entered from the opposite side and called out, "Hey! Hare Krishnas! Where have you been? I haven't seen you guys in years!"

"We've got so many other pressing things to do," Aindra replied. "*Important* things like bill-paying and crisis management!"

"Well, come on!" the businessman said. "Get it together! We miss you guys! We really need you out here!"

"Did you hear that, prabhus?" he implored the audience of forty or fifty devotees. "Let's go out on *hari-nāma-saṅkīrtana*! They really need us out there!"

Quite a few of the devotees joined him for *hari-nāma-saṅkīrtana* that day, but before long he was again going out alone.

One morning, as Aindra was chanting at Columbus Circle, at the southwest corner of Central Park, another African-American New Yorker stopped to listen. He had a dignified manner and said he was on his way to attend law school. He was paying for it himself, he said, working whenever he could.

"Come play this drum," Aindra invited.

The man knew very little about Krishna consciousness and had never touched a mridanga. He was surprised by the offer, but, responding to Aindra's simple, happy countenance, he climbed aboard, picked up the mridanga, and chanted with him for several hours.

Before long, the man was initiated as Chaitanya Priya das. He moved into the New York temple and helped Aindra every day, until the temple authorities insisted that he stop and go out collecting instead.

This became the norm. A new devotee would join Aindra for a few weeks but soon have to stop to go out and solicit donations. Most of them eventually left the temple, but Chaitanya Priya stayed on, and some years later he made—and completed—a vow to do *nāma-saṅkīrtana* in the capital of every state in the U.S.

❦ ❦ ❦

In October of 1984, *Back to Godhead* published a photo and short blurb about Aindra's temple on wheels:

Devotees Bring Temple to New York Sidewalks

An Indian-style temple at the foot of a Manhattan skyscraper? Not for long. Aindra dāsa's van, transformed into an ornate temple, appears at different places in New York City every day. To the accompaniment of instruments, Aindra and his group chant the holy name of Kṛṣṇa, distribute books on Kṛṣṇa consciousness, and offer free refreshments to passersby.

❦ ❦ ❦

Aindra would usually start off in the Indian neighborhood of Jackson Heights, in Queens, where people would take off their shoes and bow to the kirtan on the sidewalk, or donate bags of rice, fruits, and vegetables, but his main spots were in Manhattan: Bryant Park; Columbus Circle; Times Square; Herald Square, on 34th Street; down by Wall Street in the financial district; and in the West Village, especially on West 4th Street near New York University and Washington Square Park. When he chanted at night, young people would gather around the truck, sing, dance, and join in with their own instruments.

"I was going out every day for eight, ten, twelve hours—no less," he remembered. "On Saturdays, I was doing *nāma-saṅkīrtana* for fifteen hours. We would go to Queens for six hours, then pack up our program and go to West 4th Street in the West Village and stay there all night long, until around 3:30 in the morning. It would take me twenty minutes to pack up, and then we would roll in for *maṅgala-ārati*.

"It was great—full-on kirtan in New York City! I was doing that every day for five years."

On Sundays, when several hundred people visited the temple, Aindra would return by mid-afternoon and lead kirtan until five, when the main program began. Afterwards, he would resume the kirtan while everyone was eating and then chant into the night, often joined by people who had come to the temple after seeing him on the streets.

He began with a core group of followers—Ramabhadra described "Aindra's gang" as consisting largely of Indians impressed by his spiritual dedication, eccentric guys with long hair and clarinets, and "yoga women" mesmerized by the chanting—but over time, more and more people of all stripes found inspiration in Aindra's chanting and mobile-temple program.

One Sunday, a man walked up to the truck and introduced himself. He was a guitarist, he said, and had been seeing the devotees for years but had never gotten involved.

"I'm a guitar player, too!" Aindra responded. The two leapt into a discussion of Hendrix and other guitarists and their styles. As the conversation drew to a close, Aindra asked, "Can you come to Tompkins Square Park tomorrow morning? I could really use some help."

The next day and almost every day for the next several months, the man played kartals in Aindra's kirtan. Eventually he too received initiation, as Murali Krishna das.

"Aindra invited me to serve in a practical way, by helping him," Murali Krishna remembered. "Every day, he'd tell me where to meet him, and I'd meet him there and sit with him in the truck, playing kartals. He explained that he preferred not playing chords on the harmonium; he preferred raga style and trained me how to play in that style."

Each morning, Murali Krishna helped Aindra lift the panels and set up the truck. "I don't know how he managed," he commented. "It was a lot of work. He'd frequently have to repair the panels, because they would get damaged from the constant assembly and disassembly. I'd help him carry them down to the temple basement, where he had his workshop with all kinds of tools, paints, and glues.

"He showed me how to take care of the Deities properly, with respect. 'They're not just statues,' he'd say. People would donate *bhoga*, or we would buy fruit and nuts, and we would make an offering to the Deities and distribute the *prasādam* from the truck.

"He always tried to maintain good relations with the police and authorities. He'd give them *prasādam* and be friendly with them. He always got the proper permits to park and use amplification. Cops in New York could be rough, but they liked him. They would bother all the other devotees, but not him.

"One time, an intoxicated man became violent, throwing stones and cigarettes at Aindra and the rest of us. I jumped out of the truck, wanting to beat him up, but Aindra stopped me. We just continued chanting, and the guy left. Aindra really trusted that the Lord would keep the devotees safe.

"Sometimes, at the morning program at the temple, if someone was playing kartals off beat, he would stop the kirtan. He'd go around showing everyone how to play in time. He was fearless, and people respected that. I admired that fearlessness."

༺ ༺ ༺

Aindra observed Cāturmāsya *vrata* alone that year and increased his austerities, even while chanting up to fifteen hours a day and setting up and taking down the truck's hundred-pound panels.

"*What?*" asked Ramabhadra in disbelief. "*Another vrata?*"

"Srila Prabhupada mentions it in the *Bhagavad-gītā*," Aindra replied. "You eat only fifteen bites on the full moon and decrease by one bite every day. On the new moon you totally fast, and then you increase by one bite per day."

"My God!" Ramabhadra exclaimed. "You're out there on your truck all day long and you're still doing *this*?"

"Yeah."

"Where do you eat, anyway?"

"In the truck."

"You just sit there in the truck and eat off the floor?"

"I don't sit," Aindra said. "I eat on my knees with my hands behind my back."

"You're treating yourself like an animal!" Ramabhadra told him. "You gotta stop torturing your body like this."

"But he kept doing it," Ramabhadra remembered. "It was like something straight out of the *Caitanya-caritāmṛta*. If he had a commitment to do something, he would never give up, and if he made a pledge to somebody, he would always carry it through. He was very responsible. So, he was continuing with his vows, all while doing his service. I don't know how he was able to do it."

※ ※ ※

Aindra still had to find a way to repay Bhavananda's loan. *Saṅkīrtana* donations barely covered daily expenses and the truck's repairs. He turned to Ramabhadra, who managed Radha-Govinda's account, for help. "Can you give me $800 for the monthly payment?" he asked.

"The only money I have is Radha-Govinda's," Ramabhadra said. "I can't just give it to you; you have to do some service."

"Well, what do you need?" Aindra offered.

Ramabhadra was in the midst of redesigning Radha-Govinda's altar and kitchen. Art-deco peacocks now adorned the doors, the walls were painted in a lavender shade, and one-inch turquoise tiles checkered the floor. That's where he had run into a snag. He wanted to finish the tiles with hot-pink grout, but there was no grout made in that color. The only way to do it would be to mix hot-pink paint into standard white grout, but that could ruin the turquoise tiling if it wasn't done right.

"I need hot-pink grout in the Deity kitchen by tomorrow,"

Ramabhadra said. He explained the challenge and offered to give Aindra the $800 when the job was complete.

Aindra couldn't disturb the devotees serving Radha-Govinda, so he showed up after they were finished, around ten that night, carrying pink paint, grout, and a new toothbrush. Then he got to work.

A little after three in the morning, Ramabhadra came into the kitchen to prepare for waking up Radha-Govinda. And there was Aindra, still grouting and scrubbing away with the toothbrush.

Aindra looked up through a delirium of fatigue. "You know," he said slowly, "this is a lot harder than I thought it would be."

Ramabhadra didn't reply.

"I think it's probably worth a lot more than $800," he suggested.

Ramabhadra just went about his service. Whenever he walked past, Aindra would make another remark about how hard the job was, and how insufficient the payment.

It was almost *maṅgala-ārati* when Aindra finished. He barely managed to stand up, looked Ramabhadra in the eye, and asked, "Are you going to give me an extra $800?"

"I don't think so," Ramabhadra said. "We agreed on the amount, and it's the Deities' money."

Aindra just stood there, glaring. With one eyebrow sharply up and the other sharply down, he strode off, pronouncing Ramabhadra a rascal for not paying extra for what he thought was extra-hard work.

CHAPTER TWELVE

AINDRA DID HIS best to collect as much money as possible during the holiday season. Devotees revved up their fund-raising activities during the Christmas marathon, but most of them were still selling hats, t-shirts, or stickers, or collecting donations for semi-fictitious causes.

He sometimes went into the subway posing as a disheveled, homeless man who couldn't speak. With Prabhupada's kirtan playing on a cassette player, he would shuffle through the train cars handing passengers pieces of paper on which he had written that he was disabled and couldn't keep a job. Once someone had read it, he would gesture for them to flip the paper over, and on the reverse side he had written, "Please give $1–$2. God bless." If the person gave only a dollar, he would point to the $2—and often receive the difference.

One time while he was collecting, Aindra was robbed by a mugger who threatened him with a knife and grabbed his bag, in which were his *japa-mālā* and a few personal items. As the mugger turned to run, Aindra implored him, "At least give me back my prayer beads!"

"Huh?" the man called back. Prayer beads? Then he looked in the bag and, seeing that it contained nothing of "value," threw it to the ground and ran away.

Santa Claus was always a good draw, and during one season Aindra and another devotee went around to bars both dressed as Santas. The other devotee would go in first, declaring, "Ho! Ho! Ho! Haribol!" to the drunk crowd, who would be thrilled to welcome Santa to their party. And then Aindra-Santa would enter and repeat the same line. Seeing the other Santa and pretending to be shocked, he would shout, "Hey! Who is that impostor? *I'm* the real Santa!"

The ensuing argument between Santas would escalate to the brink of a fistfight until one of them would shout, "Wait! This is just wrong. We should work together to bring good cheer to all mankind!"

"Yes!" the other Santa would agree, "Let's all work together to bring the *supreme* good cheer to all mankind!" And then the two Santas would collect money from the revelers.

One day, Aindra and Subala dressed up as Santas and went down into the subways to "Ho! Ho! Ho! Haribol!" through the stations and cars for donations. Wherever they went, however, it seemed like another Santa had already claimed the territory. They wound up finding vacant turf in Chinatown, but they couldn't drum up much business and finally gave up.

On the way back to the temple, as they passed a row of Italian restaurants on Mott Street in Little Italy, a man with a thick Italian accent called out to them, "Hey—Santa Claus!" He was standing outside a restaurant and urged them to come over. Then he opened the restaurant door and announced, "Hey, look! Santa Claus is coming to town!"

There was a big party inside, full of guys in suits smoking cigars. It looked to Aindra like a mafia Christmas party.

"Hey! *Two* Santas!" the men called out. "Whatchu guys doin'?"

"We're collecting donations for Food for Life," Aindra told them. "It feeds poor kids in India, but we've been out all night and haven't had any success."

"That's awful!" an important-looking man said. "We'll help out." And, turning to the others, he announced, "*Everyone* should help!"

At that, all the men got up from their tables and started pressing large bills into Subala and Aindra's hands. The two collected enough money that night to fund the kirtan project for the entire year.

Aindra collected like this a few times a year, but for many other devotees, it was a daily practice.

❦ ❦ ❦

In its early years, ISKCON had been both inspired and managed by Srila Prabhupada. In time, Prabhupada's followers took over most of the movement's practical activities, but Prabhupada still oversaw things and kept everything on track and moving forward.

After his departure, it was inevitable that there would be challenges. Three of ISKCON's eleven initiating gurus were suspended, and by 1985 much of the Society was in disarray. In just one year, the New York temple went from almost 150 residents to only two dozen. Some dropped out of the movement entirely; others remained but separated from the New York community.

Some devotees left the U.S. for India, especially Vrindavan. Hamsa Rupa das invited Aindra: "You should come! I am here, Tosan is here, Kurma Rupa is here—all your friends." There had been talk of reestablishing Vrindavan's 24-hour kirtan. "This is a perfect service for you; they need someone to organize it and head it up." The offer appealed to Aindra, but he wanted to "hang in there as long as possible," he said, for his preaching.

At that time, *Back to Godhead* was not officially funded by ISKCON. Several disciples of Satsvarupa dasa Goswami, the magazine's editor in chief, were among the Society's top book distributors and were lending financial support, but the publication was on the verge of bankruptcy. Determined to save it, late that year the group—Rama Raya das, Nama Sankirtan das, Mahaprabhu das, Vidura das, and Partha Damodar das—organized a Save the *Back to Godhead* Magazine party, based in a little office in the temple basement.

When Aindra had announced that he wanted to do daily *harināma*, Rama Raya, who in subsequent years became one of Aindra's closest friends and most dedicated followers, had recognized him as a dedicated *saṅkīrtana* soldier, and the group became his comrades in arms. Every month, a new issue of *Back to Godhead* was published, and the first box of each shipment would go to Aindra to distribute out on the streets. The group also donated magazines to Bhakti Tirtha Swami for his burgeoning preaching program in West Africa. Rama Raya was often away on *saṅkīrtana*, but he and Aindra established a strong solidarity and close friendship that flourished and deepened through the years.

❧ ❧ ❧

Crowds of people still gathered around Aindra's mobile temple, but when he saw that many who joined the temple were pressed into collecting more than chanting, he was concerned about their spiritual progress. "What I saw," he later said, "was devotees losing their inspiration in Krishna consciousness due to not gaining a taste for congregational chanting of the Holy Name, because the congregational chanting of the Holy Name was being so much de-emphasized in our movement."

He counselled devotees and tried to keep them focused on their *japa* and kirtan. "If it weren't for Aindra," Murali Krishna remembered, "I probably would have been among the people who left—if he hadn't shown me what was really important, what was really at the core of the movement: the pure chanting of the Holy Name.

"He was like my coach, telling me what was important in devotional service and helping me put Prabhupada's teachings into practice. He was critical of what was going on in the temple, but he didn't want me to lose faith and leave. I was new to the movement, so he was very careful about what he would tell me. He would reassure me about Krishna consciousness but ask me to be sure to stay with him and do kirtan.

"While we drove the truck, he'd preach to me about the *saṅkīrtana* movement, how kirtan was the *yuga-dharma*. All the devotees were doing other things; some were doing book distribution, but most of them were selling stickers. Aindra would just shake his head and say, 'What Prabhupada wanted was *hari-nāma-saṅkīrtana*. That's what we need to do.' He just went out with his shaved head, *śikhā*, tilak, and dhoti, chanting Hare Krishna.

"There was friction between him and the temple, but I was a new devotee, and all he would tell me was, 'I'm not getting support.' "

Eventually Aindra's frustrations became too much to bear. Murali Krishna, Subala, and Vishnu Rata das would maintain the mobile-temple program for another five years, but in the truck at Columbus Circle one evening that December, disheartened by developments in the movement and the lack of participation from devotees or cooperation from the temple authorities, Aindra told Rama Raya, "I'm moving to Vrindavan, prabhu, and this time I'm not coming back."

PART
TWO

Vrindavan

CHAPTER ONE

IN MARCH 1986, at the Radha Krishna Temple on Soho Street in London—the home of Sri Sri Radha-Londonisvara, the movement's first full-size marble Radha-Krishna deities—Riddha das heard singing coming from the temple room after a morning program. Peeking in, he saw an odd-looking devotee in a saffron T-shirt and dhoti sitting alone playing mridanga and chanting the *mahā-mantra*.

Riddha left, but when he returned at lunchtime, he could hear the devotee still singing, so he went into the temple room and introduced himself.

"I'm Aindra," the devotee said. "I'm on my way to Vrindavan. I'm just stopping here to collect enough *lakṣmī* for the rest of the trip."

Riddha was impressed by Aindra's devotion. They were godbrothers, it turned out, and Riddha, a travel agent, thought he might be able to help; he was often able to get inexpensive flights and help arrange visas for devotees.

When Riddha got back home, he told his seven-year-old son, Gopal, about Aindra. "You have to hear him do kirtan," he said. "He's a great singer."

Aindra stayed in the brahmacari ashram, and after a few days Riddha was able to obtain a voucher for a ticket from London to Delhi

Aindra could hardly believe it; he beamed with appreciation. But as he read the voucher's details, his smile faded. The name on it was William Ehrlichman. "This is for Bhagavan Goswami," he pointed out.

"A ticket is a ticket," Riddha said. "You have a valid passport and visa, so maybe they'll let you through. Anyway, it's worth a try."

They went straight to the airport, and, to Aindra's happy amazement, the airline issued him a ticket to Delhi.

When Riddha returned home, his son asked if he would take him to the temple. "I want to hear that devotee doing kirtan," the boy said. But it was too late; Aindra had left for Vrindavan.

❧ ❧ ❧

From Delhi, Aindra would travel the last two hundred kilometers by bus. When he approached the ticket window and reached for money to pay the fare, however, his pockets were empty. While he'd been racing through the station's jostling crowd lugging two trunks filled with his Deities, sound system, instruments, and personal items, he'd had his pocket picked, and there was nothing left.

The bus was leaving, but Aindra, trunks bouncing behind him, managed to jump aboard just as it pulled out into traffic. When the conductor came to collect tickets, Aindra could only fold his hands and plead his case: "Please, sir, I just need to get to Vrindavan."

"Your ticket," the conductor insisted.

"Please," Aindra begged. "I was pickpocketed at the station. They took everything. I have no money. I just need to get back to Vrindavan."

"Where is your ticket?" the conductor repeated.

Aindra fell to his knees in tears. "Please!" he repeated, "I just want to go to Vrindavan."

"Not without a ticket," the conductor insisted. He wouldn't budge.

Fortunately for Aindra, some of the passengers sympathized with him, appalled to see his treatment at the hands of the conductor. "What kind of man are you?" they demanded. "He's a sadhu! He is begging!" So, the conductor was forced to move on, and Aindra made it the rest of the way to Vrindavan.

❧ ❧ ❧

When Aindra finally arrived at Krishna-Balaram Mandir, he had to ask the manager to pay the rickshaw wallah who had brought him to the gates. He moved into a room on the third floor of the *gurukula* building with Bhuvanesvara das, a friend from New York, but just a few days after he arrived, the two prepared to leave for Mayapur, for the 500th Appearance Anniversary Celebration of Sri Chaitanya Mahaprabhu.

"Why so much baggage?" Bhuvanesvara asked when he saw Aindra heaving his two large trunks onto a rickshaw bound for the Mathura station.

"My Deities and personal stuff are in this one," Aindra explained. "The other is full of instruments and amps."

Who would drag his own sound system to a festival? Bhuvanesvara wondered. But he could see that Aindra did things his own way.

In Mayapur Aindra set up his equipment on the lawn in front of the temple and arranged instruments in a circle—an invitation for others to join in. Gopinath, a Dutch-Indonesian rock musician who had known Aindra from the Seventh Avenue temple in New York and had given up his career to join him on the kirtan truck, sat with him chanting eight hours a day, but he was practically the only one.

The Mayapur gathering was a grand, festive event with significant results: the zonal-acharya system was dismantled, and the GBC approved twenty initiating gurus. But Aindra was disappointed that devotees hadn't joined him for kirtan, and he saw that the discord he had experienced in America extended throughout the movement. His hope and effort had been to unite devotees in *hari-nāma-saṅkīrtana*, but the Mayapur meetings were contentious, with devotees engaged in institutional warfare instead of cooperating together, as Srila Prabhupada had instructed.

❧ ❧ ❧

After the festival, Aindra went with the *gurukula* students on a pilgrimage to Haridwar, where forty million people—yogis, *paṇḍits*, and devotees from the subcontinent's myriad traditions—gathered over a three-month period for the Kumbha-mela festival, culminating on the most auspicious day, when ten million bathed in the holy Ganges.

The *gurukulis* set up camp and began performing elaborate fire *yajñas*, but Aindra wanted to perform *saṅkīrtana-yajña*, and each morning he would march through the camp beating a drum and calling out, "*Saṅkīrtana-yajña! Yuga-dharma hari-nāma-saṅkīrtana yajña!*" Then he'd just sit by the altar, and, along with whoever joined him, do kirtan for the rest of the day.

As the moment for the Kumbha-mela's main sacred bath approached, Aindra found himself packed so tightly in the middle of the crowd that he was lifted up off his feet and for the next two hours barely made contact with the ground. When the gates to the river opened, there was a stampede. Aindra saw a woman just ahead of him stumble and fall. Dazed, she couldn't get up; he could see that she would be trampled. But he managed to stop in front of her, then lifted her up onto his back and carried her away from the worst of the crush.

❦ ❦ ❦

When Aindra got back to Vrindavan, he was still broke. "I didn't have a penny," he recalled. "Not one paisa. Just a couple of amps and my instruments." But he'd also brought blueprints for a new design for a mobile temple, and he had a master plan: he'd travel through India's cities, towns, and villages doing kirtan and then apply for sannyasa and submit a proposal to the GBC to build a whole fleet of mobile temples to traverse India like the Radha-Damodara Party had crossed the United States. The trucks would be even better than in New York, each like a wheeled peacock carrying a multi-domed temple on its back.

There wasn't any funding for the project, though, and its practicality was uncertain. "I thought it sounded too tough," Kurma Rupa remembered. "India is too disorganized. I told him to go for it, but I just couldn't picture it; I didn't think it was a good idea." The matter was decided when Aindra looked for the blueprints he had brought from America. They were gone, lost except for a small side-view sketch.

❧ ❧ ❧

Even more disappointing was the state of kirtan at the Krishna-Balaram temple. Aindra had left America because of the lack of support for *hari-nāma-saṅkīrtana*. "One of the things that made me come to Vrindavan," he remembered, "was sheer frustration with the condition of the movement everywhere else." He had expected different in Vraja. But he found that beyond devotees chanting during *āratis*, *guru-pūjā*, and festivals, there was no real kirtan program. "There was no kirtan here at all," he said. "Nothing."

Srila Prabhupada had first instituted a 24-hour kirtan in Los Angeles in 1970. "This is very auspicious," he had told the devotees. "In the temples in India this is what they do, and you should do this." In 1975 he had directed that one be started in Vrindavan, and in June of that year Nitai das had reported to him, "Twenty-four-hour kirtan is going on there regularly," with devotees from different temples taking the shifts. The Atlanta devotees had taken two shifts, in the early morning and the afternoon, and Visnujana Swami had volunteered to chant from midnight to 2 a.m. "Everybody had a shift," Jaganama das remembered, "but Visnujana Swami's shift really rocked."

"This 24-hour chanting is very encouraging to me," Prabhupada wrote temple president Aksayananda Swami and Dhananjaya das. "Please continue all as I have given you."

In September 1976, when Aksayananda had told Prabhupada, "We have the 24-hour kirtan—I've requested everyone who comes to do at least one hour per day," Prabhupada had responded, "There is no question; that is the condition." Then he specified, "One batch [three] hours. From morning six to nine. Another batch from nine to twelve. Another batch twelve to three. Another batch three to six."

"Twice one batch," he had added: each group could take two shifts. "One batch attending once in the morning, once in the evening."

"At the installation of the temple, Prabhupada wanted the devotees to keep this 24-hour kirtan going," longtime Vrindavan resident Daivi Shakti dasi recalled. "But some of the managers misunderstood that to mean that every single person in the temple had to take part. So every devotee who lived here—and there weren't many of us—we all had to come and do our hour or two hours; we were assigned." But not everyone wanted to do it, or could. "The managers would go to Prabhupada and complain, 'This devotee refuses to do kirtan. They say they are making garlands for six hours a day, so how can they do kirtan.' So Prabhupada clarified: 'If he has no work, he can chant Hare Krishna here. If they are not engaged in service, then they should be engaged in 24-hour kirtan' "

"Srila Prabhupada had wanted 24-hour kirtan in Krishna-Balaram Mandir," agreed Brahmananda das, one of Prabhupada's first disciples. "Different leaders in charge of the temple tried to organize it, tried different schemes, but it never sustained. What was required to chant Hare Krishna twenty-four hours a day was someone who himself was prepared to chant Hare Krishna twenty-four hours a day."

Battling against feelings of hopelessness and defeat—at one point he even considered surrendering his body to the Yamuna, which he had heard could uplift one to Goloka Vrindavan—Aindra resolved to do what he had done in Mayapur. Whenever he wasn't serving the Deities, he would sit and chant all day every day, instruments displayed around him to invite others to join.

"Aindra was the first," Brahmananda said, "because he was prepared to chant twenty-four hours a day. And he did it. In the beginning he was one man alone. But that's all that was required—even one man who was determined."

"I had originally come with the intention of doing a traveling *nāma-haṭṭa* program," Aindra remembered, "but I was thinking, *What's the use of going around inviting people to come to the temple when there is no kirtan going on here?* Without kirtan, for the public it was kind of like a wax museum—historical events, but the atmosphere was relatively dead.

"I had a harmonium, a *dholak,* kartals, whompers [plate-sized cymbals], shakers, a couple small, rechargeable amplifiers, and microphones and stands all packed into a metal box that I took along on a little hand truck with big wheels, and I spent eight hours a day just chanting alone in the temple. I was in Vrindavan-dhāma, trying to renew interest in kirtan, but nobody was helping me; there was nobody interested.

"I just wanted to get something going, so I took help from wherever I could get it. It was mostly not ISKCON devotees; whomever I could get, I considered Krishna's mercy—from the 'outside' or the 'inside' didn't matter. I would sit down in the temple room, set up the harmonium, and just grab anybody, whoever it was—just grab them, pull them over, sit them down, and get them to help somehow or other. If some old baba came through the door for darshan, I would say, 'Hey you, come, sit down, play this mridanga!' 'But I don't know how to play.' 'Play it anyway!' And then another baba would come in and I'd say, 'Sit down, play these kartals!' and in this way somehow or another get some kind of kirtan started—just so I could give the appearance of something going on. It wasn't the ISKCON devotees who were helping me in the beginning.

"Then, gradually, a couple of Indian brahmacharis would come, because they saw that something was happening. After eight months or so like that, more devotees started recognizing that there was a regular happening, and they would come and help out. And then there were about eight or nine ISKCON brahmacharis helping."

❦ ❦ ❦

One morning in October, just after breakfast *prasādam*, Srila Prabhupada's elderly *vraja-vāsī* follower Kapoorji, whom Prabhupada had appointed to handle the temple's financial accounts, approached Aindra, tears streaming from his eyes down into his bushy grey mustache. "He told me that he'd just had a dream of Srila Prabhupada," Aindra related. "Prabhupada had been crying in his dream, and that had made Kapoorji cry, too. "In the dream, Prabhupada had been imploring him, 'Why is there no 24-hour kirtan going on in my temple?' And as he was telling me about the encounter, it was affecting my heart, and I started crying, too.

"I could understand that it must have been something real: Kapoorji was telling me that Prabhupada was crying in his dream, and Kapoorji himself was crying, and he was telling me, 'Aindra, please! Start a 24-hour kirtan for Srila Prabhupada.'

"So I thought, *Okay, let's try.*"

CHAPTER TWO

AND SO, ON October 12, 1986, Vijayadashami, the anniversary of Lord Rama's defeat of the demon Ravana, Aindra re-initiated Krishna-Balaram Mandir's 24-hour kirtan.

He was determined not only to get the 24-hour kirtan going again, but also to make it last. He felt that there were three reasons why previous attempts had been short-lived: devotees had not been assigned full time, the schedules had not been maintainable, and the kirtans had not been integrated into the temple culture. So he established a core of a half dozen or so devotees for whom the kirtan was their main service, though early on, especially during the hot summers and cold winters, when there were fewer temple devotees, they also distributed books, helped on the altar, and worked for the Deity department.

The first devotee to participate was Gopinath, having overcome objections from his guru, who had not wanted him to "become a *bābājī*," "just chanting" in Vrindavan. Over the following years, a few dozen young men joined, at least for a time. Among the early members—almost all Indian—were Jagadish; Avani from north India; Devakinandan, from West Bengal, who, like several devotees, had joined in Mayapur but migrated to Vrindavan; Nanda-nandana, who had been living in Gaudiya Maṭha temples for over a decade; Ananda Chaitanya, a young Nepali recently graduated from the *gurukula*; and Sodhana Krishna, a disciple of Srila Prabhupada's godbrother Bon Maharaja.

One evening a devotee named Acutya das approached Aindra after his kirtan. "I was studying architecture in a university in New York," Acutya said, "and I saw your kirtan-truck on the sidewalk. I thought to myself, *Wow, mobile motif architecture!* I was so impressed that I stuck around to hear the kirtan and found out about the Sunday feast at the Brooklyn temple. I went to the temple that Sunday, but you had already left and come here. The other day, I told someone my story and they said it was your truck, so I wanted to introduce myself and say thank you. I'm living here in Vrindavan now. I'm an architect, and they want me to stay and help complete Prabhupada's samadhi." *Well*, Aindra considered, *maybe I wasn't completely useless in New York after all.*

Most of these first devotees were trained in classical Bengali-style kirtan, but there were initially so few that Aindra had to divide the day into four-hour shifts—each party member, including Aindra, manning two, for a total of eight hours, often alone. Further, the temple staffing was so tight that the kirtan devotees were regularly enlisted to serve on the altar and in other aspects of Deity worship. Gopinath, for instance, would do his shift, take a shower and change into clean cloth, cook and offer *bhoga* to the Deities, offer Them *ārati*, honor a little *mahā-prasādam*, and then take another four-hour shift.

Eventually, when Srila Prabhupada's letters, lectures, and conversations became available online, and Aindra learned more about Prabhupada's instructions for organizing a 24-hour kirtan, he formed eight three-hour shifts manned by three teams, each devotee participating in two shifts, for six hours of devotional service. The ideal was that each team would comprise at least three devotees—one to lead the chanting and play harmonium, one on mridanga, and the third on kartals. If only one man was available, he would accompany himself on mridanga; if there were two, one could play mridanga, the other kartals.

Again following Prabhupada's instructions, they would sing only the *mahā-mantra*—no other prayers or *bhajanas*. "I want people all over the world to understand the power of the Hare Krishna *mahā-mantra*," Aindra said. The *mahā-mantra* embodied the Divine Lovers' romantic drama. "The resplendent personality of the Holy Name of Radha (Hare) compassionately folds me into Her bosom, besprinkling the *kuṅkum* from Her breast onto the lotus of my heart to gracefully confer upon this aspiring maidservant the *adhikāra* to passionately kiss, embrace, and intimately satisfy the Holy Name of Her all-enchanting lover, Lord Gopipriya. Thus, under Her auspices and for Her absolute pleasure, I enthusiastically sing the thunderous *saṅkīrtana* of the Holy Names—Hare Krishna, Hare Krishna, Krishna Krishna, Hare Hare/ Hare Rama, Hare Rama, Rama Rama, Hare Hare."

"I always emphasize the importance of chanting the Hare Krishna *mahā-mantra*," he later shared. "Although Prabhupada said that the Six Goswamis' songs are the extensions of the *mahā-mantra*, still more important than all of them is the *mukhya-mantra*, the chief mantra. So many times devotees become sidetracked because of their lack of taste for chanting the *mahā-mantra*, due to not chanting enough. They are thinking that the kirtan is boring if you don't switch to 'Govinda *Jaya Jaya*,' or 'Radhe, Radhe,' or whatever *jaya, jaya, jaya*. Undoubtedly, Srila Prabhupada's instruction is that the main focus of the kirtan should be the *mahā-mantra*. Here in Vrindavan for the 24-hour kirtan, we chant the *mahā-mantra* exclusively. That is the main and best *saṅkīrtana* mantra for this age."

He recounted how Prabhupada, in Vrindavan, had responded when he had been asked what could be sung in kirtans. " 'Is it okay to sing "Haribol?" ' the devotees asked. 'Or "Nitai Gaur Haribol"?'

"Prabhupada said, 'Mostly chant Hare Krishna.'

" 'Is it okay to sing the songs of the predecessor acharyas?'

"Prabhupada said, 'Yes, but mostly chant Hare Krishna.'

" 'Is it okay to chant Jaya Radhe?'

"Prabhupada said, 'Yes. But mostly chant Hare Krishna.'

"At least five or six different things were asked, and Prabhupada kept saying, 'Yes, but mostly chant Hare Krishna.' Every time, he was bringing it back: 'Mostly chant Hare Krishna, mostly chant Hare Krishna, mostly chant Hare Krishna.' So it is obvious that what Prabhupada was trying to say was, 'Mostly chant Hare Krishna!' "

Only on Radhastami would Aindra make an exception and sing to glorify Srimati Radharani. In reference to other songs or combined mantra forms that Prabhupada had not introduced, Aindra was unequivocal: "Prabhupada was not interested in allowing such mantras, or such concocted form of mantras, to be chanted."

And he was firm in his insistence that both the mantra and instrument policies be followed, checking the temple room at random times to see how everything was going. When he heard a team member playing harmonium on a solo shift one night, he went down and asked the devotee to play mridanga instead.

"But it's my harmonium," the devotee retorted. "I'll play it if I want to."

Aindra just picked up the harmonium and threw it into the courtyard, where it broke into pieces on the marble floor.

With three-man teams, the kirtans could always have harmonium, mridanga, and kartals. But for that to be constant, Aindra needed nine men, and including himself, he had only seven—sometimes, especially in the hot summers, only five or six. It was suggested that musicians from outside the temple could make up the difference, but when he tried to include local professionals, he found that most would sing for a while, flaunt their skills, and then ask, "So, how do you like me?" and haggle for compensation: "How much are you paying? What, so little? Pagal Baba pays more." The experiment lasted less than a month.

❧ ❧ ❧

One of the next devotees to join was Nitai das, who had met the devotees near the end of a Kumbha-mela in Nashik, in his native state of Maharashtra. He had been with a group of family and friends from his village but had been so attracted to Krishna consciousness that he'd joined the devotees on the spot and when they left had gotten on the bus with them back to Bombay, where he'd been engaged in service by the movement's publishing division, the Bhaktivedanta Book Trust (BBT).

One morning Aindra heard a sweet, beautiful voice leading the *guru-pūjā* kirtan. Nitai, he learned, had given up a career as a professional singer to become a devotee and was visiting Vrindavan on BBT business.

It didn't take long to convince Nitai to move to Vrindavan full time, and Aindra paired him up with Devakinandan. In kirtan he would sit behind the harmonium in total absorption, his eyes closed, oblivious to what was going on around him. Sometimes he would man the late shift by himself.

One night, still in discussion upstairs in his room, Aindra heard the faint sound of kirtan—Nitai's voice accompanied by harmonium, mridanga, and kartals. But something seemed different. Then it occurred to him: wasn't Nitai on the shift alone?

Down in the temple room, he found Nitai sitting like a one-man orchestra: his left hand playing the big head of a mridanga, the strap of which was rigged so he could pump the harmonium bellows by rocking back and forth; his ankles wrapped in bells, which he played by tapping his feet; and his right hand on the strings of a tambura.

Rooms 89 and 90 on the third floor of the *gurukula* building became the 24-hour-kirtan ashram. Each department had to be self-supporting—at first the temple authorities wouldn't even pay for a mridanga—but the kirtan party didn't have enough funds to pay the rent, so Aindra had to find ways for the kirtan-party members to make themselves useful. They might not earn money, but they could serve on the altar, do building improvement and repair, and clean bathrooms.

❧ ❧ ❧

Aindra's goal for the kirtan party's members was not just to train musicians; he wanted to develop a core of solid brahmacharis. "We're not doing *hari-nāma-saṅkīrtana* because we're musicians!" he told them. "We're doing *hari-nāma-saṅkīrtana* because it's the *yuga-dharma*!"

And anyway, he said, "We can never be proud that we're good musicians. Compared to the best musicians in this world, we're nothing. And the best musicians in this world are nothing compared to the musicians in the heavenly planets. And the best musicians in the heavenly planets are nothing compared to Lord Shiva. And the best musicians of all are the *gopīs* of Vrindavan. So, we can never be proud."

"You've learned how to sing very expertly," he told one popular, accomplished classical Indian singer. "Now you should learn to sing with devotion."

To join the party, a candidate should at least be able to play kartals and follow a basic rhythm. And he must be willing to work—to put in the effort. "In this age you will not get anything without *nama-sankirtana*," he told one new devotee, "and not just a little lip-service to *nāma-saṅkīrtana*, half-hour here and half-hour there, but sitting down for hours and hours and hours for kirtan together as a practice of *bhajana*!"

But the bottom line was one's devotion. "Purity," he said, "is the main thing. Musical style is secondary." If one's heart is "steel framed," he quoted from *Śrīmad-Bhāgavatam*, then "in spite of one's chanting the Holy Name of the Lord with concentration, [it] does not change when ecstasy takes place, tears fill the eyes and the hairs stand on end." If hearing and chanting are properly performed, he read from the purport, "there will follow the reactional ecstasy with signs of tears in the eyes and standing of the hairs on the body. These are natural consequences and are the preliminary symptoms of the *bhāva* stage, which occurs before one reaches the perfectional stage of *prema*, love of Godhead. If the reaction does not take place, even after continuous hearing and chanting of the holy name of the Lord, it may be considered to be due to offenses only."

"So why do we have to remain as an offender?" he asked. "We cannot claim that we have actual attachment to the Holy Name of Krishna, which is not different from Krishna, if we're not beginning to manifest direct reactional ecstatic emotions in relationship on the basis of that attachment. The attachment is not at a standstill; it is something which naturally flows and brings one to the ecstatic position.

"If we actually have attachment to chanting of the Holy Name, there must naturally be a softening of the heart as a consequence of that attachment to Krishna. The attachment to Krishna is what causes *vipralambha*. That is what causes the preliminary anxiety for meeting with Krishna, for being with Krishna. And due to that attachment, if we're actually attached to Krishna, the personality, then when we chant His name, that name makes us think of Krishna, the personality that we're attached to. Because the name is non-different from Krishna. Our attachment to the name should be as much as what we're attached to Krishna the person. We should be attached to the name in *śānta-rasa*, in *sakhya-rasa*, or *dāsya-rasa*, or *vātsalya-rasa*, or *mādhurya-rasa*, in the same *rasa* that we're attached to, even if it's in the aspiring stage, that same *rasa* will be seen in our relationship with the chanting of the Holy Name and the feelings toward the object of our *rasa* or the subject of our *rasa*, meaning to say, Krishna is the subject. Our feelings that we will have toward Krishna based on our attachment to Krishna in various ways will be the object of His pleasure.

"To see Krishna's name or hear Krishna's name—to think of Krishna's name automatically necessitates our thinking of the person, and it should manifest as a particular kind of attachment, which is growing in our heart to that person, which should manifest as feelings of separation from Krishna, which is preliminarily manifest as the anxiety or the anticipation of meeting Krishna, of gaining His association, gaining His company, and not feeling happy without it. Which should bring a certain degree of intensity of desires within the heart, which will cause us to naturally cry for His association! That should be coming in our chanting as a result of properly hearing and chanting the Holy Names.

"If it's not coming, then it should be understood that we ourselves are not properly hearing and chanting the Holy Name. And it must be due to some impropriety in our attachment, in the attachment of our mind, in the attachment of our heart. That we're maintaining material attachments somehow or other, subtly or grossly, even after understanding so many instructions on this matter, which is the basic, let's say, bottom line in offensive chanting....

"When there's attachment to the principal of *ahaitukī bhakti* to the extent that we don't mind whether we have to again and again and again take birth, we don't care for *mukti*, we don't care for moksha. We're interested only that we should again and again and again relish the practicing of pure devotional services.... That comes after there's the constant chanting, proper constant chanting of the Holy Name. But mind you, it is symptomatic of the proper constant chanting of the Holy Name affected by accepting the humble attitude, being tolerant, giving respect to others without expecting any respect for ourselves, which is the basis for offenseless chanting. The symptom is that within our heart we will not desire any such things as *dhanam*, wealth, *or janam*, followers, people; or this *sundarīm*, adoration, people applauding us for our deeds in devotional service. We don't want profit, *dhanam*; we don't want distinction, *janam*; and we don't want adoration, *sundarīm*. Nor do we want moksha."

"We want *prema*," he said. "And the basis of the cultivation of *prema* is *ahaitukī bhakti*. So, by *ahaitukī bhakti bhajana*, it's expected that we should be developing some attachment to the subject of that *bhajana*, namely Krishna. From *ruci* comes *āsakti*. And *āsakti* is the preliminary stage of *bhāva*; it is the basis of *bhāva*. And all this is taken in terms of proportionate degrees. When there's a proportionate degree of freedom from *anarthas*, of which offenses again the Holy Name are one type.... to that degree we will become steady in our devotional practices. To the degree that we're steady in devotional practices, to that degree we will be developing something—taste....

"We're virtually living in a realm of ever-increasing, simultaneous hopelessness and hopefulness. Our hopefulness is based on expectation of Krishna's mercy, and our hopelessness is based on the realization of the futility of our efforts to express our attachment to Krishna, because there's virtually very little attachment. Therefore, crying because we can't cry based on attachment. If we can't cry for Krishna when we're chanting the Holy Name, if no tears come to our eyes, then we should at least be crying because we can't cry, realized by our decrepit destitute downtrodden position. And those tears of crying because we can't cry or are crying because we can't cry because we can't cry, those tears will melt away the hardcoredness of our heart. And those tears will be the beginning of our actual crying for Krishna."

❧ ❧ ❧

Along with following Srila Prabhupada's instructions to chant exclusively the *mahā-mantra*, Aindra also mandated that the 24-hour party satisfy His Divine Grace's desire that the kirtan be continuous—*akhaṇḍa*, without interruption. The kirtan devotees had to be punctual and remain for their entire shift. "He was emphatic," one remembered, "sometimes shouting at the top of his lungs that we should be doing kirtan *ahaitukī, apratihatā, akhaṇḍa nāma*—unmotivated, uninterrupted, and unbroken. And uninterrupted devotional service meant that when we sat down to do kirtan, we shouldn't get up for any reason whatsoever; we should stay for the entire duration of the shift." They should visit the bathroom beforehand, bring drinking water, and request someone else to save *prasādam* for them. And no chatting or speaking on cell phones. Even when one devotee complained that he had a cold and couldn't sit on the marble temple-room floor during the chilly winter night, Aindra told him to bring a blanket or even a sleeping bag—but not to ever neglect his duty or stop the kirtan.

"Why *akhaṇḍa nāma*, 24-hour kirtan?" Aindra asked. "Because people are forced to become pious by even entering into an atmosphere where a kirtan had been performed, as the ethereal atmosphere still remains purifying. So, how much more one is forced to become pious when one walks into a place where the kirtan performance is going on and one hears the Holy Name. And how much even more purifying is the place where the Holy Name is being heard 24 hours a day, nonstop. When you chant nonstop in a place, the power of that place simply increases, increases, and increases, but when the kirtan breaks, it loses power.

"The *akhaṇḍa* kirtan also forces people to surrender more, because they can't just start talking about something or even stop to eat. One has to sacrifice. There is also a greater degree of responsibility toward the other members of the team, as they are working very hard to keep *harināma* continuously manifest in the atmosphere.

"If you are doing *akhaṇḍa nāma* kirtan for years and years, the atmosphere that has been generated by the continuous manifestation of *nāma* becomes so powerful that it not only purifies one from material contamination but purifies the egoism of the soul, bringing the soul to its original egoism, the mood of a resident of Vrindavan."

Kirtan was a serious *yajña*, he stated. One should do it with full heart, with full energy: body, mind, heart—everything into it—and be there for the full duration.

"I don't just want people to come here and do kirtan," he stated. "I actually need people to come here and help us maintain this *akhaṇḍa nāma*—that's what I need here; that's what I want. We are doing this *akhaṇḍa nāma yajña* for Srila Prabhupada."

"For so many years," he said, "so many devotees have been making the effort to keep the Hare Krishna *mahā-mantra* chanted in the temple room without any break—for so long—and then some rascal comes along—it just takes one rascal—and just carelessly breaks the *akhaṇḍa nāma* and destroys all of that." Each member of the party had to be responsible and vigilant.

Maintaining the *akhaṇḍa* kirtan was one of the reasons why Aindra insisted on keeping the 24-hour-kirtan department in the *gurukula* building. The top-floor rooms could get blazing hot in the summer, and sharing the building with almost two hundred children was far from ideal, but he wanted to be within hearing distance of the temple room so that he could keep tabs on the kirtan, that it would never stop.

For the kirtan to go on uninterruptedly, for twenty-four hours a day, it had to continue even during other temple programs. If there was an activity, such as the morning *Bhāgavatam* class, that the kirtan would disrupt, the team members would chant quietly on their beads on one side of the temple, just behind Tulasi. Then, immediately after, they would resume. Initially, they did gentle kirtan during the two hours after *maṅgala-ārati* when devotees chanted *japa* together in the temple room, but when that was seen as a distraction, Aindra settled for just a few minutes of kirtan right before the Deities' darshan, understanding that the Holy Name was being chanted throughout.

Chanting from the 4 a.m. shift was the first thing devotees heard each day as they assembled, and it helped establish the right spiritual atmosphere for the morning program. Aindra specified that the kirtan then should be sung in a sweet, gentle *maṅgala-ārati* melody, even if the tempo sometimes up-shifted toward the end. At first he took the midnight-to-four shift himself, when in the solitude of the empty temple he could develop new tunes, work out beats, and chant without restriction; eventually he settled into leading the early-evening kirtan, right before *gaura-ārati*—his regular slot.

❦ ❦ ❦

Another of the challenges devotees faced when they joined the kirtan party was Aindra's insistence that all the musicians chant while playing, which they weren't all accustomed to doing. Most of the drummers concentrated on their mridanga playing, some just on producing fancy beats. But Aindra was firm. "Your mridanga playing is zero if you don't put a one before it," he said. "And that one is Krishna; that one is the *mahā-mantra*."

He would chastise any devotee who wasn't chanting—give him what one devotee called his "stare of death" or yell at him right in the middle of a kirtan, no matter how many people were listening. "Prabhupada said that the instruments should not be played in a way that one cannot sing along with them at the same time," he instructed. "Sometimes devotees become so absorbed in trying to play their instruments in a complicated way that they can't chant while they play. That means they haven't learned to play them properly. If one is not competent, or if one did not learn properly, he may know how to play intricate beats on the mridanga but not how to sing at the same time—which is a hundred times the benefit of only hearing.

"So, if one is playing the mridanga properly by following the kirtan leader and serving the Holy Name and at the same time hearing, that's great. But higher than that, better than that, is being able to play the mridanga and sing at the same time, at least as much as possible.

"Sometimes when the kirtan gets very heavy and it's really taking off, the mridanga player may have to back out of chanting to execute the changes the kirtan leader is putting the kirtan through. But that should be the exception, not the rule. As a general rule, as much as possible, the mridanga players should also respond with chanting.

"As far as the kartal players are concerned, I have seen people playing the kartals, or playing the gong, or playing the whompers, or playing the shakers, or banging on instruments just for their own high, completely oblivious to the fact that they should be chanting. And honestly speaking—that just boils my blood!"

"It was a little difficult in the beginning," one kirtan devotee remembered, "because we were so used to just playing mridanga and not singing. You had to coordinate the mouth with the hands. The mouth is doing something and the hands are doing something else, and sometimes the mind is thinking of something else. So it was a lot to deal with." When one of the party members complained about it, however, Aindra replied, "Just tighten your belt!"

Further, everyone in the kirtan had to follow the chanter's lead—mridanga first, then kartals. "If the kirtan leader is singing without playing an instrument," he said, "or if he's playing the harmonium, which is not a rhythmic instrument, then the mridanga player should be following, trying to tune in and pick up on where the kirtan leader wants to go with the kirtan. The idea is for the mridanga player to serve and enhance the mood of the kirtan leader. Then the kartals should follow the mridanga. The mridanga player should not be so self-centered that his mridanga playing becomes more important to him than the kirtan, forcing the kirtan leader to surrender to whatever *he* is doing.... There is a need for cooperation among the various performers. And because there is a leader, the idea is to follow the leader. If you become a good follower, then you can become a good leader. Because you'll know what is required in following.

"If there is a competent leader, then if someone endeavors to hear and pay attention to where the leader is at, trying to pick up on his *bhāva*, he can develop his own leadership skills. He may have a different mood, because every soul is different and is going to have some nuance of expression of his own unique mood."

In other words, there was plenty room for self-expression, innovation, and artistic finesse—for different styles and approaches. When there was a complaint from one of the kirtan devotees about how another was leading the pre-*mangala-ārati* chanting, Aindra said, "But he's doing it nicely." And when the devotee pointed out that Aindra had always done it differently and that they had been doing it the same way for years, Aindra told him, "Yeah, and the person that you remember leading the kirtan like that is telling you right now that I like the way he does it!"

"The cool thing," he said, "is to put your own spin on it!" While their role in the kirtan was to follow the leader, the other musicians also had room for their own individuality. "After all," he said, "even though the kirtan leader is the leader, it is not his performance alone; it's not that Krishna is looking only at him. *Saṅkīrtana* is a congregational effort; everyone is in it together. Love is always a two-way street. In real kirtan there is thus a give and take among the performers. Sometimes the mridanga player has a good idea, or the kartal player has a good idea. And if it is a good idea, the kirtan leader benefits by surrendering to what the mridanga player has to offer. There is natural reciprocation between good kirtan performers. That's called jamming. It's sharing inspiration with each other. That sharing brings the kirtan to another dimension of spontaneous dynamism, which increases the inspiration, enthusiasm, and appreciation of each other as cooperative constituents in Lord Chaitanya's *līlā*."

Not all of Aindra's accompanists could do it. "Some," he said, "are neither interested in nor capable of understanding my mood or musical preferences; they just can't pick up on what I am doing to effectively inspire and engage others."

Everyone had to play along. "Play something!" he shouted at one kirtan devotee who was only chanting. When, after searching for a pair of kartals, a gong, whompers, a shaker—anything—the devotee told Aindra that he couldn't find one not being used, Aindra said, "Then clap your hands!" And with gestures, shouts, stares, and glances, he would lead the musicians as he sang and played, like a conductor directing his orchestra.

※ ※ ※

Aindra's kirtans had an immediate effect on the entire temple. "It's hard to imagine now," remembered Bhurijana Prabhu, who had in 1987 established the Vrindavan Institute for Higher Education (VIHE) to fulfill Srila Prabhupada's desire for an educational institute in Vrindavan and encourage deep, systematic shastric study, "but in the '80s, no one used to come to Krishna-Balaram Mandir—not the Western devotees, not the Indian devotees. Even during Kartik there was no one here except the devotees who lived here. The Damodara prayers would have maybe twenty, thirty devotees—it was completely different."

Attendance at the evening *ārati* was particularly sparse, but when Aindra took over the lead, it almost immediately picked up. Word spread, and more devotees and pilgrims began coming. Everywhere they went, book distributors would meet people who had been impressed by the Krishna-Balaram kirtan, or who had heard about it from others. "The word in Delhi," one devotee remembered, "was that 'You have to go to Angrezi Mandir'—the English temple—'for *sandhyā-ārati*' and hear this Western devotee chanting renditions of classical Indian ragas with which they were familiar and to which they could relate." Aindra's kirtan became a trademark for the temple—the temple was known for them—and Krishna-Balaram was one of the only temples in Vraja where kirtan went on continuously.

"And then," Bhurijana continued, "very much because of kirtans specifically, especially Aindra Prabhu's kirtans, the temple became famous throughout India. They were so powerful, and everyone would dance and chant, and it had such an extreme effect."

CHAPTER THREE

AINDRA BECAME INCREASINGLY interested in raga theory, but he was almost entirely self-taught and relied on his ear and experience. "I'm not so expert," he admitted. "If a musical pundit came to my kirtans, he may be able to criticize me for taking liberties and breaking certain rules of the ragas I'm singing. But I'm doing what sounds good to me."

Raga, he learned, was essentially a collection of notes used as the basis for creating melodies, like a painter's palette. He was fascinated by how a raga palette could have a varying number of notes, from five to seven, and how there could be different notes in a different order for the ascent to higher or the descent to lower pitches.

"*Raga* actually means *rasa*," he said. "And *rasa* means a mellow. So a raga is a configuration of notes which produce a certain mellow. There are different vibrations, a certain number of vibrations allotted to different notes. Of course, it's a rather complex science with respect to Western music because there's much more subtle vibrations taken into consideration."

His approach was kinesthetic, mixing sound and sight: "The *rasas* produced can be related to various colors in a painting. Certain notes carry with them certain vibrations and can be given a color-value system, so to speak. It's just like if you have so many blues together, different shades of blue. There may be a little touch of purple and a little touch of red and maybe a small amount of green and yellow—something like that—and the kind of mood that you get, the effect it has on the viewer, is different than if you have a lot of red, a picture with a lot of red and orange. So, there are different ragas—millions of ragas—though today there are very few, maybe forty, used out of the sixteen thousand mastered by the *gopīs*."

"The classical Indian system of ragas is thus certainly useful in kirtan," he said, "but real raga kirtan goes beyond just musical consideration. It is kirtan on the platform of *bhāva*, devotion with spontaneous feeling.

"*Raga* means attraction. Affectionate attachment. In kirtan it refers to melodies that create an attractive atmosphere to affect the heart and increase affection. Different ragas generate different varieties of atmospheres that increase one's affection toward Krishna, toward the Holy Name."

That was all from the standpoint of the person chanting. "But when we speak of audience and generating an attractive atmosphere to increase the affectionate feelings that the audience has toward our kirtan performance, who is the audience? Krishna. Krishna is the audience—Radha-Krishna. So, the idea is not so much that we are attracted to the kirtan; the idea is to perform kirtan in such a way that attracts Krishna to the expression of our love expressed by the atmosphere that we generate for His pleasure. So first of all we should have some idea of what pleases Him. Of course Kṛṣṇa doesn't need our *patraṁs* [leaves] and *puṣpaṁs* [flowers]—He is after our bhakti. So here again the bhakti element is the most important consideration.

"And that principle of attraction extends. When you satisfy Krishna, you satisfy the whole creation. Thus, everyone is automatically pleased and attracted by performing *saṅkīrtana* solely for the pleasure of Krishna.

"Simply for the consideration of Krishna's pleasure, without any other consideration involved—that is raga kirtan. It has to go beyond just the musical consideration of raga."

"And in the matter of Krishna's pleasure," he said, "the main ingredient is the heart. To sing from the heart. To sing out of a desperation to somehow or other get Krishna's favorable, merciful glance."

"Of course," he noted, each devotee was different. "Practically any answer can be given from different angles of vision, and some people will appreciate one angle of vision more than another. It's all basically individual, as to what an individual is able to ascertain to be favorable for his progress on the path of *uttamā-bhakti*. Real raga kirtan means to perform kirtan with the greed to follow in the footsteps of the *gopīs* of Vrindavan who perform kirtan exclusively for Krishna's pleasure in many varieties or ways, with many varieties of complex musical accompaniment."

Ruci, Aindra considered—taste—was a matter of "attraction and of affection," and he described two types mentioned by Srila Chakravarti Thakur in his *Mādhurya Kaḍambinī*: "The first, lower form is when one is attracted to the *performance* of kirtan (or the performance of Deity worship), meaning the quality of musical instrumentation and singing (or the standard of paraphernalia)—if someone is singing nicely and there is nice mridanga playing, or a nice classical raga with perfectly executed *alaṅkāra*, ornaments. But these are all accoutrements. If someone's attraction to the kirtan, or taste for chanting in kirtan, is based on accoutrements, which are based on one's own relishment, then that is considered a lower form. Because if the accoutrements are not there, one becomes disinterested, loses his attraction. He doesn't gain any taste from it, because his taste is based on externals, in consideration of one's own, personal preferences. Some people's accoutrements will be heavy metal; others' will be classical Indian raga—depending on one's personal tastes and appreciation. Beauty is in the eyes of the beholder.

"But then there is a higher type of *ruci*: the taste one derives in devotional service, when one experiences attraction simply by chanting without consideration if it is a so-called good kirtan with nice accoutrements—by the relishment of *nāma-bhajana*, regardless of whether or not a tone-deaf, not-so-good singer has much musical skill—simply taking pleasure in participating in the kirtan on the basis of his attraction to *nāma*. He wants to relish the *harināma saṅga*. He is not interested either one way or the other, not concerned whether it is ornamented nicely or not ornamented at all; he is simply concerned with relishing the performance in the association of *nāma*. That is a higher form of *ruci* than *ruci* based on externals.

"But by watering the root of a tree, all the leaves and branches are automatically satisfied, so the real principle of raga kirtan is not a discussion concerning either the higher or lower grade of *ruci*; it is a discussion concerning how to perform *saṅkīrtana* to attract Krishna's attention toward you."

The externals, he pointed out, were like a bunch of zeroes, "but if you put *śuddha-nāma* before the zeros, then the more zeros you have, the better; you get ten, a hundred, a thousand, a million times the benefit. "Purity is the force. That's the point. And if you are lacking purity—in other words, if you are not chanting *śuddha-nāma*—then you should consider how effective is our kirtan anyway: not very effective, not very forceful."

Aindra had broadened his approach since his days in New York, when he had kept to more strictly traditional melodies. "He was always increasing his vocabulary of ragas," observed Rama Raya, who had first come to Vrindavan in 1986 by invitation and eventually stayed most of every year. "If you look at the tunes he was singing over the years, he kept bringing new ones forward. He would either discover a tune or compose a tune or some combination of both. He would choose a particular tune and then relish the *bhāva* of that tune for some period, usually months or part of a year, and then, when he felt that he had sufficiently utilized, or worshipped, that tune properly, he would chant another—another one would come. So, there was an ever-increasing vocabulary of tunes that he had at his command."

Over the years, Aindra sang the *mahā-mantra* in almost a hundred different melodies. Some came from hearing other *kīrtanīyas*, such as Vrindavan's renowned Kokan Baba, whose kirtans Aindra recorded and then studied in his room. "He used to come and make so many cassette recordings of our kirtans," Kokan remembered, smiling.

Other melodies came to him when he was chanting. "From his *japa* would come a melody," one of the kirtan devotees described. "It would just appear—out of the Holy Name. And to be able to keep hold of that melody, he would have to grab the harmonium and play and record it, because as quickly as it would come, it would go, like a stream of thought. He'd have to catch the tune, record it, and then carry on with his *japa*. And then sometimes he would expand on it later. One recording is even called the *japa* tune, and at least three others came out like that."

Melodies could come from almost anywhere—songs he heard through his window; Bollywood tunes; kirtans from visiting musicians; one from a Muslim who wrote devotional songs dedicated to Krishna; even India's national Republic Day anthem, the melody of which he adapted for the Deities on Republic Day, or "Jingle Bells," which he sang one Christmas morning—and he would sometimes combine melodies from different sources. "Prabhupada said that any tune is okay," he said, "as long as the chanting is sincere. And I live by that instruction. If I do happen to sing some that are supposedly film tunes, they are generally ragas. And anyway, those rascals stole those tunes from Krishna. They all belong to Krishna. So, I'm stealing them back and using them in Krishna's service to help inspire *hari-nāma-saṅkīrtana*. And following in the footsteps of the *gopīs*, who mixed ragas and created new ragas beyond the old established ones, sometimes I mix the tunes like a melody just to create variety for Krishna's pleasure."

He was capable of a wide range of musical variety and always strove for something new, something fresh, something different, something sweet and interesting. "Why is it that we offer Krishna a feast and not just *kichari*?" he asked. "Every day, just *kichari* and *kichari* and *kichari*? Of *course* Krishna was satisfied to eat Sanatana Goswami's wheat balls without any salt—because it was offered with devotion—but that is all he had. But do you think the *gopīs* offer only *kichari* to Krishna every day? Why is it that Radharani never cooks the same milk preparation twice? To entice Krishna, to whet His appetite, to enchant Him, to make Him think that She really loves Him. So, in the same way, when we make a nice feast for Krishna, we offer Him nice samosas, pakoras, chutney and at least ten varieties of *sabjī*: bitter *sabjīs*, sour *sabjīs*, salty *sabjīs*; sweet rice: *kheer malai*, *kheer mohan*; *gulab-jāmuns*, sweet balls, *lāḍḍus*... so many different varieties."

He also compared performing kirtan to dressing the Deities.

"*Harināma* is our Deity," he explained. "Just as we decorate the Deity with clothing and flowers, we decorate *harināma* with different tunes and musical ornaments."

There should be a variety of outfits—something new, something fresh, something different in each day's decoration. And a raga could be used to enhance the particular aesthetic.

"If Krishna enjoys only simple presentations, then why do we change the Deities' dress twice a day?" he asked. "It is the same Krishna, but the new dress allows us to appreciate Him in a fresh way.

"Similarly, when we see Krishna decorated in different ragas or tunes, the attractive atmosphere created enhances our appreciation of the beauty of Krishna in the form of His name. Instead of decorating Him in only one dress, a red dress all the time, we decorate Him sometimes in a blue dress—and Krishna looks really far out when He is dressed in blue—or a yellow dress, which contrasts so stunningly against His black body. Or sometimes in a pink dress, which brings out His beauty in a slightly different way.

"Sometimes Krishna is dressed with simple ornamentation, sometimes with complex ornamentation. The simple ornamentation makes His bodily form look a little more complex, whereas the complex ornamentation brings out His simple beauty and sweetness. In the same way, we can bring out the unique beauty of the Holy Name with various decorations of ragas."

Still, though Aindra's knowledge and use of a wide variety of ragas extended and deepened over the years, he never lost his appreciation for the first melodies that Srila Prabhupada had introduced, which had been sung exclusively when Aindra had joined in D.C., and he would recommend them as the best place to start. When a new 24-hour-kirtan member shared his uncertainty about what tune to sing during his shift, Aindra replied, "The best melody is Srila Prabhupada's melody," referring to Prabhupada's simple classic.

Although some ragas are associated with different times of the day—"That raga is sung in the early morning," he corrected one kirtan member at the end of his evening shift—he didn't always keep that connection. "Sometimes," he said, "but not always. Because my precedence is the passage in the *Govinda-līlāmṛta* where the *gopīs* and Krishna, during the *rāsa-līlā*, in the middle of the night, were singing all ragas without any consideration of time or season."

"Depending on how you look at it, there are basically only ten or eight different parts of the day," he pointed out. "But the idea is that Krishna has what is called *aṣṭa-kālīya-līlā*, eightfold pastimes. So, the different ragas ultimately are meant to complement His various moods in the performance of His different pastimes."

Aindra also had his own personal preferences. When he heard Shyamananda das, a classically trained Indian musician, practicing Raga Bhimpalashri in his room one day, he told him how pleased he was to hear someone singing so expertly. It was, he said, "my favorite raga." And later, in Mayapur, when Lokanath Swami was leading a rousing kirtan with a raga-based melody in front of the Pancha Tattva and the crowd chanted in thunderous response, Aindra turned to a godbrother who was more into Western melodies and said, "See? That's the power of a raga. That's the power of singing melodies based on the raga system."

Over time, he incorporated different elements in his kirtans and developed a new style. "Just like there is progressive rock," he said, "I have more or less named my way of doing kirtan as 'progressive kirtan'—a mix of Bengali-style kirtan and down-home, stompin' *vraja-vāsī* kirtan, which is inimitable—you can't imitate it."

"I have been influenced by a northern-Indian classical style of kirtan called *khayal*, which as far as I understand means "fantasy"—a devotional style requiring great proficiency, in which a singer can express a raga elaborately, in different tempos, allowing the musician to expand on the raga for long periods of time.

"I haven't gotten deeply into the *khayal* style, but I have incorporated elements of it in my humble attempt. It leaves more room for improvisation than, say, the *dhrupad* style. The *dhrupad* style is more rigid to the rule, to the letter of the law, whereas the *khayal* accentuates the spirit of the law. In the *khayal* style you may bend the rules—add an extra note to a raga, for example, for the purpose of generating inspiration or *bhāva*. That kind of reflects the *gopīs'* mixing of ragas or creating new ragas. The basic principles of the raga remain intact, but some extra note may be added to enhance the flavor, to show the rest of the raga against that note. In that way, it tends to enhance the beauty of a raga."

He distinguished between two types of kirtan, which, he said, "can be compared to the *mahā-rāsa-līlā* and Sharad Purnima *rāsa-līlā*.

Kirtan with many new people, guests, people from different lines, people who are strangers to one another—that is comparable to the *mahā-rāsa-līlā*, in which Krishna was dancing with so many types of *gopīs* from so many different groups. Kirtan with a more intimate gathering of like-minded devotees can be compared to the Sharad Purnima *rāsa-līlā*, in which Krishna was dancing exclusively with Radharani and Her girlfriends."

The key factor was that kirtan be offered exclusively for the pleasure of the Deities. Aindra compared kirtan to food, which the cook must offer to Krishna before enjoying. "Some people like to hear themselves singing," he noted. "But if you are so busy liking yourself singing, then maybe Krishna doesn't like to hear you singing so much, because you are already enjoying that which is actually meant for His enjoyment.... The *gopīs*' only focus was to perform kirtan for His pleasure."

"I could see the growth of his kirtan," Kurma Rupa noted. "When you paint by numbers, that's not being creative. But Aindra's kirtan started to evolve. He wasn't confined by singing someone else's tunes; he started expressing these wonderful melodies.

"But few musicians could stay with him," and, as had been the case in New York, not everyone appreciated Aindra or his efforts.

"In fact," remembered Rasesvara das, who began attending Aindra's kirtans in the late eighties, "during that time, into the early nineties, there were very few people who really appreciated him, even among his godbrothers."

CHAPTER FOUR

LIFE IN VRINDAVAN wasn't easy. Many devotees came for visits, but few could tolerate the austerities for very long, and there were only twenty or so full-time resident devotees when Aindra initiated the 24-hour kirtan.

"It was really austere," Bhurijana Prabhu remembered. "There was no electricity most of the time, no bottled water, and no money coming in.... There were six weeks in the middle of the winter when there was no water in the *gurukula* building." There was little clean drinking water; Aindra and the rest of the kirtan party drank the "hard" local water—salty with dissolved minerals—from an old, sometimes contaminated well that was later closed, opposite Srila Prabhupada's samadhi. Even in later years, they had to carry ten-liter jugs of filtered water from a tap near the Fogla ashram back to their quarters.

Vrindavan's winters were damp and chill, with a dense, wet fog that could obscure the sun for weeks. Without electricity, which in any case would have been too costly to run, the kirtan party's rooms were almost as cold inside as it was out. Especially when they awoke, before dawn, the floors, walls, marble temple and courtyard floors—everything—was freezing cold and wet. They didn't even have beds yet—everyone slept on the concrete floors.

Aindra was especially vulnerable, and when he caught a cold, he'd lose his voice. Eventually Tosan Krishna, who was about to leave Vrindavan, gave him an old cast-iron stove, which eventually was decorated with a smiling, tilak-adorned face drawn with a *gobar*, cow dung, mix and named Bhakta Stove. Aindra assembled it near his altar, for his Deities, and it kept his room baking hot and dry. But going outside in the winter for even just the minute or two it took to go bathe or use the bathroom was enough for him to get sick.

Summers were even tougher, with temperatures over 40 degrees Celsius, no air-conditioning, few fans, and long, frequent electric outages. The *gurukula* had a generator, but once the students left for summer break, it was rarely turned on.

During much of the day—from late morning until early evening—when the heat was most intense, Vrindavan's shops shut down and life in town went into suspension. The few people who were out shaded themselves with umbrellas, and walking barefoot on the blistering sand that still covered most of Vraja, or on the black asphalt of the town streets, was practically impossible; even rubber sandals would begin to melt.

The heat and humidity were hard on Aindra's light, sensitive skin, and during the wet season he was tortured with prickly heat and covered with rashes. When he didn't drink enough water, he suffered from dehydration; when he did, his rashes would burn from the salt of his sweat. He suffered every summer, but when devotees suggested that he sleep on the roof, he refused. "My Deities wouldn't be safe there," he said, "and I couldn't enjoy the cool air while They suffer in a hot room. But They are getting prickly-heat rash, just like me!"

Aindra's room was sweltering even by Vrindavan standards. He tried to keep his Deities more comfortable with a wet cloth and a peacock-feather fan, a basic version of a "swamp cooler," and a Delhi businessman once offered him a manufactured cooler, but Aindra was reluctant to accept it.

Eventually he did, but when it soon stopped working, he threw it away and went back to the peacock-fan technique. When devotees tried to convince him to install real AC, he replied, "Until Radhe-Shyam get air conditioning, I won't even consider it." But even after a system had been installed for the Deities, he still refused: "It will just make others feel jealous and envious, and besides, I don't want to be known as Vrindavan's first air-conditioner *bābā*!" It wasn't until years later, when it was clear that his health and service were being threatened by his body's reactions to the heat, that he finally relented, and even then he wouldn't turn on the unit until after devotees had turned on the air-conditioning for Sri Sri Radha-Shyamasundar on the temple altar.

He also developed his first case of kidney stones—one of the many physical ailments from which he suffered—common for devotees who lived in Vrindavan full-time and drank the local water. When he followed his friend Padmalocan das's advice that to get rid of the stones he should take an Ayurvedic medicine and fast from everything but eat as much *peṭa* (pumpkin soaked in sugar syrup and crystalized) and drink as much Kinnow mandarin-orange juice as possible, his clothing became mottled with orange-juice stains, but he did pass the stones.

His facilities were spare, but he didn't consider himself humble; on the contrary, he thought he was too indulgent, his eleven-by-twenty-foot room too luxurious. He slept on a straw mat over a concrete floor but felt extravagant for living under the roof of a big building. "A real Vrindavan devotee would sleep under a tree, in the dust of Vrindavan," he said. So he hauled three bags of sand from the banks of the Yamuna, dumped it all into a wooden frame, and tried sleeping in it—his way of living like the Six Goswamis—though as he soon found out, the sand already had its inhabitants: hundreds of tiny insects.

Next he covered his floor with the dust of Vraja and slept on that. This time he didn't use raw riverbank sand, but made a paste like the locals did, mixing Vrindavan's dustlike sand with straw and *gobar*. Ammonia from the dung would rid the sand of bugs, and the straw would make the mixture strong, supple, and insulating. A mix of 50 percent cow dung and clay covered his room's walls, keeping them warmer in winter and cooler in the summer and helping to repel mosquitoes—creating what he called "my transcendental cow-dung palace."

Aindra didn't just tolerate Vrindavan's austerities; he embraced them as spiritual blessings. He liked drinking from the well, since Srila Prabhupada had drawn from it. About Vrindavan's salty water, he said, "When Akrura took Krishna away from the *gopīs*, the *gopīs* became so overwhelmed with feelings of separation that they shed unlimited tears, which muddied the ground and created pools of salty water, salty tears. And the salty tears soaked into the ground and created a salt bed. And that is why the water here in Vrindavan is salty. So, if we try to drink some water and it tastes salty, we should understand that we're getting a taste of the *gopīs*' separation from Krishna.

"And every time we bathe in the salty water, we should be conscious of the fact and meditate on how it is that Vrindavan is so merciful that in so many ways it is facilitating our advancement in Krishna consciousness. Vrindavan will be facilitating our bathing in the remnants of the *gopīs*' *vipralambha-prema*."

※ ※ ※

When some devotees objected to Aindra taking up residence in Vrindavan rather than preaching in the West, he handwrote an article entitled, "We're Doing this for YOU!" explaining that residing in the *dhāma* was not just a selfish endeavor and establishing the primacy of *harināma saṅkīrtana* as the most powerful process of devotional service in Kali-yuga:

> Sri Vrindavan Dhāma is the most powerful place. Saṅkīrtana, or any other devotional service performed in Vrindavan has 1,000 times the potency of the same service done anywhere else in the world. The establishment of 24-hour kirtan at 1,000 different centers around the world might only begin to compare to the magnitude of international benefit derived from establishing 24-hour kirtan in Vrindavan. Therefore 24-hour kirtan performed in Vrindavan can be recognized as 'mahā-saṅkīrtana yajña'—the utmost powerful means of cultivating devotional service.

Just as the sages of Naimiṣāraṇya resolved to perform a 1,000-year sacrifice to benefit the people of this fallen age of Kali, similarly Srila Prabhupada instructed his disciples to uphold the continuous performance of akhaṇḍa nāma yajña at our Kṛṣṇa-Balarāma Mandir. Our performance of this kind of harināma mahā-yajña has far-reaching effect. The purpose is to help insure a spiritually strong and healthy Kṛṣṇa conscious atmosphere and thus spiritually benefit the Vrindavan ISKCON community, the visiting international community of devotees, as well as the public at large, and to help strengthen everyone's inspiration and commitment to advance in pure devotional life."

To act "without any consideration for one's own happiness," he said, "that is Vraja life, that is Vraja-*bhāva*. You can cultivate that *bhāva* anywhere in the world, but by cultivating that *bhāva* in Vraja you get a thousand times the results and make yourself *jaldee* [quickly] fit for going back home, back to Godhead, entering into Krishna's *līlās*.... So there is no harm in living in Vrindavan for the rest of your life—that's what I am doing! Most devotees do not understand that ... But I am doing it for the benefit of others, not that I am living in Vrindavan for my personal benefit. I may not be very good at doing benefit for others but that's the intention! My heart is in that place."

He often emphasized the specific rewards of chanting *japa* in Vrindavan-dhāma, especially during Kartik, even specifying what kind of beads were most beneficial. "You can chant hundreds and hundreds of *mālas* anywhere in the world," he stated, "but you get a thousand times the benefit here in Vrindavan! You get a million of times the benefit by chanting in Kartik-month in Vrindavan, and if you will chant on mridanga-shaped beads ... you get the benefit of chanting one hundred rounds with every round that you chant. So, that's one hundred million rounds during Kartik for every round you chant. You get one hundred million rounds worth of transcendental credit in your spiritual bank account, which makes it easier for you to come to the platform of dancing with Krishna, playing with Krishna, as cowherd boys and *gopīs*."

"Actually," he said, "the greatest offense is to leave the *dhāma* after one has obtained the *dhāma*. The only way in which it may not be considered as an offense is if one leaves with the exclusive purpose of preaching the glories of the holy *dhāma*.

"... When you come to Vrindavan, by putting one footstep in this land of Vrindavan, immediately you are eternally duty bound to preach the glories of Vrindavan. As soon as you put one foot on this dust! From that moment on you have an eternal responsibility to preach the glories of Vrindavan: either while remaining in Vrindavan, or outside, if you have to go out. This is the *sampradāya* which is bound to preach the glories of Vrindavan as per the instructions of Sri Chaitanya Mahaprabhu to the Six Goswamis."

"In this way," he told another devotee who was about to go back to his home country, "serve Vrindavan by educating people about the truth of Vrindavan-dhāma. And by encouraging others to come to Vrindavan. Otherwise, what's the meaning of preaching if we don't encourage others to come to Vrindavan? ... It's very necessary to come to Vrindavan as often as possible. Rupa Goswami says that you should live in Vrindavan—if possible, physically live in Vrindavan—and follow in the footsteps of an eternal associate of Krishna. In this way, one can cultivate the mood of Vraja-bhakti, which basically means pure unalloyed exclusive selfless devotional service which is exclusively dedicated to the pleasure of Radha and Krishna. That is the meaning of Vraja-bhakti. And that's what Srila Prabhupada is trying to teach, train us up from the very beginning....

"This is so important—that we should recognize that no matter how big we are anywhere else in the world, when we come to Vrindavan our real position is to come crawling in with straw between our teeth begging any menial service, because any menial service which is done in Vrindavan-dhāma is greater than the greatest service done anywhere else in the world.... And when you will come to Vrindavan and spend some time in Vrindavan, you will realize that Radharani Herself gives inspiration as to how to serve the *dhāma*, how you can serve Her and Krishna individually."

When one devotee said that he wanted to live in Vrindavan but had been assigned service by his guru maharaja in his home city of Delhi, Aindra clarified that a devotee must also remain faithful to their spiritual master and to Srila Prabhupada—and to their instructions. "Many people say that Aindra is a fanatic," he said. "We have a preaching movement, but he is calling everyone for chanting in Vrindavan. You should live in Delhi and do your service there. Your spiritual master has taken on so many services and projects for the pleasure of Srila Prabhupada, and if his disciples don't help him, how will he be able to please him? So, you should live there, but keep coming regularly to Vrindavan."

"How can I always remember Vrindavan while I am in Delhi?" the devotee asked.

"Read *Śrī Vṛndāvana-māhimāmṛta*. There is so much about Vrindavan and *mañjarī-tattva*; you will get so much from that book. Have you ever read it?"

He hadn't.

Then Aindra paused for a moment. "Wait a minute," he said. "Have you read all of Srila Prabhupada's books?"

The devotee waffled a bit; he still had some left.

"*What?!*" Aindra shouted. "Then don't touch *Vṛndāvana-māhimāmṛta*! What are you doing in this ISKCON movement if you haven't read all of Srila Prabhupada's books?! I read them all in my first three years as a devotee—all the big books, all the small books, even all the *Back to Godhead* magazines. Go and read all of them first; *then* you can think of anyone else's. Without reading Srila Prabhupada's books, you cannot understand any others!"

CHAPTER FIVE

AINDRA BEGAN HIS Vrindavan pujari service on Krishna-Balaram's altar, but a year after restoring the 24-hour kirtan, he was shifted over to Sri Sri Radha-Shyamasundar's. His approach on the altar, his cultivation of loving relationships with the Deities, had developed since his service to the Deities in Chicago in the early eighties, but its essence hadn't changed: everything he did, he did for Their pleasure.

Increasingly over the course of his years in Vrindavan, Aindra's interactions with Their Lordships, inspired and nourished by his deep attachment to the Holy Names in *japa* and kirtan, were more than worship or service; they were exchanges of spontaneous love, manifestations of his inner *bhāva*, which, as a pujari, he was able to express personally in a direct, physical way. "*Sevā* is based on the principle of love," he said. "It is for Krishna's pleasure. So, *ārati* is for His pleasure, and in consideration of how to please Him, we should associate those things that are pleasing to Him with the thing we are trying to do."

His affection was evident in every glance and gesture. He would weep, put his head on Their Lordships' feet and embrace them, whisper into Their ears, reach out and, holding Their arms, gaze deeply, lovingly, into Their eyes.

"When he was coming to dress the Deities, there was a certain passion and excitement in him," Govinda dasi later remembered. "Like he was coming to rendezvous with his beloved Lords."

As with any loving relationship, however, things didn't always go smoothly, and every now and then Aindra would have to lovingly chastise Krishna. Having dressing problems as darshan time approached one morning—Shyamasundar's turban was sliding back on His head, its flowers and decorations slipping off, almost as if He were playfully dropping it—Aindra scolded Him, "Come on, Krishna! Behave Yourself! Don't give me such a hard time!"

"He was immersed in this affection day and night," another devotee described. "It was not a metaphor, not imaginary; he had a real relationship with Them. And his Deity worship was the inspiration, the inner generator, for the spiritual potency behind such powerful kirtan."

"He was not just doing external Deity worship," agreed Mukunda Datta das, from Switzerland, who had served with Aindra in New York. He moved to Vrindavan in 1988, spent a great deal of time with Aindra on the altar—Mukunda Datta dressing Radharani while Aindra dressed Shyamasundar—and in 1992 became the temple's head pujari, a position he has held for almost thirty years. "He worshipped the Deities with the internal aspect of being absorbed in *vraja-bhāva*."

Aindra's *bhāva* was most visibly expressed in the way he dressed and decorated the Divine Couple. He saw dressing Radharani as service to Shyamasundar, and dressing Shyamasundar as a service to Her. Before placing a garland on Her, he would touch it to Krishna's hand, so as to imbue it with His fragrance and thus increase Her pleasure—and vice versa. He wanted to please Shyamasundar by helping Radharani be as beautiful as possible, and he wanted to please Her by making Krishna attractive to Her eyes. His method was to configure everything—the painting, flowers, garlands, ornaments, cloth, the

Deities Themselves—into a tableau vivant, a living picture of Radha-Krishna's eternal *rāsa-līlā*.

Just as Aindra's kirtans had had a transformational effect on Krishna-Balaram Mandir, his Deity service on the altar had an immediate effect on the temple's standard of worship. "There was a difference," Bhurijana Prabhu noticed, "and the difference was very clear. As soon as Aindra's influence started showing up on the Deities, everything was in motion and everything was curved. The Deities' garlands were going like this, and the garlands were going like that—from one side to the other. And Shyamasundar's crown was off to Radharani's side. Before, it was very linear, but this was spontaneous.

"And because of him and his dressing and his training [of other pujaris], Their attractiveness, Their unique attractiveness, really took off. It was quite amazing. Everyone's appreciation grew so much more. And the Deities were part of the cause of the increasing popularity of Krishna-Balaram Mandir."

The days Aindra dressed Radha-Shyamasundar "were like a festival—very special," Govinda dasi agreed. "The expressions on the faces of the Deities when he dressed Them were so gorgeous, so exquisite, that you would just want to look and look and look at Them. In those days, he was also doing kirtan in the morning, and that too was enhancing the mood."

"You could really see how happy and absorbed he was on the altar," another devotee described. "He was dressing Them in such a way that They were smiling, dancing, playing, really moving around. Every time, it was an adventure. The garlands were flowing, and everything was fluid, causing Radhe-Shyam to move either toward or away from each other, like a moving photograph, full of life."

"The best ideas I got for dressing the Deities," Mukunda Datta acknowledged, "I got from Aindra Prabhu."

It took some time, however, for Aindra to gain acceptance from some of the other pujaris. The way he expressed his devotion to Radhe-Shyam was uncommon, and at times it crossed the line of what they deemed acceptable. Sometimes, for Their Lordships' pleasure, he would massage Radha and Krishna's feet, but one morning, when he was seen kissing Radha's, one of the pujaris objected. "Do you know what Aindra is doing?" he complained to Mukunda Datta. "He is kissing Her feet!"

"Good!" Mukunda Datta replied. "At least someone around here has some devotion!"

The pujari took his complaint to the temple president, but again Mukunda Datta stood by Aindra and was able to settle the unrest. "In *Bhāgavatam*, we hear that even Dhruva Maharaja says that he wants to kiss the feet of Vishnu," he said. "So, what to speak of *vraja-bhāva*!"

Aindra's only desire on the altar was to please the Deities and not disturb Them. During the summer, for Shyamasundar's comfort when the altar doors were closed, he would keep Him undressed for as long as possible. "Are you going to make Him stand there in His *kaupīna* all day?" another pujari questioned. "Aren't you going to dress Him?"

"Give Him a break!" Aindra replied. "It's hot!"

The pujari started to admonish Aindra, saying that having Krishna undressed for so long was indecent.

"But Krishna is hot!" Aindra told him. "This is for ventilation. You're a mundane moralist!"

"Don't do anything to your Lordships that you wouldn't want done to yourself," he instructed. He disdained the use of matches on the altar because of their sulfurous smell and its effect on the Deities. "All the sulfur dioxide goes right in the eyes and the nose of the Lord."

"It's a common-sense thing," he said. "If I want to do something for the pleasure of my Deity, I should consider whether He is satisfied, whether He is pleased, because He is a person and is more sentient than we are! These senses of our body are dead, and for the soul to perceive things through the agency of mind and senses is a tough job! Because really, although something is coming through, it is basically a distortion of a reality. What *He* perceives is the reality!

"One person may have a higher developed sensibility than another. Usually that person who is more spiritually advanced has more highly developed sensibilities and can perceive things that the neophyte can't. But it doesn't take much advancement to perceive that the gross disgusting smell which the lighting of matches produces can hardly be pleasing to the Deity. That means that they are not considering that the Deity has a nose to smell, which means that they are basically impersonalists.

"The neophyte is basically an impersonalist. He does customary worship of the Deity and does not consider the beauty of relationships with Vaishnavas. Therefore he squabbles in politics in relationship with Vaishnavas in order to usurp the position of using the Deity as a commodity for fulfilling his particular demands, which are usually sense-gratificatory. That's called a neophyte or *prākṛta-bhakta*, a materialistic devotee. Such person is quite capable of doing puja, but what we want is *sevā*! We want to increase our *sevā-bhāvanā*. And especially in personal Deity worship, it is a greatest opportunity for allowing your heart to melt in the experience of your personal relationship with Krishna, who has come to your own hands, by the grace of guru, by the grace of the Vaishnavas! Krishna has come into my life, and He wants to encourage me to deepen my internal *sevā-bhāvanā* toward Him. So, it is important that we always think in terms of *sevā*."

Another time, during a Radhastami festival, when someone had placed a speaker right in front of the altar, Aindra spoke in the Deities' defense: "What is this? Who put this speaker there? Can't you understand? It's blaring in the Deities' ears! It's too loud—it's disturbing Them!" When he was told that the speaker could be removed later, he countered, "Not later—NOW!" and when no one moved to take action, he grabbed the scissors he'd been using while dressing the Deities and cut the speaker wires himself. A visiting pujari protested, but Aindra said, "I don't care! If it disturbs the Deities, it has to be stopped!" He wouldn't tolerate any disturbance to Them, whether it be noise from fans creaking, doors slamming, pots banging, or people talking too loudly.

Some complaints about Aindra's Deity service were expressed with outright disrespect. When one of the pujaris' wives wanted Aindra to drape the Deities with grape garlands but he refused, on the grounds both that the grapes would stain the Deities' dress and that there was no shastric support for Krishna ever wearing grape garlands, she yelled at him in front of the pujaris and other devotees and cursed him: "If I am a chaste wife, he will fall from his position!"

After another accusation by a pujari, that Aindra was using too many big pins and thus was pricking Shyamasundar, the temple president himself came onto the altar to check on Aindra as he was dressing the Deities.

Eventually the pujari's wife repented and begged Aindra's

forgiveness, and the other charges were proven false. But these were just a few of the many times Aindra was disrespected or challenged, including by devotees without authority. Not everyone seemed to heed his decades of preaching, book distribution, kirtan, mentoring, pujari work, and other devotional service.

❧ ❧ ❧

One morning when the altar curtains opened, Shyamasundar's hands were empty. Murmurs arose from the devotees gathered for morning darshan. "Who dressed Krishna?" one asked. "He forgot His flute!"

Then they saw it—in Radharani's hand. The scene before them, several recognized, portrayed the *līlā* in which Srimati Radharani's friends steal Krishna's flute.

"Haribol!" someone called out. "*Jaya* Sri Radhe!"

Others were not so happy, and Aindra was again called in for a talk by the temple management. "Two things must always be on the Deity of Krishna," he was told. "A peacock feather and a flute. If you do something like this again, we may have to bar you from Deity worship."

Aindra reacted strongly. He had been dressing Sri Sri Radha-Shyamasundar every day for the previous eight months, but the next afternoon, upset by the reprimand, he asked Mukunda Datta to take over his services for Sri Sri Radha-Shyamasundar, and he did not return to them for almost two years, until Mukunda Datta became head pujari and asked him to resume the service.

❧ ❧ ❧

When the curtains opened one morning in the winter of 1989, Aindra was amazed by what he saw. Srimati Radharani's eyes were newly painted. And they were incredible, more beautiful than ever. "Who painted them?" he asked Radha-Shyamasundar's pujari Bhaktisiddhanta das.

"One of the brahmacharis," Bhaktisiddhanta had replied.

Aindra knew something was off. No pujari, no artist he'd ever known, would have been able to paint Radharani's eyes with such *bhāva* or spiritual expertise. "No way," he challenged. "Who painted them?"

Bhaktisiddhanta held fast; he wouldn't identify the source of the transformation. But when Aindra kept asking, Bhaktisiddhanta finally revealed the secret: a renowned South African devotee artist, Arca Vigraha dasi, who had come to India to find themes for her work but was then diagnosed with cancer and remained to spend her final days in Vrindavan, had noticed that the temple Deities were in need of repainting and done the work.

But there had been an obstacle: as was standard, even in ISKCON temples, in India, women were not allowed on the altar. But Bhaktisiddhanta, who had created the bronze bas-relief panels in Srila Prabhupada's samadhi *mandir* and was himself an accomplished artist—classically trained in Europe and America and a successful commercial artist in New York—had felt that the Deities deserved Arca Vigraha's talents and come up with a plan. "I'll arrange for you to do this service," he had told her, "but you have to do it in complete secrecy." Indians especially, but also other pujaris and many devotees would have disapproved of a woman doing the service. "I'll leave the key to the Deity room on the ledge above the door. Don't use it any earlier than 10 p.m. By that time, everyone except the boys on night shift for the 24-hour kirtan should be asleep."

"How will I get in without them noticing?" she had asked. "They sit so near the door."

"I don't know," he'd said. "That's a challenge."

A little after ten, Arca Vigraha had been hovering around the door to the altar, waiting for an opportunity, when Aindra had suddenly appeared beside her. "Do you need something, *mātājī*?" he had asked.

"No, no ... thank you," she'd replied, and left out the temple's side door.

A little while later, the electricity had gone out (it frequently did), and under the cover of darkness Arca Vigraha had slipped back into the temple and onto the altar, where she had spent the night painting the Deities' faces, hands, and feet, then sneaking out before the pujaris came to prepare for *maṅgala-ārati*.

The drama had resumed each night for two weeks. On the final night, Arca Vigraha had painted Srimati Radharani's eyes.

"Where is she?" Aindra demanded.

"Prabhu, calm down ..."

"Where is she?" he persisted. "If you don't tell me, I'll find out from someone else." And, learning that Arca Vigraha was staying in the guesthouse, he rushed over.

When Aindra knocked on Arca Vigraha's door, he heard a faint "Come in" and entered.

Arca Vigraha was lying in bed, visibly weak and ill.

Aindra went straight to her feet and touched them with respect. "How did you do it?" he asked.

"Do what?" she replied.

"How did you paint Radharani's eyes like that?"

"I don't know," she said. "I just painted what I was inspired to paint."

"How do you know what Radharani's eyes look like?"

"I *don't* know what they look like. I just painted them by inspiration."

"You painted them exactly as I envision them every day in my own meditations!"

CHAPTER SIX

THE PRIMARY DEITIES in Aindra's room ("on the center stage"), Sri Sri Nitai Saci-suta, came to him as the result of a rescue mission—or, as he put it, "I stole Them fair and square!" Longtime Vrindavan resident Deena Bandhu das and Pundarik Vidyanidhi das had had the neem-wood forms of Gaura-Nitai—each standing about 150 centimeters tall, with one arm raised—made for the ISKCON-Vrindavan book-distribution and preaching bus, to travel throughout north India displayed in a rear glass enclosure, but during an outing one summer the bus was in a crash. The driver passed away, and the bus was towed back to the lot behind the *gurukula* building. The Deities were still inside, unharmed by the accident, but They were just left there in the wreckage for days in the scorching summer heat.

When Aindra saw that the Deities had been abandoned, he reacted with anger, then concern. He gave Them water, with Bhuvanesvara offered Them food from the temple kitchen, and performed *ārati*. And when some days had passed without anyone else acting on Their behalf, he decided to rescue Them. So, one night when everyone was fast asleep, he took Them from the wreckage and brought them to his room.

When, eventually, the bus was repaired and the book distributors finally noticed that the Deities were missing, rumors led them to Aindra's room. "Give Them back," they demanded.

"Absolutely not," Aindra replied.

"They belong to the book-distribution party," they said. "Bring Them back."

Aindra furrowed his brow. "There is no way I will ever give Them back to you heartless people. You left Them out there in the sweltering heat and forgot about Them. So forget about getting Them back!"

As it turned out, the first time the bus went out again after it was repaired, it was again in a bad incident, this time falling off the road and rolling over and over down an incline. It was completely destroyed, and if the Deities had been on it, They might not have survived.

For the rest of his life, Aindra worshipped and cared for Nitai Saci-suta faithfully and with loving devotion. "Look at Them," he'd say, "my golden Saci-suta and my buttercream Nitai. They're so beautiful—I just marvel when I see Them." He consulted Them regularly, and received guidance from Them both while awake and in his dreams. "If I were forced to make a choice between the two," he once said, referring to Sri Sri Saci-suta and Sri Sri Radha-Shyamasundar, "even though I dearly love Radha-Shyamasundar—and I would never have to make the choice, because I'm going to have two [spiritual] bodies, one in *gaura-līlā* and one in *kṛṣṇa-līlā*—but if push came to shove and I were forced, I would get a tight handle on the feet of my Saci-suta." He lay behind Them every night to rest, and in the end he surrendered completely at Their lotus feet.

※ ※ ※

One day Aindra invited Bhaktisiddhanta Swami up to his room to see a recently arrived Govardhana *śilā* and a new arrangement he had constructed for his Deities. A quarter of the room was now taken up by a waist-high tabletop altar made from plastered bricks and a white slab of marble holding an ornately carved wooden temple with arches and domes. "I got Him from Punchari, the tail of the peacock of Govardhana Hill," he told Maharaja, indicating the new *śilā*. "Giriraj is the topmost Deity because ultimately He represents the love Krishna has for Radha and the love Radha has for Krishna."

Impressed by Aindra's devotion and standard of worship, Bhaktisiddhanta Swami later returned from a visit to Nepal with over a dozen *śālagrāma-śilās* from the Kali Gandaki River, a tributary of the Ganges in the foothills of the Himalayas, bearing the markings of different Vishnu avatars. And soon after, Laksmivan, Aindra's old friend from D.C., who had just returned from a Nepal trek, brought several more.

At the final count, Aindra had 2,240 *śālagrāma-śilās* and 28 other Deities: Govardhana *śilās*, Radharani, the *aṣṭa-sakhīs*, Gopisvara Mahadeva, his big Nitai Saci-suta, Jahnava Devi, and the small Gaura-Nitai, Srila Prabhupada, and Bhaktisiddhanta Sarasvati who had been with him in New York. Hanging from around his neck in a silver locket was a tiny square Govardhana *śilā*, Vijay-Gopal, to whom Aindra offered water and *prasādam* before honoring it, and who would accompany Aindra to daily temple kirtans, to home programs, on *parikramā*, and to the Yamuna and Radha Kund (Aindra bathing Him before taking bath himself).

Devotees would sometimes ask why Aindra was collecting so many *śilās*. "I'm not *collecting* them," he replied. "They are coming to me and offering me the chance to give Them shelter. How can I say no? How can anyone say no to Krishna? I can have only two hours with Shyamasundar on the altar, but that's not enough; there is no limit to how much blackishness I can have in my life!"

"But Salagrama is not Krishna," someone commented. "He is Narayana."

"*Śālagrāma* worship is no less *mādhurya-mayī* than Govardhana worship," Aindra said. "It's simply a question of the worshipper's ability to accommodate the Vraja conception of Salagrama."

He told the story of *śālagrāma-śilā's* origin from the *Padma Purāṇa* and the *Brahma-vaivarta Purāṇa*: For enjoying pastimes with Krishna, Tulasi-*gopī* was cursed by Radharani to be born in the material world, and there she married the demon Sankacuda, who, as Sudama, had been cursed to appear there and had conquered the demigods on the strength of a boon granted him by Lord Brahma that he would always be victorious as long as his wife was faithful to him. Finally Lord Narayana assumed the form of Sankacuda and seduced Tulasi in that guise, thus nullifying Brahma's boon and leaving Sankacuda vulnerable to attack from Lord Shiva.

When Tulasi discovered what had happened, she cursed Narayana to turn to stone, "because," she accused, "your heart is as hard as stone!" And thus Narayana became Salagrama and Tulasi became the River Gandaki.

"But who is this Narayana?" Aindra asked. "It's the same prankish Krishna, as only He enjoys *parakīya-rasa*, sporting with another man's wife!"

"Our Gaudiya *sampradāya* was founded by Sri Chaitanya Mahaprabhu," he pointed out, "and the Six Goswamis of Vrindavan worshipped Krishna *exclusively*. If Salagrama is not Krishna, then why did Mahaprabhu appear in a dream to Gopal Bhatta Goswami and tell him to seek Krishna's mercy in Nepal, where twelve *śilās* leapt into his waterpot again and again? If Salagrama is not Krishna, how is it possible that one of those twelve *śilās* became the Radha-Ramana Deity worshipped here in Vrindavan?"

"In *śālagrāma* worship there is some important *tattva* to be understood," he continued, "and we can refer to *Hari-bhakti-vilāsa* for the basis of our discussion. It is mentioned there that any *śālagrāma*, regardless of external characteristics, such as various chakras—any Vishnu-tattva form—can be worshipped in any *śālagrāma*. Those who are *sakāma-bhaktas*, who have material desires ... some may worship *śālagrāma* because by worshipping a certain kind of *śālagrāma* one may get good progeny.... [but] Sanatana Goswami recommends that a pure devotee will worship any *śālagrāma*, even the broken ones, because he knows that Supreme Absolute Truth is all good and that there can never be any inauspiciousness or auspiciousness in Krishna, that Krishna is worshipable in all circumstances, whether happy or sad. Worship Krishna; whether there is a good result or a bad result is not important. The real principle is to try to please Krishna in pure devotional service.... So, anyone who will worship Krishna with that *niṣkāma*, pure devotional, mood, is eligible to understand that, regardless of the external *lakṣaṇa*, characteristics, the Supreme Absolute Truth, *svayaṁ-rūpa*, Krishna, is within every *śālagrāma* ... Some *śālagrāmas* by external characteristics may be ascertained to be a Matsya *śilā*, or a Laxmi-Narayana *śilā*, or a Kurma *śilā*, or a Nrsimha *śilā*, but They all reflect various aspects of Krishna's personality."

All *śilās* were perfect, he said, but it took a special devotee to see this. "From the standpoint of a *sakāma-bhakta*," a devotee with personal motivation, he told a visitor viewing one of his *śilās*, "there are may be so many faults in this *śilā*. The *sakāma-bhakta* will likely reject this *śilā*, or decline to worship this *śilā*, because he will be thinking that there are so many faults—so many cracks, so many breaks. And because it's broken, he thinks it will not be auspicious to worship. But we should understand clearly that the *śālagrāma-śilā* is Krishna Himself, and when Krishna says, 'ye yathā māṁ prapadyante tāṁs tathaiva bhajāmy aham,' He means, 'As they approach Me, I will reward them, I will reciprocate.' So, if someone thinks, 'Oh, this is Krishna, but this Krishna is having so many faults! I will not worship this Krishna, because I am seeing so many faults in this Krishna,' it means that the *sakāma-bhakta* is not seeing Krishna!"

"And even if Krishna *is* full of faults," he continued, "a pure devotee loves Him for His faults.... If I will love Krishna, if I will love Him without seeing His faults, if I will not see the faults of Krishna and love Him for what He really is, as the darling son of Nanda Maharaja, the sweetheart of Srimati Radharani, if I will overlook His faults and see the essence of the truth about Krishna in this *śālagrāma-śilā*, that He is the same all-perfect, all-good, completely lovable personality Shyamasundar Krishna, then do you think that *śālagrāma* will not understand and notice my mood, my *bhāva*, my service attitude? That I will serve Him and love Him in spite of all His faults, will not take seriously any of His faults, not think to notice His faults, not take these faults as noteworthy? Then I can hope that Krishna will overlook my faults, that Krishna will love me, too, in spite of all my faults, that Krishna will not take my faults seriously or consider that these faults are noteworthy.

"If I will only worship *śālagrāma*, Krishna, when He is faultless, then what is my vision? If I will worship *śālagrāma* only when I see that He is faultless, then I should expect that He will love me only when I am faultless. Actually, I am full of faults. If I am to think that

I should see the faults in Krishna and Krishna will also be seeing my faults, then what hope is there for me? I am full of faults. My hope should be that Krishna will see even one good thing about this wretched soul. If Krishna will see even one good thing about this wretched soul and magnify that good quality, then there is hope for me! But how could I think that Krishna will take that attitude toward me if I cannot think to take that attitude toward Him, who is actually faultless in spite of His apparent so many 'faults'?"

He worshipped even those *śilās* that, according to Srila Sanatan Goswami's *Hari-bhakti-vilas*, could be detrimental to his health, acknowledging Their danger but dismissing it in favor of Their benefits. "I have two red *śilās*, which is maybe why I'm always having trouble with my throat and stuff," he admitted in a lecture, "but it's a small price to pay for love of Godhead."

"By worshipping the red *śālagrāma*," he said, "according to shastra the result is that increased bodily diseases will come to us. This kind of *śālagrāma* is to be worshipped only by *niṣkiñcana-bhaktas*, not by the *sakāma-bhaktas*, because by worshipping this *śālagrāma*, you may get any number of diseases. But if the *niṣkāma-bhakta* or the *niṣkiñcana-bhakta* will be worshipping this *śālagrāma* only with the aim of augmenting his love of Godhead, then he will consider that some increase in bodily disease—it doesn't say how much the bodily diseases will be increased ... only that it will be increased. But if someone is worshipping with his heart and with the prayers to augment, or to increase, his love for Krishna, then he will consider that this increase of bodily diseases is a small, small price to pay." He followed Sri Chaitanya Mahaprabhu's invitation to the Lord: "Let Him trample Me or break My heart by never being visible to Me. He ... can do whatever He likes, but still He alone, and no one else, is the worshipable Lord of My heart."

After accepting one such *śilā*, Aindra became extremely ill, and when he recovered, he picked up the *śilā* and admonished, "Stop making me sick! I've had enough of it, please! If You keep doing this, I'll send You back. Do You want to go back to the Kali Gandaki and sit in that freezing cold river up in that mountain? Can't You just be happy in Vrindavan? Just think how fortunate You are! Do you want to go back to the Himalayas? I'll send You back, so just stop it right now!"

CHAPTER SIX

When a few years later Aindra was in Nepal to renew his Indian visa, a process that put him through extreme anxiety at the thought of having to leave Vrindavan, he visited the Kali Gandaki River himself. Venturing further and further upriver, he shouted, "Shyaaaaama-suuuuundar" but heard only echoes in reply.

Then, seemingly out of nowhere, two Chinese soldiers emerged from a jeep and pointed shotguns at him. Apparently he had wandered into a restricted zone in Chinese-occupied Tibet. "You are under arrest!" they barked in English. "Get in the car!"

They took Aindra to a security checkpoint, where an officer accused him of being an American spy trying to infiltrate their territory in religious disguise.

"No," Aindra defended himself. "I am a worshipper of Krishna; I'm a monk."

"What is your mission here?" the officer demanded.

"I'm searching for Krishna," Aindra replied.

The officer held up a map. "This map shows where you cannot go! You went anyway!"

"I'm simply trying to search for Krishna!" Aindra exclaimed. "What is this map going to do for me? What is the meaning of the lines you draw on maps? Bewildered by the material energy, you think one country belongs to you and another country belongs to someone else. Everything belongs to Krishna! I am Krishna's devotee, so I will search for Him anywhere and everywhere. Your map means nothing to me!"

Eventually the officer released Aindra, recognizing that he really *was* a religious pilgrim and knowing that detaining an American would likely be more trouble than it was worth.

When in 1994 Aindra was again in Nepal to renew his visa and ventured to the holy site of Muktinath, he was both saddened and angered to find shops in the town selling *śālagrāma-śilās* to tourists and pilgrims.

"This is sinful!" he told the shopkeepers. "The *Padma Purāṇa* says that anyone who makes a business of selling *śālagrāma* sends themselves and generations of their family into the darkest hells."

"No, no," the shopkeepers defended themselves. "We have done nothing wrong."

"You've done wrong by making Krishna into a commodity for

your business," he chastised them. "You have no idea what these tourists will do with the śilās you sell them. They might use Them to crack nuts! They might crack Them open, looking for gold! You are ultimately responsible for all these offenses!"

When the shopkeepers started to get worried, Aindra offered them a solution: "Look—give me a few of your best ones. I will take them to Sri Vrindavan-dhāma and worship Them there. They will be very pleased, and this will free you from a huge percentage of the sinful reactions you incur by running this business. A percentage of the benefit I get by worshipping your śilās in Vrindavan will be shared with you."

Almost every shopkeeper agreed to give Aindra a half dozen śilās, and he returned to Vrindavan with nearly a hundred, adding to the dozens already in his room. He hadn't intended to bring back so many, but he had wanted to rescue as many as he could. He felt that he just had to help the śilās—and any other Deities he found in adverse circumstances—so he adopted Them.

The same thing happened in Vrindavan: when he saw shopkeepers in Loi Bazaar selling śilās, he would reproach them for their sinful activity and offer them mahā-prasādam or a donation for the śilās' rescue. He never had it in his mind to keep so many; that just sort of happened.

❦ ❦ ❦

With all the śilās in his care, Aindra had to come up with a system to worship Them. He set aside several primary śilās to receive daily care and worship with ṣoḍaśa upacāra, sixteen items. The rest he arranged on gold-plated platters, and each day, he cleaned Them all, applied fragrant oils suitable for the season, bathed Them in a gentle spray of water, offered candana and flower garlands, and brushed Them with a bunch of tulasi, having noted that shastra defined the basic foundation of śālagrāma worship as a bath of at least three drops of water and the touch of tulasi. In the winter, when fresh tulasi leaves were scarce, he would gently tap each śilā twice with a tulasi twig. "Reminding Them of my existence," he'd say with a smile. And thus he managed to give a little personal attention to each. "They are Krishna," he said, "who needs our love and care."

No matter how many Deities Aindra had, he remained faithful to Them, was attached to Their service, and hardly ever let go of one that he had begun to worship. "He made a promise to any *śālagrāma-śilās* who came to him," Rama Raya remembered, "that 'You've come to be with me in Vrindavan, and any who come to me will stay with me.' Devotees would sometimes come begging for *śālagrāma-śilās*—even GBCs and other senior devotees—and, with few exceptions, Aindra would refuse on that basis."

Once, after Rasesvara had been begging for a *śilā* and had a series of dreams confirming that one should come to him, Aindra finally relented, but when handing over the *śilā's* care, he broke into tears of separation. It would be all right, Rasesvara assured him; many other *śilās* would come to him. But Aindra, distraught to lose the association of *this śilā*, couldn't help but express his love and attachment. Similarly, when a tulasi plant—whom he worshipped daily with devotion—left her body, he grieved, crying, "She left me!" and kept offering Her *ārati* until a new one grew.

Aindra understood that even if he served only as a go-between to help a devotee obtain a *śilā*, he was still responsible for the *śilā's* worship and would incur the reaction for anything that ensued. So he was extremely careful about who was an eligible recipient, based on the devotee's level of training and experience and ability to provide Them a good home. If he determined that someone was qualified, he would either arrange for a *śilā* to come to them, instruct them in the proper way to approach a *vraja-vāsī* brahmana with their request, or give them one that he had received but had not yet begun to worship. Their transfer would be accompanied by a lecture, usually hours long, covering the proper mood, practicalities, and regulations of Their worship, the spiritual significance of *śilā* worship in the Gaudiya Vaishnava *sampradāya*, and the determination that the devotee must have to maintain that worship with love and care for the duration of their life—often accompanied by a few days' intensive training.

"This is Tadiya Nrsimhadeva," he explained to one sannyasi who some years later requested a Nrsimha *śilā*. "*Tadiya* means 'belonging.' This *śilā* is Lord Nrsimha because it belongs to Lord Nrsimha, and that which belongs to the Absolute is non-different from the Absolute. Actually, that which belongs to the Absolute is an even better object of worship than the Absolute Himself. Lord Shiva told Parvati that it is even higher to worship the *tadiya* of the Lord than to worship the Lord Himself.

"The devotee is *tadiya* because the devotee belongs to Krishna. This *śilā* is *tadiya* because it is a piece from the gigantic pillar in the mountains of Ahovalam, said to be the pillar of Hiranyakasipu's palace from which Lord Nrsimha burst out.

"As you can see, this *śilā* has the shape of a nail—Lord Nrsimha's nail. Look here at the tip ... see this red streak? That is the blood of Hiranyakasipu. So, this is an Ugra-Nrsimha *śilā*. A devotee gave Him to me some time ago, and now I will entrust Him to you.

"We are Gaudiya Vaishnavas," he continued. "We worship only Vrajendra-nandana Shyamasundar Krishna. We worship even Nrsimhadeva in that Vrindavan mood. In Vraja-bhakti we conceive of Nrsimha as the son of Nanda, Vrajendra-nandana Shyamasundar, the lion among young men, fearless as a lion in fulfilling his desires. So, you see, we do not need to abandon the Vrindavan mood to worship Nrsimhadeva. It is not that you should take some mood of awe and reverence.

"The *gopīs* also worship Nrsimhadeva. They see the essence of all the avatars within their beloved Shyamasundar Krishna. In the *Haṁsadūta*, Srila Rupa Goswami has written about a very special pastime in which the *gopīs* address Krishna by the names of all the different avatars, giving a special interpretation for each name. The *gopīs* saw Nrsimhadeva within their Shyamasundar Krishna, and we should follow in their footsteps and worship Nrsimhadeva as Shyamasundar."

"Radha-Krishna worship," Aindra instructed, "is in the mood of establishing the intimate connection between the bhakta and the service of Radharani and of Krishna for those aspiring to enter the realm of Vraja. Begging Govardhana Hill in the mood of Him being Haridasa-*varya* to please manifest Himself in such a way that I can see by His grace the beautiful attractive form of my Lord, none other than my dearmost, dearer than my own life. In this way, it is a most intimate form of worship and the most elevated form of worship. Devotees generally don't start out with the most elevated, but even for *sādhakas* the whole idea is that we have to intelligently pursue in such a way as to augment the attraction of the heart toward Radha and Krishna.

"So, it is necessary that we hear the attractive descriptions of Radha and Krishna's forms, qualities, pastimes, *dhāma*, etc. And all of these have been given to us by Krishnadas Kaviraja Goswami in *Govinda-līlāmṛta* and by Vishvanatha Cakravarti in *Kṛṣṇa-bhāvanāmṛta*. These books are meant for solacing the heart of persons who are actually beginning to experience the feelings of separation in terms of intense longing for at long last getting the direct darshan of Radha and Krishna in the *līlās* of the Lord. These descriptions are meant for people who are damn serious about giving up the connection with this material world and all the foolishness that goes along with the considerations of superfluous external duties of varna and ashrama and all these things and simply focusing on going home back to Godhead.

"Forget about the rest of it, because the rest will come and go anyway, but eternal relationship is the mainstay. We can take or leave the rest of it, but we can't leave the consideration of abject need, the ultimate necessity of the *jīva* in the matter of getting *prema* and being absorbed in the prospect of getting facilities in terms of *vastu-siddhi*, or the realization of the substantial spiritual body with which to give a full expression to that *prema* in the eternal *līlās* of the Lord.

"A full expression cannot be given in the *sādhaka-deha* while wandering around in the material world. Full expression is given in a *siddha-deha*. So, it is essential that in our worship of Govardhan-*śilā* that we hanker and pray like madmen or madwomen for the ultimate realization of our *siddha-deha*. At least for starters to be revealed to us, within and without, the true nature of our *siddha-svarūp*, which will in our *sādhaka-deha* be characterized by *svarūp-siddhi*, not *vastu-siddhi*. But the ultimate perfection is to attain the eternal substantial *sad-cid-ānanda-vigrahaḥ siddha-deha* and go home back to Godhead....

"The whole purpose of sadhana is to develop a selfless service attitude of a *vraja-vāsī* who is prepared to go to hell for the pleasure of Krishna.... Let me get kicked out of Vraja, let me go to hell, let me suffer unlimited anxieties in pangs of separation from Krishna, but let me at least be satisfied with knowledge that Krishna is pleased. That's real *prema*; that's *vraja-prema*. The *prema* of other realms is *jñāna-miśra*; it is not *kevala-prema*. Śrī-guru-carana-padma, kevala bhakati-sadma. It is *kevala-bhakti*, Vraja-bhakti, that our *guru-paramparā* wants to give. And as you deepen your *bhajana* and your *nāma-bhajana* and become concentrated on the pursuit of that goal of our life, Krishna marks you! Radharani marks you! Rupa-manjari marks you! And They will do all the work; They will make all the arrangements. If you need a guru, They will give you all the gurus you need. They will make all the arrangements, sooner or later, for all the necessities for your coming to the end degree of perfection, because They want you to become perfected more than you want to become perfected. They love you more than you love Them—more than you love yourself. Their whole intention, the whole purpose of the thing is to drag you back home, back to Godhead. But it would help if we become a little interested, at least run along. And that's called *rāgānuga*—when you are a little interested in the affair and run along behind, responding to Their beckoning.

"Krishna reveals Himself to a sweet-hearted devotee, when you are non-duplicitous, non-envious. What is the *adhikār* for hearing these intimate topics of Radha-Krishna *līlā*? It is the degree of freedom from this enviousness for Krishna as a supreme enjoyer. When you become free from enviousness for Krishna, then when you hear about how He enjoys, the way He enjoys—and I am telling you, He enjoys!—it becomes so delightful and so satisfying; it pacifies us to know that there is reality to all that is reflected, an original prototype to all that is perceived in this material world: the disgusting debauchery of so-called men and women.

"If you are not envious, then when you see the original transcendental golden prototype of which iron is only a reflection—perverted, distorted, deformed—when you see the real thing, your heart will rest in peace. And you will feel so happy that there is real substance in the spiritual world that is not the exploitative, self-gratifying type of sense gratification in this material world. It is based on heartfelt anxiety to give pleasure to the other, and Krishna has this heartfelt anxiety, and His devotees have it in various ways.

"There is nothing but that going on in the realm of Vraja. That is Govardhana puja—to be absorbed, meditating on Krishna's *vraja-līlās*. And the easy way to do it is to hear *vraja-līlās* while you are doing your puja, because you have time while you are engaged in that. It will take at least forty-five minutes or an hour to do it nicely. And while you are doing it, this is your time. The rest of the time, you are bustling around, engaged with others for preaching; so how much time are you going to have? That is why I am doing puja four hours a day. Someone may think, "How can you just waste four hours for your puja?" I am not wasting my time. I am absorbed in relishing *bhāvas* being transmitted by the divine grace of the predecessor acharyas in the form of this important Goswami literature."

If someone were to take a *śilā* out of Vraja, Aindra instructed, they had to create a Vraja-like atmosphere wherever they took Him, and that was a life-long commitment, more serious than family or any other responsibilities. "You should always, at every step, have your Deity in your mind," he told Radhika Ramana das, who had helped get him high-quality Japanese microphones and was one of the few devotees to whom he ever gifted a Govardhana *śilā*. "Whether you are on *saṅkīrtana* or doing something for your Deity, your whole life is centered on Him—all of your activities. The idea is that you want to do things pleasing to Him....

"*Puja* means you are worshipping as a kind of formality—it is a formal process—but Govardhana worship is not puja; it is service. *Service* means that you are giving Him the pleasure of smelling some nice incense, so you are offering some incense to Him. You are offering a flame to Him, which is representative of your own heart's love for Him—the flame of your desire for His pleasure—and Krishna accepts that flame of your heart's desire. That's why you should light it with a tulasi stick, so that you are offering something that is worth ten million of your heart's flames of desire to please Him. And it will please Him ten times over by the grace of Tulasi. He is so pleased, so happy with Tulasi. You can hardly offer Him anything, but when you bring Tulasi into the picture, Krishna is so satisfied. He becomes satisfied with you, because you are considering His pleasure in the matter of His relationship with Tulasi.... Therefore, while offering *ārati*, we are lighting the lamp with tulasi, touching the incense. If you touch any wood with tulasi it becomes as pure as tulasi. So, when you take incense and touch it with a tulasi stick, that incense becomes purified and more pleasing to Krishna.

"Anything and everything you offer you should associate with

Tulasi. That's why you should chant on a tulasi *mālā*, because Krishna is pleased when we associate our chanting with Tulasi. We should keep tulasi leaf on our tongue so that He is pleased with our words. They are vibrated with this vile tongue, but because they are associated with Tulasi, He is happy to hear such words. Similarly, when we offer water, we should place tulasi in the water, offer tulasi water to Krishna. When we offer bath to Krishna, we should place tulasi in the water. All this because He is so pleased with Tulasi. So, as an expression of our love, we want to make the arrangements for Him to be pleasingly associated with His beloved Tulasi.

"It is a matter of considering His pleasure in everything and anything we are doing," he said, including the simplest, most practical aspects of Deity worship and treating the Deities in a caring, personal way, as one would want to be treated oneself. "Just like if someone pricks you with a pin, you will think twice about pricking someone else with a pin. So, if it hurts when you get hurt with a pin, then you dare not prick the Deity with a pin, because you know that it is gonna hurt and He is gonna feel it! It will be more distressing to you to prick Him with a pin than to be pricked with a pin yourself—because you love Him! You are willing to accept any calamity to save Him from the calamity. Before you'd dare to allow Him to fall into distress, you are willing to accept even the distress of death. His pleasure is worth more to you than your own life's breath; you are ready to give up your life for Him.... When you take a Deity into your hands, especially Govardhana *śilā*, you have to be prepared to give your life for His pleasure.

"It is not a light thing. There is no time for sleeping. You have to be prepared to give your life—that's *sevā*, that His pleasure is worth more than your own life. You have to have that mentality. If you don't, then you are not doing the Govardhana worship and you are not getting the benefit of it. You have to fully sell yourself out to the pleasure of Govardhana. If you adopt that mentality, then you are making advancement in Krishna consciousness by leaps and bounds and you will realize your guru's mercy....

"You please Krishna and became steeped by hopes and aspirations for satisfying Krishna and ultimately become overwhelmed by ecstatic love for Krishna. Pouring incessant tears, thinking of His happiness, thinking of His distress, thinking of His separation. Even the thought that you would be separated from those Deities should make you pour incessant tears."

"That fear is already there," Radhika Ramana said.

"It *has* to be there!" Aindra shouted. "If it is not, then I am immediately going to take the Deities back and place Them back on Govardhana Hill. I have the power to do that." He was especially severe with devotees who took it upon themselves to remove *śilās* from the hill—chastising them, taking the *śilās*, and having Them returned to Govardhana.

"It's a damn serious thing!" he continued. "Krishna wants His sense gratification—He demands it! And it is our business to not only seriously consider, but act on His demand! He has the right to demand. We have to command respect; we can't demand it. But *He* can demand respect! He has that position. Our position is to follow His desires, serve His desires. And He demands your love! Nothing else will do. He doesn't want anything from you. He wants your complete 100 percent absorption in love to Him. Love means *sevā*. And *sevā* means in consideration of His pleasure. That is pure devotional service; that is a pure devotee.

"I never want to experience the distress of hearing that you have allowed these Deities to be unhappy," he concluded. "I never want to hear that. Just the thought of it ..." His voice trembled, and then he fell silent.

※ ※ ※

Aindra almost always cooked for his Deities himself—often, except in the heat of summer, a spicy, strong-flavored *kichari* rich with ghee. Matsya Avatar das remembered, "He had a standard 3–4 liter bell-metal pot, took five handfuls of rice, washed it, brought it to a boil, then add chopped vegetables: green pumpkin; *tinda* ("baby pumpkin"), which he loved; radish; bell peppers; cauliflower. He loved frying things in ghee. Once, in a dream, Nitai Saci-suta asked him for it, so he always tried to get the purest cow ghee possible, which in the early days wasn't easy to find. And he would use a lot of it—for his *kichari* he would just open a can and pour it right in! He would fry cabbage until it became brownish, which lent a strong fried taste, and potatoes, and sometimes he'd fry mung-dal *bori* (dumplings) or some nuts or panir. And the spices—asafetida, cumin, coriander, fennel, ginger, and black pepper. In earlier years he used a lot of green chilies, but later and during Chaturmasya he was simpler, with just ginger, black pepper, and rock salt. And he loved offering achar, the mixed and ginger varieties, and using *kashundi* (Bengali mustard sauce) from Mayapur.

"In another dream, his Deities asked him for potato chips. So in Loi Bazar he found these dried raw thin potato slices, and he would fry them in ghee, mix in some chat masala, and offer them.

"During Chaturmasya he used only a few vegetables—potatoes, pumpkin, and *tinda*. And during the summer he'd offer cold preps: cucumbers and radish, nuts (especially cashews and almonds) and dried fruits, and whatever fresh fruits were available—melons, mango, strawberries and other berries, peaches, bananas, apples, oranges, grapes, and/or pomegranates—up to a kilo—daily.

"And always a sweet. Except during Chaturmasya he would offer milk sweets, sometimes sour *rasbharis*, sour Cape gooseberries dipped in honey, or Kinnow oranges with jaggery brittle. Sometimes he'd get items from Brijbasi Sweets or another shop—milk cake, *malai* burfi, panir, samosas, *kachoris* with chutney, or *dhokla* with marinated chilies on top—as long as it was cooked in Vrindavan. And, feeling bad that his Deities were being deprived of milk sweets, during the months of Chaturmasya he'd make a sweet from *bura* sugar (crushed brown rock candy) with nuts, dried fruit, and kernels of black pepper."

Aindra wouldn't eat or drink until he had completed his extensive puja, given the Deities a half hour to relish the offering, and then put Them all to rest, and this didn't usually happen until late at night, so sometimes he didn't have anything until the early hours of the morning. After years of this schedule, he said, he could hardly even digest anything during the day.

❦ ❦ ❦

Though he bathed regularly and kept himself clean, with all Aindra's cooking and pujas, and the room being heated by Bhakta Stove, in the course of each day his body would pick up a multitude of smells from his surroundings and the oils with which he rubbed his Deities—a distinctive mix of patchouli, Sai Flora incense, cow dung, wood smoke, musk, and camphor. He sometimes showered with his cloth on, using whatever soap—even dish-soap—was available. Then he applied tilak made from a mixture of *gopī-candana*, Radha-Kund mud, and dirt from his tulasi plants. "Shastra glorifies all of them," he said, "so I want the blessings of all three."

CHAPTER SEVEN

The first time Mahabhagavata das, originally from Ukraine, met Aindra, he was translating for a Russian devotee who was on the verge of leaving ISKCON. "He kept us in the room until almost midnight answering questions and preaching," Mahabhagavata remembered. "His preaching was intense, and even though I was translating answers meant for that devotee, I had the impression—the way he was looking at me—that he was aiming for me too.

"Some months later, when I asked him about the talk, he said that he had been addressing the other devotee's doubts but that in case the devotee failed to get it, at least I might, though I had not really asked anything myself. I never saw that person again, but the talk was not in vain."

When Mahabhagavata asked about acquiring a Govardhana śilā, Aindra said, "This worship is a very serious matter. First you should worship Gaura-Nitai, then Jagannath. Gain some experience—then you can approach Krishna, worship nicely for His pleasure."

Hearing that Mahabhagavata had been worshipping Gaura-Nitai in his brahmachari ashram, he said, "I think it would be nice if you got some more experience, and you can also help me. Why don't you come with me onto the altar." The service would help Mahabhagavata in his personal service and help train him further in brahminical standards and the proper mood of worship. Only then, when Aindra felt that Mahabhagavata was ready, would he give him a *śālagrāma-śilā* that a devotee had brought back from Nepal. And only after Mahabhagavata had been worshipping the *śilā* for over a year did Aindra give him a Govardhana *śilā*, which had been abandoned by an American devotee. (Aindra had also painted the *śilā*, as he had those in the care of several other devotees, and so the *śilā* joined a small "family" of local *śilās*, all of whom bore a common semblance.)

Entering into pujari service at the temple was competitive, though— many devotees, even sannyasis and other senior men, wanted to serve on the altar but could not—and one of the other pujaris objected to Mahabhagavata's presence. If Aindra needed help, the pujari said, he would help him; but this newcomer had to go.

But Aindra was insistent. It was a weekend, he pointed out—his days to dress Radha-Shyamasundar—and he could bring any assistant he wanted.

"No way," the pujari said. "He's not coming." And he took it a step further: "Just because you're a disciple of Srila Prabhupada, you think you can do whatever you want. But I am pujari here, and I won't allow it!"

Aindra explained that he had gotten permission from the department head, but the pujari wouldn't accept it, and the two argued for half an hour.

Finally Aindra had had enough. "Listen everyone!" he proclaimed, "I curse him to fall from his brahmachari position for his insolence!" Eventually the pujari calmed down and Aindra resumed his service with Mahabhagavata's assistance. But in time the pujari did change ashramas—and lost his place on the altar.

For the next year, Aindra trained Mahabhagavata in the service of Radhe-Shyam—as he would a select few of his closest, most trusted brahmacaris. "In his room he gave us knowledge for developing pure bhakti and taking, at first, small steps on the path of *rāga* in the line of the Goswamis of Vraja and all the predecessor acharyas," Mahabhagavata recounted. "And then on the altar he gave the best practical training of being *dāsa-dāsa-anudāsa* and using those instructions in practice. To serve Radha and Krishna under someone with that level of love and conviction, watching his mood and interactions with the Deities, his relationship with Them—nothing was more impressive. As much as we were able to imbibe due to our limitations, he really gave the best devotional training."

Aindra taught his trainees to serve the Deities in the mood of Radharani's divine maidservants, who, out of pure love, desired nothing but to please Her and assist Her in Her desire to please Krishna. Even when they served Him, he said, they did so to please Her.

"Shastra describes the elevated and pure service of the *sakhās* and *sakhīs* of Vraja at the feet of Radha and Krishna," Mahabhagavata noted, "and Aindra was the emblem of that mood—absolutely selfless, focused exclusively on pleasing Them. He was training us to develop a conscious, eager approach, to actively employ our abilities and intelligence to anticipate anything that might be required for service—to always try to please Krishna, one's guru, and the devotees not in a mechanical way but with a loving service attitude. When one morning I couldn't apply the Deities' oil before Their bath, because the metal cupboard containing the oils and other paraphernalia hadn't been unlocked, he chastised me playfully: 'You have to anticipate this and bring oil with you—you have to be a smart little *mañjarī*!' "

"What I really saw," Mahabhagavata said, "was the incredible intensity of his life. He was very intense himself with his sadhana (and his preaching), trying to offer Radha-Shyamasundar the best and purest possible service, and he demanded the same from those he taught. It was kind of hard and at the same time extremely uplifting, and it created a lasting and deep impression of devotion on one's heart. Krishna was challenging him from all sides to test his devotion, his character—whether he would be disturbed by the constant onslaughts. But he would get upset only when it disturbed the atmosphere of worship that Srila Prabhupada had taught—especially on the altar, since that could spoil Krishna's pleasure. Vrindavan is meant for the highest, purest, most self-sacrificing expressions of devotion, and Aindra Prabhu would fight against anything opposed to that mood and demonstrate his own fixed dedication to serve and try to please Krishna no matter the circumstances.

"I understood that he was generously, without ego, sharing this most sublime service on the altar. Undressing and bathing the Deities each morning was a very intimate service, and he wanted us to have that experience, too, to have the opportunity to develop the same loving affection for Them that he had. He was genuinely happy to bring other living entities to the feet of his beloved Lords—the same mood he showed in his preaching and kirtans."

Over the years, Aindra was assisted by several pujaris, who would go onto the altar when the doors were closed after the *saṅkīrtana* scores were read; remove the small Deities; place Them on a table, where They would receive Their *sevā-pūjā*; take all the pins from Radha-Shyamasundar's clothes and straighten any that had been bent; and undress Them. Then they would massage the Deities with oil; bathe Them with a wet towel; dry Them; put on Their day dress, ankle bracelets, and toe rings; arrange matching ornaments and decorations, and be prepared for Aindra's arrival.

"After a while," Mahabhagavata recounted, "we learned what he preferred and made it ready for him—small pins on one side of the cushion, big ones on the other, each item in accordance with the particular color and type of dress for the day and placed in the order that Aindra Prabhu would apply it. Everything was cleaned, untangled, ready.

"Especially on the Saturdays, Sundays, and festival days, he wanted lots of flowers—good ones—to make Krishna happy. 'The Deities really want them,' he would say. 'Especially in Vrindavan, Krishna must have fresh, nice, wonderful flowers.' There were still many growing in front of the temple back then, and tall trees with big bunches of these little yellow flowers, sweet like honey."

Whether in the blazing heat of May or the damp chill of December, Aindra would send devotees out to dozens of locations he had scouted throughout Vrindavan to pick different flowers, some rare or hard to find, chosen for their variations of form, color, and fragrance to complement the time of year and the Deities' different moods and outfits. Flowers from the *dhāma*, he knew, would be especially pleasing to Them, and in the early days of the 24-hour kirtan, before

CHAPTER SEVEN 159

Vrindavan's paths were paved and lined with new construction, there were seemingly endless varieties.

"So, we would climb up the trees to get them. There were these big orange trumpet flowers that Aindra loved, and different colors of what he called 'fleaves' [bougainvillea], flowers that looked like colored leaves. Different seasons, different flowers—there were trees and flowers everywhere."

Aindra was exacting about both the flowers and how they were used, and, as in all of his worship, he was never arbitrary in his requests; his motivation was always to please the Deities, and his reasoning always came from shastra. Govinda dasi remembered, "He wanted things done in a particular way and requested us to make Radharani's garland long so that it would touch Her feet. Sometimes devotees complained: 'Why are you making such a long garland?' So one day I went to Aindra Prabhu and said, 'People are complaining that the garland is too long!' And right there on the spot he gave me a whole hour-long class describing how Rupa Goswami says that Srimati Radharani actually has three garlands: one extended garland that's touching Her feet, one of medium size, and one smaller, delicate garland. 'Anyway,' he said, 'She deserves to have the garland extending to Her feet! Why not?' Since then, we started to make three garlands for Radharani. And I feel very confident that when people ask or complain, I can tell them that Aindra Prabhu said, 'She deserves to have Her garland touching Her feet.'

"He was also expecting that the garlands should be gorgeous—and fresh. So I would go early in the morning, sometimes in the dark, and climb trees to get special flowers and make sure to pick the best ones. I would climb the *champa* tree to get the flowers and then make the garland beautiful and special so that Aindra Prabhu could offer the best possible to Sri Sri Radha-Shyamasundar.

"Then, when the altar curtains would open and I would see two beautiful *champas* on Shyamasundar's head and flowers in Radharani's hair, I felt that this was the perfection of my life. He was like a guru teaching me how to worship Sri Radha-Shyamasundar."

※ ※ ※

Aindra's close attention to every aspect of Deity worship, no matter how minute, added to the challenge for those training under him.

"Dress for the camera," he told Giridhari das, from New York, who had joined in the Berkeley, California, temple. "It catches every detail."

One morning, after dressing Radhe-Shyam together in Rajasthani dress with a yellow border, Aindra and Giridhari stood in the temple room and surveyed their work.

"Look how you pinned Her dress," Aindra told Giridhari.

"It's how you like it, no?" Giridhari asked.

"No," Aindra replied. "Look—you don't see it? How the pinhead is sticking out from Radharani's dress?" Even from fifteen feet away, he had spotted a yellow pinhead sticking out a few millimeters from the yellow cloth.

❦ ❦ ❦

As with his kirtan crew, in his desire to inspire and instruct his trainees, to help them develop into expert pujaris, Aindra would challenge and confront them—sometimes strongly. "He was so heavy with me," Mahabhagavata recalled. " 'What are you doing?' he would chastise me. 'This is Krishna—don't you understand? This is Krishna; this is Radharani—this is no joke, no time to be playing around—this is Them! I give you the chance to serve Them, but are you worth this chance or not?' He would get especially upset if I accidentally poked Krishna or did something that would cause Him pain or make Him unhappy.

"He chastised me again and again, demanding perfection. Sometimes I was almost crying on the altar. But I knew that in his heart he was trying to train me, and I was happy just to assist him. It was an amazing, blissful experience. Being on the altar with him was really like coming into the spiritual world—super-wonderful, like nothing I've ever seen or done."

Not everyone appreciated Aindra's critiques. "To criticize or praise someone in front of Krishna is an offense," one temple pujari reproached him. But Mukunda Datta, defending Aindra, cited Srila Prabhupada shouting at devotees while the Deities were being installed in London and Amsterdam, because they had not been doing things properly.

Another pujari trained by Aindra was Annada, also from Ukraine. While he was dressing Lalita and Visakha on Sri Sri Radha-

Shyamasundar's altar, he would observe Aindra dressing Radhe-Shyam and try to glean what he could. And Aindra, noting Annada's interest and eagerness to learn, started instructing him. While Aindra was doing his dressing, Annada would take photos and videos, zooming in to see how exactly Aindra twisted a length of Radharani's dress or where he would pin it, and later, in his room, he would review the photos and recordings to analyze what Aindra had done.

Annada progressed quickly, and before long, when assisting Aindra, he knew what to give Aindra even before Aindra asked. "He knew every single thing, every single ornament that Aindra favored," Giridhari remembered. "This is the mentality of the *mañjarīs*: they don't need to be asked; they know what Radha and Krishna need right now. He knew that Aindra liked to use one particular set of earrings, one necklace or another. 'Look Prabhu, this new one matches very nicely.' And somehow he always knew Aindra's mind."

"Aindra appreciated Annada's *sevā* so much," Giridhari saw, "because he had this desire to understand Aindra's mind, what he needed." One day, admiring Their Lordships after Annada had dressed Them, Aindra said, "Actually, I think he is dressing Them now better than I am!"

One of the most important qualities of the pujaris whom Aindra trained was how they worked together. "In the spiritual world there's no question of envy," he told them. Radharani's maidservants expressed appreciation for each other's service, cooperated to maximize Her transcendental pleasure, and never put each other down.

"That was the real mood," Giridhari said, "that you appreciated the others so much: 'Wow, how much pleasure you gave to Radha! Let me try also.' In that sense, we could behave like *dasa-dasa-anudasa*, servants of the servant. If Annada would say, 'Bring this particular necklace,' I would run downstairs and bring it. In this mood, we could imagine how the Divine Couple's eternal servants feel, how they behave without having to be asked, and, when asked, immediately bring, have it clean, have it ready, take everything so that he can do his worship. As soon as he would say, 'I need a flower like this,' a helper would be standing there with a tray of flowers: 'Look, we picked these—the red ones that match the dress.'

"Aindra appreciated that so much—how we were all helping each other, not saying, 'Today's my day for dressing—why are you here?'

It wasn't like that. Whoever was there, whoever was ready to do it, whoever was most qualified—we let him do it. Even Aindra, if he came late and knew that Annada was faster and was good, would say, 'Okay, you dress Radharani today; Giridhari, bring the ornaments.' And there was never a problem."

CHAPTER EIGHT

FROM THE FIRST time he'd read the *Bhagavad-gītā*—in 1972, when he was seventeen—Aindra had been struck by Srila Prabhupada's statement that every living being had a particular, direct relationship with the Lord—an eternal constitutional position, *svarūpa*. He'd read that by the process of devotional service, one could revive that *svarūpa* and achieve *svarūpa-siddhi*—perfection of one's position. He'd noted that five different kinds of relationships were possible and had been especially attracted to the idea that one could attain a romantic spiritual relationship with the Supreme Personality of Godhead. And from the start, that had been his ultimate goal.

In America he'd had *sphūrtis*, glimpses of the spiritual world, in the form of dreams, but he had not gotten information specific to that goal; his devotional life had been focused on service to Srila Prabhupada and the Deities through book distribution, Deity worship, and *hari-nāma-sankīrtana*. In Vraja, the site of Krishna's most intimate pastimes, his desire to discover his spiritual identity intensified into a great longing—a *lobha*, transcendental hankering—to uncover his relationship with both Srila Prabhupada and Sri Sri Radha-Shyamasundar.

Aindra's mood of wanting to leave behind all material concerns and surrender fully to unalloyed devotional service to their Divine Lordships seemed to recommend him for the sannyasa ashram, which several of his godbrothers had entered. "*Sat nyāsa*, sannyasa—this is the combination," Srila Prabhupada had stated. "*Sat* means the Supreme, the ever-existing, and *nyāsa* means renunciation. That means one who has renounced everything for serving the Supreme, he is real sannyasa. He may take this dress or not; that doesn't matter. Anyone who has sacrificed his life for service of the Supreme Lord, he's a sannyasi." A change of ashrama might also help Aindra better guide and protect the 24-hour-kirtan brahmacharis under his care.

In the spring of 1989, however, when Aindra's name was submitted for sannyasa by Jagadisa Goswami, he was rejected by the GBC. "They wouldn't even put my name on a five-year waiting list," he told Ramabhadra. "They think I'm too austere."

In a letter explaining the decision, Jagadisa had mentioned concern about Aindra's "tendency towards austerities like following Chaturmasya very strictly."

"And they think my philosophy is deviant," Aindra said about one commissioner's objections to his "unusual" lectures, "and that I don't preach, I just do *bhajana*. What do they mean, I'm not preaching? Every day so many people are chanting and dancing. I think that's pretty good preaching—isn't it?"

Jagadisa had said that he thought the main issue was that the GBC didn't know Aindra well enough to understand where he was coming from. Some devotees thought him eccentric not only in his austerities and talks, but also in his devotional studies, musical passion, reclusive habits, dress, and shifting schedule—even, unaware of the irony of their speculation, suggesting that these were means of Aindra drawing attention to himself.

"People think I'm eccentric," Aindra later acknowledged, "but I'm just very, very conservative," following instructions and examples that had been laid down by the Six Goswamis and ISKCON's other predecessor acharyas.

"It may be wise for you to get to know them a little better and allow them to know you a little better," Jagadisa had suggested. "Generally, you are shy and introverted and not very prone to socializing, but taking association from senior devotees is not ordinary socializing and may be beneficial for you."

He'd assured Aindra that even though the GBC might not agree on whether the 24-hour-kirtan program was technically "preaching," they'd seemed to recognize both its value and the importance of his leadership. "I believe that everyone appreciates the contribution you have made," he'd written, "and would like to see you continue."

"My suggestion is that we wait until next year, when I will again be happy to recommend you. By then, the members will have had a chance to think about the proposal, and perhaps some of the reservations will have been worked out for them. Please don't be discouraged. I don't think you should take it personally ... given more time to get used to the idea, people will give up some of their hesitations."

"I wouldn't get bent out of shape," Ramabhadra said. "You have a good thing going here; just give it time and be patient. Prove to them that you can come up to what they consider to be the standard for a sannyasi."

"What 'standard' is *that*?" Aindra rejoined. "Less renunciation? Less *bhajana*? Should I make myself so busy flying here and there for 'preaching' that I have no time to chant Hare Krishna or read Prabhupada's books?"

"It's not like that—"

"What's the use of sannyasa, anyway? It's kid's stuff; I should aim for something higher. I should get beyond all these varnashrama titles and positions and aim for the *paramahaṁsa* level. They rejected me. That's fine; I know what I'm gonna do."

Without advertising it, Aindra dedicated himself to a life of renunciation and full surrender to devotional service and took a vow of *kṣetra-sannyāsa*—to live as a renunciant within the confines of the holy *dhāma*—to never leave Vrindavan or his kirtan service in Krishna-Balaram Mandir, which, he understood from Srila Prabhupada, contained the entire spiritual world. "I will not go to another place where I will not be able to hear the sound of the peacocks crying," he stated. "Anyway, what else would I do? What other more important things? Here in my room with my Deities—this is Vraja."

"The worst day in Vrindavan," he said, "is better than the best day anywhere else!"

In the following years, whenever he did leave Vraja—to Delhi, for instance, to produce cassettes, to lead kirtan, and, later, to publish his book—he always made sure to return the same day, no matter what time it was, never spending the night outside the *dhāma*. Mayapur, considered nondifferent from Vrindavan, was the only exception.

He changed his dress, eschewing kurtas for, at first, a simple saffron-colored cloth tied behind his neck. Some devotees objected that in ISKCON only sannyasis dressed like that, and lodged formal complaints with the temple president, but Aindra countered that many devotees—not just sannyasis—had worn that kind of top-piece in Srila Prabhupada's presence and also that ISKCON sannyasa attire included a lower garment with no back-pleat separating the legs. "Look," he said, showing off a small dhoti hidden beneath his top cloth. "Here are my pleats. I'm wearing my tail like a good monkey!"

Still, he replaced the saffron top-piece with a simple jute cloth that tied behind his neck, crossed over his chest, and extended a little below the knee. For a while, he wore only the top piece, but when devotees again complained, he added a short dhoti to cover his legs.

Over time, the color of the jute faded, and again some devotees were critical, or confused, wondering if Aindra had changed ashramas, gone from saffron to white. Did he intend to marry? Some recognized what he wore as a *bābājī* outfit; some were disturbed by the whole affair and again demanded that Kadamba Kanana, who, still a grihastha, was serving as temple president, intervene, "to determine for certain what ashrama Aindra is in."

When Kadamba Kanana asked about this, Aindra combined the names of all four ashramas: "I am a *brahmāsta-vannyāsī*."

"Don't worry about Aindra," Kadamba Kanana told the local GBC. "Leave him to me."

❧ ❧ ❧

Endeavoring for deeper internal realization, Aindra continued his intense chanting of the Holy Name in kirtan and *japa*. He also consulted senior ISKCON devotees, but, as one sannyasi pointed out years later, "What people know today when they first walk in the door of a temple, people at that time didn't know even if they were very senior. Practically no one knew what a *mañjarī* was; even the term was not there. Aindra, though, was really intense about understanding his eternal relationship with Krishna."

Seeking further insight, he tried consulting senior Vaishnavas from outside ISKCON. He was criticized for this from both sides: by some for going outside for his research—though he never sought the shelter of outside teachers or wavered in his allegiance to ISKCON or exclusive loyalty to Srila Prabhupada—by others for not staying with the teachers longer.

When he inquired about *siddha-praṇālī* from Bhaktivedanta Narayana Maharaja, who was attracting some of the most senior ISKCON devotees in Vrindavan, Maharaja replied that he could reveal the desired information but that Aindra would first have to accept his shelter.

"I refused him," Aindra later told a few of his closest associates. He had questioned the information that Maharaja was conveying and recognized that it sometimes differed both from Srila Prabhupada's teachings and from what he felt in his heart. "I said that I already had a spiritual master." And, happy with his own guru's guidance, he never went back.

"They just don't understand," Aindra said. "We're just trying to follow Srila Prabhupada *as deeply as we can.*" And the more deeply he immersed himself in serving the Deities, chanting, reading, and meditating on shastra, the more appreciative of and grateful for Srila Prabhupada's grace he became and the more he dedicated himself to propagating Prabhupada's mission.

In fact, loyalty to both Srila Prabhupada and ISKCON was a foundational principle for Aindra and one of his main preaching points. "Srila Prabhupada told me that many people will leave this Society," he told one disenchanted senior devotee, "But please don't."

"When Krishna shows you His beautiful transcendental form," he said, "when He gives you a *sphūrti*, a vision of His unlimited beauty, then you will never ever think of leaving this Krishna consciousness movement and you will never ever think to allow yourself to be distracted by any superfluous goals! ... If you ever saw Krishna, you would definitely understand the power of this ISKCON movement! I understood that by Krishna's grace more that thirty-five years ago, and because of it, my heart has become solid, like lines on a stone! I will never ever give up the lotus feet of Srila Prabhupada and never ever give up the lotus feet of Radha and Krishna!"

"Srila Prabhupada saved me," he later told a young brahmacari. "He nourished me from the beginning and can still appear to me and reveal things. Everything will come to me by his grace." Further, he said in his room one night, "He is not just a monolithic authority figure in our lives. He is our best friend!"

And one didn't have to go outside for advanced spiritual knowledge. "This ISKCON movement is complete!" he'd proclaimed in his 1987 Vyasa-puja offering, tears flowing from his eyes as he spoke. "Everything is here—if you want it. If you want to have complete perfection, you can have it, because Srila Prabhupada ... will give you all perfection. From him everything is coming!" It was the purport of both his experience and the dreams he'd had of Srila Prabhupada—that there was no need to go to other gurus for advanced spiritual instruction or information. "Everything is available in Srila Prabhupada's Society."

"We should never neglect this point," he'd continued. "We should never misunderstand under some illusion and bewilderment that we don't have all the facilities for complete perfection at the feet of Srila Prabhupada in this ISKCON movement."

Individuality was needed as well, he'd said—"everyone has to fly his own plane"—but that too put responsibility on the individual, not that one should blame Srila Prabhupada's movement, "pass the buck of responsibility to the rest of the Society," and "to individually do it together, we require good association."

"Srila Prabhupada said it, and I will repeat it," he told a devotee who was having doubts about ISKCON when things, in the devotee's words, were "getting weird in Delhi." "You. Cannot. Blame. Anyone. Else. For. Your. Lack. Of. Krishna. Consciousness!" A leading preacher who counselled hundreds of devotees had left to take shelter of a *bābājī* at Radha Kund, and the devotee, one of the biggest book distributors in one of the movement's biggest book-distribution centers, was thinking of joining him.

"There's ample facility [in ISKCON] for you to be totally absorbed in *bhajana*," Aindra advised. "Ample facility: all kinds of books to read, all kinds of time to chant as much *japa* as you want. Try chanting minimum of fifty-eight rounds. That means focusing, concentration—yoga, *bhakti-yoga* devoted to the chanting of the Holy Name, which is the only viable process for attaining self-realization, which begins with *nāma*. Self-realization begins with chanting the Holy Name. Have you read all of Srila Prabhupada's books? If not, no wonder you are having problems! You cannot blame anyone else but yourself. Why are you shifting the blame to other people?

"I don't want to hear how everything is 'weird in Delhi.' Everything may be weird in Delhi, but whether it is weird or not weird is not an excuse for anyone not making advancement in Krishna consciousness. The whole material world is weird! Probably a lot of the reason why it's weird is because they're having to deal with you, who are weird too on one level or another. As you relate to the world, that's how the world is going to respond to you. That's practically an axiomatic truth. If you are more Krishna conscious, the world will respond to you in a way that will facilitate more Krishna consciousness."

Answering a question about devotees who had left ISKCON, he said, "That's their business. If they're satisfied with what they've done, they have the prerogative to do like that. Every living entity has free will; nobody can bind anyone. Association and relationship are totally voluntary. No one can force anyone to love someone.

"The results, the fruit, of chanting the Hare Krishna *mahā-mantra* is the attainment of the realm of Vraja-*dhāma* ... simply by chanting Hare Krishna. And all the shaktis are present—all of them. The Holy Name can reveal every aspect of itself, every aspect of its shakti—just by you chanting Hare Krishna. According to your sincerity."

When the devotee said that book distribution seemed to be the only thing that pleased Srila Prabhupada, which, even as a book distributor, he questioned, Aindra told him the story of when Prabhupada had been in the Atlanta temple, which had gained his visit by winning a Christmas book marathon. All their big book distributors had been there, and the temple president had asked, "Srila Prabhupada, what pleases you the most?"

"It was a loaded question," Aindra related. "He was expecting Prabhupada to say, 'What will please me the most is if everyone distributes my books,' and everyone would go wild: 'Rah! *Jaya!* We won the marathon!' They wanted to feed their egoism. But you know what Srila Prabhupada answered? He paused for a minute and said,

'What will please me the most is if you learn to love Krishna.' That's the Srila Prabhupada *I* love.

"Now, if you love Krishna, you can express your love for Krishna by distributing books, you can express your love for Krishna by worshipping the Deity, you can express your love for Krishna by cooking for Krishna, you can express your love for Krishna by painting for Krishna, you can express your love for Krishna by going out on *hari-nāma-saṅkīrtana*, performing the *yuga-dharma*, you can express your love by chanting Hare Krishna!

"Book distribution is an important service. But even more important is learning to love Krishna. If you learn to love Krishna, your book distribution will be realized. If you learn to love Krishna, your *japa* will be realized, your *saṅkīrtana* will be realized. It will help every aspect of your devotional life."

In the end, the devotee was both moved and convinced by Aindra's response. After the meeting, he said, "I know only one *bābā* in Vrindavan, and that is Aindra Baba." And he remained in ISKCON.

The situation was not unusual. "I had friends who left ISKCON gurus and took initiation at Radha Kund," another devotee remembered. "But Aindra preached to me. He made me more confident to stay in ISKCON. And that's not a small thing."

❧ ❧ ❧

Aindra fixed his attention on his chanting, Deity worship, and study of shastra, his absorption in which strengthened and informed his preaching. He remained focused on Srila Prabhupada's books and repeatedly emphasized—insisted—that devotees should thoroughly and systematically read *all* of them, as he had done, before continuing on to those by other Vaishnava acharyas or outside authors.

CHAPTER NINE

PREVIOUSLY, FEW VAISHNAVA texts had been be available to Western readers, but as books by the movement's acharyas were translated into English, Aindra asked friends to read aloud from and, when he got a tape recorder, record them. He listened to them while doing his Deity *sevā*—along with all of Srila Prabhupada's recorded lectures, especially those Prabhupada had given in the early days at Rupa Goswami's samadhi *kuṭīr* on the *Nectar of Devotion*. "I worship my Deities for a minimum of three or four hours each day," he said, "so this gives me a chance to hear about Krishna's pastimes."

"That became a service I did for Aindra over the years," Rama Raya recalled, "recording some of the Goswamis' literatures and reading to him while he was doing his Deity worship—Bon Maharaja's translations of Sanatan Goswami's *Bṛhad-bhāgavatāmṛta* and Rupa Goswami's *Bhakti-rasāmṛta-sindhu* with commentaries by Jiva Goswami and Visvanath Cakravarti Thakur, the *Govinda-līlāmṛta* by

Krishnadas Kaviraj Goswami, *Kṛṣṇa-bhāvanāmṛta-mahākāvya* and *Prema Samputa* by Visvanatha Chakravarti Thakur, Rupa Goswami's *Ujjvala-nīlamaṇi* (translated by Kusakratha Prabhu), Raghunath das Goswami's *Muktā-carita*, and many others. I read all seventeen *śatakas* of *Śrī Vṛndāvana-māhimāmṛta* by Prabodhananda Sarasvati."

Other works Aindra studied included Visvanatha Chakravarti Thakura's *Madhurya Kadambini*, *Raga-vartma-candrika*, and *Surata Kathamrita*; Prabodhananda Sarasvati's *Radha-rasa-sudhanidhi* and *Ascarya Rasa Prabandha*; Ragunath das Goswami's *Vilapa-kusumanjali*; numerous books and articles by Bhaktivinoda Thakur and Bhaktisiddhanta Sarasvati Thakur; the *Garuda Purana*; the *Padma Purana* (from which he particularly relished the story of Arjuna turning into Arjuniya-gopī in Vraja); and many others.

He was so excited to receive a gift of Srila Kavi-karnapura's poetic rendition of Krishna's pastimes in Vrindavan, the *Ananda-vrindavana-campu*, newly translated by Bhanu Swami and Subhag Swami, that he broke down in tears over the exquisitely beautiful text. "What a wonderful book!" he exclaimed; he had longed for it, and he read and listened to it repeatedly, attracted especially to the section recounting the *pūrva-raga* (love prior to meeting) of the *gopīs*.

"At every step, he was probing, questioning, trying to go deeper," Rama Raya observed. "He listened to the Goswami literatures again and again [to the *Govinda Lilamrita* over a hundred times]—so often that he practically memorized them, which was interesting, since he admitted that his ability to memorize was poor, his Sanskrit was not strong, and he sometimes had trouble reading aloud—he would have someone else read the verse if he gave a class."

He was particularly fond of hearing about Radha and Krishna's *līlā* and different aspects of *mādhurya-rasa* and was beginning to delve into *mañjarī-tattva*, endeavoring to understand through the eyes of the shastra the devotional aspirations blossoming in his heart. A thorough and intelligent understanding of Gaudiya Vaishnava literature, he was convinced, would enable him to develop the realization needed both to chant Krishna's pure name and to go deeper into his *bhajana* and discover his true relationship with Krishna and Radharani. His study was not merely a theoretical or intellectual exercise; it was helping to guide his inner search, nourishing and confirming his developing realizations and revelations.

CHAPTER NINE 173

❧ ❧ ❧

Engaged in such intense, comprehensive study, Aindra was a font of knowledge for the 24-hour-kirtan members and other devotees, and his room became the Vrindavan hot spot for *sādhu-saṅga* focused on *kṛṣṇa-kathā* and Vraja-bhakti. "It was the coolest place in the whole world," said Akincana Krishna das. "This man was just fully on fire for Krishna consciousness. It was very exciting, and he had this personality—he was not exactly a soft, gentle, sweet sadhu; he was intense."

An evening visitor to Aindra's room would likely find a half-dozen brahmacaris sitting on the floor in semi-darkness discussing spiritual topics or listening to Aindra expound on *kṛṣṇa-līlā* as he did his puja, or to Rama Raya reading aloud from the *Kṛṣṇa* book or another Vaishnava text. Americans, Russians, Indians, devotees from England, Poland, Mauritius, Hungary, Australia—they came from all over the world to get Aindra's association, receive his training, and imbibe whatever they could of his *guru-niṣṭhā* and deep love for the Deities. As Srila Bhaktivinoda describes in *Sri Caitanya Mahaprabhu: His Life and Precepts*, "When one comes in contact with a Vaishnava whose heart has been melted by *hari-bhakti-rasa*, it is then that he loves to imbibe the sweet principle of *bhakti*, devotion, by following his holy footsteps.... *Bhakti* is a principle which comes from soul to soul, and like electricity or magnetism in gross matter, it conducts itself from one congenial soul to another."

Aindra focused his preaching to new members on just that: cultivating pure, unalloyed bhakti—how to develop a higher taste, spiritual aspirations, and, in order to remain steady over time, overcome *anarthas* on their devotional path. And they found in him a demanding but nurturing teacher and guide in their spiritual growth who cared for them like a loving parent. He spoke of principles more than of pastimes, but he was willing to answer questions that few others in the movement seemed to want to address. And he provided a living example, a role model of a devotee striving for spiritual advancement and realization—a practical education that, for these young men, penetrated more deeply than what they learned in *Śrīmad-Bhāgavatam* class. They formed, one devotee described, "a motley crew of serious, spiritual madmen whom Aindra Prabhu inspired, who gathered around him and made his association that much more fun, dangerous, crazy, and uplifting."

Some local devotees were disturbed by Aindra's focus on what they considered to be overly intimate spiritual subject matter. "What disturbed me," one said, "was that he'd discuss these things with young devotees. 'Why talk about these things to people who are not on the same level?' I wondered. 'What is the need?' I had no problem with him discussing them with his godbrothers, but when he talked about it with some kids, I couldn't understand that."

But Aindra was undeterred. He also shared such topics with senior devotees, and he inspired many of them, but one of his main purposes in relating these topics—and one of its effects—was not to lead young devotees astray from Srila Prabhupada, but, on the contrary, to encourage them to remain in ISKCON, to show them that they could find the full range of spiritual truths in Prabhupada's Society.

As Srila Sanatana Goswami had written in *Śrī Bṛhad-bhāgavatāmṛta* of Gopa-kumara's revealing his life story to a new brahmana devotee, the devotee "need[ed] to be informed that Kṛṣṇa is the goal of his endeavors and that *nāma-saṅkīrtana* is the means to achieve Kṛṣṇa.... to win the brahmana's trust, Gopa-kumāra first needs to describe his own experiences, beginning from when he also received the same *gopāla-mantra* and continuing up to the present moment. That will drive away the brahmana's doubts and wrong ideas. It will also allow the brahmana to drink the nectar of *śrī-bhagavat-kathā*, which will render his heart pure enough to assimilate the transcendental knowledge he requires.... And what would ordinarily have been a breach of etiquette will be perfectly acceptable behavior.... Many of these personal events are also too confidential to discuss freely in public, and Gopa-kumāra may be somewhat embarrassed to mention them. He feels obliged, however, to do everything he can to help enlighten the brahmana."

Also, Aindra liked to stir the waters, to disrupt people's complacency and promote their spiritual progress. "Sometimes," he said, "I intentionally speak openly about things that are generally hidden just to shake things up and somehow get people interested in *rāgānugā-bhakti*, because *rāgānugā-bhakti* is so important and so essential to our Gaudiya Vaishnava line. Krishna's intimate *līlās* are there to attract us and give us the chance to develop intimate relationships with Him. We have to speak about them. We have to hear about them. These things are the true wealth of our lineage. They have to be discussed and understood in ISKCON—but under the proper guidance of Srila Prabhupada and the previous acharyas."

"We read all kinds of books," Mahabhagavata remembered of the evening gatherings, "not only intimate matter. We would read *Śrīmad-Bhāgavatam* and the *Bhagavad-gītā*—all kinds of shastras: Bhaktivinoda Thakur's books, Bhaktisiddhanta Sarasvati Thakur's *Upākhyāne Upadeśa*, short instructive stories to illustrate Krishna consciousness, which Rama Raya read in a humorous tone while the rest of us listened and laughed.

"But the message was always the same: in any shastra, the devotee sees his *prāṇanātha*, his *iṣṭadeva* and his desired mood of bhakti, everywhere. No matter what book we read, no matter what the topic was, he was speaking about surrender, about pure devotional service, about *vraja-vāsa*, the mood of Vraja, living in Vraja with the pure intention of pleasing Krishna with all your heart—just trying to create faith among devotees."

The privacy of his room also gave Aindra more liberty to express emotions that in the temple he usually kept to himself. "Up in his room he would talk about Krishna and just break down crying," remembered Govinda das, from Hungary, who had joined the movement in New York after Aindra had left for Vrindavan. "He felt so much separation and was so sad, heartbroken. This was actually what *sādhu-saṅga* is supposed to be—you would see this and experience this, and it would leave an impression on your subtle body and awaken your soul."

"His talks could last for hours," Mahabhagavata described. "Sometimes he'd be crying—about the depth of the *vraja-vāsīs*' love for Krishna, or a devotee's hope of achieving the Lord's shelter—sometimes yelling, sometimes whispering, sometimes laughing. You could see that he was not just showing off—he was really giving himself fully, even to devotees he didn't know very well, trying to do his best to give the devotees everything, to try to bring them as high as he could right then. There was no tomorrow, keeping it for later."

It upset Aindra if he couldn't bring someone deeper into Krishna consciousness. "I couldn't convince him," he lamented after one such encounter, when he couldn't prevent a devotee from leaving the movement. He was in tears, more sad than frustrated. "I couldn't help him."

"If anyone had a question, he would take as long as it took to answer fully and elaborately," remembered Akincana Krishna. "In the temple his talks were usually at least somewhat constrained by time, but in his room there was no limit"; Aindra would put everything else aside to give his exclusive attention to a devotee he may never before have even met.

"Sometimes you would want to take association or darshan of a senior devotee but they wouldn't have time for you and you would get frustrated," Rama Raya noted. "But with Aindra, it was the opposite—you got so much, so far beyond your expectation and even your capacity to take it in. When devotees came to his room asking questions, he would preach to them for hours, leaving everything aside to help, so often they got more than they bargained for. A devotee might say that he had to leave, but Aindra would respond, 'Yes, but first...' and another forty minutes would go by."

If someone said it was getting late, Aindra would motion toward the clock on his wall, which had no hands, and say, "It's always a million o'clock here."

"When you asked him a question, he would give you an answer that was like three, four hours long," Govinda added. "He wasn't a superficial person; when he started speaking, one point would lead to another point which would lead to another thirty points. His brain was so sharp—he would bring you back to the point you asked, and a secondary point and a third point, and he would weave it all together in such a way that it made complete sense and was interrelated. And at the same time it was so deep; you never heard an explanation going so deep. It was fascinating to listen to him."

"When he spoke the philosophy, time would stand still," Rama Raya agreed, "and you would feel that you were entering into a very special dimension—Radha and Krishna's sacred space. He could speak unlimitedly, in great detail, but you never felt that it was unnecessary or too much; it was just one thing after another holding you spellbound—all very important and correct."

Aindra and Mukunda Datta would discuss the Vrindavan mood of loving Krishna. "Wherever there is *bhakti*," Mukunda Datta would say, "there is Krishna, and wherever there is Krishna, there is Vrindavan."

Vrindavan, Aindra would counter, was not produced by a devotee; it was the environment that allowed a devotee to exist. The devotee had to seek to enter Vrindavan, not imagine that Vrindavan would follow him around like a servant.

As he said during one seminar, "I could spend—and I wouldn't mind spending—all day long discussing these topics from various angles of vision."

❦ ❦ ❦

A great variety of devotees were drawn to visit Aindra in his room, and he welcomed sincere visitors seeking spiritual advancement. But like many renunciants, he was by nature reclusive. Except for his kirtan shifts and the regular temple program, he only occasionally ventured outside his room, disliking social interruptions, distractions, and anything that wasn't directly related Krishna consciousness. "If anyone asks for me," he once told a kirtan-party member before retreating behind his door, "tell them I went to Govardhana." It wasn't a lie, he said—he'd be with Sri Giriraj on his altar.

"His life was his room," another devotee described. "His *bhajana kutir*, the temple room—his service—and back to his room again. And maybe a few programs here and there."

As more and more devotees started looking for him in his room and knocking on his door at all hours and when he was busy, Aindra rigged it to look like he wasn't inside when he actually was. He'd cut a gap in the frame for padlock that didn't actually lock the door, so unless someone knew about the setup, they would see the padlock and closed latch and conclude that he was out.

Generally, he wouldn't answer the door unless he knew who was there. He assigned regular visitors individual identifying codes (Rama Raya's was five knocks in a particular rhythm). And to dissuade casual interruptions, over the years he would tape different signs to his door. One showed a fanged skull over crossbones wearing red tilak between its black, empty eye sockets. In red, underlined capitals, he had written, "NOTICE!! HIGHLY CONTAGIOUS DISEASE. ENTER AT YOUR OWN RISK." Another portrayed Aindra himself in an angry mood, smoke coming from his ears, above the warning "DO NOT DISTURB! RECORDING WORK IN PROGRESS!" Another announcement was displayed in multicolored print:

> IF...
> you have not completed
> your required minimum
> daily 16 rounds of Hari nāma
> THEN...
> you should know that
> you have no more important
> service to your Guru and
> Guru parampara than to
> FINISH YOUR
> JAPA VRATA.
> Even IF...
> you think you have
> finished your nāma bhajan,
> THEN...
> please mercifully leave me
> alone for now so I may
> HOPE TO SOONER
> IMPROVE MINE.
> y.s.

When he did leave the temple compound—later only a few times a year—it was usually to visit the sacred places of Vraja—Govardhana, Radha Kund, and the Yamuna—on specific auspicious dates. He sometimes felt uncomfortable at other temples, where he would see pujaris at work and feel separation from his own service. "I just wouldn't feel at home," he said—another reason for his reluctance to go beyond the four walls of Krishna-Balaram Mandir.

❧ ❧ ❧

One of the frequent later visitors to Aindra's room was Dvarakanath das, who owned a nearby Internet cafe. Fascinated by everything he had seen of and heard about Aindra, he had struck up a conversation and been impressed with both Aindra's depth of knowledge and his strength of conviction.

"Prabhu," he asked, "I would like my children to meet you. Would that be okay?"

Aindra blushed and looked down with an embarrassed smile. "Okay," he said. "I'm on the third floor of the *gurukula*, room number 89. You can come see me any time."

Less than a week later, Dvarakanath arrived with his young son, Shiv, and ten-year-old daughter, Preeti. Peering into the dark room through the screen door, they could just barely make out Aindra doing puja for his Deities.

Hearing someone at his door, Aindra turned, saw them, and said, "Oh! *Prabhujī*! Come in!" He wondered how Dvarakanath had managed to smuggle Preeti into the all-male ashram, but then, seeing that Dvarakanath had disguised her as a young boy, in a dhoti and kurta and covered with a chaddar, he just smiled and repeated, "Come in! Come in!"

Preeti was struck by the room's incredible heat; there was no air conditioning, not even a fan—hardly any ventilation whatsoever. It was dark, especially coming in from the bright sunlight, and she tripped over the edge of the hard clay that made up the floor.

Suddenly she began to cry and just couldn't stop. Something about the way this person looked, about the way the room smelled, triggered a response in her heart that she felt powerless to control.

Through the tears, and as her eyes adjusted to the light, Preeti began to make out the big Gaura-Nitai Deities dressed in simple dhotis, and the altar, filled with hundreds of *śilās*—more than she had ever seen; the room was *packed* with Deities. Barely one corner remained, cluttered and disorganized, for Aindra himself.

When Dvarakanath and the children had found spots on the floor to sit, Aindra opened a discourse on the devotion and sacrifice of the *gopīs*, telling one of his favorite stories. "Krishna once had a headache that could not be cured," he began. "Narada Muni was distressed, and Krishna told him, 'The only medicine that will cure me is the dust from the feet of my devotee. If you bring that dust and put it on my head, my aching headache will be cured.' "

He described how Narada went from one devotee to the next,

relaying Krishna's problem and asking for the dust from their feet. Each devotee refused; none could bear the thought of putting dirt from their feet upon the head of their beloved master.

"Finally, Narada came to Vrindavan and found Srimati Radharani and the *gopīs*. 'My dear *gopīs*,' he said. 'Krishna has a headache.'

"As soon as he said that, the *gopīs* became acutely pained. Some of them clutched their heads as if they also had headaches. Some of them fainted. 'What can we do?' they asked Narada.

" 'Oh,' Narada said, 'I don't think you will like it.'

" 'No!' they demanded. 'Anything! We will do anything to get rid of Krishna's headache!'

" 'All right,' Narada said, ready to be disappointed, as he had been so many times before. 'Krishna says that if I get the dust from the feet of his devotee and put that dust on his head, his pain will go away.'

"The *gopīs* immediately agreed.

"Narada was shocked. 'But it is an offense!' he said. 'If you put your foot-dust on Krishna's head you will go to hell for that offense!'

" 'Oh, who cares what happens to us!' the *gopīs* replied. 'Let us go to hell if it cures Krishna's headache!' "

Aindra became more and more animated as he told the story. He stuck out his feet and started brushing the dust off their bottoms, saying, "The *gopīs* immediately stuck out their feet—'Here! Here! Take it! Take it!' Then they shooed him off: 'Hurry up! Put it on His head! What are you waiting for, you dullard!' "

The conversation lasted three hours, during all of which time the kids remained quiet and patient. Finally, Dvarakanath stood up to leave, but first he had a request. "Prabhu," he said, "my daughter is chanting a little bit, but my son is not chanting very much. Can you say something to him before we go?"

Aindra bent down and spoke into the boy's ear: "Hare Krishna."

The boy's sister, Preeti, was also listening, and later she remembered feeling the sound of Aindra speaking the Holy Names go straight to her heart.

CHAPTER TEN

AINDRA SPENT HOURS in his room worshipping his Deities and preaching to devotees, but even more of his time—as many as twelve hours a day—was taken up by his chanting of the Holy Names in *japa* and kirtan. Expounding on the difference between the two, Aindra said, "There are two prominent ways that the *gopīs* are absorbed in the services of Radha and Krishna. *Japa* is in *nikuñja-sevā*, in which one serves Radha-Krishna alone, and kirtan is *rāsa-līlā*—dancing and singing and serving Krishna with all the *gopīs*.

"Similar to how all the *gopīs* have their individual *kuñjas* for individual personal service, we chant *nāma-japa* in the mood of *nāma-sevā*, to assist in personal intimate service. *Nāma-japa* is thus like facilitating the meeting of Radha and Krishna alone.

"So, *nāma-japa* is a more secluded, personal affair; it's not so extroverted. You may even pull your *chādar* over your face so that no one can see you crying. And softly mutter the Holy Name to yourself. It's your own relationship with Radha and Krishna, without considering the idea of sharing your Radha and Krishna with others. That comes later—that's *rāsa-līlā* and *saṅkīrtana*. But whether you're doing *nāma-japa* or whether you're doing *nāma-saṅkīrtana*, the principle is to serve Radha and Krishna for Their satisfaction. Whether it is your endeavor to satisfy Radha and Krishna by your personal *sevās* or your transcendentally altruistic *para-upakāra* mood of cooperating with others to bring about the pleasure of Radha and Krishna, in both cases the aim is never a self-aggrandizing affair. The aim is not to gain some personal satisfaction; the aim is to satisfy Radha and Krishna, and moreover to bring about the satisfaction of the devotees of Radha and Krishna. That's what brings *saṅkīrtana* to a different level.

"But in *nāma-japa* one is free to allow the heart to flow and express one's desperation for the eternal loving service to the Holy Name in a way that one can't do in public assembly.

"For practicing devotees, it's powerful to chant *nāma-japa* in the mood of separation—especially a type of separation called *pūrva-rāga*, which means the intense, desperate anticipation—hopefully sooner than later, but at least eventually, after millions of millions of lifetimes of endeavor, devotional struggle—to actually meet Radha and Krishna. The idea is that you meditate on the types of services that you would like to do for Radha and Krishna in the *kuñja* and pray, 'When, oh when, will that day be mine?' That is *pūrva-rāga*.

"*Saṅkīrtana*, on the other hand, can be performed in the spirit of Krishna's *rāsa-līlā*. The *rāsa-līlā* acts as an appetizer to whet Krishna's appetite for more intimate reciprocation with his *gopīs*. In Rupa Goswami's *Ujjvala-nīlamaṇi*, however, there is a description that says that the *rāsa-līlā* generates in Krishna a happiness that far surpasses even the experience of His complete intimate union with Srimati Radharani and the *gopīs*.

"One may ask, 'How is it possible for *rāsa-līlā* to be the highest, when the culmination of all the *mādhurya-līlās* is that *samprayoga* when Radha-Krishna are finally united and enjoy Their pleasure pastimes in the *kuñja*?' The answer is *vipralambha*; it is the mood of separation. So close, yet so far. Krishna is dancing with the *gopīs*, but He is not making love with the *gopīs*. So one's hairs are standing on end—the *gopīs* and Krishna in the ecstasy of dancing *rāsa-līlā*, and now Radha and Krishna's impending embrace. The *rāsa-līlā* is thus like the hors d'oeuvres served before a feast. The feast is the real objective, but the hors d'oeuvres can be more transcendentally tantalizing, more piquant and full of *rāsa*, than the feast itself.

"From *nāma-kīrtana*, Krishna also sees that you are serious about sacrificing your egocentricity for the purpose of helping others to gain access to the Holy Name. An attraction thus naturally awakens within Krishna to the soul who is performing that *yajña*. It induces Him to relish deeper with that devotee even more intimate, loving reciprocation in the form of *nāma-japa*. In that way, *nāma-saṅkīrtana* and *nāma-japa* are always inter-supportive."

"The culture of *hari-nāma-japa-yajña* is said to be a disciple's first and foremost essential obligation at the feet of Sri Guru," Aindra wrote. "Though apparently bearing a relatively small radius of *para-upakāra* audibility, a disciple's offenseless chanting of at least a fixed minimum number of Holy Names daily unquestionably constitutes the top-priority, most substantial service to Sri Guru and his institution. In fact, the guru imposes no more imperative order than to regularly complete one's prescribed personal *japa-vrata*. Such is the incontrovertible status of *nāma-japa's* enormous significance."

"Make sure you chant your sixteen rounds a day," he instructed a developing *kīrtanīya*. "Otherwise, your kirtan won't have any power." The first question he'd ask any devotee having trouble with their chanting in kirtan was, "How is your sadhana?" The potency of one's chanting of the Holy Name in kirtan depended on first completing one's sixteen rounds of *japa*.

In one short article, Aindra emphasized the special importance of chanting *japa* in the modern world:

> Some misinformed people say that chanting Hare Krishna is a kind of brainwashing. We, however, suggest that most so-called human beings don't have a brain to wash. Hare Krishna chanting is not brainwashing; it is brain-giving.
>
> Those who have a brain will understand this. Those who do not can at least try chanting Hare Krishna, which will give them a brain with which to understand the immense value of chanting the Hare Krishna mantra.

In this era of ever-encroaching wholesale pollution and inane carelessness, people with good brains will welcome the chance to gain relief from the lying propaganda of misguided materialistic politicians, scientists and superstitious religionists—all of whom more or less broadcast their own variety of systematic selfishness, eroding the finer internal sensibilities of almost everyone.

The transcendentally potent Hare Krishna vibration of timeless names of Godhead cleanses the heart of all these vicious material pollutants, allowing us to actually perceive the eternal nature of our inner spiritual being, bringing into reach the natural inner peace and happiness for which we are always anxious. Thus, chanting Hare Krishna is not brain-washing so much as it is heart-washing. It gives a brain and cleans the heart.

And if your brain thinks you haven't the heart for it, don't worry: Hare Krishna chanting will give that also.

When asked what he thought about when he was chanting, he said, "The essence of what I think about and strive for runs on two parallels. One is the external mood, the mood relevant to my external situation of not being capable to meet Krishna. I base this on *Jaiva Dharma's* instructions to think of myself as a *gopī* who is bound by her mother-in-law, who constantly prevents me from meeting with my Shyam. But by making many clever excuses, I can somehow slip away to do my *sevā* to Radha and Krishna. From there I can go into the internal mood, where I meditate on Radha and Krishna's eternal *aṣṭa-kālīya-līlā*, but with the mood described in the books of Raghunath das Goswami."

"There is a strong need to go deep in our understanding of *tattva*," he said. "Otherwise our *nāma-bhajana* will never go deep, will never be filled with *bhāva*."

❦ ❦ ❦

As much as Aindra chanted, and as deep as was his realization of and attachment to the Holy Name, he was never satisfied with either.

"I'm *three hundred and sixty-three* rounds behind my quota!" he bemoaned one night in frustration.

"That's because you're trying to chant so much, besides doing kirtan eight hours every day and spending so much time worshipping your Deities," a devotee pointed out.

"That's not why I can't finish my quota!" he insisted. "The problem isn't that I'm too busy—the problem is that I have no taste for chanting."

He was chanting sixty-four rounds a day, trying to increase his love for Srimati Radharani, but even after undergoing so many austerities in the effort, he still felt inadequate to the task, and his desperation for spiritual answers kept building. Internally, he begged for greater taste, deeper realization, and especially deeper realization of his eternal spiritual identity and service.

One day, while he was chanting, he heard a voice in his head—"First deserve, then desire." The words were Srila Prabhupada's, from a purport in *The Teachings of Queen Kunti*, which Prabhupada had often repeated, and a theme on which Aindra often preached. But it was also a phrase that had been twisted by temple managers wanting to avoid answering his difficult philosophical questions.

The phrase kept repeating, first intermittently, then every minute, then faster, almost nonstop, over and over. Finally he threw his bead bag against the wall and yelled "Damn it! When will I deserve to desire?" When would he receive response to his inquiries?

And then he heard a voice—thunderous, coming from everywhere all at once and resounding all around him, filling the room and resonating throughout the ether: "WHEN YOUR DESIRE IS BIG ENOUGH!"

Awestruck, Aindra ran outside and asked devotees in other rooms if they had heard anything. But they hadn't—the voice had been for only him.

❧ ❧ ❧

Frustrated by his inability to gain further realization of his spiritual identity, Aindra's endeavor to further increase his taste and desire manifested in the *vratas* that he had begun in New York and increased in Vrindavan, even to the point of risking his health and physical well-being. In his effort to serve and please guru and Radha-Krishna and his *lobha* to discover his spiritual identity and empower his preaching from his eternal position in relation with Them, bodily considerations were secondary.

"It's likely that one will get weak," he acknowledged, "and because of that weakness it's possible for one to become diseased. But to get diseased by performing such *vrata* for the purpose of curtailing sense gratification with the aim of augmenting the hopes of attaining prema in this lifetime ... is much better than to have the disease of lust within the heart and within the senses. If you strictly follow Chaturmasya, you will find that your senses become pacified, and it's advantageous in the matter if it's performed properly with a proper attitude. If one is abstaining from the object of senses while contemplating those objects within, he is a pretender and a first-class nonsense."

Knowing the spiritual benefits of following particular *vratas* was important, he said, but "even more important than considering scriptural vows and their results is to consider our attitude, our purpose, the motivation behind performing all of these *vratas*."

"Just like one vow is to fast from six tastes," he said, "sweet, sour, salty, pungent, bitter, and astringent. These six tastes agitate the mind to again and again taste those things. So it's mentioned that if you fast from these six tastes, the result is that you will have no objectionable body odor.... But that's not such an important benediction, just not to have body odor. But those who practiced this particular vow, what they actually experience is something a little different and more practical in terms of achievement of the goal of life.

"We should have within out heart the mood that whatever is favorable for cultivation of unalloyed devotional *bhajana*, that is to be accepted. And the things which are not favorable we should not concern ourselves with. So fasting from six tastes certainly does, as scriptures say, reduce the body odor, but there is a more important result in that the fasting from six tastes makes it that your tongue becomes acclimated to the idea that it will not get varieties of palatable foodstuff; thereby the mind becomes used to not chasing after varieties of palatable foodstuff, which helps us in the matter of 1) controlling the tongue and 2) freeing us of *aparādha* against the *mahā-prasāda*, that 'This *mahā-prasāda* is palatable for the gratification of my taste buds, so I accept it, and this *mahā-prasāda* is not palatable; thereby

I reject it,' which is equivalent to rejecting Krishna. This is *aparādha* on both cases.

"*Mahā-prasāda* is not meant for our sense gratification. Otherwise, if one can control the tongue, one can control all the senses, and when senses come under control, then it's possible to push back the influence of *kāma* that is residing in the senses, mind, and intellect, as described in the *Bhagavad-gita*."

Material benefits were never the goal: "Whatever *vrata* we may be taking—just like if you read *Ekadasi Mahatmya*, you will see that it is mentioned many times that material results were obtained by people who either knowingly or unknowingly performed *ekādaśī-vrata* in various instances. We should understand that ultimately we are not aiming to achieve any material benedictions."

Even the goal of cleansing oneself from sin was not primary: "It is very necessary, or useful, to reduce our bodily activities in terms of sense gratification and to increase our *bhajana* so that by the influence of that *bhajana* we may become so much free from sin. Fasting on these days of Krishna's appearance or on the appearance days of various incarnations and Ekadasi helps the devotee to become free from sin, but becoming free from sin is an insignificant fruit in the matter of chanting the Holy Name.... The real business is the fact that performing Chaturmasya *vrata* or Kartik *vrata* or Bhiṣma-*pañcaka vrata* in Vrindavan yields the benefit of unalloyed devotional service."

Certainly, one should not be motivated by the desire to cultivate an austere image, to be "recognized as an austere devotee, *tyāgī*. Because if one becomes attached to superfluous fruits, such as name and fame, profit, adoration, and distinction, these things will automatically undermine the real purpose for which such vows are to be undertaken. One should be very careful with these kinds of *vratas*, because the tendency is that if someone will strictly follow Chaturmasya, he may look down on other devotees who are not following so strictly. Or if someone is cultivating knowledge, then the tendency is to look down on others.... As soon as one thinks that he is better than anyone, immediately the results of his austerities, his knowledge—the benefit of his service—becomes very much diminished."

Further, "gaining mastery over the senses or performances of austerities has no value in and of itself. Austerity or penances or *tapasya* in and of itself is not an *aṅga* of pure devotional service. So we don't have much concern with austerity for its own sake, just like Narada Muni says something to the effect of, 'What is the use of performing austerity if bhakti has not arisen?'

"But that does not mean that we should not practice austerity. Especially in the vanaprastha ashrama it is useful in order to curb our tendency toward sense gratification as we are accustomed to in grihastha ashrama, to whatever extent we have allowed ourselves to become acclimated to the mood of enjoying the senses."

"Ultimately," he said, "what we really want to see is whether our devotion is increasing."

When one devotee questioned his practice, noting that Srila Prabhupada hadn't emphasized such penances, he had replied, "Yeah, but what if they work?"

"If our *bhajana* increases," he said, "then we can understand that our acceptance of any vow is favorable.... Because ultimately it is not what we do, but our attitude." We should maintain the mood that " 'I am not very qualified; I am not as qualified as other devotees, because they are advancing in pure devotional service without having to accept such superfluous or extraneous modes of life—they don't have to perform such severe austerities to gain control over the senses. They are much better than I am.' ... *Tapasya* may be useful in the beginning by helping us to get a foothold in the house of bhakti, but ultimately the *tapasya* is not what's important."

In his early years in Vrindavan, during the four months of Chaturmasya Aindra would offer his Deities only a handful each of raw soaked rice and mung dal, salt, and ghee on the side, and a little fruit or *miśri*, rock candy, mixed with anise seeds, with raisins for variety, and would honor only the rice and dal, which he ate off the floor without using his hands. The lack of salt in his diet was especially impactful, as he was constantly dehydrated and weak from not being able to retain water. His liver would weaken and he'd suffer from jaundice.

Even in later years, and for the rest of his life, during Chaturmasya he abstained from all dairy except ghee, which, according to Srila Sanatan Goswami in his *Hari-bhakti-vilas*, bestowed the benediction of going to Goloka-Vrindavan at the end of one's life.

Beginning on Guru Purnima, he would not shave his face or head for two months, then shave at the midpoint, on Visvarupa Mahotsava, and then not again for the second two months.

For Kartik and the month of Puruṣottama, which, when it came around every three years would increase the summer fast to five months, he would have only Ekadasi prasādam, and during the final five days of Kartik, the final month, he would observe the Bhiṣma-pañcaka vrata: complete fasting except for a teaspoon of one type of cow-product each day: cow dung, cow urine, ghee, curd (yoghurt), and milk.

"It is told that if you follow this fast," he said, "you don't even have to endeavor for unalloyed devotion, but unalloyed devotion comes to your hand. So, it is also another facility for advancing in Krishna consciousness which has been mercifully bestowed upon us by Krishna Himself."

On the last day of Kartik, he would have a massive offering prepared for the Deities and host a feast that he would personally serve to the devotees that evening—after the last *Dāmodarāṣṭaka* kirtan, which he usually led—outside his room, on the veranda. And then, for another month, he would adopt "Katyayani's Vow," meant for obtaining a good husband and followed by the *gopīs* and by the sages of Dandakaranya to attain Krishna as theirs, eating only unspiced *kichari* and chanting extra rounds of the mantra used by the *gopīs* to worship Katyayani:

> *kātyāyani mahā-māye*
> *mahā-yoginy adhīśvari*
> *nanda-gopa-sutaṁ devi*
> *patiṁ me kuru te namaḥ*

"My respects unto Katyayani, the great controller, great mystic, and great power of the Supreme. Please, oh Goddess, make Nanda-gopa's son my husband!"

In the mornings, despite the cold winter temperatures, he would go down to the Yamuna to bathe. One morning, Bhagavata das met him there and asked why he braved the elements and came so early. "The sun was up," Bhagavata described, "but it was still early and, of course, cold, as it usually is at that time of year. I asked him why he didn't come to bathe later, when it got warmer.

Aindra replied, "Young *gopīs* and *mañjarīs*, following their *vrata* were coming to take their early morning bath, and there was nowhere they could warm themselves, no one to take care of them—such was their vow. Their determination was unwavering. We have to follow that example."

At noon, with Rama Raya, he would take a rickshaw to the *ārati* at Vrindavan's Katyayani temple and make an offering (in later years he also went in the evening). And on the last day of the *vrata*, he would take the 24-hour-kirtan devotees, do a big *saṅkīrtana*, and hold a feast.

❦ ❦ ❦

Altogether, Aindra observed significant austerities for almost half of each year. During one *vrata* he got so sick that all he could do was lie down in his room. Another devotee helped by serving his Deities, but it didn't go well (a tiny *śilā* was accidentally thrown out), and Aindra was so upset that he vowed that nothing like that would ever happen again and scaled down his austerities for the sake of his Deities and service. "If our *bhajana* suffers," he said, "(of course there will always be a little weakness; it may affect us to a certain extent, and that's to be expected), if one sees that his service is drastically reduced ... then it is better to take some *prasādam* and go on *saṅkīrtana*.... We have to regulate, moderate even in the performance of Chaturmasya *vrata*. There are at least four hundred different *vratas* and you can't take all of them."

By that point, he had been strictly observing Chaturmasya *vrata* for over fifteen years and at least twice had fasted almost to the point of death. "I accepted such an austere vow and didn't want to break it, and my *bhajana* may sometimes have suffered," he admitted. "So I basically learned the hard way to concentrate only on those most important vows which are useful in my culture of *kṛṣṇa-premā*, or at least in the culture of hope of augmenting such prospects for getting *kṛṣṇa-prema* by Their grace. It's not that it is caused by our activities. Ultimately it is by Their grace, by Their special mercy that we are elevated to such a status when They see that we have cried hard and long enough that They mercifully bestow Their *prema-bhakti-śakti* on us."

❦ ❦ ❦

Inspired by Aindra's example, some young devotees also began to follow *vratas*, especially during Kartik and Purushottama. Aindra was concerned that they perform the *vratas* correctly, however, and so would instruct them however possible, posting detailed explanations with quotes from shastra and making announcements in the temple room after *maṅgala-ārati*. He stocked and distributed fast ingredients, such as for Bhiṣma-*pañcaka vrata*, which required exclusively cow products, some of which could be difficult to obtain. And when it came time to break the fast, he instructed devotees to go around the temple to distribute sweets, juice, and various presents and donations to honor the brahmanas and Vaishnavas.

CHAPTER ELEVEN

ALL OF AINDRA'S years of *saṅkīrtana*, *japa*, Deity worship, preaching, *vratas*, shastric study—even his book distribution—had been imbued with his urgent desire to understand his eternal relationship with Radha and Krishna. "[T]he basic unconditional service attitude practiced at the very onset of a novice's humble surrender to the acharya's external missionary training program," he later wrote, "may be easily adapted and internally applied at a more mature stage to fittingly promote the true, cognitive, esoteric evolvement of one's eternal constitutional ... *vraja-svarūpa*."

"Okay, so we are not this body," he'd say. "Then who are we?"

'*Jīvera "svarūpa" haya—kṛṣṇera "nitya-dāsa"*—every living entity is constitutionally an eternal servant of Krishna'—but that's not enough!"

"He was probing, in a period of his aspiration where he was really wanting to realize his eternal identity," Rama Raya remembered, "and he was in great anxiety about it all the time."

"What would be the use of it all," Aindra wrote, "if we could not become factually freed from the insanity of not clearly knowing who we really are in terms of the intricacies of our ultimate, intrinsic, eternal spiritual identity?"

This was not merely a selfish search for personal spiritual advancement, he wrote. "[T]he internally perfected realization of one's eternal spiritual identity ... would immensely enhance one's preaching proficiency and efficacy."

Ultimately, the success of such an endeavor was dependent on one's attachment and surrender to the Holy Name: "If we seriously want to go well beyond the bodily concept of life, to realize the highest constitutional spiritual identity of the self (*vraja-svarūpa*), then we would do very well to set all worldly considerations aside, take shelter of Śrī Caitanya Mahāprabhu, and do more *harināma-saṅkīrtana*!"

In 1993, striving for further realization, which, he knew, could come from only Srila Prabhupada, Aindra engaged in *ājagara-vṛtti*, the Python's Vow, as had been practiced by Madhavendra Puri and by Bilvamangala Thakura—to make no endeavor to eat, but to rely on the grace of his spiritual master and accept only what was offered to him without request. "Let my guru maharaja reveal this knowledge to me," he said. "If not, there is no reason for me to live."

He continued to offer *bhoga* to his Deities, but, without telling anyone, he distributed all Their *prasādam* to other devotees and ate only every few days, and only when something was given without him asking. He was determined to fast until either Prabhupada granted the knowledge he so desperately desired or his body wasted away. "Will my guru kindly reciprocate?" he asked. "Will he show me the mercy?" Without it, he said, he saw no reason to live.

He followed the *vrata* strictly for a couple months, but his body weakened, and one morning when devotees went to see him, there was no reply to their calls. "We kept knocking," Rasesvara recounted, "but he wouldn't answer. So we broke the door open and found him on the floor, pale and semi-conscious. We took him to the hospital, and they put him on a drip. 'If you had found him just a little later,' the doctor said, 'he wouldn't have survived.'"

CHAPTER ELEVEN 195

❧ ❧ ❧

After Aindra's *ājagara-vṛtti*, his dreams reached another level of revelation. Even though "such things are basically unverifiable subjective experiences," he had said, "if they are in keeping with the *siddhānta* of our acharyas, they may be accepted for inspiration, encouragement, and even guidance."

The dreams were nourished by Aindra's years of dedication to japa and kirtan, both of which deepened his relationships with Srila Prabhupada, the Deities, and the Holy Name. "Srila Prabhupada has appeared numerous times in my dreams and given me so many instructions regarding the progress of my spiritual life," he said. "Whether that's actually Prabhupada coming in my dreams or whether it is *antaryāmī* manifesting within the mental quantum by manipulation of the subtle energies in the form of the acharya *svarūpa* of Srila Prabhupada, whom I accept as the authority of my spiritual life, and speaking through that acharya *svarūpa* a message that *antaryāmī*, whom that acharya is representing anyway, wants to relate to me a message, so many instructions he has spoken to me in the dreams, which I keep as my life and soul." During one period of especially lucid dreams, "I was looking so much more forward to being asleep than being awake, because I was getting so much more enlightenment in my dreams than I was during the time I was awake."

The dreams in which Srila Prabhupada appeared "profoundly increased my fervent attachment to his lotus feet." During one, Prabhupada told Aindra, "You are not qualified to worship Giriraj. This is the highest type of worship, and you have no qualification for that." "What do you mean?" Aindra asked. "What should be done to be qualified?" Still in the dream, he began weeping. "I just want to be a new devotee with no position or conceptions about himself." "Now you are qualified," Prabhupada replied.

Aindra yearned for a revelation of his spiritual identity. "When," he wrote, "by a flood of unprecedented tenderheartedness, will the cowherd girls of Vrndavana bestow upon this wretched person the most blessed birth within the cowherd community of Varsana? When, by the mercy of my beloved guru, will I appear as a resplendently delightful young damsel of Vraja?"

Srila Prabhupada had said that the guru revealed a disciple's *siddha-deha* when the time was right. "How to qualify? Who will give?" one devotee asked. "Guru will give," Prabhupada replied. "You just chant Hare Krsna." The revelation did not even have to come in the guru's physical presence: "Guru will give. There is no material consideration about Guru is here or there. When you reach that level, Guru will give."

Some months after he completed his vrata, Aindra had a series of dreams revealing the information he'd been seeking. Most often it came from Srila Prabhupada—once from an old woman whom Aindra took to be Paurnamasi-devi—identified in Srila Rūpa Goswami's *Śrī Rādhā-Kṛṣṇa-gaṇoddeśa-dīpikā* as "the incarnation of the Lord's Yogamāyā potency" who arranges for the performance of Krishna's pastimes.

Finally, in one dream, Srila Prabhupada disclosed, "You are a follower of Ananga Manjari." Few devotees spoke about Ananga Manjari, a shakti expansion of Lord Balaram, and Radharani's younger sister, who in *gaura-līlā* appeared as Nityananda's wife Jahnava Devi. So Aindra searched out any information he could find, but he didn't have to look far. In his song "Kabe Mor Subhadina Hoibe Udoy," Srila Bhaktivinoda Thakur writes, "Bhaktivinoda's incessant longing is for the shelter of the lotus feet of Sri Ananga Manjari "in "Ha Ha Mora Gaura Kisora" that "The merciful Ananga-Manjari, catching the hands of this maidservant, will take me to offer me in devotion unto Sri Sri Radha-Madhava, and my eyes will be brimming with pleasure to behold the beauty and sweetness of Them both." He was so serious in his study of Ramachandra Goswami's *Ananga Manjari Samputika* that in addition to tracking down an English translation from the Bengali, he commissioned another so that nothing was left out or mistranslated.

Along with his extensive japa, kirtan, and strict spiritual practice, Aindra's dreams and revelations continued unabated, and with further study of works such as Prabhodananda Sarasvati's *Radha-rasa-sudhanidhi*, Raghunatha Dasa Goswami's *Vilapa-Kumsumanjali*, and other writings by Vaishnava acharyas, he came to understand how his internal aspirations were in accord with Ananga Manjari's *bhāva*. In her faithful service to Srimati Radharani and under Radharani's shelter, with Her express permission, and for Her supreme pleasure, she also had direct association with Krishna. And in that same mood, on the altar Aindra dressed Shyamasundar, serving Him in service to Radha: "For the pleasure of Srimati Radharani I am giving pleasure to Shyam! For the pleasure of Radharani I am soothing the limbs of love-tired Sri Krishna. They sported the whole night, and when it is time to rise during maṅgala-ārati, His limbs are so tired and Their ornaments are entangled. So for the pleasure of Srimati Radharani, to give Her ultimate pleasure, I am serving Shyam! Radharani is the queen of my heart, and Krishna is the treasure of my heart. Radharani can give you the treasure; you can't take it by yourself. She is my queen, and I serve Her, and She gives me the treasure—that's Shyam."

"According to the acharyas," he related, Ananga Manjari—whom he thenceforth worshipped as his *guru-rūpa-sakhī*, his spiritual master in the eternal *mañjarī* form—"is even considered to be a virtual second Radha—directly Radha, who is accepting the position of a maidservant of Herself to relish the transcendental position of *dasi dasi anudasi*."

CHAPTER TWELVE

THE 24-HOUR KIRTAN had faced financial challenges since its inception. Without a regular means of income, Aindra had barely been able pay the rent, but even later, when he was no longer charged for the brahmacaris' quarters, he had to cover the cost of instruments, equipment, medicine, clothes, and the basics of daily maintenance. Anything beyond that was a luxury. When a devotee ran out of toothpaste, Aindra suggested salt; when one needed a toothbrush, he pointed to the twigs of a tree. Instead of soap, they could use soil from the *gurukula* grounds.

Friends sometimes helped, and Mukunda Datta arranged for Aindra to get a thousand rupees per month for his pujari service. Aindra didn't like accepting money for *sevā*, though, and after a few months he told Mukunda Datta that he could manage. Instead, describing himself as a "poor Indianized beggar," he sent out a chain letter to godbrothers requesting donations, but there wasn't any response.

When the temple adopted a policy that each department had to be self-sufficient, Aindra didn't know what to do. "How can the 24-hour-kirtan department be self-sufficient?" he asked. "We don't make any money. We don't even collect donations."

"Why don't you record kirtan and sell the cassettes?" Kadamba Kanana suggested.

"The Holy Name shouldn't be sold," Aindra replied—a point he made many times. "Kirtan is meant to be done purely as *yajña*, for the satisfaction of Krishna, without expectation of anything in return."

When a few members of the party asked about the kirtan at a nearby ashram that paid its *kīrtanīyas*, Aindra said, "It's nice to listen to if you don't mind being infested with millions upon millions of material desires."

He asked, "By our performance of kirtan are we endeavoring to generate an atmosphere that is conducive to the evolution of *prema* or not? According to all the bhakti shastras, the substance of *prema* is based on the principle of selfless sacrifice. It doesn't matter what ashrama or what varna one is in; all devotees need to be doing selfless sacrifice to advance in pure devotional service.... Sacrifice done for the purpose of material results and sacrifice with the pure intent of satisfying Krishna without any expectation of material gain do not yield the same result. A gram of gold is worth more than a ton of fool's gold. Similarly, a little kirtan performed purely as selfless sacrifice for the pleasure of Lord Vishnu is worth thousands of mayic kirtans performed with the aim of gaining profit, adoration, and distinction."

The practice would affect not just the musicians and kirtan, but the audience as well. "Where an attitude of selfless sacrifice is lacking," he pointed out, "we can hardly expect to see constituents attuned to the desired selfless, pure devotional mood. When someone does kirtan for money, the one who does the kirtan, the one who hears the kirtan, and the one who pays for such so-called kirtan to be performed all become infected by material desires and get sinful reactions."

There were also the considerations of how merit should be determined and with whom payment should begin and end. "Which kirtan artists will get paid and which won't?" he asked. "And what determines which one? We all know that kirtan is not just about the kirtan leader. So, what about paying the mridanga players and the kartal players and the people clapping their hands? Why not pay the whole audience, who are all singing, dancing, and participating in the kirtan? Should we be paying the kirtan artists on the basis of who is apparently prominent or most popular? Wouldn't it make more sense to offer the most money to those who are strictest in following pure devotional principles?"

"We are all clear that it is generally appropriate for brahmana beggars to receive donations so that they can maintain themselves," he acknowledged. And householders had to maintain their families. "It is also appropriate that we cover some transportation costs. But it is against the pure devotional principles of Srila Prabhupada and our acharyas to charge money for a kirtan program." It was not even most profitable, he said. "One of the problems with charging for kirtan is that it puts a limit on what people give. Someone may be ready to give more, but because you've put a price tag on your kirtan, they'll just give what you're demanding."

"We do not use the Holy Name of God for our sense gratification or material purposes; we chant the Holy Name without any personal ambition, simply to glorify and serve the Holy Name. If someone gives you money for doing kirtan, you should cry and think, I wanted *kṛṣṇa-premā*, but all I got was this lousy money!"

"But you're not selling the Holy Name," Kadamba Kanana countered about marketing tapes to supporting the kirtan department. "You're selling cassettes. Srila Prabhupada sold books about Krishna and described them as 'recorded kirtan,' so why shouldn't you sell recordings of kirtan too?"

Aindra saw the point. He had to fund his department somehow, and he wanted to give devotees all over the world the opportunity to hear the Vrindavan kirtans. But he still favored donations over sales. Distributors might offer the cassettes at a market rate, but if someone approached Aindra directly for a cassette, he would tell them the cost of production and say that any reciprocation beyond that would help fund the 24-hour-kirtan party.

Everything was recorded in his room. He wanted the kartals really soft, so he had them played in a wicker basket. He chanted both the lead and backup vocals and played the harmonium. A few brahmacharis were brought in to record another set of backup vocals near the end of the process.

The next step was to make and package the cassettes, and for that he needed equipment. As Sacinandana Swami recalled, "A devotee came to me and said, 'A disciple of Srila Prabhupada has made it his mission to establish the 24-hour kirtan in the Krishna-Balaram temple. Seeing his determination, it seems he will be successful against any odds. He needs to generate some financial foundation for the project, so he wants to record kirtan and make the cassettes available for sale. He asked if I could find someone to donate a four-track recorder. Would you do it?'

"I didn't know who Aindra was, and at the time sending something to Vrindavan was like throwing a message-in-a-bottle into the ocean, but for some reason I purchased the recorder and sent it."

As soon as he received the equipment, Aindra set to his task. He had worked in multi-track recording studios as a musician in D.C. and had some experience with sound engineering. Recording in Vrindavan was a challenge, however—the power surged and cut off in seemingly random intervals—and as it turned out, the four-track wasn't enough.

Shortly thereafter, in Bhurijana Prabhu's room one day, he spotted a higher-end recorder and mic. "Where did you get this?" he asked.

"It was donated to the VIHE," Bhurijana told him.

"Can I borrow it?"

Bhurijana hesitated, but it was off-season for the institute, so he loaned Aindra the equipment for four days, and Aindra hacked it into the four-track that Sacinandana Swami had sent and resumed recording.

So that he could return the equipment on time, Aindra worked tirelessly, practically without sleep. His first attempt—produced in his room—was a recording of the Pancha Tattva mantra and an adaptation of a popular Bengali *bhajana* melody to the *mahā-mantra*. But the tape didn't even come close to Aindra's standards, and he made only six copies—what he called "my biggest flop." When he brought a copy to the temple gift shop, the manager listened for only a few minutes before agreeing. "This is garbage," he said. "I can't sell it."

Undaunted, Aindra moved on to his next project: compiling two hours of his most popular kirtan melodies into a double cassette, *Cintamani Nam*. One of the recordings' distinctive elements was the use of an *esraja*—a bowed string-instrument. He also incorporated a swarmandal, an Indian Autoharp, playing melody lines rather than its usual chords. The kartals rang out trills and rapid grace notes, and the mridanga held it all together and ushered the kirtans through sophisticated rhythmic changes.

He included the high-pitched, drawn-out melodic sections—alaps—that characterized Bengali kirtan, but by limiting them to half a mantra and keeping the mantra going in the background while the lead vocal elaborated on the melody, he avoided the vocal showmanship that sometimes obscured the mantra itself. On one track Gopinath led and Aindra played mridanga—a rare recording of him on the drum.

When the master of the second cassette came back from Delhi, Aindra found that the duplicator had boosted the midrange so much that although the vocals were clear, they were pitched too high. The recording was over-compressed and muddy, and the kirtans—unusual anyway, with their long, slow sections and complex structures—faded in and out. Always the perfectionist, he was tempted to just trash it all and start over. But calmer heads prevailed, and the cassettes of *Cintamani Nam* were released in 1992 and circulated widely throughout ISKCON, attracting attention with its new techniques, and, more importantly, attracting to Vrindavan devotees who wanted to join the 24-hour kirtan.

❦ ❦ ❦

For his next recording, Aindra was offered time in a Delhi studio, but he declined. "I don't want to go to Delhi," he said. "I want to sit down here in Vrindavan, chant Hare Krishna, and get a thousand times more benefit sitting in Vrindavan and influencing the whole world just by sitting in Vrindavan."

The main idea of the recording, which he entitled *Vrindavan Mellows*—from Srila Bhaktisiddhanta Sarasvati Thakur's and then

Srila Prabhupada's use of the Late Middle English word *mellow* (ripe, sweet, juicy) to help translate the idea of *rasa,* the sweet taste of a living being's relationship with the Lord—was to give the world Vrindavan.

But for that, he would need better equipment, which could not be obtained in India. "I can't keep recording with rinky-dink stuff," he told Ramabhadra in a phone call to New York. "I need a real system."

"And you want me to help, right?" Ramabhadra asked.

"We'll reimburse you," Aindra replied. "Jada Bharata [a *BTG*-party devotee and friend from New York] will guarantee the reimbursement; he's here with me right now. We just need you to pick it up from the shop in New York and bring it here to Vrindavan."

"What do you want me to buy?"

"The Alesis ADAT multi-track digital recording system."

"What's that cost?"

"Three or four thousand dollars."

"I've carried expensive things to India before," Ramabhadra said. "I know what can happen. It could get stolen, it could get confiscated ... I'll only do it if Jada Bharata guarantees to reimburse me no matter if I can get it to Vrindavan or not."

"I want to make field recordings around Vrindavan to capture the sounds of the *dhāma,*" Aindra said. "If you see some good equipment for that, maybe you can bring it." Ramabhadra arrived soon thereafter with a top-of-the-line field recorder, the Sony TC-D5M, which was eventually replaced by a donated Alesis system.

With the addition of an equalizer, digital sound-effect processor, and mixer, Aindra transformed his room into a multi-track digital recording studio. It was a demanding process. The power kept going out, and even when he used the battery and an inverter for backup, the power changeover was marked by a click in the recording. He was a perfectionist about the music, and even with the better equipment, the work to achieve the perfection of detail he desired was painstaking—"the most tedious thing," he said, "I ever did in my life."

The main recording was done in the temple, in front of the altars, both for the reverb produced by the size and arrangement of the room, and, more importantly, for the Deities Themselves, Their spiritual potency.

Each night, Aindra would mount the equipment onto a rack and he and the crew would carry it down the three flights of stairs. "We would lock the temple door from the inside and tell the chowkidar not to let anyone in," Devakinandan remembered. "It was really difficult, because Aindra Prabhu was very professional and wanted to make a good, clean recording. We had to play each song thirty or forty times, so it would take a week or two, recording every night from 10 to 3:30." When Aindra recorded his singing and harmonium playing with a mridanga, for instance, every time the mridanga player faltered—or any time Aindra would misplay something on the harmonium—they would have to start over. He had Nitai sing one tune over and over, after each saying, "That was good, but ..." pointing out something that could be just a little bit better.

By the time the crew was done with a track, they would be so tired—and tired of it—that they couldn't even listen to the recording. The next day, they would hear what had been completed the night before and then lay down the kartal tracks, along with the rest of the rhythm section—shakers and the bells. Sometimes they'd add clapping or a gong. Aindra played the string instruments—an Indian banjo and the swarmandal—and the background vocals were added last. In one kirtan, one can hear voices that sound like women's, beautifying and balancing the singing, but they came from Aindra and a few brahmacharis singing in falsetto, what he called *gopī* voices, and by speeding up the recording. The final version sounded like there was a big kirtan with a crowd singing, clapping, and calling out "Haribol!" and "*Jaya* Radhe!" but it was all accomplished with just four or five devotees.

When the main structure of a kirtan had been captured on tape, Aindra did the engineering in his room, mixing in instrumental overdubs, backing vocals, and samples of sounds of Vraja. He wanted to flavor the recording with the essence of Vrindavan by blending ambient sounds of Vraja into the music. He and his assistants would go out in the evening, when animal sounds reached a crescendo and artificial noise was at a minimum, and record birdsongs and other sounds of the forest. He recorded a tonga wallah, who carried people to Vrindavan in a horse cart, intoning "Vrindavan, Vrindavan, Vrindavan, Vrindavan." The goal was to make Vrindavan come alive, to bring the listener into the holy *dhāma*.

The full production of *Vrindavan Mellows* took six months. It opens with the sounds of Vrindavan's natural landscape: chirping crickets and cooing night birds, the cries of a peacock and screeching of an owl. Inside the cover—the title, handwritten and embellished by Aindra in sandalwood paste, arching over an oval painting of Krishna framed by a leaf plate, standing under a tree on the bank of the Yamuna, holding a flute to Radharani's mouth—is a message:

> May this cassette serve to remind you of Vrindavan, the perfect place to lead a spiritually progressive life. It is the home of Lord Kṛṣṇa, as well as the home of His pure devotees who know the meaning of unalloyed devotion. In this dark age of quarrel, such rarely achieved devotion, self-realization, and God realization (Kṛṣṇa Consciousness) are greatly facilitated by the natural yet superb method of singing these sweet names of the Lord congregationally. Always live in Vrindavan, at least mentally, and happily absorb your thoughts in the delightful pastimes of Kṛṣṇa by constantly chanting:
>
> Hare Kṛṣṇa Hare Kṛṣṇa
> Kṛṣṇa Kṛṣṇa Hare Hare
> Hare Rāma Hare Rāma
> Rāma Rāma Hare Hare

Devotees had never heard anything like it. Describing his amazement on hearing Aindra's recordings for the first time, in Mexico City, Radha Krsna das, the youngest member of the party when he joined in 2006, echoed responses from listeners around the world: "I was, like, *Who is this?!* ... *How many? Where are they singing? In the temple? In the street? What is going on?! All these peacocks and cows—are they singing in a stable or something?*"

The tape was an overnight sensation, and Aindra's reputation—and following—began to grow. Over the next three years, he produced *Vrindavan Mellows II* and *III*, both with a similar sound and style. He and the kirtan-party members distributed the cassettes themselves, especially during Kartik, when Vrindavan was filled with visiting devotees, and the recordings were soon picked up by the movement's emerging mail-order businesses, such as Krishna Culture in the U.S.

As distribution of the studio recordings, along with others of live kirtans, increased, Aindra's name reached out to the world beyond Vrindavan and spurred interest in the 24-hour-kirtan program. Participation in the evening kirtan swelled, and, as people began taping it with portable equipment, independent recordings spread worldwide.

During one of Aindra's kirtans in 1994 someone clipped a small mic to the end of a bamboo pole and recorded for two hours. The kirtan, Aindra felt, had been really fired up, so he'd gotten the tapes and compiled them into a live album, processing the best portions through his ADAT multi-track and adding instrumentation—flutes, horns, and strings—and releasing it (without cover art) under the title *Kirtan is our Bhajan*.

In the spring of 1997 he released *Prayers to the Dust of Vraja*, recorded digitally for greater fidelity, mostly in his room, where he could more easily separate the tracks and had finer control over the sonic details. He overdubbed tracks, playing all the instruments except the mridanga and *shenai* himself—including flute, which he hadn't played since his days in D.C. One of the biggest production challenges was power outages, which were frequent and random and could ruin an hour's work in a second, as the machine would shut down without saving what had been done. So some of the sessions were recorded in an apartment in the nearby MVT complex, which had its own generator, though that required carrying and dragging over all the heavy equipment.

Prayers was a natural sequel to the *Vrindavan Mellows* trilogy, continuing the themes of Vrindavan sounds but with shorter compositions in intricate patterns—not always following his standard tempo progression—and exotic instrumentation, with a dreamier and more ethereal sound. There was a noticeable improvement in the audio quality—the instruments, voices, and samples being more distinct than on the previous recordings—and on more than one occasion, Aindra expressed that it was his favorite, most successful studio recording.

In 1999 Aindra released *Vraja Vilasa*, a double CD, which, even with its beautiful instrumentation and long free-form, almost dreamy, sections, conveyed the vibrancy—the impact and excitement—of his live festival kirtans.

Still rooted in traditional kirtan, Aindra was moving forward with a musically nuanced style of sit-down kirtan that was attracting listeners with backgrounds in contemporary Western music—a sound they could feel, with which they could connect. The recordings were at the forefront of a developing worldwide kirtan culture—a progressive, even revolutionary, movement that was bringing back an enthusiasm especially but not only among young devotees for the kind of spiritually surcharged *nāma-saṅkīrtana* that had marked the early days of ISKCON.

CHAPTER THIRTEEN

"THERE'S A BIG kirtan guy up on the third floor," Jiva, a recent *gurukula* graduate, told Gopal das, a new arrival from Bhaktivedanta Manor in England. "Everyone is crazy about him."

Because of Aindra's unusual appearance and fiery demeanor, some of the *gurukula* boys were afraid of him, at least until they got to know him better. But one spring, the eldest boys, who had experienced both his kirtan and his more affectionate side, invited him to an end-of-year evening program. Several of them were graduating, and they personally requested him to come down and do kirtan with them before they left.

When Aindra arrived in the *gurukula* garden—the first time he had come into the school to do a program—the students spontaneously all stood up and gave him a long ovation. He was touched by their welcome, had the older boys play mridanga, and included everyone. "Throw out everything else you've learned," he told the group. "The only thing you have to learn in life, you have: chanting the Holy Name in Vrindavan."

❧ ❧ ❧

Gopal had been only eight when he'd first seen Aindra ten years before, a year after his father, Riddha, had met Aindra in London, but he'd been mesmerized by his singing. *I've never heard anything like this*, he'd thought, and the devotee's singing had struck a chord deep inside him. "What attracted me to his kirtan," Gopal later remembered, "was that his chanting felt really pure. When I heard his kirtan, it really touched my heart. Even at that age, I felt a heart-moving experience."

After the kirtan had been going on for a while, Aindra had leaned toward one of the other kirtan members and said, "I've gotta give my voice a break; you take over."

When he'd seen Gopal's father, he'd broken into a big smile. It was Riddha, the travel agent with the voucher from London! Aindra had been thrilled to see him, and with his back to Gopal, he'd put down his mridanga, turned to Riddha, and became absorbed in conversation.

Gopal had learned how to play one or two simple drum beats. The mridanga had been just lying there on its side, and the devotee, he'd thought, would be happy to have someone playing. So he had reached forward, taken hold of the strap, and gently tugged the drum to where he was sitting on the courtyard steps.

As he'd been speaking, from the corner of his eye, Aindra had seen the mridanga rolling toward the steps. He'd lunged for it, and found young Gopal pulling it by the strap.

"What are you doing?" Aindra had admonished.

Gopal had frozen.

"You gotta be more careful or you'll break it!"

"Gopal!" his father had chastised. "Why are you touching people's things?"

Gopal had burst into tears.

"Anyway, prabhu," Aindra had said to Riddha as he'd placed the mridanga back on his lap, "I have to get back to my service. It's great to see you."

Gopal hadn't realized that he had just met the devotee his father had heard chanting in London the year before. And now, ten years after that, he didn't realize that Aindra was the kirtan devotee on the third floor.

Jiva was helping Gopal develop his mridanga skills, and the two would sit and play together for hours. That's what they were doing on the first day of Kartik when Niranjana Swami came into the temple room to sing the *Dāmodarāṣṭaka* prayers.

As the kirtan shifted into the *mahā-mantra,* some of the devotees began to dance, including one who Gopal thought looked unusual. He had a stubbly beard, unkempt hair, and razor-sharp eyes and was leaping around in thick woolen socks with a childlike smile on his face.

"Whoa!" Gopal exclaimed. "That's the dude! The one who freaked me out when I was a kid! That's him!" And, he realized, it was probably the kirtan guy from the third floor.

Carried away by the kirtan and enthused by the devotees dancing, Gopal put the mridanga aside and stood up to play whompers, imitating the way he'd seen devotees strike their edges against each other in complex beats.

But no sooner had he begun than the kirtan devotee came over, leaned in to Gopal, gestured toward the whompers, and said, "That's a no-no, kid."

Gopal softened his playing, brushing the whompers' flat surfaces against each other, but after a few minutes, when he thought the devotee wasn't watching anymore, he started playing them on their edges again.

As soon as he resumed, the devotee came back. "You'll crack them if you keep doing that!" he warned.

꧁ ꧁ ꧁

One day soon thereafter, Gopal glanced up toward the third floor of the *gurukula* building and saw smoke pouring from one of the rooms. He ran up and looked inside, but he couldn't see anything through the smoke. "Haribol!" he shouted. "Is everything all right? Is there a fire?"

"That's the problem," a voice called out. "There's no fire."

Gopal was confused. "Are you okay?"

"Yeah, I'm fine ... 'Where there's smoke, there's fire,' right? Wrong. There's no fire here, just smoke."

"Should I do something?" Gopal asked.

"Yes," the voice replied. "Help me get all this damn smoke out of the room!"

Gopal began swinging the door open and shut, but whatever was causing the smoke was creating it faster than he could get it out.

"Nothing's working!" he shouted.

"I know ... Just forget it. We're gonna have to wait for the smoke to clear at its own pace."

Who would ever stay in the room? Gopal wondered. He ventured in, keeping close to the floor, his eyes burning, but he couldn't see through the smoke.

"Who are you?" the voice asked.

"Gopal," he replied, and as the smoke cleared, he began to discern the form of the speaker. Then he recognized the unusual clothes and piercing eyes, now bright red and pouring tears ... it was him, the wild kirtan guy!

"I'm Aindra." Behind him, the fuel in the iron stove wouldn't catch fire, and it was spewing out a fountain of smoke.

"Why don't you get out?" Gopal asked. "Why are you just sitting here in all this smoke?"

"Look how many Deities I have," Aindra said. "I can't take Them all out. And if They have to tolerate the smoke, how can I leave?" He stood up and turned to the trays of *śilās* behind him. "Come back in the evening, after the *gaura-ārati* kirtan. Have *prasādam* with us."

When Gopal returned that evening, the room was filled with devotees seated on the floor, listening to Rama Raya reading from the *Kṛṣṇa* book. A curtain hid the altar, but from the sounds and smells and the legs beneath the curtain, Gopal could tell that Aindra was behind it, making an offering.

The room seemed to be from another era, another realm—its floor of packed clay and dung; its walls decorated with *gobar* reliefs of trees, vines, flowers, honeycombs, and bees; it's ceiling sky-blue, "the sky," Aindra described, "of Goloka." Near the door, a pot of *kichari* sat on a small wood stove.

A warped, wrinkled painting of Radha and Krishna extended

from the floor to the ceiling, surrounded by an ornate frame. Musical instruments were scattered amidst piles of books. There was a bare, stripped tree trunk reaching up toward the ceiling, scraps of cloth hanging from the stumps of its truncated branches.

Gopal found a place to sit and turned his attention to the reading. "Krishna was very expert in playing the flute," Rama Raya read, "and the *gopīs* were captivated by the sound vibration, which was attractive not only to them but to all living creatures who heard it. One of the *gopīs* told her friends, 'The highest perfection of the eyes is to see Krishna and Balaram entering the forest and playing Their flutes and tending the cows with Their friends.' "

Aindra stuck his head out from behind the curtains just long enough to add, "And Visvanath Cakravarti Thakur comments that the *gopīs* mean to say, 'My dear friend, if you simply remain shackled to your mundane family life, what will your eyes ever get to see? Lord Brahma has given us eyes, so let us satisfy our eyes by looking upon the most wonderful thing there is to see—Krishna.' "

After a while, he emerged from the altar and began serving out *prasādam*. Rama Raya continued to read, and the others listened quietly as they ate.

Aindra's *kichari* was packed with ghee and was so spicy that Gopal felt as if he were swallowing fire, and to make matters worse, it came with a super-spicy pickle. Placing the pickle on Gopal's plate, Aindra told him, "This is the same *ācār* Krishna was holding in his hand when Brahma came to apologize for stealing all the cowherd boys." Somehow, Gopal managed to get it down.

Once Aindra had served everyone else, he made a plate for himself, sat down, and focused on honoring the *prasādam*. After a few minutes, he looked up and said, "Srila Bhaktisiddhanta Sarasvati Thakur says that one who approaches *mahā-prasādam* with an enjoying spirit, to satisfy his tongue and belly, is an offender. Taking *mahā-prasādam* with an enjoying spirit results in taking another birth in the material world, because it's only in the material world that one approaches *mahā-prasādam* in an enjoying spirit."

Aindra valued *mahā-prasādam* greatly and was adamant that it be fully honored and never thrown away. "If you bring even a few grains of this *prasādam* anywhere else, they will say, 'Oh, it's Vrindavan *prasādam*!' and honor it with great respect, but here we just throw it away in the dust bin," he said. "For this offense one would have to be born as a monkey here in one's next life—to learn to treat *prasādam* respectfully."

He had gotten very upset when he'd once found that 24-hour-kirtan members had thrown *mahā-prasādam* onto the veranda ledge and left it for monkeys. He had retrieved it and eaten it himself. "This is a sacred *mahā-prasādam* from Govardhana- and *śālagrāma-śilās*, and they throw it away like that!" he had said. "I'm never giving them any again."

When he was finished, he swished his hands around in a cup of water and said, "Prabhus, I have to wake up by two in the morning to finish my quota of *japa*, so please excuse me." Then he drank the water and lay down to sleep with his head at Nitai Saci-suta's feet and his feet near the stove.

On the way out, Rama Raya told Gopal, "For Kartik, he chants sixty-four rounds before sunrise."

※ ※ ※

Gopal began spending more time with Aindra in his room and in kirtan. While watching Aindra dress Nitai Saci-suta one day, he noticed that Nitai had only one earring.

"Prabhu," he said. "You forgot one of Nitai's earrings."

"Really?" Aindra asked. Then he turned to Nitai and politely inquired, "Nitai, do You want another earring?"

After a moment, he said, "Okay" and gave Nitai a second earring. Then he turned to Gopal and asked, "How did you know?"

"Well ... I just saw that He only had one."

"Yeah, but maybe He only wants one," Aindra said.

"Well, Mahaprabhu wears two."

"Yeah, but that's Mahaprabhu. In the Tenth Canto, Balaram is described as having one earring: '*eka kuṇḍala*.' The *Hari-vaṁśa*, *Viṣṇu Purāṇa*, and *Bṛhat-saṁhitā* all confirm it. Nitai is non-different from Balaram. Therefore our acharyas clearly describe that Nitai—"

Just then there was a loud *clink* from the altar. Nitai's second earring had fallen off.

Aindra smiled from ear to ear. "You see!" he said, "I told you!"

※ ※ ※

"Prabhu, why is there a tree in your room?" Gopal asked one day.

"Well, not too long ago, a terrible thing happened," Aindra explained. "The tamal tree in the courtyard died, and they chopped it into pieces to get it out the door. They planted a new one, but the original is special because Srila Prabhupada himself saved it from being cut down while the temple was being built. I didn't want to be separated from that tree, so I found the biggest, most beautiful piece and took it up here. You must be knowing how the *gopīs* mistake tamal trees for Krishna and embrace them."

"Notice the sawdust?" Gopal asked. "Termites are wrecking it!"

When he looked closer, Aindra saw that Gopal was right. So he flushed out the termites and sealed the wood with a thick layer of lacquer to prevent further damage. "Do you know why I selected this particular part of the tree out of all the pieces they had cut it into?" he asked.

"No, why?"

"Look at it," he encouraged. "You can't see it?"

"See what?"

"Look how it has a threefold bending form, just like Krishna! The branches are just like Krishna's arms holding the flute to His lips."

Gopal looked around the rest of the room, wondering what other hidden treasures he might find. "What about the ceiling?" he asked. "Why did you paint a sky up there?"

Aindra seemed embarrassed. "Well," he explained, "a real *gosvāmī* would live without a roof and sleep outside beneath the trees of Vrindavan. I really want to do that, to sleep under the tamal tree in the courtyard, but I'm too weak. But I thought I could at least emulate that mood in my room." Motioning toward the altar, he said, "That's the temple room, and here we are standing in the courtyard with the tamal tree, out under the open sky."

"And what are all these sticks?" Gopal asked, pointing to the branches propped here and there in corners or against walls.

"They're *kalpa-vṛkṣa*. They can give *kṛṣṇa-premā*." He joked, "They're my *tree-daṇḍas*," like the *tri-daṇḍa* staffs sannyasis carried, made of three rods signifying service with mind, body, and words. He had picked them up at Seva Kunj and worshipped them as representing different *sakhīs* who had been present during the *kunj's* nocturnal *līlās*.

"That painting is beautiful," Gopal said, indicating an old framed painting on the wall. "But why is it so warped and wrinkled?"

"It used to hang in the temple on the wall of the tulasi *maṇḍap*. A few years ago they took it down and threw it away. I saw it sitting in the garbage, and my heart just broke. You know? It's so awful to just throw away such a beautiful, big painting of Radha and Krishna. I yelled at them about it and carried it up here to my room."

It *was* beautiful, Gopal agreed. Radharani and Krishna were standing side by side, each with an arm around the other, Radharani holding Krishna's flute to His mouth while He covered Her shoulder in His *chādār*. "What do you like most about it?" he asked.

"Look at Krishna's eyes," Aindra pointed out. "They have such depth of expression. I like to do my *nāma-japa* looking at this painting."

"Why don't we fix it up?" Gopal suggested.

Aindra's face lit up, and the two of them began gathering bricks, buckets, and hammers; carried everything up to the roof; and after paying obeisances, laid the painting flat on the ground and flattened it out.

❦ ❦ ❦

Gopal joined the 24-hour-kirtan party and stayed in the ashram through the winter. Knowing it would be too cold for him, he had brought an electric heater, but the outlet in the ashram didn't work and anyway wasn't compatible with the pins on his heater's plug. Late one night, unable to tolerate the cold, he knocked on Aindra's door.

It was past two, but Aindra grabbed a few tools, ran over, repaired the outlet, and changed the pins on the heater's plug. "There you go," he said with a smile, and returned to his room.

"Prabhu," Gopal appealed in the middle of another night, having again knocked on Aindra's door and awakened him. "I just had a really heavy ghost nightmare!"

Aindra brought him inside, sprinkled him with *śālagrāma* water, and said, "Don't worry, Uncle Aindra will always be here for you. You can always come to me."

❦ ❦ ❦

Aindra had always been handy, making things with his hands and working with musical instruments and equipment, employing what his bandmate had called his "construction logic." To play just one part of one track of an album, he had taken a small *panch tara*, a five-stringed instrument from Bengal, and fitted it with a handmade fretboard—a long, tedious procedure requiring close attention to exact detail and measurements.

When he was playing it in his room one day with the door open, Gopal heard him from outside. "Hey, prabhu, what are you doing?" Gopal asked. "Just jamming out?" Aindra started playing the melody of "*Jaya* Radha-Madhava," and Gopal picked up a *dotar*, like a Bengali banjo. Aindra tuned it to the same key and plucked out a simple rhythm, and the two started jamming together.

"We were having a great time," Gopal remembered, "but then some brahmachari walked past and started saying something—criticizing, passing judgment—and that spoiled the mood."

Aindra shooed the devotee away and shut the door. "You see?" he said, "I need to soundproof the room."

"He would get into his deep *bhāva* in his room," Gopal described, "playing harmonium and just crying out to his Deities, and he didn't want to feel that someone outside might hear him—it would interfere with his expression. He needed to know that he could just express himself in his own space without anybody's negative vibration."

Aindra had also been disturbed by sounds coming *from* the outside. "I can't sleep," he told Gopal one morning.

"Why not?" Gopal asked, concerned. He kept watch on Aindra's health, knowing that his getting at least some rest was essential for his whole kirtan program.

Aindra was very sound sensitive, and, trying to catch up with his sleep with a few hours after *Bhāgavatam* class, he had been kept awake by noise from a classroom in the *gurukula* below. As the boys had been moving around, their chairs had been scraping against the floor and screeching.

Rama Raya had brought velvet pads from the U.S., and Aindra tried attaching them to the bottom of the chairs' legs, but that didn't work. Gopal went to speak with Ananda Vrindavaneswari dasi, the *gurukula* principal, and she acknowledged the problem but didn't know what to do about it. It was driving her nuts, too, she said; she didn't know how the teachers could teach with it.

From Aindra's perspective, the best solution was to do what he had suggested: soundproof the room. It would help him get rest, allow him to concentrate while chanting, reading, and writing, and keep out external noise when he was recording. First he got special, unbreakable, triple-paned glass for the back window, behind the Deities. Then, researching online, he found a company in America that manufactured soundproofing equipment for studios and carried a rubber pad with foam that could be adhered to the door. He ordered it to be shipped to New York, and Prabhupada das, who was coming to Vrindavan for VIHE courses, brought it with him.

There was a full manual for installation. "Aindra had his toolbox and everything," Gopal remembered. "He got the door off its hinges and laid it out on the walkway, and we were trying to figure out how to put it all together. The mat had this peel-off sticky part, but it wasn't sticking properly. It wasn't working, and Aindra was getting kind of frustrated. After a while he said, 'Okay, I guess we'll just have to look at this again tomorrow.' And for the next week he had no door up—just the screen and a dhoti for privacy."

Finally Aindra got a carpenter up to his room, found and brought up yet another door, nailed the screen door to that, and attached the American soundproofing to the inside. Then he went to Mathura, got another kind of rubber mat, and attached that to the outside. The whole process took a full week, but once everything was in place, he had a triple barrier—the American pad; the Indian mat; and two wooden doors, rounded at the edges, with the screen door attached—between him and the outside world.

The insulation was airtight, and the soundproofing was perfect. There was only one problem: "What happens if something happens to you and we can't communicate with you or get in?" Gopal asked. "You're going to need a cell phone."

"No cell phone." Aindra was firm.

They argued back and forth, but Aindra wouldn't relent, so Gopal thought of installing a dog flap, like what was used to let pets in and out of a house.

"Why do we need that?" Aindra questioned.

"So that this dog can get in there sometime, if you have a medical crisis or something."

Aindra took the lower-right panel off the outer door and had the carpenter cut a small trap door in it, behind the screen, enough for ventilation and just big enough for a small person to slip through. When he cooked, he could leave the inner door open, prop open the trap with a stick, and allow for air to flow through the screen. But you couldn't tell from the outside.

❧ ❧ ❧

During his early years in Vrindavan, Aindra had been quite regulated in the hours he kept, taking rest by ten or so at night and getting up by two or three in the morning. Until 1999, he made a point of attending *maṅgala-ārati* every morning, chanting *japa* by the railing in front of Sri Sri Radha-Shyamasundar's altar, and afterwards chanted while circumambulating the temple or in his room. For *Bhāgavatam* class, he would stand on the side of the temple room, behind the other listeners, or lean on the railing, always softly chanting.

As had been the case practically since he'd joined the movement, when he had a question or comment for the person giving class, he would begin with a preamble. On some occasions he'd add a point or a clarification or explanation; on others his questions were challenging, pointed at some error in the speaker's philosophical presentation, regardless of their stature or position, and he wouldn't let go of a point. As one devotee speaker recalled, "He would either ask a very difficult question or, more often, simply give his own *Bhāgavatam* class, picking up on what he wanted to say." Sometimes he would follow up with the speaker after class, approaching the *vyāsāsana* for discussion.

As years passed, his schedule became less fixed. He would listen to class from his room via the radio broadcast and go down only if he had a query or comment. When he did hear something he considered questionable, he would rush down to the temple room to confront the speaker. "If you were giving class and you saw him walking in," one devotee recalled with a laugh, "you'd think, 'Uh-oh!'"

As his preaching and rounds of *japa* increased, Aindra's chanting could continue through the day and into the night and early morning. "There was always something going on in which he was involved," Rama Raya remembered. "Some project, decorating the ashram or putting an album together or, later, working on his book. Sometimes he would wake up his Deities and perform Their puja during the day, but when he was engaged in something particularly demanding, he might not get to it until late at night. Everything was quieter then, too, and he was less likely to be disturbed. He'd try to move his Deity worship earlier, but after a few days, things would inevitably slip back to where they had been.

But even in these later years, he was still regulated in his chanting and Deity worship; he just followed a different clock. "We're on a 24-hour-kirtan schedule here," he told the kirtan devotees, "so just make sure your sixteen rounds are completed." It was a shifting schedule—the specific timing might vary day to day—but the 24-hour requirement was fixed, and he would always finish his *japa* and puja within that time, after which the clock restarted.

※ ※ ※

When Aindra made daytime appointments, he was frequently late, usually leaving his room at the arranged time to arrive, regardless of how long it might take to get to his destination. And at night, with all his projects, his tendency to lose track of time when preaching, and his extensive Deity worship, he didn't eat or do anything else until very late. Invited for an eight-o'clock supper at a devotee friend's family home one night, he said, "I'll finish my puja and come soon" but didn't arrive until 2 a.m.

He typically slept only two or three hours each night—from around two until *mangala-ārati*—was only rarely able to catch a few hours during the day, and sometimes didn't get to sleep at all and wouldn't sleep for a few days running, especially when he was scheduled to dress Sri Sri Radha-Shyamasundar.

One time, running late for his pujari service, he raced onto the altar after shortening his ritual purification—mantras and some drops of water—instead just pouring the whole *ācamana* cup of water over his head.

He was strict about 24-hour-kirtan members' attendance at the morning program, and before *mangala-ārati* he would check the kirtan-men's room to make sure everyone had gone down. "Wake up, prabhu*s*!" he would call out, rubbing their heads to rouse them. "Krishna is waiting for you in the temple room. He wants to see you." Or, like an Army drill sergeant, he would yell, "GET UP! GET UP! DRESS! DRESS! GO! GO! GO!" In the temple room, he would point at each devotee to count that they had all arrived and, if satisfied, raise his arms in triumph and silently call out, "*Haribol!*"

One morning, Amala Harinam das—the son of the American cook Apurva das and his book-distributor wife, Kamalini dasi—who had joined the party later, in 2008, after having listened to Aindra's recordings all his life, was still putting on his tilak when Aindra walked by. Amala knew he was in trouble. "When Aindra Prabhu was going to chastise you," he remembered with a smile, "he would move slowly, stalk you—like predator!"

"What are you doing?" Aindra asked. "Why aren't you taking this service seriously? When you go down there, do you see Krishna on the altar?"

Amala had no reply.

"That's the problem. You haven't come to the point where you see Krishna really there, on the altar; you don't actually believe that He is present. Srimati Radharani doesn't accept the *bhoga* offering if it's even one minute late. You have your service, your offering, at four o'clock. But if you are even one minute late, who is to say that Radharani will still accept your service?" Then he sat down, in a serious mood.

"He wasn't shouting or anything," Amala described. "He was just talking to me like a concerned parent."

"Do you ever think that maybe Radha-Shyamasundar are down there waiting for you to sing for Them?" Aindra continued. "Maybe right now Krishna is thinking, 'Where is Amala? I can't wait for him to come and sing for Me.'

"Radharani has given you this service. How many people can say that they've had the opportunity to reside in Sri Vrindavan-dhāma? And of those, how many can say they've been given the opportunity to do kirtan for Radha-Shyamasundar, Krishna-Balaram, and Gaura-Nitai here in Krishna-Balaram Mandir?

"You know, Amala, maybe some people are too dull-headed or spaced-out to grasp what I'm saying, but I expect you to get this, because you have great potential to be a leader in this Society."

Amala saluted, responded, "Yes, *sir*!" and marched out, both enlivened and encouraged in his service.

In his assessment of the kirtan members, Aindra valued their ability to adhere to the schedule as well as their musical expertise. One new devotee in the party wasn't much of a musician, but Aindra still valued and praised him, because he was punctual. "I really appreciate him," Aindra told the other members. "He doesn't know how to play kartals nicely, he doesn't know how to sing nicely, and he doesn't play mridanga nicely, but he's on time for his kirtan every day."

"Even if a person wasn't very musically talented," one member remembered, "if he had that sense of responsibility for the service, Aindra really appreciated that."

At the same time, prospective members had to show some potential. There was a need for musical excellence, expertise, and Aindra didn't appreciate bad musicianship or unharmonious kirtan. "If this *harināma* party came through my village," he said of one rough-sounding group in front of the temple, "I would throw rocks at them!"

"Srila Prabhupada expressed great pleasure with Acyutananda's mridanga playing," he remembered. "At that time, Acyutananda was pretty expert compared to most of the rest of us. Prabhupada complimented him, telling him, 'You are playing just like a professional.' That wasn't a criticism, trying to cut him down to size—'What the hell are you doing trying to play like a professional?' He was complimenting him: 'Your playing is like a professional's.' He was exhibiting a certain level of competence, and Prabhupada appreciated it. Not that professionalism supersedes the principle of purity, but there is need to understand the instrument you are playing.

"There is also a need to tune the instrument you are playing. I personally demand that devotees who are playing the mridangas understand that the first lesson in playing any instrument is how to tune it. Just like if you are going to play a guitar, or a sitar, the first thing you have to do before you start playing it is you have to tune the instrument. Similarly, a mridanga needs to be tuned properly to have the proper vibration.

"And similarly, it is important to understand what it is to have a tuned pair of kartals. If one kartal is lower in pitch than the other—if they are not the same pitch—then it can create an awfully discordant vibration that breaks the ear. And rather than attracting people to the kirtan, it drives them away."

"When someone wanted to join, we would test them," Vrindavan remembered. "Many people came to his room and asked if they could join the kirtan party. And Aindra Prabhu would tell me, 'Bring your mridanga.' He would give the person a set of kartals and tell him, 'Okay, you play this beat,' and he would have me play a series of beats on the mridanga, and we would see if the person could follow—he would test each one in that way. That was the basic musical prerequisite for joining, that at least he could play kartals, all the standard *tals*.

"He would test their singing too—sing a note and see if the person could sing the same note, just to make sure they weren't tone deaf.

"Still, even if someone couldn't play them all, if Aindra Prabhu felt the person had the ability to learn, he would give him a chance—he would say, 'Okay, we'll try you out for a month. If you are improving, then you can stay. If you're not able to improve, then you should find another service.'"

"Usually there was a standard of being able to play kartals and mridanga at least enough to keep a kirtan going, before you could move into the ashram," Amala remembered. "But the main criterion Aindra was interested in seeing the devotees have was enthusiasm to do *hari-nāma-saṅkīrtana* sincerely and to sincerely learn to use the instruments in that service." Last, all the kirtan members had to know, or learn, English—so they could communicate.

Aindra's standards for devotees leading kirtan always went back to the basics—and to their ability not to lead but to follow. "If someone is not expert in following in a kirtan," he said, "he may pose as an expert leader, but he is actually not an expert leader. An expert leader is expert at both leading and following. It is not that he puts on a big show of being the kirtan leader, but when someone else is leading, he is either disinterested in or incapable of following others. Just like someone may be able to play the harmonium by the book, looking at the book and reading, but real expert means hearing—everything begins with the ear. A real expert is able to accompany other leaders—when someone else is singing, he can follow the tune. That is actual expertise."

Regardless of a devotee's musical expertise, however, to lead kirtan—or even play mridanga—in the temple, they had to chant at least sixteen rounds of *nāma-japa* daily and follow the regulative principles. But Aindra couldn't always keep track of all the members, and although he could generally maintain the party's standards, on occasion some of the boys strayed.

During kirtan one evening, Gopal leaned toward Aindra, indicated one of the mridanga players, who looked fully absorbed in the kirtan, unaware of anything else, and asked, "Are you really going to let this guy play with you?"

"Of course," Aindra replied. "Why not? He's great."

"Look at him," Gopal said. "He's stoned!"

Aindra looked more carefully. "Yeah," he said, "but he's a really good drummer."

"But he's totally stoned," Gopal repeated. "Ripped and red-eyed."

Handing the lead chanting to someone else, Aindra tapped the drummer on the shoulder, startling him out of his trance, and asked him to step outside.

"Are you stoned again, kid?" he asked.

The boy just nodded.

"Come on!" Aindra said. "I thought you cleaned yourself up?"

There was nothing he could say.

"Well, you can't play here when you're stoned," Aindra told him. "Come back when you're clean."

It was neither the first nor the last time that Aindra had to speak with a young kirtan member about their behavior. Some came from the West with loose habits; others, having come from prominent Indian devotional families, felt entitled and flouted Aindra and the temple's rules and regulations. But he would not compromise the kirtan-party's standards. When he confronted one devotee about to lead the evening *ārati* while intoxicated, Aindra was met with insults and even physical threats. But he held firm to the kirtan standards.

CHAPTER FOURTEEN

AINDRA WAS AMONG ISKCON's strictest renunciants, which led some devotees to think that he was anti-woman. "They think that I am against women," he said, "but I am serving Radharani directly as a woman myself, as a maidservant. They say sometimes that I am disrespectful to women, but they don't understand that in my true form I am completely surrendered to the Supreme form aspect of womanhood: Srimati Radharani!"

When a big book distributor gave *Bhāgavatam* class in the temple one morning and said that it took a real man to distribute books, Aindra laughed and asked, "Then why should *anyone* distribute books? No one but Shyamasundar is a 'real man.' And besides, some of us *prefer* to be women!"

One day, Aindra visited a bookstore in Loi Bazaar, Vrindavan's downtown marketplace, with Subhekshana das, a brahmana brahmacari from Mayapur who had come to spend time with him. On the way out, Subhekshana, who had purchased a volume of Vaishnava teachings, was shocked to see Aindra emerge with only one book: *Hair Styles for Women*. "What's this, prabhu?" he asked.

"You wouldn't understand," Aindra replied. "It's for my next life." He was learning how to best adorn Srimati Radharani.

And sometimes, when a brahmachari was trying to get to the temple altar, Aindra would block the doorway, arms crossed over his chest, and declare in mock formality, "No men allowed! Women only, puh-lease!"

At the same time, he supported the temple's injunction against pujari service being performed by female devotees. In principle, he said, there was nothing wrong with women serving on the altar, but if it were practiced at Krishna-Balaram Mandir, the Vrindavan *gosvāmīs* would chase the ISKCON devotees out of Vraja. When one devotee argued that women not being allowed on the altar signified that the *gopas* had defeated the *gopīs*, Aindra questioned her material designation of gender and replied, "It's not possible for the *gopas* to defeat the *gopīs*, and I'm not a *gopa*; I'm a *gopī*. Maybe you are a *gopa*, and I have defeated *you*!"

He also saw the danger of his kirtan-party brahmacaris having young women around them, and for a long time he urged them to avoid marriage and, whenever possible, women in general. Even later, he opposed the practice of men and women regularly singing or playing in kirtan together. "The original standard, in Mahaprabhu's time," he said, "was that men would have a kirtan group and ladies also could have a kirtan group. No problem. But you would never have a kirtan group with men and ladies playing together."

When, in 1995, the temple management had asked for residents' visions for ISKCON-Vrindavan's development, Aindra had echoed Srila Prabhupada's 1976 statement that living in Vrindavan was for brahmacharis and retired male devotees fully engaged in devotional service. Only serious devotees should live in the holy *dhāma*, and unmarried women should serve in Vrindavan only if they were serious, mature Vaishnavis who followed strict vows of renunciation.

"Our broad ISKCON movement has plenty of other facilities to accommodate women seeking husbands," he had written. "ISKCON Vrindavan is not the place for them ... Vraja-vasa is meant for those who have retired from the grhamedhi mentality, materialistic pursuits and the bodily conception of life. Not that we make Vrndavana the business capitol of the world, the International Livestock Exchange for Pimps and Prostitutes Chewing the Thorny Twigs."

He was especially concerned about the increasing fraternization between young men and women in the *dhāma*. The temple was being used as a meeting place for young singles, and his kirtan party members didn't all have his strength—or spirit—of renunciation. He knew that not all of them had given up their sex desire or practice, and as members of the kirtan party they were regularly approached by interested women; some were even using their place in the kirtan to attract them.

❦ ❦ ❦

During kirtans, Aindra asked that women stay at a distance from the brahmacaris. "Better chaste than sorry," he said to one who he felt had been sitting too close. When, later, he heard that another, Sabina, from Switzerland (later named Sandesh), was singing and playing kartals near the kirtan musicians after *Bhāgavatam* class one morning, he came down from his room and requested of her, "*Mātājī*, could you please sit at more of a distance and play your kartals more softly? Some of the boys here are feeling disturbed by your presence. They're not *paramahaṁsas*, you know!"

"But *prabhujī*," Sabina said, "I just want to be part of the kirtan!"

"*Mātājī*," he repeated, "I really don't want to offend you, but please just sit at a little distance," and then went into the pujari room. After a couple minutes he came out, walked up to Sabina, smiled, bent down, and placed a few fragrant *parijata* flowers in her hand. Subsequently she sat near the 24-hour-kirtan party throughout the day, singing and playing kartals, but at a respectful distance, and later she participated in the ladies' kirtan at Srila Prabhupada's samadhi.

The kirtan ashram was like a fortress protecting Aindra and the other brahmacaris, but women found other ways to approach them, and when they were in the temple room for kirtan they were more vulnerable. One day, Aindra told Giridhari's wife, Ati Sundari, "Some woman sent me a letter arguing that there was nothing wrong with being lusty like Kubja," referring to the young hunchbacked woman whom Krishna had transformed into a beauty and who, overwhelmed with gratitude, became filled with a burning desire to offer Him her newfound charms. In *Bhakti-rasāmṛta-sindhu*, Rupa Goswami cites Kubja as the epitome of *kāmaprāya-bhakti*—"devotion that borders on lust"—a substandard example of someone having a romantic relationship with Krishna: lust in the context of *bhakti*, unlike the *gopīs*' bhakti in the context of lust.

Ati Sundari identified the Kubja fan—a young woman who sat close behind Aindra during his kirtan, decorated with lipstick and other ornaments—and that evening she saw the woman position herself surreptitiously on the other side of the door Aindra always exited through after kirtan. "Tell Aindra to go out the other door," she told one of the brahmacaris. "The lady who sent him that weird letter is waiting for him outside."

On their way out, Aindra and his crew made a detour out another door. But the woman saw them and started rushing in their direction.

"She's coming," Ati Sundari said. "Run!"

Aindra wasn't much of a runner, especially carrying his harmonium, but they made it to the safety of the stairway leading up to the brahmachari ashram.

"What should I tell her?" Ati Sundari asked from the entrance.

"Tell her to go jump in Kaliya's lake!" Aindra shouted back.

Hardly a second later, the woman arrived, calling, "Aindra Prabhu! Aindra Prabhu!"

Ati Sundari stopped her in her tracks and asked, "What do you want?"

"I just want to talk to Aindra Prabhu."

"He gave me a message for you," Ati Sundari said.

"Really?" The woman's distress was suddenly replaced with hope. "What did he say?"

"He said ... that you should go jump in Kaliya's lake!"

"What does that mean?" the woman asked.

"It means you should get out of here and leave him alone!" Ati Sundari ordered.

"But I am so beautiful!" the woman insisted.

"Hare Krishna!" Ati Sundari, said, and she turned and left.

Another time, Aindra used Madhumangal das as a shield. "A young *mātājī* wanted to speak to him after a lecture one day," Madhumangal recalled. "She wanted to ask him about *mañjarīs*, and she was trying to come closer. So he caught my hand and brought me closer. And the closer that *mātājī* came, the closer he brought me. When she got very close, he almost embraced me. As long as she was there, he was holding me. And then, when she finally left, he said, 'Okay, now you can go, too!' "

❧ ❧ ❧

At least in part because of how dramatically Aindra expressed himself, his position on gender issues—or others' perception of it—sometimes led to controversy and even confrontation. During Kartik of 1998, when he was accused of preventing a young woman from leading a kirtan, he wrote an official reply to the GBC inquiry:

> My approval was requested for one of the ex-gurukulis to lead the Damodarastaka kīrtana that evening, as it was earlier announced to be "ISKCON Youth day." I said I didn't have any objection, as long as he was competent to actually get the kīrtana fired up and was relatively pure in habits. Then [I was told] that it wasn't a "he" but a "she."
>
> I had reservations about this, because I have observed significantly increased general looseness among a lot of the ex-gurukulis, increased promiscuity among the young men and women, and did not want to contribute to the situation. I expressed this ... and concluded that I would accept whatever the management committee decided.
>
> Thereafter it was decided that I should execute the majority decision of the management committee, which was *against* allowing the girl to lead. I requested Ghanasyama prabhu to lead the *kīrtana*, whom I recognize to be quite a capable *kīrtana* leader, and whom the ex-gurukuli youth should be able to at least respect as an ex-gurukuli himself.
>
> That evening I was confronted by an angry mob just before the *Damodarastaka kīrtana* was to begin. Even after repeatedly trying to explain to them that I was only executing the decision of the temple management, they denounced me time and again as an insensitive male chauvinist pig. One

of the alumni, Sanjay prabhu, viciously barked in my face, "You're just a frustrated brahmacari!!!"

Later that night, as I was returning to my room, I again met Sanjay prabhu on the first-floor terrace of the gurukula. He said, "Prabhu, I don't think it's right what you did tonight."

I told him, "I'm neither a brahmacari nor am I frustrated." I said that since I prefer to think of myself as an eternal associate-adherent of Srimati Radharani, it could not be possible for me to act as either a male chauvinist or a frustrated brahmacari. Thus I privately tried to demonstrate to him the superficiality of his view that I was an ogre, a male chauvinist pig, a frustrated brahmacari, or whatever.

Later, the temple authorities called a meeting and requested that I apologize to the gurukula alumni. In the course of my apology I reiterated the point I made to Sanjay, and, seeing them worked-up over it, tried to say something humorous, "I am very fallen, but I would venture to say that I have probably realized myself to be more spiritually 'female' than a lot of the women in our movement."

A few days later, when the young woman in question, Chakrini dasi, did lead the *Dāmodarāṣṭaka* kirtan, Aindra was enthusiastic in his response, jumping up and dancing—rare for him—and swirling his *chādār* in the air. Afterwards, he congratulated her on the quality of her kirtan. When he joked, "I didn't think a girl could do so good!" she just laughed. "How is your *japa*?" he asked. "Are you reading *Srimad-Bhāgavatam*? Have you heard of Jahnava Mata?"

At the end of Kartik, after she had performed *daṇḍavat-parikramā* around Radha Kund, Chakrini approached Aindra and gave him a donation of gold. "I feel like I was just a pawn in a political move," she said, "and I am sorry I got involved in so many people saying bad things about you."

❦ ❦ ❦

In many ISKCON temples at the time, the women were relegated to the rear during classes, *āratis*, and *guru-pūjās*. In Vrindavan, the temple room was wider than deep, and there was no back wall—just archways leading out to the open courtyard—so when there was a big crowd, the women were sometimes pushed out.

Guru-pūjā and lectures were held on the left side of the room, so the area in front of Sri Sri Radha-Shyamasundar, whose altar was on the right, was open. And during *gaura-ārati*, the focus was on Gaura-Nitai's side, so again the women could be in front of Radhe-Shyam.

But *maṅgala-ārati* was a problem. When a group of senior women proposed to the temple management that halfway through the *ārati* the men should move aside from in front of Radha-Shyamasundar's altar and let the women forward, the temple president agreed to give it a try.

For years, Aindra's regular spot at *maṅgala-ārati* had been on the railing of Radhe-Shyam's altar, but he complied. Then, during Kartik of 1998, a group of female residents decided that the whole front area of the altar should be reserved for women for the entirety of *maṅgala-ārati*.

That arrangement lasted for a year, until just before Kartik of 1999. The temple would be much more crowded during that period, and the management announced, "Many sannyasis will be visiting for the festival, so we request the devotees to observe the agreement made last year: during *maṅgala-ārati*, the ladies should come up in front of Radha-Shyamasundar's altar *after* the ghee-lamp has been passed around."

A few of the women refused to change their practice. The temple management tried to force the issue by having the 24-hour-kirtan men occupy the space throughout the night and into the morning, but this resulted in name-calling and even a small skirmish.

The management offered to reserve Gaura-Nitai's half of the temple for women during *maṅgala-ārati* and Radha-Shyamasundar's side during *gaura-ārati*, but one dissenting woman and her supporters would not accept anything less than the space in front of Radha-Shyamasundar for all of *maṅgala-ārati*.

When the management gave up trying to keep the area open to everyone, Aindra informed them that he would no longer attend *maṅgala-ārati*.

"But you have to attend!" they appealed. "If you don't, it sends a message to every devotee in your department that it's okay not to."

"It *is* okay," Aindra replied. "If you're going to let it be a circus where women press their breasts and rub their legs against sannyasis and brahmacharis, then it is better for us to listen to the *maṅgala-ārati* on the radio."

Many of Vrindavan's resident female devotees did not support the women's group's protest. Visakha Priya dasi, a senior disciple of Giriraj Swami who had been a preaching pioneer in South Africa and managed the Kirtan Ashram, a residence for visiting and retired women, declined to participate in the controversy and advised residents to stay calm and cooperate. A few days after the skirmishes, she stood at Radha-Shyamasundar's railing in the evening when an outstretched hand appeared in front of her and dropped a tulasi leaf into her open palm. It was Aindra. "He didn't say anything," she remembered. "He didn't smile. I didn't smile or say anything, and we both went back to looking at the Deities. It was his way of thanking me for not taking part in the controversy."

Aindra was not unaffected by the conflict—or by how he was perceived—and was particularly conscious of avoiding any offense. "If I offend them," he said, "if they are thinking that I'm hating them, then I may also become implicated in the offense. They really dragged my name through the mud, but at least now, more women are for me than against me."

"Aindra Prabhu was like a father for us," remembered Divya Shakti dasi, from Moscow. "At first I was afraid of him, because I heard that he was a woman-hater, that you should stay far away from him and not look him in the eyes. I was surprised to find out that it wasn't like that. From the very beginning, he was very friendly and kind. On the first day when we met, we were standing on the cold floor for about forty minutes, bitten by the mosquitoes, but nevertheless he answered questions and also asked some questions himself. I could see that he was interested in helping us."

In collecting material for the current volume, Akincana Krishna reported, "I interviewed ladies from all different eras of Aindra Prabhu's life, from the '70s, the '80s, the '90s, and the 2000s, and they all—every single one of them—said the exact same thing: 'I was so afraid of Aindra. I thought he was going to be so heavy; I thought he was going to be so mean. But when I spoke with him, he was the nicest person.' "

Even when he would "burst through the [*gurukula*] office door" with some urgent need, "flying in, his kurta flying," remembered Ananda Vrindavaneswari, he was "always very respectful, not demeaning or demanding, just intensely enthusiastic ... always a gentleman in his dealings with me."

Yamuna Devi dasi—one of Srila Prabhupada's first disciples and the movement's pioneers and leading *kīrtanīyas*, whose recorded "Govindam" prayer Srila Prabhhpada had directed to be played every morning at the beginning of every *śṛṅgāra-ārati* in every ISKCON temple around the world and who had been part of the Krishna-Balaram Mandir since its inception—told Akincana Krishna that even though Prabhupada had so strongly desired to see a 24-hour kirtan at the temple, it had been a challenging program to start and devotees had not been able to maintain it. "I prayed and I prayed and I prayed to Radha-Shyamasundar to please send somebody that can establish this 24-hour kirtan," she said. Based on reports from some of her godsisters, she'd had mixed impressions of Aindra. "But now that I've read this interview with Aindra Prabhu [the one Akincana had conducted with him about kirtan], I'm really appreciating what a beautiful devotee They sent."

❧ ❧ ❧

One day, Aindra was talking to Giridhari about the tulasi he was getting from local suppliers. "They're not good enough to offer to my Shyam," he complained.

When Giridhari mentioned the issue to Ati Sundari, she said, "Maybe I can collect tulasi for him."

Giridhari was doubtful; he knew that Aindra didn't have regular contact with women. But Ati Sundari convinced him to at least try. "Okay," he said, "we can go and ask him."

When they met Aindra in the temple and Ati Sundari asked, Aindra, as expected, said, "No way. I don't accept service from women."

"I know," she replied. "But I'm not 'women'; I'm married."

Aindra wasn't impressed. "Still."

It took a while, but Ati Sundari persisted, and eventually Aindra gave in. "Okay," he said, "I accept your offer, but only through your husband. You pick the tulasi and give it to him, and then he can give it to me."

Over time, Aindra became more comfortable with Ati Sundari, and his friendship with Giridhari expanded to include her. She joined in their conversations, and Aindra eventually spent as much time speaking with her as he did with Giridhari. "Prabhu," she once told him, "the astrologer told me that in my last life I was a sannyasi who was very harsh with women, and that's why I became a woman in this life."

Aindra was impressed. "Oh, really!" he said.

It seemed to Ati Sundari that Aindra was becoming at least a little more open in his dealings with women. He didn't want women to think that "I have some mundane feelings for them," he explained to her, but as he later told a group of devotees, "I know I should try to keep up my reputation as a 'woman-hater,' but I have become a lot more open toward women over the years because, you know"—he turned to look at Ati Sundari—"I don't want to become a woman in my next life."

CHAPTER FIFTEEN

By the early '90s, pilgrims, Delhiites, and devotees from all over the world were coming to Vrindavan, especially during Kartik and festivals—many attracted to Krishna-Balaram Mandir to participate in Aindra's kirtans, some to join the kirtan party. He made a striking first impression on newcomers, many of whom just didn't know *what* to think. More than one was surprised that he was a white Westerner; his voice had sounded so Indian on his recordings. And then there was his hair and beard—unconventional for a devotee. "The first time I saw him," one devotee described, "his hair was long and his beard was grown out, and his eyes were on *fire!*"

"He had his style, his own look," Govinda described, laughing. "The first time I met him, I was a fresh devotee, a two-months'-old bhakta, and I came for *gaura-ārati* one night and saw this man playing these big whompers—'Haribolllll! Haribolllll!'—and jumping up and down, with his outfit and all this red hair, and I was like, *Who is this guy?!* Even for a seasoned devotee, it was quite a scene, and I was young.

"But that's how Aindra Prabhu was—always intense. He had his sweet moments and emotional moments, but he was always very intense. And many devotees couldn't really handle it; they had a whole different conception of what Krishna consciousness should be, how a devotee should act.

"Sometimes people would criticize him, but he said, 'Yes, I'm going to dress like this, and if people judge me because of my externals, then I want those people to avoid me. Therefore, I dress like this. Anyone who wants to know me should come to my room and speak with me man to man. I'm available, and I'm ready to sit and talk with you.'"

Bhagavata Purana das, an American disciple of Satsvarupa Maharaja, had done his share of commercial "*saṅkīrtana*" in the States. "I was being driven on a highway to a home program one snowy winter night," he remembered, "when the temple commander popped a tape-deck recording into the car's cassette player. It was one of Aindra's tapes. The night-raga sound vibration that came into my ears felt spooky. My instinctive impression was that I was listening to the weeping of Jimi Hendrix and his Fender Stratocaster guitar howling at the full-moon night."

He just showed up in Room 89 one day in 1993 and asked, "Can I join?"

Aindra studied him for a moment. "First you'll have to pass the electric Kool-Aid acid test," he said in jest, referring to tests of people's mettle, which in the '60s had been conducted in San Francisco by taking hits of LSD at the countercultural gatherings led by Ken Kesey's Merry Pranksters that led to the Mantra-Rock Dance event Srila Prabhupada attended in 1967.

"Um ... what?"

"Find the *gurukula* go-down," Aindra explained. "In the back-right corner, behind the brooms, there'll be a bunch of plastic canisters of cleaning acid. Use them to clean the bathroom up here on the third floor every day. Then we'll see if you can join."

Before leaving, Bhagavata Purana asked, "They say you chant sixty-four rounds. Can I do that, too?"

Aindra studied him again. "Why don't you chant sixteen rounds first?"

"I do chant sixteen rounds," Bhagavata Purana replied.

"*Really?*" Aindra asked.

"Yeah."

"*Really?*" Aindra pressed. "You chant sixteen rounds of *pure harināma?*"

❧ ❧ ❧

Aindra welcomed Madhumangal in a similar manner. When Madhumangal arrived, "he gave me a broom and told me to remove all the chipped paint from the ceiling. It took about an hour, and then he gave me a bucket and told me to clean the rest of the bathroom. 'Without cleaning the toilet, no one can attain gopi *bhāva*,' he explained. 'This ashram is given to us by our spiritual master, and this toilet is a part of this ashram. If we're not taking care of the toilet, it means we're not taking care of the ashram; it means we're not taking care of our guru maharaja. How can we attain *gopī-bhāva* if we neglect our guru maharaja? This ashram was given to me by my guru, so I will take care of it to attain *gopī-bhāva*.'"

Bathroom duty became a requirement for all kirtan-party applicants, and for a while every new member had to fulfill one of his two shifts by cleaning bathrooms three hours a day for a month or two. "Even a GBC would have to do it!" Aindra declared. And when new arrivals to Vrindavan—even those not there to join the kirtan party—asked what service they could render in the *dhāma*, he would tell them that they should clean the bathrooms.

Whatever he demanded of the kirtan devotees, including toilet duty, he also asked of himself. In fact, he had been cleaning toilets when Madhumangala had arrived. One Janmastami he had dreamed that Srila Prabhupada came and told him that the standard of cleanliness at the temple should be first class but that the bathrooms were dirty. "It's sad that I can't even find a proper man to keep the bathrooms clean," Prabhupada had said. So, the next day, on Prabhupada's Vyasa-puja, taking his spiritual master's words in the dream as instruction, Aindra had decided that his offering would be to clean the bathrooms—unheard of for a brahmana or pujari—really, for anyone other than members of India's untouchable caste.

He started on the third floor, scrubbing the toilets, sinks, and showers with acid and a hand brush. He would start on the ceiling and work downwards along the walls to the floor. There was so much dirt and slime that before long he developed boils and weeping sores, which covered his body, arms, legs, and hands and became so painful that he could hardly sleep. He had to stop his cleaning, but after a few days his sores began to heal, and he proceeded to clean the rest of the bathrooms in the building—every one, on every floor. "We appreciated that a lot," one of the *gurukula* boys later remarked.

When the head of the *gurukula* saw Aindra climbing a shower wall wielding a scrub brush with a crazed look of determination and asked what he was doing, Aindra replied, "I'm doing what every leader, every sannyasi, every GBC, and every guru *should* be doing— I'm cleaning the bathroom!"

❦ ❦ ❦

When Bhagavan das, another American, looked out the window of the *gurukula* building's second-floor stairwell, he saw what he thought was an odd-looking devotee in the courtyard dressed in what seemed more like a rag than a dhoti. He had ankle-bells strapped over thick woolen socks, and reddish stubble sprouted from his face and head. A clean-cut, respectable-looking sannyasi was engaged with the man in what seemed like deep conversation. *So, Bhagavan thought hopefully, maybe you don't have to be a conformist to be a good devotee!*

"That's Aindra," Bhagavata Purana told Bhagavan as he passed by. "You should meet him. He lives in Room 89, on the third floor."

Aindra?! Bhagavan had been listening to *Vrindavan Mellows* every morning for more than a year. So, he went up to Room 89, but the skull and crossbones and rough warning posted on the door discouraged him from knocking.

"Have you seen Aindra yet?" Bhagavata Purana asked later that day.

"No," Bhagavan said. "I made it as far as his door and got scared. It didn't seem like he wanted anyone to bother him."

Bhagavata Purana laughed. "It's okay," he said. "I'm sure he'd be happy to talk to you."

The next day, Bhagavan knocked. A metal bar-lock inside clanged.

The door opened slightly, slowly, and from behind it, out peeked Aindra.

He invited Bhagavan in, sat him down, and began asking so many questions so rapidly that Bhagavan felt as if he was being interrogated and Aindra was trying to gauge his mental state and spiritual standing. "What's your service?" Aindra asked.

Bhagavan pulled a locket from under his shirt. "Well, I chant internally most of the day to send loving mantra vibrations to this *girirāja-śilā* I carry around my neck."

"Me too!" Aindra said, pulling out his own locket. He introduced Bhagavan to his Deities. "You know," he said, "your Giriraj is pretty small. You should really worship a larger one. And you should get a stone from Varshana too."

"How can I get a larger *śilā*?" Bhagavan asked.

Feeling merciful and in one of his more spontaneous moods, Aindra reached behind his altar and pulled out a few. "Here," he said. "I'm not worshipping these. You can have one."

"Wow, thanks!" Bhagavan said. "Is there anything special I should do to install Him?"

"Give him lots of sweets on the first day of puja."

Bhagavan went back to America but returned in 1996, looking for service.

When he heard that Bhagavan was back, Aindra enlisted him in the 24-hour-kirtan party and gave him the late-night shift and another *śilā*.

After the kirtan each evening, the group would move upstairs to Aindra's room and have *prasādam*, and he would talk about Krishna. By midnight, often only Bhagavan remained, listening to Aindra explain the nuances of *rāgātmikā-bhakti*—the pure devotion for Krishna in the hearts of the eternal, ever-perfect devotees of Vrindavan—as was his practice, relating its *tattva*, foundational principles, rather than telling specific Radha-Krishna *līlā*. Then Aindra would put his Deities to bed and occasionally fall asleep himself, even while still talking. Sometimes they would talk until *maṅgala-āratī*—even *guru-pūjā*.

"We just have to chant Hare Krishna here in Krishna-Balaram Mandir," Aindra said one night. "Then we will get everything. We will realize everything. The name will clean the mirror of your heart and reveal everything: *siddha-deha* [eternal spiritual identity] and everything."

"Did the name reveal your *siddha-deha* to you?" Bhagavan asked.

"Yes," Aindra told him.

Bhagavan was amazed. "What did you find out?" he asked. "Are you a *gopī*? What is your name?"

Aindra leaned in close with a serious, grave look. Then his face bloomed into a mischievous smile, and he tugged on the bead-bag hanging around Bhagavan's neck. "Keep chanting Hare Krishna."

"Oh, come on, prabhu!" Bhagavan begged. "Please tell me something!"

"Bhagavan das ..." Aindra said, taking a deep breath. "In the *siddha-deha*, service is natural and effortless. It is such a wonderful feeling. In my *siddha-deha*, I sing for Radhe-Shyam and effortlessly hit any note, no matter how high. I can perform the most amazing, intricate *alankar* to ornament any note. Whatever I desire to sing for the pleasure of Sri Sri Radhe-Shyam, it automatically manifests in my voice."

"So, in the spiritual world, we don't have to learn how to sing?" Bhagavan asked.

"Learning is also there," Aindra explained. "Lalita-devi taught me to sing like that."

Bhagavan was speechless; he felt like he could barely breathe.

Aindra gazed at him for some time, then said, "There is a whole lot of nectar over here, Bhagavan. You just gotta jump in. Chant Hare Krishna."

One morning, Bhagavan was in his room worshipping his *śilās* when Aindra came in, crying.

"What is it?" Bhagavan asked. "Did something happen?"

Aindra nodded. He motioned for Bhagavan to continue with his puja and sat beside him. When he had composed himself, he spoke in a faltering voice. "I just made a flower garland ... and gave it to another young *gopī* ... who passed it along ... and I watched ... as Sri Radhika put it on the neck of my Shyamasundar!"

"When was this?"

"Just now."

"What? Where?"

"In my room ... I was chanting *japa*."

❧ ❧ ❧

Among Aindra's most enthusiastic followers were those from Russia and the former Soviet Republics, where for years devotees had suffered persecution, harassment, and physical attacks for their practice—in the early days of the movement even imprisonment and torture in labor camps and psychiatric hospitals. One night in 1994 Aindra was resting, half-asleep, when his Deities came to him in a vision. He was in his room with a fan on, and through its whirring he heard a voice, but he didn't know its source. When he looked up, he saw that his Nitai Saci-suta's lips were moving. It was such a beautiful sight that he couldn't move; he just gazed in amazement. *Oh, my God*, he thought. *They probably want to tell me something!* So he turned off the fan and heard Nitai Saci-suta speaking, but in a foreign language that he didn't recognize and couldn't understand. *What are They saying?* he wondered. He said, "I don't understand," but there was no reply.

The next morning, Aindra awoke to a knock at his door. It was Eduard, from Moscow, who had come to join the 24-hour-kirtan party. He spoke to Aindra in halting English, and suddenly, hearing his accent, Aindra realized that his native language, Russian, was the one his Deities had been speaking the night before. "My Nitai Saci-suta speak Russian!" Aindra proclaimed.

❧ ❧ ❧

Eduard became the first Russian devotee to join the kirtan department. He had been a member of the Rostov-on-Don temple, which had been attacked by the local Orthodox Christian Kazakh militia, and when he had tried to fight back and protect devotees, he had suffered a savage beating that almost killed him, landing him in the hospital's intensive care unit for months, with head injuries that plagued him the rest of his life. Aindra gave him the name Adi Rasa, which, he explained, was the original mellow of pure conjugal love, "so that we don't have to call you by a material name and we can all meditate on something uplifting."

Adi Rasa had heard Aindra's kirtans on cassettes that Russian devotees had brought back with them after visits to Krishna-Balaram

Mandir. "I always made a copy," he remembered, "and I was constantly listening to them." He arrived in Vrindavan speaking little English and without knowing how to play any instruments, but with diligent practice during the night shifts, when no one else was around, he soon improved and became a regular kartal player in the kirtan, serving until his passing in 2012. He had hypoglycemia, so he needed to eat regularly, or else he could have a seizure, pass out, or even die, and Aindra took fatherly care of him, ordering him to never fast and making sure he was properly fed. On a number of occasions, when Adi Rasa was sick from low blood sugar, Aindra would feed him by hand.

One day at Radha Kund, having gone against Aindra's advice that he remain at the temple, where he could eat and be cared for, Adi Rasa nodded off while chanting *japa* on a roof and fell to the ground below, unconscious. He was taken to the hospital, and at one point his heart stopped beating. The doctors were able to revive him, but they determined that he still might not survive.

Aindra had mixed feelings about the incident. On one hand, he was deeply concerned; Adi Rasa was like a beloved family member. On the other hand, Adi Rasa had practically left his body at Radha Kund during Purushottama Masa—what would have been a spiritually auspicious passing. Perhaps that was best. Still, Aindra beseeched the doctors to do everything they could, no matter the expense. Over the next few months (it took him almost a year to fully recover) someone always had to be at Adi Rasa's side, and Aindra visited him regularly in the hospital. He helped pay for his care, and when the funds ran out, he went to *maṅgala-ārati* and appealed to the devotees, who helped make up the cost. "I will soon have no money to get flowers for offering to my Deities!" he complained in jest. "What will I do then? I will offer them the flower of Adi Rasa."

❦ ❦ ❦

From then on, there were always a few Russian devotees in the kirtan party, and one of the ashram rooms was dubbed the Russian Room. The next to join, Ijya das, from Moscow's Begovaya temple, had also been attracted by Aindra's early cassettes. He was the head of his temple's *saṅkīrtana* department, and when he returned to Russia, he began inspiring devotees there to go out on *harināma* and dive deeper into their spiritual lives.

Another devotee to bring Aindra's *harināma* spirit back to Russia was Sundar Madhava, a householder from Moscow, who visited Vrindavan several times with his family. Aindra preached to him that life was short and that he should thus devote his energies to relocating to Vrindavan and developing his relationship with Krishna, primarily in His form as the Holy Name. And eventually, following the principle that "When a sadhu gives you an order, simultaneously he gives you power to follow it," Sundar Madhava was able to quit his job in Moscow and spend more time in Vraja. One year when he was not able to visit and sent a donation in his stead, Aindra accepted it gratefully but said that he regretted Sundar Madhava's absence and would have preferred that he'd spent the money on himself and his travel and come to Vrindavan for the sake of his spiritual benefit.

"Sri Harinam is not dependent on our tongue to make His divine appearance," Aindra told Sundar Madhava on his first visit. "It's not just by articulating the syllabic sounds with this fleshy tongue that the Holy Name must appear. The Holy Name is independent as much as Krishna is independent." He told him about a related experience: "Once, a tantric was showing off his magic tricks on the street in front of the temple, and all the people there were very impressed by him. After the performance, I told him that Krishna is the Supreme mystic and that he should not show himself off in Vrindavan but instead acknowledge Krishna's supreme position. He became angry. And then, some time later in my room, I was suddenly overcome by the tantric's tamasic power and I became paralyzed, similar to the way one can become paralyzed if he is attacked by ghosts. I understood that it was the tantric's mystic power overcoming me. I was unable to escape; I realized what was happening too late to try to counter the effect of the thing, and I was overwhelmed. The purpose of the yogi was to put me into a comatose condition, and it was a very dangerous situation.

"Suddenly from the sky above me the *mahā-mantra* in a very pure and clear sounding voice descended upon me. I can't even begin to try to reproduce the sound vibration! The *mahā-mantra* was independently descending. The Holy Names came to protect me, and as soon as They came to me, immediately the tantric's influence was dissipated. My experience was that there wasn't anyone who was chanting the Holy Name, but that rather the Holy Name, who is a person, an independent spiritual sound vibration, came Himself.

"In other words, the Holy Name doesn't require someone to chant Him in order for Him to manifest. Rather, the Holy Name is an independent spiritual sound vibration, a manifestation, who has His own free will and unlimited, omnipotent abilities.

"So, I had a direct experience of the Personality of Godhead in His Harinam *svarūpa* descending and appearing to save me. Even now, that experience, that sound, is ringing in my ears. I can never forget the experience of the divine appearance of the Holy Name in my consciousness at that time.

"On account of that experience, I came to the rather profound realization that the Holy Name can appear even without the vibration of our tongue. In other words, He doesn't need us to vibrate 'Hare Krishna, Hare Krishna ...' with this fleshy tongue for Him to make His manifestation within this world. It is only because of His special causeless mercy upon certain devotees that He may choose by His own free will to manifest by using their tongue as an instrument. By engaging them in His *sevā*, He may choose to manifest by dancing on the tongue of a pure devotee.

"The point I am bringing out is that we should feel very privileged if Sri Chaitanya Mahaprabhu, who is a personification of the Holy Name, decides to use any of us as an instrument for the propagation of the Holy Name in the world."

When he returned to Moscow, Sundar Madhava began a *nāma-haṭṭa* program and attracted dozens of young, interested people, quite a few of whom were materially successful, including musicians, producers, and writers.

Among the attendees were Mukunda Murari das and his wife, Divya Shakti, who later helped Aindra with his book, facilitated his preaching to Russians in Vrindavan and over the Internet, and brought large groups to Vraja. "The atmosphere in Sundar Madhava's *nāma-haṭṭa* was very different from any other devotee-run programs in Moscow at that time," Mukunda Murari remembered. "We had very long, nice kirtans; discussed philosophy deeply; and while taking *prasādam* (Vrindavan-style *kichari*) listened to Aindra Prabhu's kirtans. Sundar Madhava told us a lot about Aindra Prabhu as a sadhu who had dedicated his life to serving the kirtan of Holy Names and Deities in Vrindavan and found absolute shelter there."

"The mood was very friendly, almost homely, and steeped in devotion," Divya Shakti agreed. "We studied books of Srila Prabhupada and many other acharyas, we discussed the philosophy of kirtan and *saṅkīrtana*, and we spoke a lot about chanting."

With Aindra as its *saṅkīrtana* exemplar, Sundar Madhava's *nāma-haṭṭa* grew so fast that it eventually had to branch out into several programs. Devotees learned how to play mridanga and lead traditional kirtans, did regular *hari-nāma-saṅkīrtana*, developed traveling *saṅkīrtana* groups, and organized kirtan festivals in other Russian cities and nearby countries.

Inspired, many of the *nāma-haṭṭa* devotees visited Vrindavan. On one visit, before meeting Aindra, Mukunda Murari remembered, "at Srila Prabhupada's samadhi I started praying, asking for mercy: 'Please give me a sign which way I should take, because I myself cannot understand. I do not know whom can I trust, but I am sure that I trust you.' We had heard a lot about Aindra Prabhu from Sundar Madhava. We knew him as a saint and a sadhu, devoted to the kirtan of Holy Names. And now, eight or nine months later, we were finally in Vrindavan.

"At the time, I was thinking of leaving ISKCON. I had a lack of trust in the leadership and was looking at different *saṅgas* and sadhus in Vraja, spending time in Mathura, Govardhana, and Radha Kund. I opened my heart to Aindra, but he never told me that my doubts were bad, that my feelings for other *saṅgas* were bad. He just said, 'Whatever problem you have, you can only solve them if you intensify your *bhajana*. Just switching *saṅgas* won't help.' It was exactly what I needed.

"When I asked him a few questions about points I had heard, he gave me *Nectar of Devotion* and told me that all the answers were there. He also gave me Bon Maharaja's translation of *Bhakti-rasāmṛta-sindhu* and Srila Bhaktivinoda's *Jaiva Dharma* and suggested that I could check the acharyas' commentaries. He said that there was nothing new I could receive from other *saṅgas*—Srila Prabhupada had already given us everything.

"He was extremely devoted to Prabhupada—cent percent

convinced that there was no need to get any association outside of ISKCON. Prabhupada had given everything, he said, and there was no need to get inspiration from any other lines.... I understood from him that I all I had to do was chant and pray to Srila Prabhupada.

"Very naturally and simply, all the questions that had not allowed me to rest—philosophical, psychological, ethical—were resolved. 'Why do you doubt that Srila Prabhupada can lead you to perfection?' he asked me. 'Why do you wander here and there in Vraja? Do you really think that this is the way to find a guru, to get answers to your questions about our *siddhānta*? Srila Prabhupada never approved it; better to take your beads, choose a place for yourself in his samadhi mandir or in front of Tulasi, chant, and read Srila Prabhupada's books. This is all you need. Prabhupada said that in one grain of earth surrounding Tulasi in the Krishna-Balaram Mandir there are all the holy places of Vrindavan. I generally don't go anywhere. I worship the Deities in my room, chant the Holy Name, go downstairs only to participate in kirtan and get the darshan of the Deities, and that's it. I do not like to go here and there to look at my surroundings with my eyes. What for? I can listen, chant, read books and that's enough.'

"He was a real missionary to the depth of his heart. It is often said that he did not conform to the traditions of ISKCON. In fact, he took responsibility for serving the entire mission. He often said, 'It hurts me that so many Vaishnavas in ISKCON cannot understand my missionary spirit.'

"I personally observed on a number of occasions how when devotees wanted to join the kirtan, when they met Aindra Prabhu, he would immediately start to preach to them. 'This service, kirtan,' he said, 'we do not do for ourselves. We do not live in Vrindavan simply for the sake of purification and personal spiritual benefit. This is the service to all ISKCON!' He said that this *kīrtana-yajña* nourishes Srila Prabhupada's body, since Prabhupada said that ISKCON is his body. All the time, he stressed that this *yajña* is for the benefit of the whole society. He was in this state, mood of commitment to this *yajña*, and he inspired other devotees in this service.

"And he loved the Russian devotees very much. Although he was strict with them, there was always a certain reason. He said that

Russian devotees are very wonderful, they have so many talents, but they are too sentimental. So he gave them a lot of attention and care.

"One day, he called me into his room after the morning kirtan and asked, 'Is everything okay with your wife?' He had seen us speaking to each other in a cold manner the evening before, and he was disturbed by this, because if we fought, our spiritual life would suffer and we would not be able to live in Vrindavan. He said that he had no ready solution at hand since he was a *bābājī* and was busy with his service, but I had to do something about it. That really touched my heart—that he was concerned with our life and our relationship, because it affected our spiritual life. He was taking care of us in all possible ways."

When Mukunda Murari and his wife returned to Moscow, they opened their own *nāma-haṭṭa* program—like Sundar Madhava's, influenced by Aindra's preaching and mood—and a couple years later, Mukunda became president of the Moscow temple. Then, beginning in 2005, Mukunda remembered, "we started to hold regular outdoor *hari-nāma-saṅkīrtana* throughout the summer—a manifestation of Aindra Prabhu's desire and inspirational preaching. They were very lively and enthusiastic, and it was done as an offering for his pleasure. He was so happy about it, and every time I saw him he loved hearing all the details—how many devotees were going out for how long, and all the small details. Thus our successful *nāma-haṭṭa* preaching and *hari-nāma-saṅkīrtana*, which many devotees remember with fondness till this day, were directly brought into life by Aindra Prabhu's great inspiration."

The kirtan revolution was spreading across Russia, even to remote places like Siberia. Despite the harsh climate, devotees were going out on the streets regularly on *hari-nāma-saṅkīrtana*, and there were several traveling *saṅkīrtana* parties. A kirtan academy to train musicians had opened in the southern city of Novorossiysk, and devotees from there would write to Aindra or go to Vrindavan for his advice.

Other Russian devotees to join the 24-hour-kirtan party and stay long term were Premamrita das; Sivananda das; Maha-muni das; Vedakarta das; Param Purusa das; Vishishtha das and Radhe Syam das, from Siberia; and Tamal Krishna das, a professional musician and DJ who helped Aindra edit his audio recordings and produced over half a dozen kirtan DVDs.

Srila Prabhupada with devotees in Potomac, Maryland, July 1976 (Aindra in back center).

In kirtan with Ganapati Swami in the U.S.

Street kirtan on New York's Broadway.

Kirtan in the Temple on Wheels.

Devotees Bring Temple to New York Sidewalks

An Indian-style temple at the foot of a Manhattan skyscraper? Not for long. Aindra dāsa's van, transformed into an ornate temple, appears at different places in New York City every day. To the accompaniment of instruments, Aindra and his group chant the holy name of Kṛṣṇa, distribute books on Kṛṣṇa consciousness, and offer free refreshments to passersby.

Back to Godhead feature, 1984.

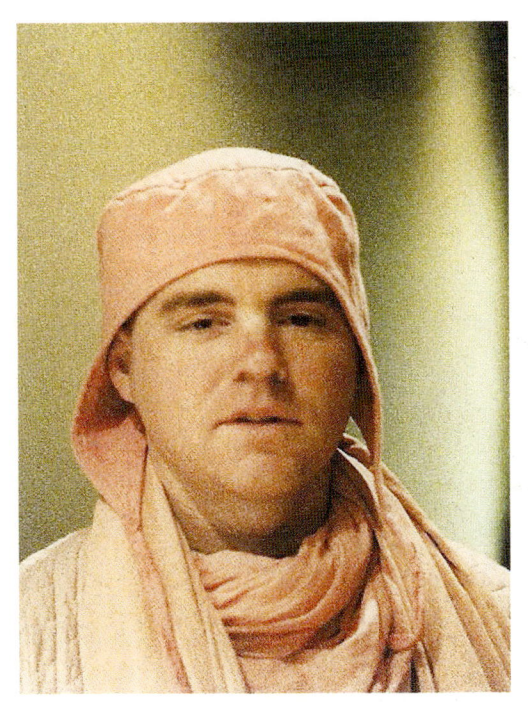

Brahmachari days.

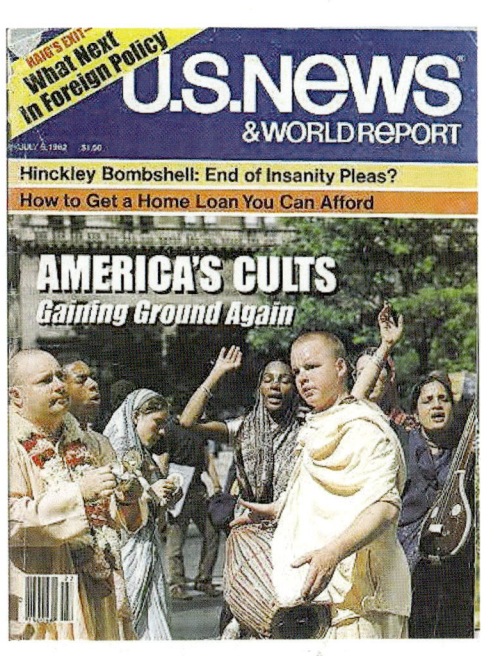

1982 *U.S. News and World Report* cover highlighting "cult" article.

Temple-courtyard kirtan, 1987.

The initial 24-hour kirtan team and supporting devotees, late 1980s.

Aindra's personal Deities, whom he carried around his neck. On the right, Vijay-Gopal *śilā*; on the left, one of the primary *śilās* from his altar.

Radha-Krishna painting in Aindra's room, which he rescued and reconditioned and before which he chanted *japa*.

Giving talk in Krishna Balaram Mandir.

Aindra's beloved Sri Sri Nitai Saci-suta, whom he stole "fair and square."

On the altar dressing Sri Sri Radha-Shyamasundar.

Sri Sri Nitai Saci-suta and Aindra's room altar.

Chanting *japa* by Govardhana Hill.

On the bank of Radha-Kund during Parama Ekadasi, 1999.

At Govardhana Hill.

Viewing Sri Sri Radha-Shyamasundar from the altar railing.

At Ma Jahnava Baithak, the sitting place of Sri Jahnava Devi,
on the bank of Radha-Kund, February 1997.

Leading temple kirtan.

Sign handwritten and posted by Aindra on his door.

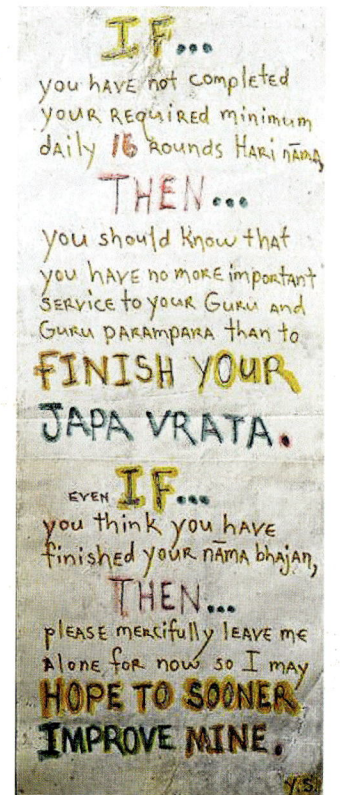

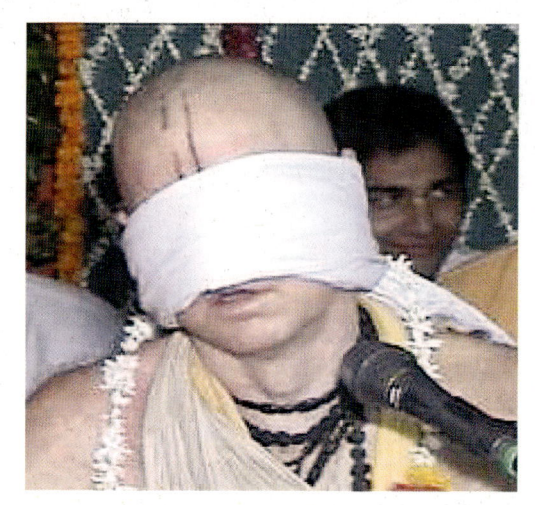

IF...
you have not completed your required minimum daily 16 rounds Hari nama
THEN...
you should know that you have no more important service to your Guru and Guru parampara than to
FINISH YOUR JAPA VRATA.
EVEN IF...
you think you have finished your nama bhajan,
THEN...
please mercifully leave me alone for now so I may
HOPE TO SOONER IMPROVE MINE.

Blindfolded kirtan at Delhi wedding.

Leading kirtan before the evening *ārati*.

Leading Damodarastaka prayers during Kartik.

Aindra's Gaura-Nitai, Jahnava Mata, Srila Bhaktisiddhanta Sarasvati, and Srila Prabhupada.

Serving *prasādam* to godbrothers during his birthday program at Giridhari's house.

Sri Sri Radha-Krishna and the *aṣṭa-sakhīs* on Aindra's altar.

Carrying Srila Prabhupada around the Krishna Balaram temple room on *parikramā*.

Distributing sweets after evening kirtan during Govardhana-puja festival.

Speaking with Radhanath Swami.

Speaking with Gopal Krishna Maharaja.

Doing kirtan while Bhakti Charu Swami, with Mukunda Datta Prabhu, performs *ārati* during Deities' installation.

Bathing with Bhaktisiddhanta Swami in Radha Kund.

Spontaneous kirtan at Srila Prabhupada's samadhi
after the evening Damodarastaka prayers.

Chanting at Katyayani temple on the last day of Katyayani-*vrata*.

Leading kirtan before the evening *ārati*.

Leading festival kirtan in Krishna Balaram
temple courtyard.

In room speaking with Bhakti Vijnana Goswami, 2007.

Sitting beneath his 2,200 *śilās*, leaning against Bhakta Stove, 2007.

With Dr. Radha Madhava at Thompson Press in Delhi, examining cover proofs from *The Heart of Transcendental Book Distribution*.

Kirtan with Sivarama Swami at Radha-Syamasundara boat festival in Krishna Balaram Mandir.

Devotees gathered around Aindra's body in the passageway outside his room.

Passing through the Krishna Balaram temple room.

Devotees and well-wishers carrying Aindra's body to the Yamuna.

Cremation on the bank of the Yamuna, led by Mukunda Datta Prabhu.

Aindra's samadhi, in his room in the *gurukula* building.

CHAPTER SIXTEEN

IN NOVEMBER OF 1998 Aindra was among those who would speak as part of Srila Prabhupada's disappearance-day observance. Throughout the day, one after another, Prabhupada's disciples made their offerings, but as had sometimes been Aindra's experience, to delay—or avoid—any controversial comments he might make, he was not called upon until late at night, after the gathering had shifted from the temple room to Prabhupada's quarters. It was almost midnight, even grand-disciples had already spoken, and most of the devotees—all but a dozen or so—had left.

The whole room, especially Prabhupada's bed, was lavishly decorated with flowers, featuring bunches of pinkish-red roses. "These roses remind me of my dream of Srila Prabhupada," Aindra began, describing the dream he'd had a few years' before, after his *ājagara-vṛtti*. "In it, I was sitting at the feet of Srila Prabhupada, who was sitting at the low desk and doing his book translation work. I was breaking off thorns from the roses, as we used to do before offering them to Deities. After I finished, I offered them to Srila Prabhupada, who glanced away from his work, accepted the roses, and deeply smelled in and savored the fragrance. Then he said, 'Ah ... now my life is complete. Now, Aindra, you are *nitya-siddha*.'" And without elaborating, he said that Srila Prabhupada had revealed to him things that he needed and desired very much.

"Usually these things are not discussed openly," he admitted to the devotees, "Neither do I want to proclaim myself *nitya-siddha* or boast of this special fortune. What I really want to do is to try to share with you a conviction, try to instill in you faith that for a real disciple, for any of you, guru is always available and Srila Prabhupada is always available. He is always there for us, no matter that physically he may be far away or even may have left this world. If a devotee really so desires, he is always in touch with guru, and all spiritual perfection is available at the feet of guru and especially at the feet of our Srila Prabhupada. So you should never think that he has left and is no more, that we are cut off from his mercy. His mercy, his presence, is always available. He is always here for us."

The reaction was almost immediate, with one devotee reporting and rumors flying that Aindra had said that he was a *nitya-siddha*. An official investigation ensued into "Aindra Prabhu's activities, and, more specifically, his philosophical outlook."

Aindra was asked to explain himself, and in response, over the next two or three months—he wanted to have it done for the Gaura-purnima GBC meetings—he composed a 28-page letter, quoting from Srila Prabhupada's books, letters, conversations, and lectures:

> On Prabhupada's disappearance day, almost invariably, all the "big guns" naturally get their opportunity to glorify Prabhupada during the morning session but generally don't seem to place much importance on attending the evening session. It is obvious to me that, for whatever reasons, my concerned well-wishers could not possibly have been present when I spoke (it was about midnight, as I was the last initiated disciple of Srila Prabhupada to have the opportunity to speak that day). Or, if they were present, they must have been dozing off or too tired to grasp what I actually said.

Brajisma prabhu and his good wife, Mother Draupadi, mentioned in their offering that they are compiling a book to be entitled "Prabhupada Now" and requested that devotees send them accounts of any metaphysical experiences, such as dreams, in which Srila Prabhupada had appeared. I thought to myself, and even expressed, that such things are basically unverifiable subjective experiences; yet even so, if they are in keeping with the siddhanta of our acaryas they may be accepted for inspiration, encouragement, and even guidance. I became inspired by them to share one such dream-experience of my own, although normally I wouldn't think to do so.

I wanted to share an experience which profoundly increased my fervent attachment to the lotus feet of Srila Prabhupada, because it has always broken my heart that many of my godbrothers would become disenchanted and think that this movement was incapable of delivering them to the topmost perfection in devotional life.

Aindra described the dream and events leading to it:

Not wanting anyone to get any wise ideas that I am a "nitya-siddha," I said, "I am the same dirty ol' dog I've always been and always will be until I fully surrender and become the object of my Guru's grace, but at least I was considerably pacified and became very hopeful, and I wanted to share that guru-nista with all of you.

Here is a brief sketch of my activities. Srila Prabhupada stated that the whole spiritual world is within the four walls of the Krishna-Balaram Mandir. In an effort to realize the truth of this statement, I mostly relegate my existence to the confines of the temple room, my living quarters, and, unfortunately, the bathroom.

I rarely ever go to the guest house, what to speak of the restaurant, and you will never find me loitering at Bihari

> Lal's drinking Coca-Cola. I always scrupulously avoid any dealings with women, as far as possible, although I don't despise them. I am keenly aware of the simple truth that I'm not very advanced and I don't have much longer to live. So, I spend most of my time doing my level best to engage continuously in chanting the Holy Names of Krsna with the hopes of eventually elevating myself to the pure stage of nama-bhajan. In whatever time remains, I absorb my heart and soul in relishing krsna-katha by attending Srimad-Bhagavatam class and discussing the philosophy of Krishna consciousness as I have understood it from my spiritual master. I also usually spend at least three hours daily hearing my favorite stories from Srila Prabhupada's Krsna book while doing my personal deity worship.

Then he turned the inquisitors' spotlight back on them, questioning the value of what he saw as a prevalent practice in the movement—preaching without internal qualification—and highlighting the need to develop such qualification and "save oneself":

> I am basically a spiritual derelict. I know I'm not very qualified. I never present myself as an uttama-adhikari. Instead, I decline to accept even one disciple until I'm thoroughly convinced I have well attained that qualification.
>
> "Hip, hip, hurray!" for all our "preaching," but to what extent has it made devotees so enchanted by Krsna that they seriously pursue prema, aspiring for the heartfelt devotional mood (seva-bhavana) fit to be relished by Rasaraja Sri Krsna? Instead, if anyone even inquires about such topics, we reply with some version of, "Shut up and get back to work! Don't ask these kinds of questions. 'First deserve, then desire.' 'Just try to understand you're not that body.' " How convenient! Pass the potatoes when they get too hot to handle, put 'em on the back burner, or just smash 'em right there.
>
> "Work now, samadhi later." But work at what?

"We have to preach, prabhu!" But preach about what?

"Preach about preaching about preaching that we're supposed to preach about preaching about how we're supposed to preach." We have no time to think about what we're preaching about. That's for bhajananandis, heaven forbid. We're workaholics, and that's good enough ... isn't it?

In one famous letter, Srila Prabhupada tells, "As devotees of Krsna, being engaged in the practical work of spreading Krsna consciousness, that is already the highest realization. That's all right, that is our real mission, to deliver the world by preaching Krsna's message to others; but even higher realization, the highest realization, is to save oneself."

To "save oneself" is the best contribution anyone can make to the Guru's mission, for without doing so we lack the fitness to really save anyone else.

He then replied to the request for information about his "philosophical outlooks and inlooks":

> My foremost desire is to live and die in Vrndavan-dhama singing "Hare Krsna, Hare Krsna, Krsna Krsna, Hare Hare, Hare Rama, Hare Rama, Rama Rama, Hare Hare" at the top of my lungs for the pleasure of Guru and Gauranga.
>
> Srila Prabhupada said we should have high aspirations. Sometimes, in my enthusiasm to pursue those aspirations, I naturally tend to internally see myself in terms of what I want to be for Krsna. If you see any fault in that, please forgive me.
>
> When we get something nice, naturally we want to share it with others. But at the same time, we don't want to share with just anybody, save and except those who will actually appreciate it. Sometimes, in the midst of my ardor for eternal devotional service, I may now and then give expression

of my heart's inspirations to someone. Generally, however, in my better moments, I try to camouflage them. At any rate, please know beyond any doubt that I would rather be born as a worm in the stool of a pig in Vrndavana than to become a queen in Dwaraka or a servant of the Lord of Vaikuntha. In Vrndavana at least there is a hope of hearing Krsna's flute, and what's the use of a Krsna without the flute? What's the use of a Krsna without Radha?

I hope to someday actually see Krsna and His young cowherd boyfriends going in the morning to the gosala to milk the cows. I hope to see Krsna and his friends enjoying the blissful breakfast cooked by Radha and her friends and served by Mother Yasoda and Rohini devi. I pray to someday see Krsna and Balarama going to the pastures with Their cows and boyfriends, followed by practically the whole of Vraja. I long to catch a glimpse of His sidelong glances toward His priya-gana. When will that day come when I will fortunately witness with my own eyes beautiful Krsna playing ball with bael fruits, wrestling with His friends and relishing so many other pleasing pastimes in the middle of the day? I hope against hope to someday get the chance to see the Lord of my heart coming back to Vraja at the end of the day, appearing to be fatigued, like a swaggering elephant, with His fine, curly locks dusted by the hoof-dust of the cows, as He slowly enters His home. To get a glimpse of these pastimes, we should be prepared to lay down millions of our lives for preaching the sankirtana movement of Sri Caitanya Mahaprabhu and His sena-pati bhakta, Srila Prabhupada. I long to someday be seen by Them as an object of Their pleasure; and I pray that day will come to all of us.

The topic of *rāgānuga-sādhana* and its goal, *vraja-prema*, was a major factor in the investigation:

Raga basically means "attachment" or "attraction." We

should not be surprised if devotees become attracted to Krsna, since small pieces of iron have practically no choice but to be drawn toward a big magnet.

If we are not intensely attracted to the beautiful vision of Krsna, our iron hearts must be corroded. If we remove the corrosion from a piece of iron, it becomes more sensitive to magnetic influence. Similarly, by following the regulative principles of devotional service and discarding our inordinate and superfluous attachments to maha-maya, the rust is scrubbed off our hearts and raga (attachment) more and more naturally fixes upon the lotus feet of Krsna. Thus the practices of vaidhi-bhakti serve to ensure the healthy initial growth of the natural Krishna conscious raga of the soul.

If we don't deeply understand this ultimate purpose of the vaidhi-bhakti program that was given to us by our Srila Prabhupada, then we are prone to one of two problems: We may foolishly disregard those regulative principles in our less-than-fully-eligible, unauthorized pursuit of wrong-headed, so-called raga-bhajan. Or, to the other extreme, we may become grounded by excessive, fear-based, over-attachment to the rules and regulations, not recognizing that their function is to help us be fixed-up enough to merit gradually going beyond vaidhi-bhakti. The first mistake causes us to unfairly criticize ISKCON as being exclusively concerned with reverential devotion, discarding it like a fool who discards a brown paper bag without looking inside to find the precious gems it holds.

The second mistake leads to raganuga phobia. I have seen many times that supposedly more advanced senior devotees unnecessarily fear allowing themselves to actually be captivated by the beauty of Krsna and Krsna's lilas. We should not fail to allow ourselves to be attracted and enchanted by the sweetness of Krsna, for if we do not become infatuated with hope to eternally serve Krsna in one of the five primary rasas, then it is no wonder that we will plunge headlong into, or at best keep struggling to ignore, our attachments to the perverted rasas of this mundane sphere.

The unfortunate warring that apparently goes on sometimes between persons on both sides of the mistake plainly stems from inadequate knowledge of the subject, either from one side or the other, or both. Very often I have seen that devotees mistakenly equate raganuga-sadhana with bhava-bhakti—the stage at which one becomes a siddha-bhakta above the state of bondage and beyond the clutches of the illusory energy. This is clearly a misconception. The mistaken notion that one cannot follow the path of raga-bhakti unless he is perfectly liberated and fully self-realized obviously arises from overly casual, careless, or unedified reading of our acaryas' teachings. In Bhakti-rasamrta-sindhu Rupa Goswami delineates three stages of bhakti: sadhana, bhava, and prema. The higher two stages, bhava and prema, are the domain of perfected souls, siddhas. The initial stage, sadhana is the stage in which an aspirant earnestly engages in practicing bhakti, aiming to attain such perfection. Rupa Goswami clearly defines that sadhana-bhakti has two categorical departments: vaidhi and raganuga. Thus raganuga is clearly not a perfectional stage; it is a type of practice.

He then tied the discussion to the misconception that since he considered himself an associate-adherent of Srimati Radharani, he must think of himself as a perfected being:

> Siddha-bhaktas at the higher stages of bhava and prema have fully actualized their siddha-svarupa. Sadhakas have not, but those who have fortunately gained entrance into raga-bhajan know something about who they are or aspire to be, because their sadhana necessarily involves internal contemplation of such, as confirmed or conferred upon them by the spiritual master. Thus, the raganuga-sadhaka may "know" who he/she is, but he/she has yet to fully realize the thing.

I have yet to attain the liberated stages of bhava and prema, but still, I should hope to have received at least a little mercy on account of all this Hare Krsna chanting. You should try it. Loudly sing "Hare Krsna, Hare Krsna, Krsna Krsna, Hare Hare, Hare Rama, Hare Rama, Rama Rama, Hare Hare" from a desperate heart, for a minimum of 6–12 hours, every day, for 15–20 years, and see what happens to you!

CHAPTER SEVENTEEN

AINDRA'S MAIN CONCERN for ISKCON was never in doubt. "It has always put me into anxiety," he wrote in an article titled "Bring the Bliss Back," "that Hari Nāma Saṁkirtana has been carelessly neglected, practically at the expense of the basic spiritual foundation and bliss of our Movement. It may not be so easy for us to immediately have faith in such a subtle and apparently simplistic principle, that simply by chanting Hare Kṛṣṇa all of our problems will be solved, and that simply by regularly going on Mahā Nāma Saṁkirtana all the problems of our society will be solved, but if we do it vigorously, with the right motivation to purify ourselves and others so that we may become fit to give and get Kṛṣṇa-prema, then certainly we will quickly perceive the effects.

"We cannot really spread the Krishna Consciousness movement by our material calculations, but this chanting and dancing will lead to the desired goal, both individually and collectively. Don't think it will not. It WILL!"

❦ ❦ ❦

On the last night of Kartik one year, the kirtan just kept going. The *Dāmodarāṣṭaka* prayers—Aindra usually led at least the first and last ones of each Kartik—had finished and the altar doors had opened and closed, but Aindra and the dozens of other devotees were so immersed that they wouldn't stop chanting, even when the cleaners appeared with hoses, buckets, and squeegees. He got upset when the cleaners sprayed the kirtan devotees, and berated the head of security—Vrindavan das had never seen him so angry—that the kirtan should never be disturbed or interrupted, especially during Kartik. He had already complained to the temple management about hiring outsiders: "Why are we selling off our devotional credits? We have the opportunity to clean our hearts by cleaning Krishna's temple. Why are we paying others to do it?"

But the cleaners continued. When the devotees wouldn't move, the cleaners just kept spraying the floors, soaking the chanters. So Aindra stood up, strapped his harmonium over his shoulder, and led everyone dancing in the puddles.

The group danced into the courtyard, out the temple's front door, and into Srila Prabhupada's samadhi mandir, the energy picking up. From the samadhi, the group sang and danced their way out the front gate, onto the road, and to the shops across the street, where they were joined by gathered locals and pilgrims. They moved shop to shop, the proprietors welcoming them with smiles and donations, piling cloth on Aindra's shoulders and rupees on his harmonium.

Awakened by the uproar outside their windows, the *gurukula* boys leaned over their balconies to see the devotees chanting and dancing in the street. Finally Aindra led the group back under the samadhi's marble arches, where the kirtan came to a close. Everyone sat on the pathway, stretched out their legs, and gazed up at the full moon. "Oh well," he said. "That's another Kartik done. At least tonight was ecstatic, right? That was fun!"

❦ ❦ ❦

During Kartik of 1998 Aindra attended the Bahulastami-night bath festival at Radha Kund. A few of the kirtan devotees were also there, along with others who had been on the Vraja Mandala Parikrama, among the thousands of pilgrims who packed the area to bathe in the sacred *kuṇḍa*.

As they had planned, the kirtan devotees met up afterwards at Bhaktisvarupa Damodara Goswami's Gopalji Mandir. "It was well after midnight," remembered Akincana Krishna, who was still a new devotee, twenty years old, and had just taken his first-ever bath in Radha Kund. "It was mystical—with just one light coming off the altar." Aindra picked up a pair of whompers and began to play a slow half-time three-beat and chant. Another devotee joined him on mridanga, Gopal took down a big Manipuri gong hanging from the wall, and the fifteen or twenty devotees sat around them.

"Aindra wasn't sitting or standing," Akincana remembered. "He was crouching. And the way he sang—shaking his head back and forth—it was a whole emotional thing. Musically, it was completely over my head, but it was magnetically attractive and interesting and inspiring—a powerful, passionate kirtan.

"Everyone was sitting, but at one point, when the tempo came to a crescendo, it was impossible to stay down anymore. My body just forced me to get up and dance. It was absolutely ecstatic, so incredibly powerful. It was the most powerful, beautiful, inspiring, uplifting, life-affirming, amazing thing I'd ever experienced—way more than the best hardcore show or any other type of music. I'm not so sentimental, but it was like some energy forced me to my feet—and not just me, the entire room—and it was just total ecstasy. The kirtan was roaring, amazing—a life-changing experience."

When Aindra sang, "it was a super-desperate call to Krishna, like nothing I'd ever seen before.... the way he was just crying out to Krishna, and his singing was so beautiful, and there was so much style to his expression, and when I saw it I understood: Ah, *this* is what kirtan is supposed to be. Now I get it—this is what it is—someone completely crying for the mercy of Krishna."

That night, Akincana recalled, "it all became immediately clear to me. I completely switched off any hesitation, any kind of doubts I had, and I thought, *Whatever it took to be here, whatever sacrifices I had to make, was 100 percent worth it. This is exactly where I need to be, and whatever it is that those guys did—whatever sacrifices they made, whatever austerities they performed, whatever music they took the trouble to learn—that's what I need to do, that's what my life is about, that's what it's for; this is what I want in my life.* It was very, very clear to me."

As Aindra chanted, Gopal was transported back to the first time he'd heard him. The sound of the mantra drew him in just as powerfully as it had then, as if the kirtan had opened a portal to the spiritual world and a torrent of mercy was pouring down. "Prabhu," he asked Aindra afterwards, "How about that kirtan?"

"That was the most amazing kirtan I've ever been in in my entire life," Aindra replied.

Gopal was struck by how Aindra was without pride or any sense of ownership, of being the "doer." He saw himself as just one of the people who had participated in connecting to the divine.

"I was seeing the *gopīs* and Radharani dancing in the *rāsa* dance," said Subekshana das.

"Oh yeah, mate!" Nandulal das agreed in his Aussie accent. "That was better than sex!"

Everyone burst into laughter, and Aindra agreed, "You got *that* right!"

Years later, in New York, Akincana asked Gopal when he had gotten into kirtan, when he had known that it was what he was into. What had inspired him to do it?

"Everything changed for me on one particular night," Gopal replied. "It was on Bahulastami in 1998—Aindra Prabhu in a kirtan at Gopalji Mandir after the midnight bathing. That kirtan changed everything. Right after that, I thought to myself, *Okay, this is what it's all about for me. I gotta get serious about the mridanga, I want to join the 24-hour kirtan—this is what my life is for.*

Even during the kirtan, Gopal had wondered what it was about it that was so different, why it was having such an effect, but he had let it go, an inner voice telling him to stop thinking and just chant.

Now, years later, Akincana considered that the one thing that had made the kirtan so remarkable was that every person in it had just taken a midnight Bahulastami bath in Radha Kund. "That," he said, "combined with the shakti that Aindra had was something really powerful, really special." Both he and Gopal felt sure that it was the best kirtan they had ever experienced.

CHAPTER SEVENTEEN

And in the months following the Bahulastami kirtan, Gopal became more and more serious about both his mridanga playing and *sādhana-bhakti* and moved into the kirtan ashram to live as a brahmachari.

❦ ❦ ❦

One day, Gopal saw Aindra emerge from his doorway wearing a military gas mask and go from room to room making comical pig noises and declaring, "Varahadeva! Varahadeva!"

After a while, Aindra took off the mask, looked at it, and said, "Maybe I should put tilak on it?" And after applying tilak between the eyes of the mask, he resumed his fun.

"Who wants to go to Delhi with me?" he called out.

"Why are you going?" Gopal asked.

"Festival season is coming, and devotees want recordings."

Gopal agreed to go and get more cassettes produced.

Aindra wore the gas mask for hours, into Delhi, as people gawked at his apparent lunacy. "Delhi's pollution wrecks my voice," he explained.

When they arrived at the reproduction factory, Gopal was shocked at the poor quality of the facilities. "This place hasn't updated their equipment since the '80s," he said. "You can't keep working with this rinky-dink stuff, prabhu. You have to come up to modern standards."

"I really want to," Aindra replied, "but how will I pay for it? No one's helping. Anyway, it's better than it used to be. When we did *Vrindavan Mellows*, I went by train with Bhagavata Purana, without a ticket. We didn't have *any* money. We just told the ticket-man, 'Radhe-Shyam' and hoped he would let us stay on the train. We couldn't afford to have the cassettes assembled, either, so we took all the parts up to someone's attic and put them together ourselves."

Moved by Aindra's state of affairs, Gopal sponsored the purchase of five or six cassette-reproducing machines, which, installed in Aindra's room, became the kirtan department's first in-house reproduction system.

❦ ❦ ❦

Aindra felt that the recorded versions of his kirtans could give listeners an even clearer sense of his vision than hearing them live. "In the temple kirtans," he said, "what is mostly on my mind is to go out there and make people chant, clap, and dance." The musical qualities of the kirtan were less prominent. "If you want to see what my kirtan is really like, listen to my recordings. *That's* the real me, offering my full artistic presentation."

The recordings were well received and became more popular over time, but the kirtan department couldn't afford to produce very many cassettes, and donations generated only about 20 percent of their basic needs.

"Our cassette program has had some success," Aindra wrote to a godbrother, "but remains insufficient as of yet to meet the need. Last year from the temple bookstall alone we distributed not less than 500 cassettes at RS50 each. Thakur Haridas of Krishna Culture bought 600 pieces at RS40 each. We could have done much more had we the capital to invest."

He added a plea for donations to the inside cover of the *Vrindavan Mellows* cassettes but got only two replies. One was a postal order for 280 British pounds, which he wasn't able to cash. The other was more significant: Abhirama das donated enough to cover the department's operating expenses—about $5,000 per year—for two years.

Aindra's kirtans had begun to attract a worldwide audience and exert a greater influence, but Bhagavan felt sure that there had to be a way to generate enough money at least to keep the kirtan party afloat. Maybe CDs were the answer. Their audio quality was higher than cassettes', they were becoming more popular and available, and hardly anyone had the equipment needed to bootleg them, which had become a significant problem.

Aindra liked the idea, and they developed a plan. Bhagavan would go back to the San Diego temple and get *Vrindavan Mellows* and *Cintamani Nam* digitally remastered. Then, over the summer, he would travel with the Festival of India, sell the CDs at festivals and Ratha-yatras across America, and return with the proceeds by Kartik. The plan would cost over $3,000 U.S., more than they had, but the temple vice-president, Pancagauda das, agreed to loan them the funds.

Before Bhagavan left, however, he got cold feet. He hadn't had any experience with that kind of responsibility. Hoping to ease Bhagavan's nerves, Aindra took him to see Raghunatha Yogi, a well-known mystic, in Mathura, and with a small group of kirtan devotees, they wound their way through the labyrinth of the town's twisty alleyways. When they finally found the right door, they were greeted by a small boy, who took them in past the family's Radha-Krishna Deities to a large room in the back.

After some time, the mystic entered, his long white hair and beard draped over a yellow kurta, with a white lungi beneath, and sat at a desk at one end of the room

Aindra paid obeisances and touched the mystic's feet. "Our 24-hour-kirtan party requires funds," he explained. "To get them, this boy, Bhagavan das, will go back to America and create new versions of our kirtan recordings for CD, compact disc. He will travel to Ratha-yatras, selling the CDs. Then he will return with the money he raised. Can you ask Devi if this will be successful?"

"Maybe it is too late to ask," the mystic said, "but I will ask Her anyway."

He rang a bell to call his wife, who brought a big strand of Rudraksa beads, which he hung around his neck under his kurta. Then he closed his eyes and began chanting mantras.

When an oversized black desk phone rang, the mystic answered, spoke for a few minutes in Hindi, hung up, and then returned to his meditation. Eventually he opened his eyes and said, "Yes, Bhagavan das will be able to do this thing ..."

Everyone breathed a sigh of relief.

"... but not at this time."

Their hearts sank.

"When will he do it?" Aindra asked.

"After fourteen years," the mystic explained. "At that time, he will be capable of doing this thing."

"Why so long?" Aindra asked. "What will happen in those fourteen years?"

"All the knowledge he has gained will be lost," the mystic explained. "He will become like a riven cloud. Devotees will not give him a place—that begins the problem. *Karmīs* will not give him a place, either. He will be having no place, no home, wandering here and there in madness. He will be starving, falling victim to intoxication and so many temptations of the material life. Many times, he will lie at the doorstep of death."

"Is there any remedy?" Aindra asked.

"A ring," the mystic said. "Tiger's eye, set in gold."

They were baffled. A gold ring? They hardly had enough money to buy a plane ticket! Aindra turned to Bhagavan and said, "I think you should just take shelter of the Holy Name and your *girirāja-śilās*."

Bhagavan agreed, and Aindra gave him funding, letters requesting the assistance of ISKCON San Diego and the Festival of India, a new saffron shoulder bag, some incense, the masters of *Vrindavan Mellows* and *Cintamani Nam*, most of whatever cassettes remained, a tablecloth, and a big picture of Radha-Shyamasundar and sent him off.

In San Diego Bhagavan rented a small apartment downtown with two young brahmacaris, and Aindra kept in touch with him there, at what became the U.S. office of "KBM records." One of the brahmacaris was a sound engineer who could remaster the recordings, but the studio was booked for weeks, and Bhagavan was not able to muster further support.

"This just isn't working," Aindra told Bhagavan over the phone. "Come back to Vrindavan while you still can. It's not a total loss."

Bhagavan had spent all of the money Aindra had given him, but he started working at a vegetarian restaurant and moved into a cheaper room in another apartment. When Aindra tried calling, he wouldn't answer. "Bhagavan Prabhu," Aindra implored in a voice message, "come back to Vrindavan. Your Krishna consciousness is more important than the money. Come back now while you still can. We can figure out a new plan when you get here."

But it was too late. Bhagavan put his *śilās* in a box and gave Them to a friend. He recovered his old clothes from his parents' house and got involved in the rave scene. And, lost in the clubs and partying, he spiraled into depression. The mystic's vision was unfolding exactly as described.

Months later, Aindra tracked Bhagavan down and was able to reach him by phone at an apartment in Los Angeles. "Come back to Vrindavan, Bhagavan. Please! Don't worry about anything. Just come back!"

Finally, Bhagavan agreed. His parents bought him a one-way ticket, and in the middle of the night a few weeks later, he again knocked on the door of Room 89.

When Aindra saw Bhagavan, he teared up with relief. "I thought

I was never going to see you again," he said. He fed him, and they discussed everything that had transpired.

Just before they both fell asleep, Aindra said, "Don't worry about your failure. Just pick up the pieces. Start chanting again and resume your Giriraj *sevā*. We'll figure everything else out here, in Vrindavan."

But although Bhagavan had made it back, he couldn't shake his depression. He spent most days sleeping, unable to get out of bed. One day, he confided to Aindra, "I think I have to leave."

"Stay here with me in Vraja," Aindra said. "Everything will work out."

But Bhagavan was having a hard time returning to devotional life.

Aindra became morose. "It's my fault," he told Bhagavan. "I should never have sent you away. How will Krishna ever accept a person who treats devotees like I treated you?"

On the last night of Kartik, after a feast in Aindra's room, Bhagavan gave his Govardhana *śilās* back to Aindra and left.

❧ ❧ ❧

Despite Bhagavan's personal difficulties, however, when he had returned from America, he had brought back the digital masters he'd taken with him, and when Ramabhadra heard *Vrindavan Mellows*, he was impressed.

"Can you help us produce it?" Aindra asked.

"I'll pay off your debt to Pancagauda," Ramabhadra offered. "What is it, about $3,000?"

"More like four, with the interest." The months during which Aindra had been paying off the loan had been even more austere than usual for the kirtan crew.

"And I'll pay off your loan from the samadhi fund. What's that, about a thousand?"

"A little less."

"Okay," Ramabhadra said. "I'll dissolve both debts. Then I'll mass-produce the *Vrindavan Mellows* recordings on CD and give you a few thousand copies that you can sell yourself. Okay?"

Aindra agreed, and not long after, while Aindra was in the temple room one day, absorbed in kirtan, Ramabhadra walked up nonchalantly, squatted down, and held up a CD.

Aindra stopped singing and playing.

On the CD cover was a photo of a scruffy-looking Aindra cooking, dressed in a lungi and looking at the camera with a big, goofy smile. Superimposed on the photo were the words "Vrindavan Marshmellows, by His Divine Grace Aindra Das Petapada Baba."

"This is a joke, right?" Aindra asked quietly.

"Joke?" Ramabhadra said. "We've already sent a hundred thousand to distributors worldwide!"

After the kirtan, Aindra looked everywhere for Ramabhadra. He found him an hour later, headed upstairs accompanied by two men carrying trunks. "I've got two loads of CDs for you!" he announced.

"Please tell me you didn't use that cover," Aindra begged. When Ramabhadra opened the trunks, Aindra was relieved to see the real *Vrindavan Mellows* cover on all the copies.

As it turned out, Ramabhadra and Vaiyasaki had decided to trash what had been done and work from the original cassette masters, remastering them for digital reproduction at a studio in New York.

Aindra was eager to hear them, so they gathered around a stereo in his room and listened through the whole thing. "It's good—much better than before," Aindra said. "But why aren't Nitai's kirtans here?"

"We had to fit all three cassettes onto two CDs," Ramabhadra explained, "so we decided to take some of Nitai's out. Otherwise it wouldn't fit."

Aindra didn't like that, but at least they had high-quality recordings they could market.

❦ ❦ ❦

When Nandi Mukhi dasi, a Russian devotee, heard that the 24-hour-kirtan department was short of funds, she decided that even though her painting sales had been slow, she would give Aindra a quarter of the profits. As soon as she made her decision, business suddenly picked up, and she soon found herself on the way to Vrindavan with a sizable donation.

Nanda Mukhi was introduced to Aindra by a Russian translator. When she handed him the donation, his gratitude and affection took her by surprise. "Thank you!" he told her. "You are like a beautiful flower at Krishna's lotus feet."

The translator too was surprised—in his case, to hear Aindra, the strict renunciant, speak to a woman in such a manner. Everyone knew that he was reserved with women, didn't entertain them, and was very selective about whom he would even speak to. "It's impossible to understand a pure devotee of Krishna," the man commented in Russian.

Aindra was inspired by Nandi Mukhi's offering, and after kirtan that evening, he gave her two CDs and some tulasi leaves as tokens of his gratitude. "These leaves are from the feet of my Nitai Saci-suta," he told her. "A tulasi leaf is more valuable than the wealth of the whole universe."

CHAPTER EIGHTEEN

"OH MY GOD, he's white!" the woman exclaimed. Nalini Jani had been singing a melody from *Vrindavan Mellows* for months, and here was this devotee, singing the exact same tune with the exact same voice she had heard.

Srila Prabhupada had been both proud of and strategic with the way his "dancing white elephants," his Western disciples, inspired Indians to rediscover their faith, and likewise, Aindra was fully aware of the impression he made as a white-bodied devotee in Vrindavan. People were especially impressed that he had taken the time and trouble to learn Indian styles of singing and embellishments. "When Indian people take darshan of the Deities and then turn around to look at the kirtan party," he said, "they're surprised to see that it's a white man leading the kirtan. That's a very impressive thing for them, to see that a white man has really embraced their style and their culture, and they really appreciate that."

People were also impressed by how Aindra had sustained the 24-hour kirtan over the years. "Indians appreciate something done steadily over time," Bhurijana Prabhu noted. "That, they know, is devotion. Anyone can do some devotional service for a short time and then something else takes over. The fact that he did that for so many years had such an effect. You can't do something steadily like that without devotion. Because life is just too hard, especially life in Vrindavan."

Incredulous that a Westerner could generate such natural and authentic kirtan, Nalini bought all Aindra's CDs and listened to them constantly. She began writing letters to him and was delighted to receive handwritten replies. When she and her family came to Vrindavan the following year, she offered him full *daṇḍavat* obeisances, her entire body flat on the floor. And when she stood up, she asked him to be her guru.

"Continue listening to the recordings," he told her, "and keep doing kirtan. That's how you can follow me and serve me."

The next day, Nalini gave her husband a donation and asked him to bring it to Aindra, and her teenage nephew went along with him and their son to Aindra's room. On arriving, the three found places among the young men sitting on the floor listening to Rama Raya read stories from the *Bhagavad-gītā*. At one point, Rama Raya's recitation became somewhat dramatic and humorous, and Aindra, who was cooking, interrupted: "I think everyone is paying more attention to the way it's being read, not what's being read!"

When Rama Raya mentioned sowing one's wild oats, Aindra turned to the boys and asked, "Do you know what that means?" They didn't. "You have to control it," he explained. "Try to control your wild oats, especially because you are young. Don't waste your energy trying to mix freely with women. You won't get self-realization that way."

❦ ❦ ❦

Aindra hadn't heard from anyone in his own family for years. His parting with his father had been acrimonious, and the two hadn't been in touch since. Then one day a letter came from his brother John: "Dad is on his deathbed."

Aindra was a renunciant, having given up even his family ties, and his relationship with Art had never been good. Still, it was his father. But what could he do? He was living in Vrindavan and doing everything he could to become a pure devotee. Art, he knew—his whole family—would benefit from that. "If I can go back to Godhead and if I really love him, that's the best thing I can do for him," he said. "So, it's better if I don't divert my focus."

There was also the question of parenthood seen from a Krishna-conscious perspective. "I've had so many parents," Aindra said. "Dog parents, cat parents, ant parents ... and anyway, Radha and Krishna are my real parents." He decided not to respond to his brother's letter and went about the day.

But just before dawn the next morning, he had a dream. An effulgent, angelic male figure came before him and said, "Why didn't you contact your father? You don't know it, but in his previous life he was a fallen disciple of Bhaktisiddhanta Sarasvati. You took birth in his family for the purpose of liberating him. Contact your family and do the needful to deliver him."

Aindra was startled awake. *What should I do?* he wondered. What was "the needful"? Then he remembered the *Padma Purāṇa's Tulasī-māhātmya's* glorification of Tulasi's purity: "If there is a single piece of tulasi wood in the fire of a cremated person, then that person, regardless of how sinful he or she may have been, immediately attains the spiritual world."

After confirming that his father was to be cremated, he sent a strand of tulasi beads, along with several tapes of kirtans he had led and a ten-page handwritten letter to his brother, with Dhanurdhara Swami, who would bring it all to America to be delivered to John. "Please give these beads to our father as a token of my gratitude for his putting up with me in my childhood," he wrote, "and ask Dad to wear them, as an expression of my love. Please make sure the beads are with him when he is cremated. It will liberate him from all his karma."

He told John that life in Vrindavan was like a festival every day. "I'm leading the chanting on all of the cuts," he wrote, "but I didn't put my name on the cassettes—to avoid any unnecessary self-aggrandizement." He had known that John had gotten into Buddhism, so he also included a few philosophical points challenging impersonalism and establishing Vaishnavism.

Art had renewed his Christian faith after Aindra had left, and the family already had burial plots set aside in a cemetery, but Aindra felt confident that his brother would communicate everything properly. Later, John informed him that Art had accepted the gift of tulasi beads, worn them to the end, and said that he wanted to be cremated with them around his neck, which he was. In later years, when their sister, Carlyn, was dying from cancer, John gave her tulasi beads as well—a set that Aindra had given him in the '70s, from when he was first visiting the temple.

CHAPTER NINETEEN

AINDRA WAS WELL known both for his love of and knowledge about esoteric spiritual topics and literatures, especially those regarding the divine love between Radha and Krishna, and for his tendency to expound upon them at length.

Whether he was giving morning *Bhāgavatam* class or speaking at a festival, he could never keep his talk to the allotted time. "If I ever get the chance to speak," he prefaced one Radhastami talk, "I'm usually accustomed to speaking for longer than what I'm supposed to."

"In order to help us to appreciate the importance of Radhastami," he began, "there is some necessity to appreciate the person of Srimati Radharani. And I think the best way to appreciate the beauty of Radharani's personality is, first of all, to hear something from the mouth of Srimati Radharani about Herself, about Her love for Krishna, and about the love of the *vraja-gopīs* for Krishna."

"Why am I relating these pastimes?" he asked. "Because I want to give you some idea of the intensity of Krishna's attraction to Srimati Radharani, and Radharani's attraction to Her beloved Krishna."

"I'm not going read the most intimate parts, so don't worry," he assured his listeners. "That's for you, in the privacy of your *bhajana*. But we should understand that our Radha-Shyamasundar, whom Srila Prabhupada mercifully brought to us by installing the Deities of Radha-Shyamasundar in the temple—these Deities are not just 'Deities'; They are *personalities*.

"And so, as we hear this description, we should try to appreciate that this is the description of the activities of these two personalities, our very own Sri Sri Radha-Shyamasundar. And try to enter into an understanding of the beauty of Radha and Shyamasundar's loving relationships—between Themselves and with all of Their devotees.

"You are invited to have a loving relationship with Srimati Radharani and Her beloved Shyamasundar. And the easiest way is to become gradually educated about the beauty of Their personalities."

He read from Visvanatha Cakravarti Thakur's *Prema-samputa*. Radharani, he explained, was speaking to Krishna, who had disguised Himself as a demigoddess, seeking Her guidance on the topic of pure love. She was stating that She could speak on this topic, Aindra related, because, She said, " ' "I know about love. Even those who are thoroughly learned in all the Vedas cannot understand anything about the way pure divine love manifests—what love is, or what love is not.

" ' "If one tries to describe the topics of pure love to someone desirous of knowing about it, then whatever is described as well as whatever is understood is all merely surface information that cannot possibly convey the truth of such an indescribable phenomenon as love. Purest love is such that, upon being investigated, it immediately disappears, and even if not analyzed, it also disappears....

" ' "When one's mind is endowed with affection, that is purified of all other motives. Being devoid of all forms of discrimination and nondiscrimination alike, it then ascends the lion throne of its own natural position and shines brightly there.

" ' "From this platform, one performs actions only to give pleasure to one's beloved, and whatever happiness one feels by performing such actions is indicative of the presence of pure love. Just as the lion conquers his prey and nourishes himself thereby, similarly this extremely powerful love nourishes itself by instantly consuming the limitless difficulties of all worldly things ... all the difficulties are effortlessly dispelled by pure love." ' "

" ' "This type of divine love,' " She explains, " ' "makes my dearmost beloved Krishna fresh and new from moment to moment.... This standard of pure love is found nowhere but here, in these pasturelands of Vraja." ' "

Aindra called everyone's attention to an important *śloka*: " ' "When this pure love is exhibited externally as if it were lust," ' " Radharani tells Krishna, " ' "then My dearmost beloved experiences limitless happiness. But when someone tries to make their lust look like love, then Krishna, the abode of all clever arts, certainly knows the truth right away, and He doesn't derive the slightest pleasure from it." ' "

Even when She seems to be angry with Krishna, Radharani says, " ' "This chastisement is also only for His pleasure, for it is done only out of pure loving affection for Him. In this way, you can know something about the quality of love that is exhibited here in Vrajabhūmi." ' "

All this, Aindra said, was necessary "to even begin to relish the essential nature of Krishna's *līlās* with Srimati Radharani in the realm of Vraja." And, " ' "by remembering these *līlās*," ' " he quoted Vrindadevi, as recorded in Dhyanacandra Goswami's *Gaura-govindarcana-smarana-paddhati*, " ' "even sinners will be liberated." ' "

"So, if even sinners will be liberated," he added, "then it may also do us well from time to time to take the opportunity to peek into that realm of ambrosial bliss."

When the Divine Couple saw each other, he read, They " 'became intoxicated with transcendental bliss, and Their hearts became conquered by seeing each other's limitless transcendental qualities.' "

But on the way to see Her beloved, "because of Her *mahā-bhāva*, Radharani is seeing everything in the forest as resembling different aspects of Krishna's personality and personal paraphernalia."

So, She now has doubts and turns to Visakha for help. " ' "I am bewildered," ' " She confides in Her friend. " ' "I do not know whether this is my lover, Krishna, or a blue lotus flower standing before the two bumble bees of My eyes. Please tell Me the truth: What is this beautiful object standing before Me?" ' "

Radharani, Aindra explained, had been tricked so many times in the past into thinking that a tamal tree was Krishna and embracing that tree but then becoming embarrassed before Her *gopī* friends when She realized that it wasn't Him.

As he read Visakha's response, Aindra became overwhelmed with emotion. His voice cracked and faltered, and the devotees around him were themselves moved to tears. " ' "Standing before You," ' " he managed, " ' "is the dark tilak that will be drawn in musk on Your forehead. Standing before You is the musk-dot that will be placed on Your chin. Standing before You is the black mascara that will adorn Your eyes. Standing …" ' "

He could no longer speak but just sat in silence for a long minute, tears coursing down his cheeks as he struggled to regain his composure.

"Hare Krishna, Hare Krishna …" he chanted, pulling himself back together. "Please excuse me, please forgive me."

" ' "Standing before You," ' " he continued, weeping openly now, " ' "is Your lover, Krishna. Standing before You is Your supreme good fortune." By seeing each other, the Divine Couple became overwhelmed with ecstatic love.' "

After an hour, Aindra concluded by apologizing to the master of ceremonies for going over time and "begging the forgiveness of any of my superiors who might object to my audacity in reading such things. But because it's Radharani's appearance day and She is especially compassionate—that is why Chaitanya Mahaprabhu is so compassionate, because actually, Mahaprabhu wanted to distribute this *ujjvala-vraja-rasa*, *mādhurya-rasa* especially, to the conditioned souls. So, it would do us well to become at least somewhat acquainted with it in the course of our progress in spiritual life. *Jaya, jaya* Sri Sri Radhe-Shyam!"

❦ ❦ ❦

Aindra took Radharani's statement about Krishna's displeasure over lust masquerading as love seriously. During *Bhāgavatam* class on the following Vasant Panchami, he again addressed the mingling between young men and women at the temple. "We must not exploit the romantic Vasant season for our own Tarzan-meets-Jane pleasures," he admonished. "Unfortunately, the Krishna-Balaram Mandir has become otherwise known as the international meat market, a breeding ground for licentiousness and promiscuity.

"I beg all of you to cease and desist from such nonsense. Better to take shelter of the *adi-rāsa*—the original prototype of this perverted reflection found in the material world—and experience something sublime, something sweet, something actually tasteful."

The class was on *Śrīmad-Bhāgavatam* 10.36.20, in which Kamsa sends the horse-demon, Keshi, to kill Krishna. "Keshi represents the illusion of being a great devotee, or acharya, and therefore attempting to control resources and gain political power in a spiritual institution," Aindra explained. "This tendency must be destroyed before *vraja-prema* can be attained."

But as had happened the previous year, he was interrupted by the ringing of the temple bell. It was nine o'clock, time for class to end. "It's okay," he said. "You can go for *prasādam* now. We won't think that we are better devotees than you."

Then, chuckling, he added, "But I am going to read some things ... so, if you want to hear something really good, stick around." And he launched into a reading and discussion of an incident described in *Ānanda-vṛndāvana-campū* in which Madhumangala plays the role of an omniscient astrologer and tricks the *gopī* mothers-in-law into trying to solve their sons' marriage problems by sending their daughters-in-law out into the forests to worship Kamadeva—continuing for the next two hours.

✢ ✢ ✢

One day, Preeti, several years older now, asked Aindra if there was some way she could help with his dressing of Radhe-Shyam. When Aindra suggested that she could make something out of flowers, she made flower birds.

Aindra indicated some flaws in Preeti's crafting of the birds, but he was delighted with them, and during one stretch when he dressed Radhe-Shyam for fifteen days in a row, he asked her to repeat her efforts.

Preeti made birds and other decorations, also out of flowers, intending some to be for Radharani and some for Shyam, but to her confusion, Aindra would always give most of them to Shyam.

"Prabhu," she said when she saw that Radharani had not received any of her creations, "it's not good that you are giving everything to Shyam."

"No," he replied, "this is the way. If you want to please Radharani, you have to give everything to Him." And again he indicated a few small flaws in her creations.

Every day, Aindra would point out some defect. Finally, on the fifteenth day, Preeti lamented, "Prabhu, I don't think I can ever serve you properly."

"It's not like that," he said. "I am just trying to help you become perfect."

Preeti worked at her father's Internet cafe, and Aindra would occasionally visit their home to speak with him and the family. One day, she was sitting at a computer playing a video game. Absorbed, she bobbed left and right as her game-world motorbike raced and jumped. Then she noticed a distinctive scent, and when she turned, she saw Aindra standing behind her, watching.

"Preeti," he said, "you are in maya!"

During the afternoon some days later, she was sitting in her house relaxing, watching TV and snacking, when she saw Aindra through the window.

"Mommy," she called, "Aindra Prabhu is here!" and she jumped up to greet him.

"Aindra Prabhu," she said, "what do you need?"

Her family was renovating the house, and her father had offered that Aindra could come anytime and take leftover wood for his stove. But Aindra didn't mention anything about wood; he just stared at her with big, dramatic eyes. "I don't need anything," he said, "but what are you doing? Are you watching TV again? The other day you were playing games, and now you're watching TV?"

"I'm sorry, prabhu," Preeti said. "I won't do it again."

❦ ❦ ❦

One morning, a young man knocked on Aindra's door, nervous and wondering if Aindra would answer. He had been told that this was the time of day when Aindra chanted *japa* and that he rarely opened the door for anyone. But he knocked and waited, and after a few minutes the door opened and Aindra poked his head out. "Prabhu," the young man said, "I have some questions about chanting."

Yadavendra das was just nineteen, a university student in Perth.

Like so many others, he'd become attracted to Aindra through his recordings, and he'd arranged a fourteen-hour stopover on the way to England so that he could visit Vrindavan and meet him. He had a question: he'd heard from an ISKCON sannyasi that while chanting, one should concentrate solely on the sound of the Holy Names and not think of anything else. On his mother's instructions, he'd always tried to think about Krishna when he chanted, but he had tried to follow the sannyasi's instructions, and his chanting had diminished and become dry.

When Yadavendra explained the situation and told Aindra what the sannyasi had said, Aindra replied in no uncertain terms: "That's wrong. You're supposed to think of Krishna when you chant." And he began pulling out books, opening them to earmarked pages, and reciting excerpts. He quoted *Harinām Cintāmani*, which explained that one should first meditate on the sound of the name and then, once the sound was clear, on the form associated with the sound. One should meditate on the qualities associated with the person named by the sound and then on the pastimes that express those qualities.

"Bhaktivinoda Thakur says that we must 'seek out the form of the Lord,'" Aindra emphasized. "This is proof that we have to make an endeavor to search for Krishna while chanting."

He suggested that Yadavendra chant on mridanga-shaped beads and stressed the importance of chanting quickly and efficiently. "If someone has taken brahmana initiation," he said, "he should be able to chant with enough concentration that he takes no more than five minutes per round."

How could one chant so quickly? Yadavendra asked.

By chanting on the outgoing as well as the incoming breaths, Aindra explained. To do this, one would have to chant quietly, which was a good method anyway. "You don't have to chant too loud," he added. "It should be loving, like whispering into your lover's ears."

When Aindra demonstrated, Yadavendra found his chanting to be faint and fast but still articulate. "My tongue is vibrating every syllable," Aindra said. "But even if some of the syllables are not clear to the ear, that is not a big problem. Your tongue is still vibrating those syllables." Pulling out an earmarked copy of *Prema Vivarta*, he read, "'Even if you don't hit every syllable perfectly every time, there is no offense, the chanter is not bereft of benefit.' " And, returning to the original question, he said, "You should take your favorite picture and meditate on it while chanting. That will help your *japa*."

CHAPTER TWENTY

V RINDAVAN DAS WAS only thirteen when his father, a disciple of Lokanath Swami, brought him to Krishna-Balaram Mandir. "Look," his father said when they arrived, "that's Aindra." When his father had first heard Aindra's voice from outside the temple, he had thought he was a Bengali devotee. For Vrindavan, "Aindra" was already a household name.

Less than two years later, Vrindavan joined the kirtan party as one of Aindra's primary mridanga players. "Vrindavan is a leading mridanga," Aindra told another drummer, who wasn't happy with his secondary status. "When he's not here, maybe you can be the leader, or someone else. But when he is here you have to follow him; he's my man. And if you don't wanna follow him, then you better don't play because we have to have some things solid here."

Aindra watched over Vrindavan with care. "Actually," Vrindavan remembered, "he was just like my father." But the two also shared a friendship that had nothing to do with their ages. " 'How old are you?" Aindra asked Vrindavan one night the following year. "Only sixteen? I'm fifty, but it doesn't feel like there's any difference in age between us."

"We were just sitting there, hanging out, like friends," Vrindavan recalled.

"We don't consider all those different external designations," Aindra said. "We're just people people."

Another time, when Vrindavan had been spending a lot of time with a devotee who Aindra didn't think provided the best association, Aindra said, "Why do you hang out with him all the time? I'm your friend—why don't you spend more time with me?" It was characteristic for him to express affection and appreciation for a devotee, whether his feelings were a friend's for a friend, a father's for his son, or a son's for his mother.

✤ ✤ ✤

Varun, from England, had been visiting Vrindavan since he was a child, and his family had a second home there. He would go to the temple regularly and play mridanga in the kirtan, but he always left before Aindra came downstairs.

One day in 2003 Varun stayed a little longer than usual and saw him. *Is he Russian?* Varun wondered, seeing Aindra's red beard and pale skin tone. *What a wild appearance! But let's give him a chance.* He remained seated and joined in the kirtan, chanting and drumming, struck by the intensity of Aindra's singing.

After the *ārati*, Varun was with a friend at a shop across the road when Aindra walked in to pick up some supplies. "There's that devotee I was telling you about," he told his friend.

"Hare Krishna, prabhu," he said to Aindra. "You do such nice kirtan."

"Thank you," Aindra replied.

"I'm Varun; who are you?"

"I'm Aindra das. You play really good mridanga. Where did you learn?"

"I never really 'learned,' " Varun said. "I just picked it up and started playing."

"Good!" Aindra said with a smile. "That's how to do it! A disciple once asked Srila Prabhupada, 'How can I learn mridanga?' and Prabhupada said, 'Pick it up and play it.' I would like you to come every evening and play for me."

Varun had only a few more days in Vrindavan, but he spent each evening in the kirtan. Upon returning home, he discovered that the peacock CD he had seen in his father's room was Aindra's and that his parents had a complete collection of Aindra's recordings. He listened to them over and over, looking forward to when he could return to Vrindavan and play with Aindra again.

※ ※ ※

In June of that year, Aindra was working on a new CD—*Vipralambha Nama*. It was a progression from his previous *Vraja Vilasa*, almost as different from his other recordings as they had been from everything else—colored by *vipralambha-bhāva*, the mood of separation.

The CD opens with a lonesome bowed-string instrument winding through a slow raga, joined by kartals and then harmoniums. Aindra's hoarse voice seems to cry in desperation. Gone are his upbeat harp arpeggios, enthusiastic Haribols, and showering crescendos.

"We experimented," remembered Vrindavan, who played percussion. "The stuff we played wasn't like regular kirtan—at all. The rhythmic structures were extraordinary. No one in ISKCON had ever heard this stuff."

Aindra's temple kirtan was changing, too, getting louder and heavier. More than one devotee told him, "I like the way you used to chant," but he would say, "All that mushy-gushy stuff? No. My kirtan is so much better now. It has so much more *bhāva*." And with more people visiting Krishna-Balaram Mandir, he wanted to engage them more fully in the kirtan, to get them to sing and clap and get up and dance—to get more spiritual benefit. Lord Chaitanya's kirtan parties, he pointed out, had not only singers and musicians, but also dancers assigned to each.

The heavy, even aggressive, mood of the new kirtans was not the only feature that raised questions. "Everyone loves the softer, simpler style of kirtan that you used to do," Yadavendra offered one evening. "It seems to be a lot more attractive to people. It helps them sit, get into a nice meditation, follow it, and sing along. When you do kirtan now, everyone in the kirtan party sings along, but no one else can, unless they really focus."

"Do you want to know the real purpose of kirtan?" Aindra asked. "Do you want to know why I do kirtan the way I do? Kirtan is an offering to Krishna. Before *maṅgala-ārati*, the Deities are offered milk sweets, at 7 a.m. sweets and fruits, and at 12 a full meal. It's a variety of offerings. There should be variety in the kirtan offerings.

"In the *nitya-līlā*, Krishna and the *gopīs* go through all six seasons of a year every day in just three and a half hours. First it'll be hot summer and the *mañjarīs* will bring cooling drinks and fan Krishna. Then all of a sudden, to bring an unexpected twist, it will go into winter mode and everyone has to be on the tips of their toes to bring shawls and hot drinks. It keeps changing, because variety is the spice of life.

"So, when I do kirtan, I do it in the mood of the *gopīs* in the *kuñja* with Krishna, going through different seasons. To keep Krishna on His toes (because that's what He is used to), sometimes I will change the beat abruptly, make it slow, make it fast, move into a new raga. Our Shyamasundar is used to so much variety. Just like we decorate Krishna's *mūrti* with varieties of clothes and ornaments, we also have to decorate the *mahā-mantra* with varieties of melodies and beats."

He again referred to the *Govinda-līlāmṛta's* description of the *gopīs* and Krishna singing hundreds of ragas, "all with different types of rhythms. It even describes how their rhythmic programming was very complex—it wasn't simple stuff ... complex singing and rhythmic instrumentation.... It even mentions complexity. Whatever complex musical arrangements Laxmi and Narayana and their associates performed in Vaikuntha, the *gopīs* and Krishna were also doing in *rāsa-līlā*—there are very elaborate descriptions."

Krishna's flute playing is so complex and astounding, he said, "that demigods like Lord Brahma become bewildered and Lord Shiva falls off Nandi the bull, unconscious—they can't understand the musical arrangements. It blows them away! And whatever complex musical and rhythmical arrangements are performed by Lord Brahma and the residents of the higher planetary systems, even more complex musical arrangements are performed by Lakshmi-Narayana and the residents of Vaikuntha, and even more complex are the musical and dancing performances of the *gopīs*, all without any *anyābhilāṣitā-śūnyaṁ*, any ulterior motive or desire for sense gratification—simply one motive: how to please Krishna, how to satisfy Krishna's senses. So, we can't insist that only simple tunes and melodies satisfy Krishna. Krishna enjoys a variety of flavors, many of which are intricate. So don't tell me that Krishna doesn't like complexity!"

"Some devotees complain about the complexity in my style," he acknowledged, "but I think that if you actually listen to the vast majority of my kirtan, it is quite simple if you just pay attention. One thing I try to do is keep people on their toes, forcing devotees who participate with me in kirtan to wake up and tune in and listen more attentively, instead of just putting their mind on automatic."

Adding to kirtans' complexity, Aindra would also change rhythms and melodies. When one of the party members showed him how a contemporary Western band used short cuts in a music video, Aindra said, "You see! This is how I do kirtan! The Kali-yuga attention span is short. You have to keep them on their toes. You have to keep showing them something new. Switch to a new scene, a new angle. Switch to a new melody, a new tempo. Otherwise their attention will drift off and their chanting becomes inattentive. I do my kirtan in such a way that people have to pay attention and listen carefully."

During one kirtan, he called out to the devotees, "Please be attentive while you are singing! When you are doing kirtan with me, you have to be ready for anything!"

Another time, he instructed, "When you're performing *sankīrtana* for the benefit of others, it also means considering how to engage them—how to attract them, how to bring them on board, how to keep their interest up. After all, our intention is to engage others in congregational chanting. So, there *should* be a certain amount of complexity. And people who are musically inclined will recognize when something is a little expert. So, a certain amount of expertise is useful to impressing the public. They'll know what you are doing.

"There should be some variety, because they are coming from that world where the TV has got them running; every two seconds it is changing, changing, changing. They are coming from that conditioning. So, you have to consider that.... And there are many varieties of tastes being generated, along with progressive rhythmic patterns. We use the mridanga and kartals to change up, change over, shift gears, and bring the kirtan into new dimensions. I try to use a variety of technical musical embellishments that I feel enhance the attractiveness of the kirtan.

"My practical experience is that putting the kirtan through changes gets people out of the automatic mode and into the thinking mode. Then, from the thinking mode, you can come to the conscious mode—conscious of what you are doing, conscious of how the kirtan is developing, conscious of the mood the kirtan leader is trying to inspire in the hearts of the other participants, whether the direct inner-circle participants, or the outer-circle public.

"No one said that leading a kirtan is meant to be a cakewalk. It is a sacrifice, an austerity. It is not easy. It is difficult to have the necessary clout, purity of purpose and intention in chanting to inspire people from within to come forward to help. Personally, I don't claim to be so powerful, or so expert, so I have to struggle sometimes just to wake people up to get them to chant. It's not that the tune is too complicated; it's that people are not attentive. So sometimes you have to remind those people again and again, 'Prabhu, Haribol! Chant!' because they are going to get much more benefit by participating in the responsive chanting."

Some devotees complained that the kirtans were just "too much"—too much energy, too complex. It was hard for them to follow. "The rhythm, tempo, and melody kept changing every minute or two," Visakha Priya commented, "and it was just too bewildering for me."

Actually, his shifts followed the traditional Bengali kirtan format pretty closely: he would sing a part of the melody twice, then move to the next part—two leads, two responses. "It was based on a traditional, raga, classical approach," Gopal described, "but embellished and with expressions of deep *bhāva* and *prema* for Krishna."

Still, even the kirtan-party members sometimes had a hard time keeping up. As Vrindavan recounted, "Playing mridanga for Aindra was no easy task, no joke; it wasn't something you could just do. You had to be trained for it—he was such an artist and so specific about what he wanted. His style was so intricate, and he was so musically sensitive, that in order to match his level of kirtan, you would have to be at a certain level, compatible."

It wasn't just a matter of complexity, Aindra explained; there should be contrast: "When we are dressing the Deities, we consider the colors, their relationship to each other. If I have two dark colors,

I'm not going to put them together. There is no contrast; we can't appreciate them. But if I put something brighter and something darker against each other, that enhances them both. Similarly, in mridanga playing, there is simplicity and complexity. And if you apply too much complexity all the time, the listener can't appreciate what's being played, whereas if you apply some simplicity sometimes, the complexity is enhanced."

Following Aindra's shifts, rhythms, and different melodies could be a challenge for musicians playing with him. "You've got to help us out with that one," Gopal implored when he and the others were having a hard time. "We're not getting it. Could you help us out with the response?"

"Okay, just try to listen," Aindra said, slowing down and repeating parts to demonstrate.

"And then we'd listen again and catch it," Gopal recalled. "And we'd do it a few times, we'd do it for a while, and then it would stick and become an easy tune. But it was something new and fresh when we heard him chant in a new melody—it could be like hearing the *mahā-mantra*, experiencing the Holy Name, for the first time."

With Aindra's lead, once they'd learned a tune and could play it together, the kirtan musicians became a cohesive unit, weaving a melodic texture—like Aindra's dressing of the Deities, in constant motion. That quality of dynamic unity was one of the things that had first impressed Amala Harinam. "It was mind-blowing," he remembered, "that kind of teamwork ... Aindra's Prabhu's team was like a band ... everyone was on the same page—and that really awakened the desire in me to join him and serve him in that way."

With repeated exposure, Visakha Priya—and others—started to get it, too. "Gradually I understood what he was doing," she recalled. "By constantly changing the rhythm, tempo, and melody, he was keeping us alive in kirtan. I realized that, generally, my participation in temple kirtans was on automatic pilot—like a somnambulist who walks in his or her sleep, unconscious. So, this was a very enlivening realization, and from that time I tried to attend as many of Aindra's kirtans as I could."

The popularity of Aindra's evening kirtans had grown so much that during Kartik and festivals the temple room would be filled with chanting, clapping, singing devotees. "These kirtans were so powerful—rocking," one devotee remembered. Devotees would bring their own kartals and drums and surround the core kirtan-party devotees across from Radha-Shyamasundar's altar—sometimes a dozen singers and five or six mridanga players drumming at once, creating such an uproar that even Aindra once quipped, "I've been mridanga'd to deaf!"

❦ ❦ ❦

Due to Aindra singing at the top of his lungs for so many years in the extremes of Vrindavan's climate, with dust constantly swirling through the air, his vocal cords had become strained. A doctor told him that their condition was severe enough that if he kept singing he might lose his voice permanently. So for five months Aindra stopped singing entirely and went down to the temple room only once daily to have darshan of the Deities. He became increasingly dependent on kirtan-party members to sit close and sing *with* him on lead, not just in response, sometimes inviting even devotees who were not part of the kirtan department to help. "Together, please!" he would call out. "Ram, Bhag—I need your help! Give it all you got!"

He said that when Mother Yashoda couldn't bind baby Krishna during His Damodara pastimes, she called on her older *gopī* friends to help, and cited the *Caitanya-caritāmṛta's* description of Lord Chaitanya's kirtans having six lead singers singing simultaneously in each of the four groups. "I have incorporated that standard to a large extent in my own endeavors to perform kirtan," he said, "largely because my voice has been destroyed due to so many years of very intense kirtan. My voice has its limitations, but I see that as Krishna's mercy in a few different ways.

"I can't be falsely proud about how beautiful my voice is, because it's not anymore. I ask for others to help me sing the lead when I perform kirtan, which helps to generate enthusiasm and bring more devotees on board. Devotees are naturally eager to help when they see someone needs help, and they become enthusiastic when they are part of the leadership.

"I may still give the impetus to the progressive direction of the kirtan, but for the most part, it is other people who are singing more than me. So, when we go up to the high parts, to 'kill my voice,' then other devotees come and kill their voices, too.

"First of all, it cuts my false pride in my personal ability as far as singing is concerned; second, it helps generate enthusiasm in others to participate, to come forward to help; and third, because then there is more than one person—it is not a one-man show. It is not that there is one egomaniac eager to gratify his earholes by hearing his own voice singing. Rather, it helps to break down the false ego involved in the kirtan leadership so that even if one is not chanting the pure name, still it is a lot closer to the offenseless platform than trying to exploit the kirtan for personal self-aggrandizement. And that goes a long way to help inspire others to feel that they are not just participating in someone's ego trip, which increases their enthusiasm to participate, to come forward to join the kirtan.

"Even if *śuddha-nāma* hasn't condescended to make His divine descent from Goloka Vrindavan to appear in our hearts and dance on our tongues, still there is pure motivation involved, there is a greater degree of purity of purpose, there is a greater degree of cooperation, and there is a greater degree of inspiration for at least making the effort of doing the *yajña* with the prayer that Lord Chaitanya and Lord Nityananda will ultimately have mercy on poor little pathetic us down here cooperating to generate a louder voice to cry out for Their mercy. If there is a louder voice, then there is more hope that Lord Chaitanya will hear, there is more hope that Lord Chaitanya will acknowledge our attempt to selflessly cooperate to generate that louder voice for His pleasure, with the hope that He'll bestow His mercy on us.

"Also, the mass of people are not going to be so expert at picking up exactly what tune was just sung, but if there are expert kirtan responders together singing the correct response, they can help the rest of the devotees respond by giving them the correct tune so that they too can fall into place. In that way, everyone doesn't have to be so expert, strain their brain to remember what was just sung; they have someone expert leading them in their response. That is very useful."

When devotees did come together to chant, Aindra said, "when we all get together and call out with all sincerity, begging for the merciful divine appearance of Sri Radha in our midst—Radha and Krishna, since Radha is never alone, as Krishna is never alone; if Krishna is alone, He's not Krishna, and if Radha is alone, She's not

Radha—Radha and Krishna appear together by Their special mercy upon us and dance in our hearts, dance on our tongues. And when we're dancing in *saṅkīrtana*, at least in our hearts we're dancing in the proximity of that great love flame of Radha. Where there is *rādhā-nāma*, there is Radha. And where Radha is manifest, all of Krishna's *svarūpa* shaktis are manifest, all of his *antaraṅgā* shaktis are manifest.

"So, by dancing in the proximity of the great unlimited love flame of Radha, Radha's love flame for Krishna, in the performance of *saṅkīrtana yajña*, that *svarūpa* shakti, or *antaraṅgā* shakti that's manifest in *śuddha-nāma* rekindles, reawakens the natural brilliance of our spark-like existence, so that we again come to our natural constitutional position of serving to beautify the love flame of Radha. By dancing in Her proximity. This is training, how to dance for Radharani's pleasure. To make a good show for Krishna. A good show of cooperative, loving reciprocation. Krishna just wants that little loving reciprocation from us.

"Of all kinds of kirtan, *nāma-kīrtana* is supreme. And of all varieties of *nāma-kīrtana*, *saṅkīrtana* of the Holy Name is supreme, and of all varieties of *nāma-saṅkīrtana*, *mahā-harināma-saṅkīrtana* is the topmost, absolute topmost *aṅga* of devotional service. Where hundreds of devotees, or thousands of devotees, come together and cooperate together to loudly petition Lord Chaitanya and Lord Nityananda, Radha, and Krishna for Their special causeless mercy for fallen conditioned souls like us.... Krishna is much more impressed with a group effort when he sees that we're surrendering to each other enough and we're dependent on each other enough and we realize that we're not going to be able to make it on our own. We're not standing up trying to be our own man or woman. We need all the help we can get. I'm the personification of that. I need all the help I can get. And especially the more broken down I become, I'm gonna need more and more help. So, I need all of your help. Spirit soul to spirit soul.

"It takes that much humility to get off the egocentric platform long enough, for at least a few hours a day—to come together, realizing that we're all very fallen, we're all very diseased, that we need to take the medicine, we need to take sufficient dosage, and we need to take it often enough. Once in a blue moon is not going to get us well. We're diseased; we're fallen. And Lord Chaitanya has given only one prime process: the prime benediction for humanity at large. Maybe someone can get *arcana-siddhi* and go back home, back to Godhead, but it is unlikely that will even happen if he's not also performing *nāma-sankīrtana*. Srila Prabhupada told Visnujana Maharaja that he had achieved *arcana-siddhi*. But look how much *hari-nāma-sankīrtana* Visnujana Maharaja was performing. It's not enough just to do *archana*, it's not enough just to do Bhagavat *śravaṇa*. It's not enough just to do Bhagavat kirtan. It's not enough just to do book distribution, even though book distribution is described as *bṛhat-kīrtana*. But we also have to come together and perform *nāma-sankīrtana* and really cry out from the heart for Krishna's causeless, merciful dispensation upon fallen conditioned souls like us. From the heart. *Sankīrtana* is meant to be from the heart. Praying to Radha and Krishna to please, please, please, please pick us up from this wretched condition and place us as an atom in the dust of Your lotus feet."

※ ※ ※

Aindra was sometimes asked to distinguish between his kirtans—and devotional, Vedic music in general—and Western music. "There are different ways this question could be answered," he once replied, "but from the standpoint of Krishna consciousness, actually we're not so much interested in music but in the elevation of our consciousness to our original pure state.

"Still, as you see on the streets, we're using mridanga, which is a two-sided drum, and we're using the hand-cymbals, kartals, and sometimes we're using the harmonium. We're using different instruments to produce a musical vibration in the relationship to the chanting of the Holy Names of God. So, it can be said that music does play a part, but it should be understood that we are not musicians."

"If devotees can learn how to play instruments in the Indian classical style," he said, "it goes a long way to enhance the transcultural experience of *sankīrtana*. If you learn how to play the mridanga nicely, according to a traditional mantra system, that generates the type of vibration that takes the kirtan to another cultural dimension.

"Similarly with the violin—someone may play the violin in a Western classical style, but I think for kirtan it is much better to play with an Indian classical style. Have you ever heard Indian classical guitar playing? It's outrageously good, tremendous. Have you ever heard Indian classical clarinet? It's tremendous. Have you ever heard classical Indian flute? Compared to the occidental style of flute or violin playing, the Indian classical style is much more appropriate for kirtan. When you play those instruments in kirtan in a Western style, I think it's not as harmonious.

"The same can be said for harmonium playing. Srila Prabhupada played harmonium in an Indian classical style. He didn't use chords. It's not that the Vedic culture doesn't lend itself to higher cultural expression than other so-called cultures of the world. The highest cultural expressions in the world are Vedic cultural expressions. It's not like you are going to lose something by learning how to play the instruments in accordance with the Vedic way."

When he once walked in on a 24-hour-kirtan devotee joking around by playing chords on his harmonium, Aindra chastised him, "I don't ever want to hear you playing chords on the harmonium! I don't care if you're joking; I don't ever want to hear you play like that! When you play harmonium like that, it reminds me of some kind of Churchianity, or Christian missionaries coming to India to try to convert the heathen Hindus."

Likewise, in singing, Aindra said, "We don't sing harmonies."

"Everything you learned about Western music," he told Akincana Krishna, who had been formally trained and had played in American hardcore bands, "just forget it; just forget about Western music completely and try to learn something about traditional Indian classical music. If you do that and completely forget about Western music, you will lose nothing and you will gain everything. Today's Western culture means no culture; it is a culture of ignorance and passion at best, hardly approaching transcendence in the least."

"At the time, I thought that was slightly fanatical," Akincana later reflected, "but since then, completely on Aindra's inspiration, I've studied with more Indian music teachers, and now I think he was completely right, and I'm so grateful that he saved me from having any illusions about that."

"Vedic culture is meant for elevation of the soul to higher statuses of life," Aindra stated. "So it can be said that the difference between the music used in Vedic culture and the music used in Western culture is that that goal is kept in mind in Vedic culture to elevate the consciousness of the individual to higher statuses of life, higher sensitivity, higher awareness, whereas Western popular music is generally based in sense-gratificatory ideas, which are within the realm of passion and ignorance. Generally, there's very little goodness in modern Western music, whereas Vedic music is meant for elevation at least to the mode of goodness, because from the platform of goodness, knowledge can be illumined.

"Therefore, generally devotees of Krishna don't associate themselves with music produced of the lower modes of nature—passion and ignorance. Rather, they associate themselves with music produced of the mode of goodness, transcendental sound vibrations, so that their Krishna consciousness can be awakened."

Once, when a popular *kīrtanīya* was leading the chanting in Srila Prabhupada's samadhi—a rousing, syncopated rendition of the *mahā-mantra* evoking the sound of American soul music—Aindra, there with a few of his men, remarked on the singer's passionate style. "Do you hear that note?" he asked. "That's the sex note!"

When asked what he meant, what the "sex note" was, Aindra explained it in musical terms: "the flat third"—in Indian classical music the *komal ga*.

"But Aindra Prabhu," one of the devotees questioned, "so many of your tunes have the flat third in it. What's the difference?"

"It's how you sing it," Aindra replied. One's consciousness was often revealed in one's chanting. Some *kīrtanīyas* focused less on the depth of expression, and their singing, its mood, could be more sensual.

"When I came to understand that," Akincana remembered, "I understood that someone's style can make all the difference. Two people can be singing Hare Krishna, even in the same tune but in different styles, and they will produce two different results. One might sing it in a style that expresses great devotion, the other in a sensual way, and that's what Aindra Prabhu meant by the 'sex note'—the expression of a modern, Western style that is associated with and lends itself to more sensual content and consciousness."

The *mahā-mantra* should be sung in *sattva-guṇa*, the mode of goodness, Aindra had been saying, not in passion or ignorance like an American soul singer or Hollywood crooner. *Sattva-guṇa* lets pure consciousness shine through and so was more conducive to spiritual practices.

Sattvik musical instruments, therefore, were better for kirtan. "Lalita-sakhi and Srimati Radharani play the vina," he said. "That is pure sattva, *viśuddha-sattva*, because they play directly for Krishna. The different types of vina, even sitar, are sattvic instruments. When a vina is replicated in *raja*-guṇa, it becomes a guitar, and when a guitar replicates in *tamo*-guṇa, it becomes an electric guitar," the instrument he'd been known for playing before he'd met the devotees.

Finally, though, the key element was devotion: "It doesn't matter whether one is accompanying the kirtan with kartals, mridangas, and harmonium; using a drum set, electric keyboard, and bass guitar; decorating the kirtan with flute and violin; or even just clapping one's hands. One can chant with very melodious classical ragas, or one can sing raucous, hellacious, heavy-metal chanting to attract certain people. One can sing ten tunes an hour or sing one tune every ten hours, sing in complex rhythmic patterns or simple rhythmic ones. One can have jumping, dancing kirtan or a very slow, contemplative kirtan. No matter what you do, no matter how you decorate the kirtan, if such chanting is not done with pure devotion, it will never ever inculcate bhakti into the heart of anyone."

"If you're not chanting *śuddha-nāma*," he said, "then you ain't getting no bhakti-shakti, and you ain't giving no bhakti-shakti. Sankirtan doesn't mean just putting on a big show. *Saṅkīrtana* means that you're chanting *śuddha-nāma*."

The sattvik elements of Vedic culture facilitated the manifestation of Krishna's *dhāma*, which in turn facilitated the manifestation of Krishna *līlā*, which in turn allowed the full manifestation of Krishna's *guṇā*, *rūpa*, and *nāma*. From its first verse, the *Bhāgavatam* explained that Krishna was not separable from His environment—His *dhāma*—so the aspects of Vedic culture involved in the manifestation of Goloka Vrindavan were inseparable from Krishna Himself.

Krishna played a *bansuri*, wore peacock feathers and mascara, milked cows, and ate *makhan* and sandesh, Aindra pointed out, but that didn't mean that He may not also have enjoyed all other varieties of existence, both known and unknown. But these things were not an integral part of how His intrinsic name, form, qualities, and pastimes manifested in their own atmosphere, His own *dhāma*—Śrī Vraja-*dhāma*.

"If you put Krishna in jeans and a cap, that's not Krishna!" he said. Turbans and dhotis were significant parts of Krishna's *dhāma* culture. Changing them to elements like jeans and a cap from a more *rajasika* and *tāmasika* culture changed His surrounding environment, and since that environment was inseparable from Krishna Himself, this hampered the clarity of Krishna's full manifestation.

Putting aside the question of whether or not dhotis or other articles of clothing were originally Vedic, he felt that devotees should dress in the style of traditional Vaishnava culture, since it was "Krishna's culture, the culture He enjoys most," and helped create a "transcultural experience" that was favorable for preaching. Asked about a senior godbrother's position that devotees wearing respectable clothing common to the culture in which they were preaching could help make Krishna consciousness more attractive to Westerners, he said, "I just feel he's wrong about this."

Likewise, he said, Krishna's name likes to be "dressed" in elements of sattvik *dhāma* culture. Changing from a mridanga to an African djembe, for instance, would change the environment surrounding the name and thereby cover its full manifestation. "It's just like if you have a jackhammer for digging up the street. If the jackhammer is going outside your window, it will produce an irritating effect, because it is a destructive sound vibration. The mode of goodness maintains. The mode of passion is creative with the sense of the enjoying spirit. That is symptomatic of the mode of passion, whereas the mode of ignorance is destructive. The mode of passion is very agitating, but the mode of ignorance is devastating."

In regard to the use of harmoniums in kirtan, he said, "I go by Srila Prabhupada's instruction on the matter. First Prabhupada said that the harmonium should not be played in the temple. Why did he say that? I think it was because he didn't like harmoniums being played with Western chords.

"That becomes evident by the time he wrote the third letter on this point. First Prabhupada said that harmoniums couldn't be played in temples, only for festival programs. Then he said that harmonium could be played in the temple but not during the *ārati*. And then, in the third and last letter that came out, Prabhupada said that harmonium can be played during an *ārati*, but 'melodiously.' Melodiously means following the melody line, not hanging on chords. Melodiously means following the way Srila Prabhupada taught us to play harmonium. He recorded the harmonium not just so we can enjoy hearing, but so we can learn how to play the harmonium.

"One time, Srila Prabhupada was asked what kind of instruments were in the spiritual world, and he answered, 'Well, there is mridanga, there are kartals,' and then he said, 'and there is a little harmonium.' Prabhupada appreciated the harmonium enough to import it to the spiritual world. Prabhupada himself played harmonium. And even members of the Gaudiya Maṭha appreciated that Prabhupada's playing of the harmonium was very expert. Prabhupada said that the harmonium creates a nice atmosphere.

"Therefore, I learned how to play harmonium, and I use the harmonium in temple kirtans because Prabhupada said it was okay. He gave his permission. I don't feel that it is altogether wrong to play the harmonium. But I do feel that it is at least somewhat wrong to allow the harmonium to play you.

"In other words, if you are going to play the harmonium, you should be expert enough to play the harmonium like Srila Prabhupada, or at least according to his instructions. Not that you can't get around on the keyboard and that forces your tune to conform to whatever chord you find on the harmonium. Chords destroy the raga system, or imprison it, as Vaiyasaki would say."

Actually, he said, "instruments are important, but we already have all the instruments we need—we have a tongue, and we have ears. So, we have to remember that our performance of *nāma-saṅkīrtana* is primarily based on those instruments. Everything else should be seen as supplementary, or supportive—a decoration to enhance. So, then any other instruments should actually enhance and not detract from the chanting with the tongue and ear.

"That's why I don't allow djembes when I perform *saṅkīrtana*.... It has its appeal, perhaps because it is easier to play than a mridanga nicely. But the djembe is a tamasic instrument, which totally overpowers and obliterates the beauty of the *mādhurya* mridanga vibration." When for a while he had allowed Gopal—who was expert—to occasionally play a djembe, he had seen that local Indian devotees had started copying him, playing it loudly and indiscriminately during *gaura-ārati* in the temple, and had put an immediate end to the practice.

"Of course," Aindra continued, "someone could argue that Lord

Chaitanya didn't have a harmonium, but certainly Lord Chaitanya didn't have a djembe in his *saṅkīrtana* parties. If the djembe must be used at all, it should be used outside. But even then, the tendency is for it to overpower the mridanga and to impede the beauty and sweetness of its vibration to move the heart, which in and of itself is a transcendental sound that moves the heart toward Krishna."

He also opposed the use of accordions in kirtan. "I hate them!" he said. "In my opinion, they make the kirtan leader look like a joke. And they also sound weird to me. They bring back memories of Russian bar music or something. That's why I developed this style of small harmonium—to offer an alternative."

Most important, one should not be attached to any music—be it Western or classical Indian—for sense gratification. "Krishna-conscious music is meant for producing an atmosphere that is conducive for God realization and self-realization," Aindra stated. "In this Krishna consciousness movement, certainly music plays a very big role, but it is not exactly music—it is meditation on God. The music is a part of the meditation. It's like His assistant, assisting in the meditation. In itself, the music has no value. But in relationship to the meditation on the names and forms of the Supreme Personality of Godhead, then it has so much value!"

CHAPTER TWENTY-ONE

ONE DAY IN 2004 Aindra walked into Dvarakanath's shop and said, "Please take me to your home—I really need to cry."

Dvarakanath took him home, and they sat together while Aindra sobbed and explained: "I don't want to leave Vrindavan. I don't want to go to the West each time I have to renew my visa. Please help me."

"Don't worry," Dvarakanath assured him. "Krishna will help you."

"No!" Aindra cried. "Krishna will kick me out of Vrindavan; He won't help me. I need *your* help. Please." The only way he could stay in India permanently and without interruption was if he became a naturalized Indian citizen. He had tried to change his citizenship before and had even hired costly Mathura lawyers (who had cheated him), but all without success.

This time he went directly to the American embassy in Delhi. At the interview, the official couldn't understand why an American would want Indian citizenship. The man opened up the blinds on the window and waved toward the dirty chaos outside. "You really want to renounce being an American?" he asked. "To become a citizen of *this* country?"

Aindra confirmed that yes, that was what he wanted. Vrindavan was the place of his eternal citizenship.

Even after years of paperwork, lunches, and long, tedious meetings with government officials, Dvarakanath was not able to get Aindra an Indian passport, but Aindra appreciated his effort and recognized all the expenses he had taken on for fees and other expenses. One day he walked into Dvarakanath's shop when Dvarakanath was out, handed an envelope to Preeti, and said, "Give this to your father."

When she did and Dvarakanath looked inside, he told her, "Go to the kirtan and ask Aindra to come to the shop as soon as he finishes."

An hour later, she returned with Aindra.

Dvarakanath was hiding his face, sobbing.

"What happened?" Aindra asked. "What's wrong? Are you in a *bhāva*?"

Dvarakanath slammed the envelope on the table and shouted, "What is this?"

"Something for you," Aindra said. "You helped me so much. This is just a little gift."

Dvarakanath was furious. "We are *friends*!" he yelled. How could Aindra give him money, "pay" him like it was some financial exchange? He took Aindra's hands in his, then wrapped his arms around him, and they both embraced and broke down in tears.

Finally Aindra convinced Dvarakanath to keep the money. "But I won't use it in my home," Dvarakanath stipulated. "So, what shall I do with it?"

"Use it for your Deities," Aindra suggested.

They decided to use the money to make a cottage for the family Deities, and Aindra spent the night there, measuring and planning.

❧ ❧ ❧

In the process of securing Aindra's Indian citizenship, Preeti had seen his passport, so she knew his birthday, and her family decided to throw him a party. As far as Aindra knew, he was going over with some of his kirtan men to chant for the family Deities, but when he arrived, the house was decorated, there was a feast waiting, and everyone began singing, "Hare Krishna to you!"

He was surprised but, to everyone's relief, pleased. "How did you know?" he asked.

After the meal, the family brought out a homemade cake. "Blow out the candles," Dvarakanath said.

"No," Aindra replied. "It's not good to blow on Agni."

"Come on, blow them out."

So, Aindra blew on them, and when they were all out, he looked up with childlike pride.

Suddenly the flames came back up. "You didn't blow them out," Dvarakanath said, sounding shocked.

So Aindra blew again, and they all went out ... and then lit again.

Everyone broke into laughter at the gag candles, and Aindra, laughing uproariously, blew them out again and again.

❧ ❧ ❧

Aindra and the 24-hour-kirtan department had always existed hand-to-mouth on whatever donations were offered. And what little money Aindra had he also used to help others, especially *vraja-vāsīs*, whose service he saw as pleasing to Radha and Krishna.

One day, Gopal saw a local rickshaw driver come to Aindra's door and hand him some papers. A few moments later, Aindra put money into the man's hands. When Gopal asked about it, Aindra said, "Didn't you see how yellow his eyes were? He's got jaundice, but he's just a rickshaw-walla; he has no money for medicine. So, I told him to bring me the medical receipts and I would pay the bill."

Sometimes *gosvāmīs* from Vrindavan's poorer temples, like Nityananda Vat, would come to Aindra's door and ask for donations, and it seemed to Gopal that each year more would come, and they would ask for larger and larger donations. One local shopkeeper came every year on the same day, and Aindra would buy him new clothes. "Why are you doing this?" Gopal asked. "You can't let people take advantage of you."

"It's *vraja-vāsī sevā*," Aindra replied. "They need help, and I help them. Haribol."

One family asked him to pay for the repair of their old cowshed.

He gave them ten thousand rupees, and when soon afterwards they asked for more, he gave them another five thousand.

"*Prabhujī*, they are looting you!" protested Damodarastaka das, a cultured young Indian member of the kirtan party.

"I know," Aindra replied, "but they are *vraja-vāsīs*, so I will do *vraja-vāsī sevā* and *go-sevā*."

In 2008, without major regular donors, funds were going out as fast as they came in. Aindra had paid for the renovation of the *gurukula* building, his brahmacaris' medical care and maintenance, and a score of causes and projects—or done the painting, repair, carpentry, and electrical work himself. He had fixed fans and coolers, retiled bathrooms and repaired or replaced their fixtures, installed a large monkey-proof cage on the roof for the kirtan devotees to dry their laundry, and decorated the building's walls. To solve the problems of monkeys rummaging through the building's garbage, overturning the bins and making a big mess, he had designed bins with lids that opened with foot pedals so that devotees wouldn't have to touch them with their hands, and had two made by metalworkers in town.

When asked why he was doing so much of the work himself and not delegating it to others in order to have more time for his sadhana and Deity worship, Aindra replied, "Whatever I am doing is for the pleasure of my guru maharaja and Srimati Radharani!" There was no consideration of "high" or "low" service.

"I'm just a simple sadhu," he said. "Money isn't the most important thing." But the new temple management was pressuring him and other devotees who had been in their positions for a long time to retire from their services. "They think devotional service is like a job," he scoffed. You do it for some time, and then you give it up for retirement. But what they really want is control of our departments so that they can divert whatever donations we get to their central management office. That's why they want us to retire. That would let them bring in new, inexperienced people they can control."

He was disturbed by the new direction of management and wondered what might happen. If he had to leave the Krishna-Balaram Mandir, he considered, maybe he could reestablish the 24-hour-kirtan party in a nearby place, point a loudspeaker in the direction of the temple Deities, do kirtan for them that way. "But I've taken a vow to remain in the institution of my spiritual master for at least fifty years," he said. "So when the day comes that I see Srila Prabhupada again, I can say to him, 'Well, Srila Prabhupada, at least I managed to stay in your institution for fifty years!'"

Yadavendra and his family had donated to the 24-hour-kirtan program over the years, but when he came forward with an offer of monthly support, Aindra was especially pleased and appreciative. "No one has ever done this for me!" he exclaimed with a big smile. "For years, I've wanted to prove to these people that *saṅkīrtana* is not dependent on management. It's self-sustaining, by Krishna's mercy."

Soon thereafter, he told Yadavendra, "I have an idea what to do with the money. I want to spread kirtan all over the world. My CDs have done pretty well, but times have changed. Now everything is about video. So, I want to spread kirtan through TV. I've looked into it, and it will cost two lakh rupees"—about $4,000.

"But don't trust me!" he said with a laugh. "I might not use the money for any of this. I might think, 'To hell with all of this' and use the money to redo the brahmachari bathrooms. I always have some little project going on, and I might suddenly decide to put the money into that instead."

When Yadavendra's father, Rajan Jani, came to Vrindavan with the donation, Aindra was happy to accept it but also warned, "Please don't for a second have the false ego that it is you who are giving this to me," he said. "You must understand that it's Krishna's—this is Krishna's money."

"Yes," Rajan Jani agreed, "it is Krishna's money."

"And Krishna is giving it to me." He showed him some of the video footage he'd shot. At first, he had arranged for a film crew from Delhi to come to Krishna-Balaram with their equipment. It had been an elaborate setup, and they had recorded for four or five hours and charged a hefty amount, but in the end, Aindra hadn't felt that the footage was usable.

Still, though the session hadn't been a success, he had seen how it was done. So he bought a camera with a tripod, and after that, starting around 2004, had all the major festival kirtans recorded. The first usable recording, from Janmastami of that year, was produced on DVD: "Kirtan in Sri Vrindavan Dham 1."

When it became clear that one camera wasn't enough—it would

be boring to watch one angle for the length of the full kirtan—Aindra borrowed a second, and his longtime associate Bhakta Charles had helped with the filming. Later, donations came in for two more cameras, and Devaki Kumar and Bimal Prasad (then still Arjuna Krishna), both from Ukraine, who joined the kirtan party for some years, took over.

It was a difficult project, since, as always, Aindra wanted everything to be done at a high standard, for the result to be as perfect as possible, and the temple room could be loud and the congregation unruly—talking, singing, dancing, milling around, and pushing and shoving each other in the crush. Professional TV crews had men who made space for them and guarded their equipment, but the devotees recording had to fend for themselves as they angled for the best shots and tried to record.

"Sometimes we had to push people back," one crew member recalled. "They were upset, but Indians can be very tolerant. Still, if we had been somewhere else, we would have been beaten."

Over the years, the crew members filmed dozens of kirtans, and the resulting footage improved. There was some discussion about erecting a small crane to move a camera more smoothly above people's heads, but they couldn't work out the logistics.

Along with images of the kirtan party, Aindra also wanted to include shots of the Deities, people singing and dancing, and other scenes, so two of the cameramen remained stationary, filming from two sides of the kirtan, and a third would roam the temple. Sometimes Aindra would indicate a shot with a quick nod or glance. The crew also went around Vrindavan to film temples, trees, animals, and the Yamuna, and traveled to Govardhana to film Giriraj at sunrise.

Over time, the cost of making the videos escalated to almost two lakh rupees per month, and Aindra considered downgrading from the international Aastha TV to Sadhana TV, the less expensive national station, but Yadavendra said he could raise funds for the project from devotees and other well-wishers.

A few of the people Yadavendra approached said that they would have liked to contribute but were concerned that the live kirtans, with several mridangas, were too loud and boisterous to translate well when recorded on video. They hadn't seen the footage, but they preferred Aindra's earlier recordings and wondered if he could capture that mood.

Yadavendra related to Aindra what he had heard. "Maybe if for the videos you did kirtan more like what you used to do," he suggested. "Sweeter, more melodious."

"You don't understand," Aindra said. "The kirtans are sweeter *now*; they have much deeper *bhāva*. *I've* become deeper, and so the kirtans are deeper. I've seen the kind of kirtans they put on television. They can't really change people's hearts, because they are not lively enough, not focused enough, not energetic or pure enough. I want to show the world how we perform *nāma-saṅkīrtana* in Sri Vrindavan-dhāma, in front of Radha-Shyamasundar—so that they will want to come here and participate."

"Have you seen the videos we're using?" he asked.

Yadavendra hadn't. He and the other devotees' concerns had been based on previous recordings of Aindra's live kirtans.

"Why don't you take a look?" As it turned out, Aindra had already addressed the issue. Knowing that several mridangas playing simultaneously could overpower the singing and rest of the kirtan, he'd mic'ed only one, which had resulted in a cleaner audio track.

The following evening, when Aindra sat down in the temple to lead the Kartik prayers, he said, "Okay, everyone—look lively; we're gonna record this!"

CHAPTER TWENTY-TWO

AINDRA OFTEN EXPRESSED his desire to never leave Vrindavan—not even to go to another of the holy *dhāmas*. If someone glorified Mayapur, he would say, "My room is Nitya Navadwip, because my Nitai Saci-suta are there."

But 2004 marked a special, once-in-a-lifetime occasion: huge Deities of Sri Krishna Chaitanya Mahaprabhu and His four associates, the Pancha-Tattva, were scheduled to be installed in the Mayapur temple during a grand festival two weeks before Gaura-purnima. Gopal and Bhagavata Purana were already there, taking a *bhakti-śāstrī* course.

Devotees had invited Aindra to the festival and he had declined, but as the event approached, Gopal could see how significant it would be—it was really going to happen—and that Aindra had to be there.

"It was a bit of a chess match," Gopal described. "I'd say something, and he'd counter it—that was going on for months. Then finally

I just sent him a ticket and a short note: 'Here are the dates—I'll meet you in Calcutta.'

"Aindra's argument, or question, was simple: 'With how many people am I going to be able to do kirtan, compared to what I can do in Vrindavan?' At that time of year, busloads of people were coming to Vraja, and his frame of reference was the last time he had been to Mayapur, for the 500th appearance anniversary of Mahaprabhu in 1986. After everything he had been through in New York, Vrindavan had been his last refuge, and he had taken his vow to never leave. For a long time, it was his room, the temple room, once a year to Radha Kund for a few hours, and that was it. Only later did he start going to Delhi for the day.

"So, he wanted to know how many people would be there. And I told him, 'The management has booked rooms out for ten thousand people. And I'm here, Bhagavata Purana is here, and Rama Raya and everyone else are coming. The only one missing is you.'"

Much had changed in Mayapur since Aindra's last visit. And two years before, in 2002, in the weeks leading up to Gaura-purnima, when Tamal Krishna Goswami, wanting to bring his godbrothers closer together, had hosted nightly kirtans in his quarters, the response had been enthusiastic. Devotees had overflowed the room and lined the outside walkway, so after a few nights, the kirtan had been moved down into the temple room, in front of Pancha Tattva.

Early the next morning, Maharaja had been in a car crash and left his body. But the temple-room kirtan had continued the following year, led by several of ISKCON's leading sannyasis and attended by thousands of devotees. Kirtan had become a prominent feature of Gaura-purnima in Mayapur and, at least in part due to Aindra's influence, was gaining popularity at Krishna-conscious festivals around the world.

Finally Aindra agreed. Vrindavan das accompanied him, and Aindra brought his principal *śilās*, leaving Mahabhagavata and Giridhari in charge of the rest. He brought his own harmonium. "A *kīrtanīya* always brings his own instruments," he had instructed, and wherever he went, he was prepared.

When Aindra entered the temple room, thousands of devotees were engaged in kirtan, and when they saw him, they roared in welcome. Few outside his party had known he was coming, and those who knew him could hardly believe he was there—he hadn't been out of Vraja in almost twenty years.

"Aindra Prabhu!" Radhanath Swami greeted him. "You are here! Now we can be in Mayapur and be in Vrindavan!"

Sivarama Swami, who had just finished singing when Aindra walked in, greeted him warmly, and B.B. Govinda Swami announced, "Aindra Prabhu, Welcome! Haribol!"

The next day, when the curtains to the altar were drawn open and the installation began with the unveiling of the Deities' eyes—Govinda Maharaja leading kirtan—Aindra was standing facing the Deities, one hand raised above his head, the other in his bead bag, tears pouring from his eyes.

After a few minutes, Gopal shook him from his trance and told him that it was time for him to lead the kirtan. Then, Gopal described, "Aindra got on his harmonium, dropped this double beat, and the whole temple room started jumping."

❧ ❧ ❧

Aindra's experience in Mayapur that year drew him back to the Gaura-purnima festival for the next six. He, and thus the other kirtan devotees, was almost always late for the flight. When Rama Raya called for him to hurry up one year, he'd shout back, "What's the sense of getting so angry? If Krishna wants us to go to Mayapur, we'll get there. If not, what's the loss? We'll just stay in Vrindavan with Radhe-Shyam!"

In addition to leading a packed temple of devotees in kirtan, he was also giving Deity-dressing seminars to full classrooms. "He took such a different approach," said Matsya Avatar. "It wasn't technical; it was more of an approach of *bhāva*. While teaching devotees how to dress Radhe-Shyam, he described the whole mood and outlined all the aspects of *rāgānuga-sādhana*. He was speaking with such detail—'See, Radharani actually has two braids coming down through here, and they come and join into one braid. It goes over Her left shoulder and She wears it like this ...' and so on. He said that our mood should be that we want to dress the Deities how They like and that we have to hear from the acharyas how Radharani dresses Herself and how She dresses Krishna, and we have to dress according to *Their* taste, not according to how we want to do it. It was a whole different paradigm." And when Aindra was asked to go on the altar, he dressed Sri Madhava in the same style as he did Sri Shyamasundar in Vrindavan.

"He was starting to open up," Gopal observed, "share more of himself and his realizations with others." He was associating more with his godbrothers, and with the international community of devotees. He would go around and see the festival exhibits, meet with devotees and go to their homes for *prasādam*, go for a dip in the Ganga, associate with Jayapataka Maharaja in his rooms. He would spend hours talking with his old friend Padmalocan das.

"It was a whole part of Aindra that we hadn't seen—coming out and being more sociable. It changed his perception of his place in the movement. He was seeing the impact he was having on devotees all around the world. And after that first year, he really looked forward to the Mayapur festival. We would go on *parikramā* to all the local holy places—Bhaktivinoda's house, Yoga-pitha, Srivas Angam—and it gave him a chance to just chill out."

Aindra loved Mayapur, regretting only that he had not gone sooner. He had a dream in which Srila Prabhupada told him that he had a place for him there, and could even have stayed, he said, if it weren't for his service to the 24-hour kirtan and to Sri Sri Radha-Shyamasundar.

"Great!" one of Aindra's godbrothers reacted when he heard what Aindra was doing and the effect it was having. "This is healthy for him; he needs more of this."

It was healthy in more ways than one. Aindra stayed in Gopal's apartment in Mayapur, and while he was there, Gopal made a point to engage him in some sorely needed physical exercise. In the morning, he would drive Aindra to the temple on his motorcycle for *maṅgala-ārati*, but afterwards he would leave him to walk the half hour or so back.

Along the way, Aindra would pick coriander flowers to offer his Deities. "It is," he said, "the only time I walk all year!"

CHAPTER TWENTY-THREE

SUCIRANI DASI WAS in her early fifties when she'd been diagnosed with an aggressive form of cancer. She had visited doctors and healers around the world, all without success, but when she was in Vrindavan her condition worsened. She had planned to use her ticket to go back home to Australia, but her health had deteriorated so rapidly that she could not even make it to the airport, and it became clear that she would pass away in Vraja.

Aindra was always enthusiastic to serve departing Vaishnavas, and the 24-hour-kirtan crew regularly served devotees by performing bedside kirtan in the final days and moments of their lives, but hearing of Sucirani's desire to leave the *dhāma*, Aindra decided to stay away, thinking that they shouldn't do kirtan for someone who didn't even want to be there. When he heard that Sucirani's plan had been thwarted by fate, however, he changed his mind. "Krishna seems to be making special arrangements for her," he said, "so I should try to help create a favorable atmosphere for her to go back home, back to Godhead."

The first time he went to Sucirani's room, he smiled and told her, "When I heard you were planning on going back to Perth, I told myself that I would not be bothered to do kirtan for such a nonsense."

She laughed and said, "Radharani tricked me."

"There are three kinds of *vraja-vāsīs*," he explained. "One is born here; another lives here; the third dies here. Of the three, the best is the one who dies here."

Even if one had committed offenses to the *dhāma*, he had said, "one who has the good fortune of dying in the *dhāma* is absolved of them all."

"So I feel honored to come do kirtan for someone who will become a topmost *vraja-vāsī*," he told her.

"No," she demurred. "I'm not a topmost *vraja-vāsī*."

"You're not a topmost *vraja-vāsī* now," he said with a laugh. "But when you die, you'll achieve that status." He and the kirtan party came to her room every day and did kirtan in his sweet style of the mid-'90s—which the devotees hadn't heard in years.

Sucirani left her body a few days later. Only then did Aindra let out with an upbeat, lively kirtan, celebrating her departure. "The mood was very somber," Bhurijana Prabhu remembered, "but Aindra refused to allow us to be unhappy. He refused to get on the platform of any understanding other than 'This soul is so fortunate.'"

❧ ❧ ❧

At one point, Dvarakanath also became seriously ill, and it was clear that his end was near. "Call Aindra to come do kirtan," he asked Preeti.

"We will come every night," Aindra promised. When he arrived, he said to Dvarakanath, "I need to know—are we chanting for your recovery, or are we chanting for you to go back to Godhead?"

Dvarakanath simply pointed to a painting on the wall of Krishna dancing with the gopis in the *rāsa-līlā*. And Aindra acknowledged that he understood.

On the third night, Dvarakanath's family moved him from his bed onto the floor to be closer to the dust of Vrindavan and placed a *śālagrāma-śilā* on his forehead and Govardhana *śilās* and a *mahā* flower garland on his chest. Aindra and a few other kirtan devotees sat chanting at his feet.

Dvarakanath's breathing would stop momentarily, then he would awake with a gasp. His sons started crying, but Aindra told them, "You are supposed to help your father—chant the Holy Name."

When the final moment came, Aindra was immersed in kirtan. Only when someone informed him that Dvarakanath had left his body did he pause to look around.

Seeing the entire family in tears, he told them, "This is not what your father wanted."

Preeti placed her head at Aindra's feet. He put his hands on her head and said, "Don't worry. I'll be there for you." Then he looked up and said, "Now we will all do four hours of kirtan for your father."

He came the next day as well, leading the procession from the house to the cremation grounds, and over the next month he stopped by the house frequently to check on everyone's wellbeing.

❧ ❧ ❧

Aindra went to great efforts to take care of the kirtan-party members and attend to their health and comfort as well as possible. "When I first came," one kirtan devotee remembered, "the six of us slept on thin mattresses on the cold cement floor. There was no heating, and it was hard to get up for your night shift. But at his own expense and with his own hands, Aindra constructed wooden bunk beds in all the rooms, with shelf-desks, small lamps, and electric fans. And after that, all the devotees in the brahmacari ashram also wanted the same, so he built bunks for them. Other times, when devotees got sick, he would care for them personally. When I had malaria and was feeling so bad that I thought I was dying, he assured me that if I died in Vraja, it would be very auspicious," but then he went to Loi Bazar and bought glucose and different Ayurvedic medicines, and in a few days I regained my health."

During Govardhana Puja one year, Amala fell ill. He remained in the temple kirtan but was too sick to play mridanga, so he just sat next to Aindra and tried to help him sing. But even that proved difficult.

"What's going on with you?" Aindra asked, noticing his fatigue.

"I don't feel well, prabhu."

Aindra put his hand on his forehead. "You have a fever." He took a Fisherman's Friend lozenge from his box and tossed it into Amala's mouth, then turned his attention back to the kirtan.

Afterwards, as they were walking upstairs, Aindra told Amala, "You're not allowed to be sick. You're too valuable. You have to take care of your health. Do whatever you need to do—go take rest—and get better as fast as you can. We need you in the kirtan."

"When someone tells you that you're needed, it's one of the most important feelings of acknowledgement that you can receive," Amala remembered years later. "And that's why I was there—to serve his 24-hour kirtan ... because I felt that desire, that this was my connection to Krishna, and I wanted to make Krishna happy. And so to see that Aindra was happy that I had pushed through and participated in the kirtan when I was feeling ill, and then how he encouraged me by making me feel like I was needed ... So I said, 'Okay, prabhu, I'll take rest and get better as soon as I can.' And I went up the stairs the rest of the way with a spring in my step: I just really felt loved by him."

❦ ❦ ❦

During one of Yadavendra's visits to Vrindavan, when Aindra greeted him in the temple room, Yadavendra said, "I'm sorry, I can't offer my obeisances to you. I'm having trouble breathing."

"What happened?" Aindra asked.

Yadavendra explained that he had twisted something under his ribs and that even breathing was painful.

"Have you tried homeopathic medicine?" Aindra asked.

"No," Yadavendra replied, "I'm going to a regular doctor. But it's such a shame—I wait all year to see Radhe-Shyam and be in your kirtan, and now I can't experience the visit properly. I don't know why Krishna did this to me."

Aindra smiled and said, "Well, you can hardly expect anything less from a prankster. Do you think Krishna doesn't do this to the *gopīs*? Do you think it doesn't hurt when He scratches their breasts? Do you know how many times He's scratched my breasts, so to speak? And, yes, it hurts! It really does.

"But the reason why He does this is because He wants to get our attention. Do you know why? Because we're not chanting properly.

CHAPTER TWENTY-THREE

We're not chanting with intensity. Sometimes He forces us to leave our paltry bead-bag chanting and really, literally cry out to Him for help. But don't think for a moment that I am going to let Him get away with this. I'm going to get back at Him, in my own way. When I get to the spiritual world, the first thing I am going to do is pinch His butt really hard, and say, 'There You go! Now You know how it feels!' "

"I'm confused about Vaishnava *aparādha*," Yadavendra confided later in his visit. "There seems to be a fine line between stating facts and insulting someone. Can you explain the difference?"

"There is nothing wrong with calling a spade a spade," Aindra replied. "But it becomes an *aparādha* if you exaggerate the facts, making a mountain out of a molehill, as a result of your false sense of ascendency and supremacy. For example, to say that Jagai and Madhai were the most heinous, ruthless humans is not an offense; it's a fact. It is calling a spade a spade. But there should be some purpose, some utility, to stating an unpleasant fact. Otherwise, what is the motive? If we are wasting time discussing the fallen activities of an individual, what's the point?"

"Wouldn't it just be safer if we just don't see the bad in a Vaishnava and only see the good?"

"No, that's wrong," Aindra said. "We have to see and learn from both the good and the bad. But when you see the bad, you should see good in it. When you see someone doing nonsense, you have to ask, 'Why has Krishna put this nonsense in front of me?' Then you will see the good in the bad."

Aindra and Yadavendra were standing in front of Radhe-Shyam one morning while Aindra's friend and godbrother Keshi Damana das gave the class on *Śrīmad-Bhāgavatam*. "Everyone is a bag of stool," Keshi Damana said in his Manchester accent. "Whether you are a forty-year-old bag of stool or a five-year-old bag of stool—a bag of stool, my friends, is nothing but a bag of stool!"

Aindra laughed aloud and took a long, hard look at the Deities. Then he asked Yadavendra, "Do you know the biggest regret in my life? It's 'Why do I have to be a bag of stool for Radhe-Shyam? Why can't I have a proper body with which to serve Them?' I don't want to serve Radhe-Shyam as a bag of stool, because They deserve so much better."

"If I rush to Radhe-Shyam's side to take part in *rāsa-līlā* in this present body with my coppery hair, pot belly, fierce demon eyes, and so on," he said in half jest, "They will just scatter away out of fear!"

❦ ❦ ❦

In contrast to how he cared for others, Aindra pushed himself to the edge of his physical limits and therefore often fell ill. "He got all the diseases you could get in Vrindavan," Gopal remembered, "and then some," suffering from bouts of jaundice, hepatitis, malaria, and typhoid, in addition to almost-constant colds and respiratory ailments. Gopal would check in—"How are you feeling, prabhu? How many hours of sleep did you get? Have you eaten? Have you had anything to drink?"—but it was impossible to keep Aindra to a regular schedule or get him to really take care of himself.

Ati Sundari sometimes noticed him looking weak and pale. "Oh, I'm okay," he would tell her. "I just haven't gotten to sleep or eat for the last couple days."

"What?" she'd ask, alarmed. "Why not?"

"I didn't finish my Deity *sevā* until the sun was rising, so again I had to wait."

One day, Giridhari, concerned about Aindra's health and singing voice, went to his room with a packet of electrolytes. If Aindra's vocal cords became dry, Giridhari told him, there would be more strain on them and they could crack. "How much did you drink today?" he asked.

"Not much," Aindra said. "I didn't have time."

"But the Deity water is right there."

"Somebody came in, we started talking, I lost track of time, and then I didn't have time to drink."

Exasperated, Giridhari took out the electrolytes and was about to pour them into the water jug.

"No!" Aindra stopped him. "Don't do that."

"Prabhu," he said, "you have to drink this," and he began to mix them in.

"I know," Aindra said, "but I'll do it myself."

"I'll do it," Giridhari said.

"No, no," Aindra objected. "I don't want you to serve me."

"Okay, but I'll watch," Giridhari said. "Either you do it right now and drink it right in front of me, or I will do it."

Finally Aindra conceded, stirred the electrolytes into the water, and drank it while Giridhari looked on.

He will not accept service, Giridhari realized. *What will happen when he gets old? He will never allow himself to die in such a way that will require people to serve him.*

When another devotee tried to get Aindra to drink more water, have something to eat, and get more rest, Aindra reacted, "Look, I don't need a mother and I don't need a wife!"

CHAPTER TWENTY-FOUR

AINDRA WAS TRYING to hold the 24-hour-kirtan party together, but it seemed to him like the members were being drawn away into marriage. He didn't mind if a member was married before joining, but if one was already living in the ashram and then decided to marry, Aindra could act as if the young man was divorcing him.

Although he had considered Julie to be like a wife, that had been years before, when they were just teenagers, and he had been strictly celibate ever since. As he had told his temple president in D.C., "I've renounced marriage and embraced the renounced order.... I'm just not grihastha material, period."

Still, one night in his room, replying to a letter asking for advice to householders, he said, "All right. I guess I should make some kind of meager attempt to offer some sanguine advice."

"One of the big reasons why I didn't enter into Krishna-conscious grihastha life," he said, "is because I was told by one devotee when I asked about the prospects of entering into grihastha life, 'Grihastha ashrama, or grihastha life, is like going to a feast on a fast day.'" He was remembering Ananga Manjari dasi's class from 1976. When one evening years later he had seen her in the Krishna-Balaram temple room, he'd rushed over and said, "*Mātājī*, do you remember me? I've never forgotten how you answered my question in that *Bhāgavatam* class! I asked you how to stay renounced, and you said, 'If you are trying to fast, don't go to the feast.' It was the best advice. I've always remembered what you told me, and I repeat it to my brahmacharis.... You're like a mother to me; I think of you as my mother."

"Why go to the feast?" he asked them. "If you're fasting, better to not go to the feast. That seemed to make considerable sense to me. It's just like, if you're fasting on Ekadasi, doing *nirjala*, then why go to a feast? Or if you're doing Chaturmasya *vrata*, then it's better not to go to a feast if there's any risk of breaking your *vrata*, of breaking your fast.

"I considered that for myself, being as fallen as I am, it's better for me not to run the risk of, let's say, possibly trying to enjoy in the grihastha ashrama, for fear of breaking the regulative principles, which really govern the grihastha ashrama and which actually make it ashrama. Living with maya, you can say."

"So, I think the most sanguine advice that I can offer is to quit while you're ahead." He warned the group about other demands put on a husband that could disrupt or slow down his spiritual progress: "Generally, we will find that when you get married, suddenly you don't only have mother and father, but you have mother-in-law, father-in-law, sister-in-law, brother-in-law, and so many others who come along with the package. Then you have so many friends, so many enemies that you never had before. And then the difficulty is that you have to deal with all these people!

"Whereas in the simple brahmachari life you've more or less whittled it down to a fine point: there's only one thing to deal with, and that's service to guru and Krishna. Suddenly, when you enter into the grihastha ashrama, you have to divide your attention. And sometimes it's like, 'One for Krishna, one for me,' then, you know, 'One for Krishna, two for me,' and sometimes it gets worse, until it's 'None for Krishna and all for me' as we fall more and more into the illusion of thinking that our family maintenance and all these things are more of a priority than the service to guru, to Krishna, to the Deity....

"There's nothing saying that a grihastha can't get *bhāva*, can't do the work of getting *bhāva* and *prema* in his grihastha ashrama, but he has to be very diligent! ... He has to remember that it's Krishna's pleasure that is the priority, the foremost consideration. And Krishna's pleasure doesn't mean 'Well, it's pleasing to me, so therefore it must be pleasing to Krishna.' Krishna's pleasure means that I may have to suffer; I may have to sacrifice....

"The most important principle in becoming Krishna conscious is to surrender to the Holy Name, and if you surrender to the Holy Name, if you really surrender to the Holy Name, then Krishna, who is non-different from the Holy Name—or the Holy Name, who is non-different from Krishna—will give you the intelligence as to how to conduct your grihastha affairs in such a way that you can become disentangled from this labyrinth, or network, of misidentification with the body and with bodily extensions and all these things that go along with conditional life and make good progress to the perfection of *prema-bhakti* so that you can be ... let's say, of use to the Hare Krishna movement in a real way."

"Everyone has the desire for kisses and embraces," he later acknowledged. "But for me, brahmacharya is a question of chastity. Just like a married couple are meant to stay chaste and express their desires for intimacy only within the context of their marital relationship. If they express their desires for kisses and embraces to someone other than their spouse, that is irreligious and a disturbance to society. So, my chastity is to Krishna. I will only express my desires for intimacy with Him, not with anyone else."

"But I have so many material desires," one brahmacari complained. "How will I get purified from my material desires if I don't get married?"

"Just do what I did," Aindra replied. "I went on *hari-nāma-saṅkīrtana* for twelve hours a day. I put all my energy into *hari-nāma-saṅkīrtana*, and by doing that, a person can get purified from their material desires."

He cited the example of a kirtan member who had left the group to get married and as a result had reduced the amount of kirtan he was doing: "When he was with me, he was doing kirtan for six hours a day. Now he is doing a lot less. This proves that the grihastha ashrama is an impediment to Krishna consciousness."

And anyway, he pointed out, what man was even qualified to be a husband? "Can you become a protector like Krishna?" he asked another brahmacari who was considering marriage. "Can you be handsome like Him? Can you have power like Him? Can you control like Him? So, can you be a husband like Him? No, you cannot. Then leave the whole affair. Only Krishna can become husband; He is the only purusha. Why are you trying to become husband? Why are you trying to take the position of purusha?"

❧ ❧ ❧

It wasn't marriage to which Aindra objected; it was mundane lust. And it wasn't just men about whom he was concerned; it was all devotees. "Mundane relationships just don't work," he told one young woman.

"But prabhu," the woman had argued, "ninety percent of the world is in a relationship."

"And I'm telling you that it doesn't work," he replied, "so why do you want to be part of the ninety percent? Just be different—don't do it. Give yourself to Krishna."

"But I want someone with me," she said.

"Don't you think that sometimes I feel alone?" Aindra confided. "That's why I have Gaura-Nitai, Nitai Saci-Suta. They're everything. And then I feel okay."

When he heard that Sandesh had developed romantic feelings for someone, he met her outside the temple after kirtan, sent his companions away, and administered a half-hour chastisement. "You're lonely?" he said. "So what? Everyone is lonely—it's because you are separated from Krishna. You should give everything to Him, put all your energy into developing a relationship with Him—chant at least two lakhs of the Holy Name every day and increase that to three! You should follow the example of our acharyas, of Jahnava Mata and Ganga-mata Goswamini. You should be inspired by their sadhana and renunciation and aspire to be like them."

When Sandesh talked about dovetailing her desires with her

devotional life, he retorted, "Get out of maya! Dovetail your fingers, your tongue, to chant! You're not a dove; you're a vulture! Srila Prabhupada said that a vulture has many good qualities—it can fly miles into the sky and has such good eyesight that it can see things from miles away. But for what does a vulture use these qualifications? Just to find a carcass to eat. Instead of trying to attract Krishna, you want to attract a walking carcass of a material so-called man. You are a vulture and a fool!"

Still, although he maintained that the only true love affair was with Krishna, Aindra was not oblivious to people's emotions, and a few days after berating Sandesh, happening to meet her again outside the temple, he gave her a warm smile and asked, "So, how is my little vulture friend doing today?" And thereafter, he gave her CDs of his talks to transcribe and encouraged her to stay in Vrindavan as much as possible and progress in her devotional service.

❧ ❧ ❧

Marriage, Aindra saw, just gave lust more facility, with married devotees being even less likely to remain chaste than single ones. "You're not even supposed to have relations with your fiancée," he told Aranya Bihari das. "Do you know that? Even if you're married to her, you're not supposed to enjoy her. Krishna is the enjoyer, not you. You're not telling me, but I know you're having an illicit connection with your fiancée, and you're spoiling her position as well. She's a devotee; you're spoiling her position."

How could Aranya hope to do service for Radha and Krishna, Aindra asked, if he continued in his lusty ways? "You should be very, very serious about devotional service. If you want *bhukti*, go for it; if you want mukti, go for it; but if you want bhakti, then seriously go for it!"

It was, Aranya remembered, the heaviest chastisement in his life, and it brought him to tears. But Aindra said, "If I don't tell you this, who would? You need help!" And Aranya understood that Aindra was caring for him like a loving father, saving him in his Krishna consciousness.

Even after Aranya got married, Aindra cautioned his wife: "Take a stick in your hand and push away this rascal. Don't let him touch you. You are Krishna's property; you are meant for His enjoyment, not his enjoyment. You need to help him to come out of his addiction; he should be like Bhaktivinoda Thakur."

Devotees were misusing the grihastha ashrama, Aindra thought, entering into it as a way to have sex. As Srila Prabhupada had written in his purport to *Śrīmad-Bhāgavatam* 3.22.11, "The household duty of a man is not to satisfy his sense gratification, but to remain with a wife and children and at the same time attain advancement in spiritual life. One who does not do so is not a householder but a *gṛhamedhī*. Two words are used in Sanskrit literature; one is *gṛhastha*, and the other is *gṛhamedhī*. The difference between *gṛhamedhī* and *gṛhastha* is that *gṛhastha* is an *āśrama*, or spiritual order, but if one simply satisfies his senses as a householder, then he is a *gṛhamedhī*."

"I'm not talking about *gṛhamedhī* life," Aindra told a group of grihastha men one evening. "Marriage life means no sex life. Marriage is for *stopping* sex life, not for going on and on and on with the nonsense." He advised them to be "grihastha brahmacharis," celibate married men—sex only for having children. "And how many children do you want," he asked. "One child? Two? How many can you support? How much trouble do you want to take, for rearing children and all these things? ... You have to control your senses. That is yoga. Otherwise, how are we bhakti yogis? Therefore, grihastha brahmachari: living as a detached grihastha.

"Krishna is the *bhokta*, the Supreme Enjoyer. We are all prakriti, we are all the *bhoga* to be enjoyed by Him. The illusion is that the man is thinking he can be the husband of this so-called poor excuse of a woman in the material world—not actually a woman, because it's the antithesis of genuine spiritual womanhood. Genuine spiritual womanhood wraps Krishna around her little finger by the influence of *prema*. And the antithesis of that is the false shadow reflection of womanhood in this material world wrapping the so-called husband around the little finger by the influence of her lust, which is the diametric opposite of *prema*. Basically nonsense ... two prakritis, one copping, usurping Krishna's position: 'Oh, step aside, Krishna; let me do it on your behalf. I'll be the husband—you don't have to bother Yourself, I'll, you know, play the role on Your behalf.' Diseased condition. Playing husband. Do you know what it means to play husband? It means to play the protector, to play the proprietor, to play the provider, to play the controller, and to play the enjoyer. To play God."

"Only Krishna is the male," he continued. "He's the purusha, He's the *ishvara*, He's the protector, He's the provider, He's the enjoyer, He's the proprietor. And anything other than that conception is sheer illusion. It has nothing to do with Krishna consciousness."

"Therefore," he told them, "the grihastha ashrama is simply a regulative process ... It is not a license for sense gratification; it's a license to go about another way of stopping sex life. Because as long as you're absorbed in sexual fantasies, you're not going to get Krishna. 'Cause you can't have both.... The whole thing is to stop sex life so that you can begin to make some advancement in Krishna consciousness. Begin! Without stopping sex life there's no question of even beginning to make advancement in Krishna consciousness. It's either birth and death or back home, back to Godhead. You make the choice—simple as that."

"You should see women as Radharani's agents," he directed his men. "If a beautiful woman is present, you should think that she is one of Radharani's messengers that has come to check you. If you look at her or think of her with a mood of sense enjoyment, she will report back to Radharani and tell Her, 'This devotee is not yet ready to go back to Godhead.' "

※ ※ ※

When Damodarastaka told Aindra that he was thinking about changing ashramas, Aindra was shocked. "*What?*" he asked in disbelief. "*You?*"

Damodarastaka remained silent.

"Well, who is the girl?" Aindra asked.

Again, no response.

Aindra began lambasting the concept of mundane romantic love. He picked up the Fifth Canto of the *Bhāgavatam*, said, "You don't believe me? You think it's just Aindra's opinion?" and read from one of Prabhupada's purports: "The attraction between man and woman is the cause of bondage for both. Actually both belong to the *parā prakṛti*, the superior energy of the Lord, but both are actually *prakṛti* [female]. However, because both want to enjoy each another, they are sometimes described as *puruṣa* [male]. Actually, neither is *puruṣa*, but both can be superficially described as *puruṣa*." (SB 5.14.28)

Either way one looked at it, he explained, what appeared to be a relationship between man and woman was actually a relation between two female entities, though both behaved in essentially masculine ways.

He read from another purport: "In the material world, a so-called husband is dependent on the control of the Supreme Personality of Godhead. There are many examples of a woman whose husband, being dependent on the result of his own fruitive actions, cannot maintain his wife, her children, her wealth, or her duration of life. Therefore, factually the only real husband of all women is Kṛṣṇa, the supreme husband. Because the *gopīs* were liberated souls, they understood this fact. Therefore they rejected their material husbands and accepted Kṛṣṇa as their real husband. Kṛṣṇa is the real husband not only of the *gopīs* but of every living entity. Everyone should perfectly understand that Kṛṣṇa is the real husband of all living entities, who are described in the *Bhagavad-gītā* as *prakṛti* (female), not *puruṣa* (male). In *Bhagavad-gītā* (10.12), only Kṛṣṇa is addressed as *puruṣa*....

"Kṛṣṇa is the original *puruṣa*, and the living entities are *prakṛti*. Thus Kṛṣṇa is the enjoyer, and all living entities are meant to be enjoyed by Him. Therefore any woman who seeks a material husband for her protection, or any man who desires to become the husband of a woman, is under illusion. To become a husband means to maintain a wife and children nicely by supplying wealth and security. However, a material husband cannot possibly do this, for he is dependent on his *karma*. *Karmaṇā-daiva-netreṇa*: his circumstances are determined by his past fruitive activities. Therefore if one proudly thinks he can protect his wife, he is under illusion. Kṛṣṇa is the only husband, and therefore the relationship between a husband and wife in this material world cannot be absolute." (SB 5.18.19)

"You've been given a human body for engaging in the *hari-nāma-saṅkīrtana* mission of Lord Chaitanya," he explained. "Don't exploit it for any other purpose, and don't allow anyone else to exploit it for their own sense gratification. A real, sincere, fixed devotee will never allow anyone, man or woman, to exploit him or his body."

He rarely allowed anyone to touch his own body, even for medical purposes, and he refused to take massage. "I will never allow anyone to touch this body," he said, "lest I be bound to it or compromise my search for a perfect body in any way!"

Eventually he gave up trying to discourage Damodarastaka from getting married and shifted to advising him how to have an ideal Krishna-conscious marriage: "Okay, so you want to become a grihastha. But you should try to be an *ideal* grihastha. In an ideal marriage both the husband and wife chant one lakh of names every day."

Damodarastaka burst out laughing. "Prabhu, if they can chant one lakh names every day, why would they get married?"

"Because they are in illusion when they get married," Aindra replied. "But now they have come back to consciousness. It can be done. Look at Giridhari and Ati Sundari. I haven't seen a grihastha couple as ideal as they are."

The next day, when Damodarastaka brought him something to eat, Aindra just said, "Get out of maya." He sat down at his computer, but then he turned to Damodarastaka. "How can you guys not become serious," he asked, "even after reading all of Prabhupada's books? I was engaged in illicit sex, too. I was engaged in all sorts of nonsense. But simply by reading one of Prabhupada's books, I gave it all up. Since then, there is only one goal in my life: *kṛṣṇa-premā*. Whatever gets in the way of my goal, I just kick it out. Why can't you do that?"

❧ ❧ ❧

Yadavendra was the next young devotee to tell Aindra he was changing ashramas. "Well, if you're gonna do it, do it like a gentleman," Aindra told him. "Don't be like the rest of the nonsense that's happening these days. The divorce rate in ISKCON is practically as high as in America. So, I hope it works out—I really do."

When Yadavendra's brother Birju was engaged to get married in Vrindavan, he and his fiancée wanted to have kirtan at the ceremony the day before the wedding, with Aindra leading it. Aindra was known to never do kirtan at weddings. He would for devotees' departures and other special events, but never for a wedding. When he was once invited to the Delhi temple but found out when he arrived that it was a wedding, he blindfolded himself, even during the kirtan, so as not to witness the event.

But Yadavendra tried anyway. He sent Aindra an email through another devotee (Aindra didn't have an account), making the case that it would not be a wedding kirtan because it was not the wedding day.

Aindra refused. "It's still in celebration of marriage," he replied. "What difference does it make what day it's on?" And the next time he saw him, as Yadavendra finished offering his obeisances to Srila Prabhupada and the Deities, Aindra pulled him up by the *chādār* and confirmed, "I don't do weddings!"

"Why would you even ask me to do this?" he asked. "I'm a renunciant. A real renunciant has no interest in couples getting married. Okay, Srila Prabhupada did it because he had to. But I don't, and I certainly have no interest in it!"

"But prabhu," Yadavendra repeated, "it's not really for the marriage. We have a lot of international guests who have never been to Vrindavan, and they will not attend many kirtans here in the temple room. I want them to be able to attend kirtan and hear the Holy Name from a sadhu like you. It would be a great *sevā* if you would do this for them."

"Me?" Aindra said. "What's the big deal if I come and do kirtan? Anyway, after two days everyone will forget the kirtan."

But Yadavendra didn't give up, and eventually Aindra said, "Okay, I'll surrender if I must, but just know that I'm still not happy. Anyway, bring your brother to my room and I'll explain the purpose of marriage to him."

That night, Yadavendra brought a nervous Birju up to Aindra's room. "Do you know what Srila Prabhupada said?" Aindra began. "He said, 'If someone gets married after coming to the Krishna consciousness movement, it means he has simply not understood the philosophy.' So ... you've got two days to run away."

Then his stern expression changed into a smile and he began to laugh. "Kishori is a nice girl," he said, referring to Birju's fiancée. "I wish you all the best. But the essence of your duty as a husband is to make sure that you can take her back to Godhead. Don't look at your wife as an object of your enjoyment. Consider her Krishna's and serve her spiritual progress in that mood."

He had specific advice about conception: "You have to wait for the sixteenth day after her menstruation has started. Control yourself—don't get overexcited and go for it on the thirteenth day. On the sixteenth day, you can have a child that is a real sadhu, a 'ray of Vishnu' like Srila Bhaktisiddhanta Sarasvati Thakura."

Birju appreciated Aindra's attention and advice. "No one else would give me the instructions you have given," he said. "A lot of devotees have advised me on marriage, but what you have said I regard as the highest truth."

The day of Birju's wedding kirtan was a busy one for Aindra. He had already done a special kirtan to celebrate the end of the month of Katyayani-*vrata* and had also performed his usual evening kirtan in the temple, after which he had come straight to the wedding event and performed an energetic kirtan for over an hour.

After the kirtan, during people's speeches, Paramadvaita Swami said, "We're very fortunate to have His Grace Aindra Prabhu here, because we all know that he doesn't like weddings and marriage."

Aindra made a mock sour face and gave a thumbs-down gesture, saying "Boo!" and everyone laughed and clapped.

The next morning, after the kirtan, Aindra turned to one of the devotees, pointed to Yadavendra, and joked, "Can you believe it—he made me do kirtan at a wedding!"

"Radhe-Shyam are all I want to see," he said. "They are all I have. I always want to see Them together and happy. I can't stand to see imitation Radha-Krishnas, and I can't stand having to support them by doing kirtan so that they can engage in illicit sex! It's all illicit; none of us are meant to get married. We're supposed to spend our whole lives serving Radha-Krishna. So, how can you expect me to be happy doing kirtan at weddings? It completely contradicts everything I stand for."

❦ ❦ ❦

Despite all of Aindra's warnings about the grihastha ashrama and his instructions about how to avoid it, several of his men left the kirtan party to get married. One night in Mayapur, Gopal turned to Aindra and said, "Prabhu, I think I will be changing my ashrama. My father is suggesting—"

"You know," Aindra interrupted, "if someone orders you to marry, you don't have to follow them. Even if it's your father. Even if it's your guru."

"I know," Gopal replied, "but I've also been personally considering the idea."

For the moment, Aindra didn't say anything more. But back in Vrindavan, he lectured Gopal on the shastras' opinion of marriage. "Let's be honest," he said. "You just want sex. Otherwise, what can a woman offer you that I can't? What does she have that I don't? It's not an 'intimate relationship'; if you want an intimate relationship, I can have a much more intimate relationship with you than she can, and I can take you much closer to Krishna than she can. So, what do you really want a woman for? Sex—that's all! And what does that make you? A complete *aparādhī*! We are supposed to see all women as manifestations of the pleasure potency of Krishna, as *gopīs*, as expansions of Radharani. And what do you want to do with Radharani's expansion? ... You are a complete offender!"

"But prabhu," Gopal argued, "people need physical intimacy too. It's just a requirement of our psychophysical nature."

"To *hell* with your psychophysical nature!" Aindra shouted.

"But Bhaktivinoda Thakur was married and had fourteen children."

"Don't talk to me about Bhaktivinoda Thakur!" Aindra shot back. "Bhaktivinoda Thakur was the topmost *paramahaṁsa*. Why don't you become a *paramahaṁsa*, too, and then talk about how Bhaktivinoda was a married grihastha! Let's be real—you don't want to be like Bhaktivinoda Thakur. If you did, you would want to become a *paramahaṁsa*! What you really want is sex, and that's why you are rejecting me."

Finally, after days of emotional debate, he told Gopal, "Anyway, don't worry. Even if I have to come back to pull you out of the dark well, I will." And late that night, he added, "You know, I don't have a problem with you getting married, as long as she is an Indian girl and can live in Vrindavan. So long as she doesn't try to get in between our relationship, you have my blessings."

In the end, he said, the real question wasn't one's ashrama; those distinctions were necessary only "to the extent that there are residues of the bodily conception of life. There are those amongst us in this Society who are determined to remain attached to their bodily conception of life. And they will determinately attach themselves to the *upādhi*, designation, of being a brahmacari, or the *upādhi* of being a sannyasi, parading around in their masquerade costumes, identifying with the particular role they are endeavoring to model for the benefit of others. But many, in spite of the fact that they were role-modeling as sannyasis or good little brahmacaris or grihasthas with redoubled preaching strength, fell away....

"Just the fact that someone is pigeon-holed as a brahmacari, grihastha, vanaprastha, or sannyasi doesn't guarantee that he is not going to become distracted from his pursuit of the ultimate goal of life.

"As a matter of fact, my personal observation is that over the years, seeing how so many fell away in spite of the fact that they were big this, that, or the other varnashrama-wise, the reason they fell down is because they were not sufficiently encouraged to pursue the *paro-dharma*. They were already distracted, thinking that they had to involve themselves with conditional dharmas more than what was perhaps actually required, and thereby lost valuable time."

Ashrama wasn't the issue, and Aindra didn't treat grihasthas as lesser because of their marital status or try to disturb their position. "Although he was famous for preaching brahmacarya," Amala remembered, "his message was really that no matter your ashrama, the main, most important thing was to take *hari-nāma-saṅkīrtana* seriously. That would solve all your problems."

Nor were Aindra's instructions to his men intended to demean women. Although he advised his men of the dangers of associating with women, that they would be drawn into a web of problems, he also told them to never be offensive. And that is what he modeled: not only did he do his best to apply the standards of Vaishnava etiquette, but he related to them on a whole other, higher platform, as *sakhīs*, fellow assistants to Srimati Radharani.

CHAPTER TWENTY-FIVE

ONE SUMMER AINDRA had Greg, a recent arrival from the U.S., assist him not just in cleaning the bathrooms but also in a much more demanding project. "I've had enough of living in this slum," he said, referring to the kirtan ashram's bare, chipping grey walls. "My spiritual master's ashram looks terrible, and I want to make it beautiful. Let's do something."

Thus began what would become a full renovation of the rooms, stairs, and hallways of the *gurukula* building. Aindra worked every day for months, painting and retiling walls; replacing old, damaged sinks and toilet bowls; tightening and sealing pipes; repairing and installing fixtures; pouring cement; and doing everything he could to improve the building's condition—all at his own expense.

At one point, while Aindra and Greg were carrying a door out to the balcony, Greg remembered, "one of the hinges fell and clanged on the floor. The hinges were still good, and Aindra didn't want to waste anything, so we looked all over for it, but we couldn't find it. 'I think it must have fallen into the toilet,' he said.

"Before I had even finished cussing up a storm in my own head, Aindra said, 'Well, I dropped it, so I gotta take this bullet.' And the next thing I knew, he reached right into the toilet. He was the most senior and respected man in the building—he didn't have to do anything himself; the etiquette was that someone would do it for him—but he was reaching into the toilet. When, after a couple minutes, I found the hinge behind some blocks of wood, Aindra just laughed."

The transformation, which had started with the sculpturing of the walls and ceiling of Aindra's room, spread through the rest of the ashram, along the hallway, and down the stairs. Eventually, the walls along the whole path to the temple courtyard were covered with large, framed laminated pictures of Deities and scenes from *vraja-līlā*, and *gobar*-sculpted bas-reliefs of Goloka Vrindavan: cows, trees with honeycombs hanging from their branches, vines, birds, bees, fruit, Krishna playing His flute on Govardhana Hill, *gopīs* and *gopas*, explosions of blossoms amidst lush forest groves, and the *mahā-mantra* in different language scripts—sculpted from a mixture of cow dung, clay, and glue and then varnished.

Surveying the sculpted scenery, Aindra flashed his mischievous smile and said, "I'm spreading my madness everywhere!" Above the pillar outside his door, he set a painting of Krishna and Balaram going out with Their friends to pasture the cows—a scene from the vision he'd had years before, at the end of his first week in the D.C. temple. And for the area beneath it, he directed the sculpting of a solitary *gopī*.

※ ※ ※

Martanda das, from Poland, joined the kirtan party for six months in 2006 and then came to stay a year later. When he first arrived, Aindra put him on the night shift, from 1:00 to 7:00 in the morning—six hours straight, his usual welcome to new members. "He wasn't sentimental," Martanda remembered. "He wanted to check every devotee—if the devotee was dedicated and willing enough in doing it, because it was a difficult *sevā*. If a devotee was staying for at least six months, then for half of that, or three months, he had to do the night shift.

"He was so open and humble; next to him I was feeling like I was in the presence of my best friend, my best well-wisher, even though sometimes I let him down and did not do my service very well. Sometimes he had to chastise me and preach to me, kind of even turn me upside down with his sharp remarks, but it felt like mercy. After such a chastisement, I felt encouraged, full of energy to do my duty correctly, because in his way of dealing with me, in using strong words, there was no malice, no envy, no desire to put me down. On the contrary, by his words he wanted to uplift you, to ensure that from that time you would be doing your service properly.

"Any contact with him was inspiring, whether he was chastising me or giving me nectar—such spiritual energy was coming from him. At times he could be heavy, but he was never venting out some anger on me—never. He was always talking for my benefit."

Aindra's evening kirtans at Krishna-Balaram Mandir were drawing large, enthusiastic crowds. Every evening by 6:00 (6:30 in the summer), he would come down from his room, crouch over the harmonium on the temple floor facing Sri Sri Krishna-Balaram, and, with his signature intensity, dramatic glances, gestures, and shouts, his left leg extended, banging the floor in rhythm—the room packed with devotees, pilgrims, *vraja-vāsīs*, tourists, visitors—incite everyone to surrender to the kirtan and chant the Holy Name.

Recounting his first sight of Aindra leading the evening kirtan, Martanda said, "My first impression was how much *bhāva* he was putting into it—his whole body was moving so much. My materialistic, conditioned mind could not process it, how someone could put in so much love, dedication, heart, and emotion that his whole body was moving. He was shaking his head, and he wanted to offer all his different emotions to the Holy Name, to offer them to Krishna."

"The kirtan would often start gently," remembered Kaustubha das, Tamal Krishna Goswami's disciple from New York. "So delicate and soft. As the subtleties of the melody became more apparent and everyone became more confident in responding, you could feel the kirtan grow. It might be slow, graceful, and ornate, but you could begin to feel the power just beneath the surface. Soon, under his meticulous direction, the drumbeat would grow ... and as his voice gained strength, it would become clear that although the kirtan was slow, it was massive—an elephant struggling to stand, sluggish but powerful. Step by brawny step, the elephant would push forward, growing in strength. His kirtan was a thing of beauty. You would feel your heart pulled along through so many emotions. Joy and pain, wonder and regret—all were sublime in his kirtans. They were so satisfying, nourishing, edifying to the experience of bhakti. Nightly, large, international groups of people would join together in song and become one—one group united in devotion. Smiles and tears, so many varieties of dance. It was always a joy to see large groups of Indian villagers enter the temple on pilgrimage and take such delight in his kirtan. He never failed to astonish them, this white boy with such deep devotion, playing their folk music with more energy and skill than they had ever seen. The joy in the faces of the ladies as they raised their arms and danced. The village men, smiling with their missing teeth, clapping their hands, throwing back their heads and crying out."

"It was like one body chanting," Govinda dasi agreed, "everyone chanting in one breath. He was able to unite people in that one single effort to call Krishna."

His eyes would shoot flames at the singers and musicians—gesture, correct, direct, instruct—pull them closer, deeper. "C'mon, get in there, soldier!" he would call to a kirtan devotee sitting off to the side. "*Jīv jāgo!*" Wake up! "Follow me! Clap your hands!" The crowd would be drawn in, inching closer, closer, until everyone was pressed tight, some sitting, some dancing—singing, clapping, enveloped by the Holy Name emanating from Aindra in the center.

"The kirtan would just keep growing," Kaustubha described. "It was epic, heroic, relentless, all consuming." The music and chanting would build to a thunderous roar, cresting when the trumpeting of the three pujaris' conch shells announced the beginning of the *ārati*—and finally Aindra would call out, "*JAYA, JAYA SRI RADHAAAYYY ... SHYAM!*"

❦ ❦ ❦

Varun, who had first played mridanga in Aindra's kirtans in 2003, came to Vrindavan whenever he could to participate in the kirtans.

On one *pūrṇimā*, full-moon, day, he approached Aindra in the temple room and said, "I would like to give you a donation."

"Not here," Aindra said. Following his policy to not accept payment for *sankīrtana-sevā*, if he was offered a donation during or after a kirtan, he would put it in the temple donation box, both ensuring his purity of motive and providing an example for others. "Come to my room later. The donation is for my Deities; you should give it to Them."

That night, Varun brought the donation to Aindra's room and placed it at the feet of Nitai. "Prabhu," he said, "you have inspired me so much."

"No, no," Aindra corrected him. "It's not me."

Varun was inspired by Aindra's humility and honesty, his lack of duplicity or personal motivation, and whenever he went back to the West, he was overwhelmed by a desire to return to Vrindavan and see him again.

He was also impressed with how available Aindra made himself—how, when Varun was away, he could reach Aindra by phone.

"Come to Vrindavan!" Aindra would encourage him.

"I'm coming! I'm coming!" Varun would reply.

Varun's parents had reservations about their teenage son spending so much time in Vrindavan, though, especially since the area around the temple and the adjacent MVT guesthouse had become known as a place where boys and girls would intermingle. But Aindra assured them, "Don't worry. I'm concerned about that, too. I'll look after him. I'm recording another album, and I want Varun to play on it."

"We are recording kirtan videos for TV," he told Varun, "and I want you to be the main mridanga player. Go shave off that beard and mustache and put on a dhoti."

Varun was surprised and confused. He didn't think he was nearly as good as Gopal, Govinda, or Vrindavan, Aindra's regular mridanga players. But he didn't refuse the offer. Hoping to improve his playing, he went to the *gurukula* mridanga teacher for lessons, but he was turned away. "If you play in the 24-hour kirtan," the teacher said, "I will not teach you. That kirtan is all speculation. Playing in it will spoil your hand."

Aindra was exasperated. "He always does this," he said when he heard about the comments. "What is he talking about, that if you learn from me you can't play in kirtan? The whole *point* of learning mridanga is to play in kirtan!" When, before joining the kirtan party, Akincana Krishna had told him that he wanted to take mridanga lessons, Aindra had said, "If you're going to be taking mridanga lessons, then you should also join the 24-hour-kirtan department so that you can practically apply your mridanga beats in kirtan. Otherwise, just learning mridanga beats without learning how to use them in kirtan is like memorizing *Bhagavad-gita ślokas* without preaching."

Varun became more and more attached to Aindra and came to regard him as his guru. As had been the case in New York, Aindra attracted a large number of followers, not just members of the 24-hour-kirtan party, and Varun was one of many who yearned for his shelter, even if only informally or in confidence. "Associating with him was the best experience in my life of what shastra describes as a guru-disciple relationship, in terms of how much I got from it and how much my life really changed," one devotee shared, echoing the comments of many of the dozens of young (and some older) devotees who over the years came to Aindra Prabhu's room. They came—some fresh from the *gurukula* experience, challenging any authority and frustrated with ISKCON; some, older devotees who had lost faith in their guru or had other alienating experiences in the movement; others, just ordinary devotees with doubts. And many—younger and older devotees from all over the world—who were secure in their Krishna consciousness but relished Aindra's association and were inspired and nourished by his example and by the knowledge and realizations he shared.

"For so many of us," Varun said, "he taught us the deep value of *harināma*, kirtan, *vraja-vāsa*, *bhāgavata-sevā*, and the inner spiritual meaning of Deity worship as it is taught by the Gaudiya-Vaishnava *sampradāya*. He inspired so many devotees, lit up their faith in Srila Prabhupada and our movement again, showed that you could get everything within the walls of Krishna-Balaram Mandir, from Srila Prabhupada's movement. That was an amazing experience, why so many were drawn to his room and his kirtans. He really was a guru for many of them."

Over a period of years, Varun asked Aindra again and again for initiation and enlisted other devotees to ask on his behalf. But Aindra would not give in. "I'm not going to be a spiritual master," he said. "I'm not qualified. First I want to make a deal with my Nitai Saci-suta that They have to give me *prema*. I want to stand in front of Krishna face to face. I know I'm greedy, but first I just want to experience this once. And I wouldn't want to have to keep coming back to deliver my fallen disciples."

Even though Srila Prabhupada had come to him in his dreams so many times and given him so many instructions, he said, he had never instructed him to take disciples. "If he can speak so many instructions, he could also give the instruction that I should start initiating—he has given so many other instructions. But he has never told me to give initiation to anyone."

"We had Srila Prabhupada, so we didn't have to search or wait for a bona fide spiritual master," Aindra told Varun about his own experience joining the movement. "Now it's a different situation. You may have to wait to find a bona fide spiritual master. You may have to wait lifetimes. But don't take it cheaply. To find a bona fide spiritual master is worth waiting lifetimes."

Even when Varun begged and cried, Aindra refused. "Now you see how hard-hearted I am," he said. "I cannot give you initiation, because I am not qualified. If Nitai Saci-suta personally instructs me to initiate you, only then will I do it. Actually, even if They do, even if Prabhupada comes and tells me to initiate you, I won't. Even if Radhe-Shyam tell me, I won't ... unless They promise me that I'll get *kṛṣṇa-premā* in return. If you can find a single shastra stating that a guru gets *kṛṣṇa-premā* by giving initiation, I'll initiate you immediately."

"But you are my guru!" Varun insisted.

"Don't call me that!" Aindra said. "I hate the g-word. I am nobody's guru. Not even a *śikṣā* guru."

"But you *are* my *śikṣā* guru."

"All right," Aindra agreed. "I am your *śikṣā* guru, and I'm your best friend. See me as your best friend who only wants what's best for you." And later, when he saw how serious Varun had become about his spiritual life, he told him, "You see, look at you now! Once I started to give you *śikṣā*, see how you flourished—only once I started banging on your head!"

"That made me really happy," Varun later remembered, "and it kept my heart pacified. It was hard for me to put my faith in anybody, but I could put it in Aindra."

Most important, Aindra instructed, was to engage fully in chanting with purity. "You can get all the *dīkṣās* in the world," he said. "You can get *dīkṣā* from the topmost *mahābhāgavata*; you can have one thousand *dīkṣās* if you wish, from one *dīkṣā* guru, then from another *dīkṣā* guru, a thousand times, and they may be a thousand times better than each other—this *dīkṣā* guru is better than that *dīkṣā* guru, and that one is better than the previous, and on and on and on! But if you are not chanting *śuddha-nāma*, you will not get anything from your *dīkṣā*! You'll get *bhukti* and mukti."

"Someone," he posited, "may argue, 'Do you mean to say that if we are not chanting *śuddha-nāma*, we shouldn't go out on *saṅkīrtana*? If we are only chanting on the clearing stage, *nāmābhāsa*, we shouldn't go out?' No, I'm not saying that; something is better than nothing. But we should know that we are not actually manifesting the real form of kirtan unless we are chanting *śuddha-nāma*. And it is our greatest responsibility to come to that position."

Even though Aindra refused requests for initiation, however, he was not oblivious to his aspirants' situations and emotions. "They will say, 'But where does that leave us?'" he acknowledged. "There's a bhakta floundering in the ocean of birth and death, and here is this guy [himself] saying, 'I'll be damned if I'm going to accept even one disciple, because my guru maharaja has instructed me that it's best not to accept any'!"

"But that is my guru maharaja's instruction to me. Because he wants me to go back home, back to Godhead; he doesn't want me grounded in the material world! Krishna wants to dance with me in the *rāsa* dance!"

He also questioned the qualifications of those aspiring for his shelter—how much they really wanted it, whether they were really crying for Krishna. "I don't see anyone weeping," he said. "I don't see even one person who is fit to be a disciple. Weeping means what? Weeping one drop? A cup of tears? A bucket of tears? Who is doing that?"

"Crying and crying and crying for Lord Chaitanya's mercy"— that's what was required. And even then, it was still a matter of the mercy of the Holy Name. "*Śuddha-nāma* cannot be chanted by anyone," he stated. "*Śuddha-nāma* has to descend by His own free will, to descend from Goloka to *hari-nāma-saṅkīrtana*, to dance on your tongue. It's *śuddha-nāma* dancing. It looks like the devotee is chanting, so the devotee is getting credit for being the instrument. But actually, it is *nāma*, by His own sweet will, dancing on the tongue of the devotee. It's not the devotee chanting; it's *nāma* dancing, making it look like the devotee is chanting. But in reality, it's *nāma* dancing. And only when *nāma* is satisfied—pleased in some way, generally by the *niṣṭhitā*, strongly determined, *nāma-bhajana*—when Krishna sees that you're actually serious. You're trying to do *nāma-bhajana*—you're doing *ābhāsa-nāma-bhajana*—but Krishna sees if you're actually crying. It's not that you're not supposed to cry for Krishna's mercy when you're chanting the Holy Name. At least that kind of crying—crying because we can't cry—we have to start with that. And anyone can start with it; it's not that you have to be a high, high, exalted devotee to start crying because you can't cry for Krishna's mercy."

"If I had to stay here in the material world until all my nonsense, so-called disciples were delivered," he lamented, "how many millions of lifetimes would He have to wait? Why should I keep Him waiting?"

Still, he never turned his back on any of them. "I won't initiate you," he told one admirer, "but don't worry—no matter what situation you're in in your life, I will always be with you spiritually; I'll always be there for you."

"And anyway," he added only half-jokingly, "you and I will be girlfriends in the spiritual world!"

❦ ❦ ❦

Not all of Aindra's followers were able to keep their devotional practice up to ISKCON's, let alone Aindra's standards, but for Aindra, this was not a matter for compromise. When one devotee pointed out to him that there were people who claimed they were following him who said that they didn't like *japa*, only kirtan, Aindra responded, "Come on, you know me better than that. I never preach such nonsense. I'm chanting a *hundred* and sixteen rounds per day. If someone wants to follow me, at least they can chant their sixteen!"

"Being a follower of Aindra is no small, easy thing," Vrindavan said. "And you can follow, him, but you can't imitate him. Whenever someone tries to imitate him—his dress, his austerities, his sadhana, his Deity worship, his singing—it always falls flat. It's never sustainable or real."

"The 24-hour kirtan is not cheap," Aindra told Radha Krsna. "This is the highest you can get. As a member, you have to set a higher standard than everyone else. You have to realize that you are in Vrindavan and are a part of 24-hour kirtan, which is not a cheap thing. There are many departments in the temple, but the 24-hour-kirtan members are the Special Forces of the temple of ISKCON. So if you want to be there, you have to behave as such, like a soldier, and represent what we are. Because everyone sees the 24-hour kirtan in Vrindavan as something great, and if we just come here to be famous or be respected, like 'Oh, we're powerful saints,' there's no point in it. Because Krishna is looking at you and Krishna knows what are you thinking. And you'll fall down really bad if you use this to promote yourself for some gross stuff. I don't want my men to be cheap; I want them to be sadhus. I want them to be able, if they ever have to go out, to preach to the whole world."

"One day, one of the other devotees had done something he shouldn't have, and he didn't know what to do, how to tell Aindra," Radha Krsna remembered. 'You just have to go up and tell him,' I said. 'He's gonna kill you, but in the end, he'll still be happy with you.' So he went and told him, and Aindra 'killed' him, but in the end he was really nice. And when the devotee came back down, he said, "You were right—it was really sweet in the end." Aindra was always like that—like a lion, but in the end kind ... everything he did was for our own benefit, because he cared."

Radha Krsna was one of those devotees who couldn't play any instruments very well but in whom Aindra saw great potential. "I didn't know anything," he admitted. "First I just played the shaker, but he didn't like it the way I did it. He told me to just grab the thing from both sides and do like that the whole kirtan—'chiki-chiki-chiki-chiki.' So I did that; it was my first personal instruction. But then I just fell in love with the whole thing—his kirtan.

"I learned to play the kartals, and then one day for some reason there was no one there to play good mridanga with him. Someone was playing, but he didn't like it very much. 'I wish Gopal or Vrindavan were here,' he said. 'They're a perfect combo—Vrindavan is all classical and Gopal is all funky.' So, the next day I played with him.

It wasn't great or anything, but he didn't complain; he was just, like, 'Yeah, that's nice.' And then the others came back and I lost my job. He used everything he had—even the worst!"

❦ ❦ ❦

In fact, few devotees could maintain Aindra's intense, steadfast standard of devotion in *any* area of Krishna consciousness. And although he was the inspiration for the young men in the kirtan party, most of them came from non-devotee backgrounds with many of the behaviors and habits common to young people in the West. "Without him, many of the boys would have just been guys who smoke weed and play video games," one devotee commented.

"He was always preaching to his boys about remaining celibate and developing spontaneous attachment to Krishna instead of remaining attached to mundane sex life," Rasesvara agreed. "He always tried to help them understand the highest goals and how they related to practical things like *saṅkīrtana* and brahmacarya—trying to bring them up to a higher level. In time, most of them could not live up to his expectations, but at least they got the taste for chanting and the essence of what Aindra was teaching."

Most of the boys were still attracted by and engaged in more worldly activities, and during the day, when Aindra was in his room, they would sometimes change into gym shorts and walk over to the fields by the temple goshala to play soccer.

One day, needing to inflate the ball before playing, a few of them first went down the main road to an air pump at a rickshaw stand. To their dismay, just at that moment, Aindra rode past on a rickshaw, and he didn't look happy.

"You're in Vrindavan," Aindra told Amala that night, "so you have a great opportunity to advance in Krishna consciousness. You shouldn't waste your time here. Don't wear shorts in Vrindavan. You will feel yourself in the mood of whatever you look like. If you wear shorts here, you will feel like you are in the West, and that is a waste. Even when you sleep or relax, don't wear shorts. Wear a *gāmchā*. That will help you be in the mood of living in Vrindavan."

"Don't wear shorts when you go to bed," he told Nakula das. "Wear a gamcha. When you are in shorts, you are Nikki, when you are in gamcha, you are Nakula."

❦ ❦ ❦

Aindra didn't usually teach kirtan-party members specific tunes; he preferred that they listen to a recording and figure it out themselves. But when Nakula pleaded with him, Aindra showed him a *Vrindavan Mellows* tune in a mixed *śivaranjani* raga that he referred to as the "Bengali fantasy raga."

"This note here is very important," he emphasized. "It breaks the raga rules. It's not even supposed to be in the raga, but I like it. That's my touch. You have to use this note because it makes the tune really good; it makes it sound a lot better than the ordinary raga." He often made use of various *alankaras*, musical ornamentations, giving variety to melodies, an individual touch, but subtly, careful not to distract from the chanting.

When Aindra went into an exposition on all the variations and different subtleties that could embellish the melody, it seemed to Nakula that they were more important to him than the tune itself. This one here, that one there, another one there going into that other one over there ... the combinations were endless.

During one six-hour festival, Nakula was playing mridanga but was in pain from a bad knee. He leaned toward Aindra and said, "My knee is killing me; I can't sit anymore."

"Then just stand up," Aindra told him.

"I'll stand up if you do," Nakula said, embarrassed at the thought of being the only one standing.

Aindra gave him a look, then jumped to his feet. And the entire temple room—and Nakula—leapt up in response.

Aindra sometimes rebuked Nakula for not chanting while he was playing. "Chant!" he yelled at him during one kirtan. "Chant Hare Krishna or I'll kill you!" Then he gave what Nakula described as his "pirate eye," and the two of them broke out in laughter.

He could be also be gentle, especially with new members, and he appreciated if someone was sincerely trying. "The first time I played as the sole mridanga player during his evening kirtan (Gopal was sick), I thought he would be very heavy," Akincana Krishna remembered. "But actually, he was very sweet. My mridanga playing was not very good at all, and at one point he wanted to break down the kirtan. He was singing very intensely, but then he turned to me in a gentle, sweet way and said, 'We're going to break it down now.' At the end of the kirtan, he said, 'Well, at least you kept the beat.' And afterwards, in his room, he said, 'If you want to improve, you need to play more mridanga in kirtan. And practically what that means is that you have to play more mridanga with me.'"

But he did get angry if anyone got distracted or started spacing out. "Chanting!" he would shout. "That's what I want to see! Who's interested in chanting!"

When one member's attention began to drift during a kirtan, Aindra turned to him and said, "You don't have to be here, you know." When another was once looking at a book, Aindra just ripped it from his hands and sat on it. And when a third left the kirtan at the scheduled end time, his duty fulfilled, even though the kirtan was still going on, with Aindra leading, Aindra turned to the rest of the group, and commented, "No *bhāva*."

"Why are you playing kartals like robots?" he scolded two other kirtan musicians. "Put some *bhāva* into it!"

To get kirtan members' attention, he would call out, yell, grab their instruments, even throw them. "When I first started coming around," Govinda remembered, "before I joined the kirtan party, I was playing a gong one time. I was a new devotee and was playing soft and gentle, but Aindra was telling me, 'This is not how you play it.' He was trying to instruct me how to do it. But either it didn't register in my brain or else I was just oblivious to what he was telling me, but I didn't understand, so I kept going wrong. He corrected me two times, and then the third time he just grabbed the gong and threw it into the courtyard! He was upset—lightning in his eyes—but I thought it was just hilarious. And then he started cracking up, too. That's the way he was."

Another time, he threw away an erring musicians' kartals without looking and accidentally hit someone behind him. "I'm sorry!" he said. "Please, just take it as a love bite from Krishna," trying to help the person see it, like Aindra did everything, as *kṛṣṇa-līlā*.

"He just wanted everyone to be focused and serious," said Rama Raya. "'We're not here just banging on instruments,' he would say. 'We're chanting the Holy Name!'"

Even as a newly initiated brahmachari in D.C., Aindra had been known for his stern corrections. And his fire had intensified over time.

But when he chastised one of the kirtan devotees, Bhagavata Purana observed, "it wasn't about humiliating them. Someone might see it and think he was biting the devotee's head off, but he was doing it out of love."

"He fought like an Englishman but had the heart of a Bengali mother," said Aranya, paraphrasing an aphorism from Srila Prabhupada. "Tell me something," Aindra had told him after one tough chastisement. "If I will not say all these things to you, then who will say them?"

PART
THREE

The Heart

CHAPTER ONE

IN 2002 AINDRA had had a series of dreams in which Prabhupada gave him an order: "I want you to write a book—a book about distributing books."

Aindra had been confused. He wasn't a writer, he'd said in one dream, and he hadn't distributed books in more than twenty years. "Well," Srila Prabhupada told him, "then maybe it's time you start."

"I didn't know anything about writing a book," he said; he was feeling a lot of anxiety about it. "But Prabhupada told me to write about book distribution. So, I was thinking what to do."

In 1971, referring to an order he had received from his own spiritual master, Srila Prabhupada had told Giriraj Swami, "One may temporarily suspend the order of the spiritual master, but one should never neglect it. Just like my guru maharaja gave me the order to write, but I am so busy traveling and preaching in India now, I have no time to write. But I am always thinking of his order, and when the opportunity arises, I will take it up again."

Aindra had been considering putting together a compilation of quotes about Radha-Krishna *līlā*, but when his thoughts turned back to his dream, his direction became evident. "All right," he said, "I'll write a book about book distribution ... but I'm gonna do it *my* way!"

"As more and more things came out," he recounted, "it became clear to me by the grace of my spiritual master that there was a serious need to write a book about the relationship between one's internal *bhajana* and external preaching. Prabhupada wanted me to write a book so that the whole purpose behind transcendental book distribution was justified. I could see there was so much book distribution, but how many were understanding the real essence?"

The book's title, he decided early, would be *The Heart of Transcendental Book Distribution*. "The author of this book," he wrote, "has ventured to present his own personal insights into the realm of the Absolute with a view to demonstrate for the benefit of the broad-minded individual the tangible tie between the practical performance of *mahā-mantra-saṅkīrtana* and the vital internal realization of one's constitutional *vraja-svarūpa*." It would strive "to inspire a revolution of understanding. It attempts to deepen the self-searching thoughtfulness essentially required to bridge the apparent dichotomy between a *sādhaka's* inward *bhajana* and outward preaching by illustrating the relative importance of each, as well as their interrelation. Those fortunate souls who absorb this message will find the pathway to the highest regions of *kṛṣṇa-premā* clearly open to them."

"Simply open your heart," he invited the reader in his effusive, erudite style, "and allow the substance of this presentation to transport your inner-dimensional quantum beyond the confines of vapid ecclesiastico-conservative conventionalism to a Kṛṣṇa conscious paradigm of enriched profundity."

He became totally absorbed in the project—writing, rewriting, and reading and showing sections to devotees and asking for their feedback. "Listen to what I just wrote!" he'd say if Matsya Avatar or another devotee came in, and then launch into a recitation. And then he'd listen to their feedback, always looking to improve the writing, add new points. "It's done!" he would exclaim periodically, only to then think of new ideas and new ways to express them. And with the same perfectionism he displayed in producing musical recordings, he kept refining.

It seemed that the project might never end. But over the next six years, with virtually countless drafts and revisions, the manuscript took shape. As always, Aindra's main focus was on the development of Krishna consciousness through the chanting of the Holy Name. His concern, which he had repeated for years, was simple. "The main fault of this Krishna consciousness movement," he said, "is that, especially since the time of Srila Prabhupada's departure, *hari-nāma-saṅkīrtana* has been neglected, terribly neglected all over the world and on account of that, there's so many problems in this movement." But it was also, as he said, about the relationship between his preaching and internal *bhajana*.

When asked why he had written the book, he replied, "Because I really needed to get everything off my chest."

"It was like Aindra incarnated," Rama Raya observed. "It's everything he thought about his entire devotional life."

※ ※ ※

In another dream, Srila Prabhupada had told Aindra that book distribution was not enough. "Our real business," Aindra explained, "is to become *bhajanānandī*, and, by our personal example, to encourage as many others as possible to also become *bhajanānandī*. Book distribution simply facilitates this."

The apparent dichotomy between the internal and external, between practitioner (*bhajanānandī*) and preacher (*goṣṭhyānandī*), Aindra insisted, could be resolved. "Srila Prabhupada harped on becoming *goṣṭhyānandī*," he cited, "but what is Srila Bhaktisiddhanta's definition of *goṣṭhyānandī*? He says, 'The best *goṣṭhyānandī* is the *bhajanānandī* who preaches.'"

"Ultimately," he wrote, "both real *bhajanānanda* and real *goṣṭhyānandī* spontaneously spring from the *ānanda-maya* platform under the influence of the Lord's *hlādinī-śakti* or *svarūpa-śakti*, as per the evolvement of *bhāva* and *prema* when one transcends the influence of the three modes of material nature."

The preaching efforts of a *goṣṭhyānandī*, Aindra understood, are an attempt to share *bhajanānanda*, the joy and realization they gain as a result of their realized practice. You can't give what you don't have. A person who has not realized Krishna consciousness can't spread Krishna consciousness to others. Even to assist another person in spreading Krishna consciousness, one has to increase one's own. Only realized devotees can create realized devotees.

Aindra laid out the movement's mission in the book's opening: "The great necessity in the forward march of any growing religio-cultural institution is to recognize, encourage, responsibly guide, and positively facilitate the inner spiritual development of the society's progressive pure devotional aspirants."

The problem was that the institution had sometimes focused on increasing the external measures of preaching to the neglect of increasing the Krishna-conscious realization of the preachers, thereby risking the preachers' internal *bhajana* and compromising their presentation of the philosophy. Some of the book's passages thus criticize excesses, abuses, mismanagement, and questionable practices in ISKCON, many of which Aindra experienced firsthand. But he didn't just want to criticize; he wanted to focus on the principles and present solutions. Despite the many challenges he had faced under the Society's management, he had never left, and he refrained from placing blame on any individuals or even on the Society itself. "[W]e aim not to rudely impute any wickedness to any individual or body of individuals," he wrote. After all, "Who the hell cares who becomes the next Ravana of institutional mismanagement? God will have to sort that out. The only perfect management is in Vaikuntha anyway."

"Rather, the objective is to practically illustrate how a serious devotional candidate must, when required, transcend institutional atmospheric conditions as a down-to-earth expression of the determination to achieve spiritual perfection, keeping the ultimate mission of *guru* and Kṛṣṇa in view."

Institutions, Aindra knew, are inherently challenging for individual advancement; such progress often happens "not so much because of but in spite of the institution with all its inevitable shortcomings and tribulations ... [but] ultimately, we have only ourselves to blame for our lack of Kṛṣṇa consciousness.... in all soberness, if we ourselves actually want to permanently solve the problems of life, if we seriously want to attain the goal of our *bhajana*, if we want to ascend to the terrace of *prema* and go back to Godhead by the end of this very lifetime, then we really have to surmount our mediocrity and intensely focus, focus, and refocus.... we should not idiotically ignore the obvious implication that it is *we* who have to personally learn and gradually realize the full gamut of progressive pure devotional experience."

Book distribution is ISKCON's most fundamental and classic conception of preaching. But Aindra pointed out that true book distribution means far more than just giving out books. Srila Prabhupada's books, he argued, are *transcendental*. They express concepts that the reader has not directly experienced. The reader therefore needs examples of what is in the books, and the book distributors have to lead lives that provide such examples. Since the books are about *kṛṣṇa-bhakti*, book distribution cannot be successful without the book distributors exemplifying *kṛṣṇa-bhakti*. That requires deep realization of Krishna consciousness, which requires deep *nāma-saṅkīrtana*. Therefore, the heart of transcendental book distribution is *nāma-saṅkīrtana*.

He also countered the misconception that book distribution can replace *nāma-saṅkīrtana*. The saying "Book distribution is as good as *saṅkīrtana*" reveals that they are two different, though related, activities and suggests that book distribution can only be as good as our *nāma-saṅkīrtana*.

Books are *bṛhat*-mridangas, he acknowledged, but the mridanga calls people to participate in *nāma-saṅkīrtana*. This in itself illustrates that books are meant not to replace *nāma-saṅkīrtana* but to enhance and increase it.

And since it attracts people to participate in *saṅkīrtana*, he explained, the mridanga is *gaura-līlā's* analogue to Krishna's flute, which calls the *gopīs* to participate in *rāsa-līlā*. And since a book about Krishna is like a mridanga, ultimately it is a representation of Krishna's flute-song.

If we distribute books, he continued, we call people to Krishna consciousness. But if we provide no living guidance, no tangible example, no viable atmosphere in which those attracted by the books can develop their Krishna consciousness through legitimately advanced *sādhu-saṅga*, then we are guilty of perpetrating a great fraud. It would be like Krishna calling the *gopīs* to *rāsa-līlā* but then hanging a sign on the *vaṁśī-vaṭa* tree saying, *Rāsa Dance Cancelled*. "What a disappointment!" he wrote. "What a let-down! What a treachery!

What a sham! If after so much canvassing, if after answering to so much flute-calling (transcendental book distribution), the excited *vraja-sundarīs* (*bhakta-gaṇa*) find, to their disillusionment, upon arriving at the *rāsa-maṇḍala* (the Hare Krishna movement), no *rāsa-līlā* festival (invigorating, publicly demonstrated *hari-nāma-saṅkīrtana*)! If, upon reading the advertisements (Vaishnava shastras) and expectantly joining Lord Chaitanya's *hari-nāma-saṅkīrtana* movement, having been philosophically persuaded to faithfully surrender to the idea of prosecuting the *yuga-dharma*, *hari-nāma-saṅkīrtana*, one chances to notice a pitiful dearth of *hari-nāma-saṅkīrtana* painfully persisting among the vast majority of the movement's members in most corners of the world, would one not wonder as to whether one had in fact actually found Lord Chaitanya's *saṅkīrtana* movement of the Holy Name?"

Preaching was itself purificatory, some devotees argued; it helped develop Krishna bhakti. And that was true. Still, Aindra pointed out, the "bottom line" of preaching was its efficacy, its effect on listeners. And the quality of that effect depended on the power of the preaching, which depended on the level of realization—Krishna consciousness—of the preacher.

On the topic of guru, Aindra wrote that a preacher could not be effective without being a qualified guru, since *guru*, by definition, is the person who spreads the seeds of bhakti.

Even in a preaching mission like ISKCON, we can't expect everyone to be qualified to be a guru. Aindra compared the Society to a hospital. Most of the people in a hospital are patients, not doctors, but the people who play the role of doctors had better be qualified for it—not that the patient dresses like a doctor and starts imitating one.

He explained that the qualification to be a spiritual doctor, a guru, has nothing to do with institutional tenure, rank, social status, fame, popularity, or success of any sort, nor with academic accomplishments or intellectual prowess. The true qualification of a guru is to clearly comprehend and broadcast the shastric conclusions of the previous acharyas, especially the ultimate conclusion regarding sadhana: to engage wholeheartedly in Krishna *nāma-saṅkīrtana*.

A qualified guru, he wrote, will regularly relish hours upon hours of chanting Krishna's name purely—*śuddha-nāma*—and discussing His beauty, pastimes, and qualities. An unqualified guru will not.

Thus, a qualified guru is easy to spot and does not have to be authorized by any committee.

Aindra explained that a qualified guru should be deeply realized and specific. Otherwise, disciples cannot be effectively guided toward deep and concrete Krishna consciousness. A real guru in Sri Chaitanya's line, therefore, has to practice *rāgānuga-sādhana* deeply and be ready and able to bring disciples to the same depth and specificity of practice.

If there is a paucity of fully qualified gurus, persons of lesser quality can accept stewardship of the post if they do so with utmost humility, allowing—even helping—their disciples find the guidance of more qualified persons.

❧ ❧ ❧

Aindra tried to express his understanding from the acharyas of the best way to practice *rāgānuga-sādhana*—by evoking the mercy of a pure *rasika* Vaishnava. He addressed this by explaining that sadhana was the means to evoke and absorb that mercy.

Rāgānuga-sādhana was an urgent necessity, he explained, but one did not automatically graduate to it simply by following intellect-oriented *vaidhi-sādhana*. To support this, he referenced *Caitanya-caritāmṛta* Ādi.3.16-17, Madhya.9.131; the commentaries of Sri Visvanatha on 1.2.303 of the *Bhakti-rasāmṛta-sindhu*; and Srila Visvanatha Cakravarti Thakur's *Madhurya Kadambinī*.

Rāgānuga-sādhana, he wrote, is not only for perfected souls. As the name implies, *rāgānuga* is a sadhana, a practice, not a *sādhyā*, a perfection. Is it for only extremely advanced practitioners? Aindra noted that Rupa Goswami did not depict it this way; he stated that the qualification for *rāgānuga-sādhana* is simply a strong attraction—*lobha*, greed—to gain a relationship with Krishna. And the way to achieve this is by the revelation that descends in response to deep and extremely elevated *nāma-bhajana*. One must practice, chant, out of *rāga*, intense feeling.

Aindra employed Bhaktivinoda Thakur's analysis that there are two aspects of approaching *rāgānuga-sādhana*, usually referred to as the internal and external approaches, both deriving from the teachings of Swarupa Damodara Goswami.

The external school focuses on the rituals and procedures that support internal meditations; the internal school focuses more directly on the internal emotions, employing devotional poetry and *nāma-bhajana*—particularly *hari-nāma-saṅkīrtana*—to excite devotion for Krishna. Aindra specified that "[t]hough both systems are authorized and useful, either separately or combined, upon careful scrutiny, the characteristic slant of the two distinctive approaches becomes evident." It is, he clarified "undeniably ... Raghunatha Dasa Gosvami's esoteric *antaraṅgā* [internal] method of *rāgānuga* cultivation which eminently stands at the core of Rupanuga Vaisnavism."

He also wrote about the prevalent misconception that *rāgānuga-sādhana* should not be discussed openly. He referred to *Caitanya-caritāmṛta*, in which Krishnadas Kaviraj Goswami says that Mahaprabhu's goal was to spread *rāgānuga-bhakti* to everyone in Kali-yuga and that this was not an internal or esoteric purpose of his descent but the external and exoteric aspect. Aindra called upon devotees to act as servants of Sri Chaitanya Mahaprabhu and to not lock *rāgānuga-sādhana* away in a vault, but to carefully and intelligently explain and extol it whenever and wherever possible.

The goal of *rāgānuga-sādhana* is *vraja-prema*, the divine love of Godhead found in the residents of Vraja-*dhāma*. If *vraja-prema* is not promoted, the souls of Kali-yuga won't have any hope of experiencing a truly higher taste and will forever continue to be devoured and depressed by infinite variations of impersonalism, *sahajiyāism*, commercialism, and hedonism.

❦ ❦ ❦

Finally, Aindra presented *vraja-prema*, which is intensified by the constant fear of losing Krishna, as the ultimate form of *prema*, the highest expression of love of God, and most satisfying to Krishna among all varieties of loving exchanges in the spiritual realm, embellished by both *parakīya* (belonging to someone else) and *vipralambha* (the feeling of separation from the beloved). "The *parakīya* element in *vraja-līlā*," he wrote, "certainly intensifies in various ways the *prīti-bhajana* of the Lord's *rāgātmika* associates. This enhances the Lord's *ānanda-maya* reciprocal dealings with them in a myriad of ways, making them the objects of His special consideration and affection."

Vipralambha and *parakīya* affect everyone in Vrindavan, not just the *gopīs*. Everyone knows in the back of their minds that Krishna is completely independent and can go anywhere He likes at any time.

The hearts of the *vraja-gopīs* are particularly resplendent with *vraja-prema*. Its *parakīya* nature leaves them in constant fear of being unable to meet Krishna and thereby intensifies even the slightest affectionate exchange.

The lack of availability of the *vraja-gopīs* also naturally increases and enhances Krishna's attraction to their beauty and love. Thus, *vipralambha* and *parakīya* act even upon Him and delight Him. He also wants to experience it directly—the thrill of belonging to someone else. Some *gopīs*, like Candravali, feel, "I belong to Him," but they do not delight Krishna as much as those, like Radharani, who think, *He belongs to Me*.

Even less accessible are Radharani's maidservants, the *mañjarīs*. They *twice* belong to another, first by their married state and second by their exclusive loyalty to Radharani. "Seeing the *mañjarīs*' unrivaled love for Radhika," Aindra described, "a love that has outclassed even His own, and seeing the *mañjarīs*' purest motive to intently serve to fulfill Her purposes, enthusiastic Krsna inundates her with His own amplified love-bliss, unknown even to His own devotees. Even so, the *mañjarīs* resolve to sympathetically savor Radhika's sweetest ecstasies, which exceed Krsna's *ānanda* ten million fold, keeps her always fixed and victorious."

One is the *mañjarīs*' abilities, he explained, is, by Radha's grace, to withstand Krishna's advances: "There are many times (perhaps more often than not) when a *mañjarī* must thoroughly resist Krishna's advances in order to safeguard her integrity as Radha's confidential *kiṅkarī*. The *parakīya* sense of belonging to Radha rather than to Krsna fortunately affords her the necessary footing and firmness to successfully accomplish the task. This bears special significance particularly for the *sādhana-siddha mañjarīs*, who are *vibhinnāṁśa-jīvātmās* possessed of limited potency. They are *aṇu*, very insignificant, whereas Krsna is *vibhu*, unlimitedly great and omnipotent. On her own, the *sādhana-siddha mañjarī* could hardly hope to withstand the onslaught of Krsna's unlimited attractiveness, sweetness, beauty, and handsomeness. How could she resist Him? Can a particle of iron escape the force field of a great magnet? Highly unlikely. Yet, if there is the influence of a greater magnetism, if the *sādhana-siddha mañjarī* is constantly bound by the force of greater attraction, greater sweetness, and greater beauty, she can easily deflect His absolute unlimited wantonness. That is Sri Radhika. *Daivim prakrtim asritah*. Without Her shelter, who could stand a chance?"

He also pointed out that the position of Radha's *mañjarīs* is especially relevant to the *jīva*. Devotional proximity to Sri Radha is the one compelling quality by which a *jīva* can attract the unlimited attractor, Sri Krishna. *Hare* (a call to Radharani) is the most frequently repeated word in the *mahā-mantra*. It affords us more opportunity to associate with Her and thus become attractive to the all-blissful (*Rama*) and all-attractive (*Krishna*) Supreme Person.

Krishna and the *mañjarīs* have a uniquely intimate and dynamic relationship, on the common ground that They both give Their hearts to Radharani. And because the *mañjarīs* are completely devoted to Her, they do not have any inclination toward any kind of independent romantic relationship with Krishna, though, Aindra asserts, "having not even the slightest desire to directly associate with the rascally Krsna, having no desire other than to serve Radha's lotus feet, Radha's maidservants naturally gain optimum access to the loftiest communion with Radharani's *svayaṁ-rūpa* Krsna, unimaginable to Radha's other categories of *sakhīs* and Krsna's various other *yūtheśvarī* mistresses."

Radha and Krishna therefore welcome their services even in the most personal and intimate settings, where only friends of the most heartfelt confidentiality can be permitted.

❦ ❦ ❦

The book also addresses problems within ISKCON. To the claim that the Society is beyond reproach because it is Srila Prabhupada's body and therefore any criticism of it is a criticism of him, Aindra replied that if we accept ISKCON as Prabhupada's body, then it is our duty to keep his body healthy, to point out and help remove any flaws that negatively impact what Prabhupada worked so hard and long to build.

Having flaws, Aindra wrote, doesn't mean not also having purity. He cited the Ganges and Yamuna, which remain spiritually pure in spite of the sewage that flows into them. He presented reform not as a social or political affair but as a personal and individual endeavor. The more each individual member becomes absorbed in relishing the mellows of the pure *kṛṣṇa-bhakti*, the more the entire Society will improve. And since those mellows are accessible through *nāma-saṅkīrtana*, the more the individual members dedicate themselves to *prema-nāma-saṅkīrtana*, the more easily the Society will reach its full potential.

"They who are internally advanced enough to precisely distinguish and wholly surrender to the influence of the Lord's divine loving network," he continued, "undoubtedly inherit the privilege of assisting Him as His authorized sampradayic agents. If we don't act as His instruments to purely propagate the full gamut of essential teachings of the *rūpānuga* tradition, it is not that no one will come forward to do the needful. Lord Krsna instructed Arjuna, 'Even if you do not fight, all the warriors assembled on this battlefield are already put to death by my arrangement. Therefore, relinquish your petty weakness of heart! Acting as My instrument, stand up and fight!' Similarly, Lord Caitanya has enjoined that the Krsna consciousness movement be spread to every town and village throughout the world. And 'spread' means to spread in terms of the aforementioned purpose for which the movement is actually meant—to raise people to the path of spontaneous loving devotion, principally by way of congregational chanting of the Holy Name—thus giving them the chance to evolve to the stages of *rāgānuga-bhāva* and *vraja-prema* in this lifetime, not after some future millions of births, who knows how far down the road. Mahaprabhu's purposes will certainly be fulfilled in some way or other by someone; do not think otherwise."

❦ ❦ ❦

Although bhakti is beyond social principles, Aindra wrote, the Krishna consciousness movement should conduct itself in accordance with the Vedic social blueprint, varnashrama. And the success of varnashrama depends upon having learned, objective, and humble brahmanas who inspire powerful kshatriyas to take shelter of their guidance and impartial judgment and thus successfully keep the vaishya and sudra sectors productive and satisfied. It would be a mistake, Aindra explained, to have kshatriya managers hold posts of brahmana leadership. Power must be subordinate to wisdom.

Even the Vedic philosopher-kings, called *rājarṣis* because they were both powerful (*rāja*) and wise (*ṛṣi*), submitted themselves to the guidance of the brahmanas.

❦ ❦ ❦

For Aindra, *The Heart of Transcendental Book Distribution* would be the culmination of decades of realization from hearing, chanting in *japa* and kirtan, preaching, doing Deity worship, and promoting the primacy of *hari-nāma-saṅkīrtana* in the Krishna consciousness movement. Within, he was offering both philosophical analysis and practical application, comprehensively presenting the spiritual truths of Gaudiya-Vaishnava *siddhānta*, with an emphasis on the *yuga-dharma*, *hari-nāma-saṅkīrtana*.

CHAPTER TWO

AS THE BOOK came together, Aindra had a vision for a cover that would visually convey its central theme—a painting that would show the *saṅkīrtana* of *gaura-līlā* as identical to the *rāsa-bhajana* of *kṛṣṇa-līlā*, illustrating the ultimate manifestation of the principle that *saṅkīrtana* preaching and the practices of *bhajana* are two aspects of a single truth.

The design came from a poster he'd seen in Loi Bazaar. His idea was to use lenticular imaging to show two paintings—one of *gaura-līlā* and the other of *kṛṣṇa-līlā*—at the same time. If you looked at the book cover from one angle, you would see figures in *gaura-līlā*; if you looked from another, you would see these same figures in *kṛṣṇa-līlā*.

Aindra sketched out the idea with one or two artists, then turned to a Russian devotee, Lila Sravani dasi, who had previously asked if she could help. He explained what he wanted, and for a few months Lila painted at home and then came to the temple to show him the matching paintings. "This is nice!" he said, but he wanted to add some details.

The details were too fine for the small, rough canvases Lila was using, so they decided to Photoshop them in. Getting the two paintings to align exactly would require digital editing anyway.

"We would sit together for hours and hours at a desk working with a very old, donated computer," Lila recounted. "I never felt at all shy or uncomfortable around him; he was just so simple and so serious. Actually, whenever I was with him, I always felt so artificial. His simplicity and honesty made me feel very artificial by comparison.

"I was not a very serious devotee, so I didn't always ask him very serious questions, but his simplicity impressed me. I understood that a real holy person should be very simple."

"I am a young woman," Lila once said to Aindra. "I have so many material desires. What should I do?"

Aindra told her the story of Haridas Thakur and the prostitute. "Almost everyone tells this story focused on the greatness of Haridas Thakur," he said, "but what about the prostitute? What was it like for her? What was she thinking and feeling? Haridas Thakur instructed her to chant the *mahā-mantra* in front of Tulasi, and she immediately gave up all her wealth, fancy clothes, jewels—everything—and followed his instruction. But she had memories that were not as easy to get rid of. She would remember her former lifestyle, her partners, their love affairs, and the memories troubled her with lust and material desire.

"So, what did she do? She cut her food in half and increased her chanting. That is the secret. If you cut down your eating and increase your chanting, the material desires lingering from memories of your previous way of life will decrease and you will be able to overcome them."

Aindra and Lila worked for months on the specifics of the cover. She was amazed by how much detail he wanted. Each *gopī* was a specific personality from *kṛṣṇa-līlā*, with a corresponding form in *gaura-līlā*, and he gave elaborate instructions about how to decorate each one. "Radharani should have peacock feathers in her hair," he said. "They should all wear shades of white, because it is a full moon night." "Decorate Lalita's dress, and the sleeves of her choli with white feathers." "Ananga Manjari has a very nice bindi. It is red inside and has a circle around it, and that circle is surrounded by white dots."

"This will be printed as a book cover," Lila pointed out. "It will be small. No one will be able to see the circle and dots around the dot on Ananga Manjari's forehead!"

"Maybe not," he said, "but I will know."

"We have to hide Krishna," he had told her from the beginning. "People should not be able to see Him at first. And tears should be coming from His eyes; He is not hard-hearted."

One day he said, "You know, Radharani doesn't have a waist like yours. Make it slimmer!"

She narrowed it, but it still wasn't slim enough, so Aindra did it in Photoshop. And he made the effulgence around Her head more dramatic, adding distinct rays.

He never seemed to tire. "He could go without sleeping," Lila remembered. "He could work from nine in the morning until twelve or one at night and be completely fine. But I couldn't keep up. I completely lost my health during the last days finishing the pictures. He would give me breaks, because I would ask for them. 'Aindra, can we take a break for two or three days?' I would ask. 'I want to sleep.'"

"Lila, you'll kill me for saying this," Aindra said toward the end of the process, after she had followed him through countless revisions, "but, even at the risk of my life, I want to ask you to move Radharani's face to the angle you had it in your original sketch. It shows more emotion."

And right when she thought they were done, he asked, "Please make Radharani's eyes slightly more closed. It will show that She is becoming lost in Her emotion."

One *gopī* was the particular subject of Aindra's attention. She was seated at the feet of Ananga Manjari, on Radharani's right, with Radharani's arm draped around her back and Her hand on her shoulder, and played a stringed instrument with her eyes closed in rapt devotional attention.

"Who is this?" Lila asked.

"Oh, she's just a *gopī*," he said with a smile.

When the pictures were completed to Aindra's satisfaction, he asked, "What can I give you in return?" He was extremely grateful for all the months of time and effort she had invested in matching every detail to his vision.

Lila did not request anything, but he gave her three gifts: a tulasi leaf from the *girirāja-śilā* he kept in a silver locket around his neck, three plates of *rāja-bhoga* from the temple, and three *śālagrāma-śilās*, one of which was marked with a cow's hoof-print and another of which was white. He gave her the white one because Balaram was white, and Lila had a special affection for Krishna-Balaram.

"I paint many pictures now," Lila later said, "but this painting I did with Aindra is unique. It was what I was meant to accomplish, my life's work. Actually, I don't feel like this is my painting. It is something we did together."

One morning shortly before Radhastami of 2008, Giridhari introduced Aindra to Radha Madhava das, an Indian devotee dentist from Delhi who admired Aindra and was a frequent participant in the kirtan. And after the evening Radhastami kirtan, before Aindra got up to leave, Radha Madhava slid over to him, reintroduced himself, and asked if he could help with his book.

"Thank you," Aindra said. "Hare Krishna." He didn't seem to be responding to the offer.

The two just sat there, looking at each other without speaking. "It was like Krishna was deciding my fate," Radha Madhava described.

Then Aindra asked, "What kind of help?"

"Anything," Radha Madhava said. "Any kind of service. Maybe going to press in Delhi? Or maybe, if you will allow, some financial support?"

"Well, the main thing is, I don't like going out of Vrindavan," Aindra said. On Keshi Damana's recommendation, he'd been in touch with Thomson Press, with whom Keshi Damana had published, and he'd met in his room with one of their representatives. "I've heard Thomson is good," he said, "but if you can do a little running around outside of Vrindavan, that would be appreciated."

Radha Madhava agreed, relieved that Aindra was accepting his service, and Aindra invited him to come up to his room after the *ārati*. Upstairs, Aindra read Radha Madhava a draft of the book's introduction and told him about how Srila Prabhupada had come to him in his dream and instructed him to write a book about book distribution. "I didn't know anything about writing or putting it together," he said. "And I was thinking of different ways of how I could proceed. But gradually, as one thing after another unfolded, it became clear to me by the grace of my spiritual master that there was a serious need in our movement for a book that could bridge the gap between one's internal *bhajana* and external activities related to preaching. I understood that Srila Prabhupada wanted me to write a book so that the whole purpose behind transcendental book distribution would be revealed. I could see that there was so much book distribution going on, but how many people are understanding the real essence behind it?

"At first I thought the book could be in the shape of a heart, with some quotes, one on each page. But now I can see that it is like a jewel. I don't know what exactly it should look like, but my idea is that it should be like a jewel coming out of a box, like a treasure coming out of a *prema samputa*, a treasure chest of pure, transcendental love. Can you understand what I'm trying to say?"

Radha Madhava said yes, but he couldn't actually imagine it. Still, he went to Thomson Press, where he met with the chief operating officer, Ashish Daftari, and described Aindra's situation. "This book is his life's work," he told Daftari. "He has been writing it for nearly a decade, and he wants the printing to be first-class. He has the idea that the book should be in some kind of case, like a jewel box."

To Radha Madhava's surprise, Daftari agreed to come to Vrindavan himself. He was inspired to meet Aindra personally and wanted to hear what he had in mind.

When he arrived and was brought up to Aindra's room, he thought he had entered another world. After he had regained his composure, he asked Aindra to describe his vision.

Aindra was excited that the project was finally moving forward in a real, physical way. "You must have some previous *sukṛti* to be fortunate enough to visit Radharani's Vrindavan-dhāma," he told Daftari, and he gave him some *mahā-prasādam*. "I'm a poor, simple sadhu, but I really appreciate that you have come to help, and Prabhupada and Krishna will bless you." And then he explained what he wanted.

❦ ❦ ❦

The last stage before bringing the book to press was editing the text. Aindra had been reading it to friends since he'd begun drafting, and each day, he would share what he'd written that day with Rama Raya and listen carefully to his response. He was meticulous about using the exact right words, sometimes reading a passage aloud forty or fifty times before he was satisfied. But he still needed an editor.

❦ ❦ ❦

In 1999, when I had been in Vrindavan for a few months with my family, my son, James, a slight nine-year-old with a long blond *śikhā*, had been attracted to the Krishna-Balaram kirtan, if somewhat intimidated by Aindra's intense demeanor. We had attended the kirtan every evening, and Bhagavata Purana had given him a gong or set of sticks and drawn him in to play. When Aindra had come down to lead, James had slid the instrument back into the circle, but when Aindra had noticed this one day, he'd given James a slight smile and quick nod, just enough to encourage him, and James had been happy to join in.

Now, almost ten years later, I was in Vrindavan alone for a few weeks, and after one evening kirtan, Bhagavata Purana introduced me to Aindra. I had edited books by several of Aindra's godbrothers, and Bhagavata Purana thought I might be able to help.

After the toughest job interview I'd ever endured—Aindra demanding a full accounting of my personal, professional, and spiritual behaviors and qualifications, and questioning why I didn't just give up family life and move to Vrindavan ("You haven't met my wife," I replied. "She brought me back into Krishna consciousness.")—he asked what it would take to get me to return to Vrindavan and edit his book. "Just a round-trip ticket," I said, and we agreed that I'd be back in a few months.

We were an odd couple—one a not-yet-initiated middle-aged Catholic-university professor from New York living in America's staid Midwest with his wife and three children, the other ... well, Aindra. But somehow we clicked. With both laughter and tears, we shared memories of growing up: our fathers; the music; our lives in America's counterculture; me running through the streets of New

York as he lay in his father's field, staring up at the stars—stories we couldn't share with others, that we'd never told. I felt like I'd been reunited with an old friend.

Bhagavata Purana posted a special warning notice—the usual fanged skull and crossbones but with the alert "Heavy Editing – Do Not Disturb!"—and for the next three weeks, from ten in the morning (I sometimes had to wake him up) until the last seconds before his evening shift, with just a short mid-afternoon break, Aindra and I huddled together in front of the computer and went through the book word by word, him reading aloud and me commenting and making suggestions.

The room was stuffy and stifling hot; I could hardly breathe. With the door and window shut, it was practically vacuum sealed, and the power kept going off. It smelled ... strong—a mix of sweet, earthy, and pungent scents I couldn't place. As the day progressed and it got even hotter, we hiked up our top cloths and I rolled up my kurta, but I got a rash from us sweating and sitting so close, leaning against each other, rubbing shoulders as we strained toward the monitor.

I knew I couldn't fully comprehend Aindra's knowledge or realization; I couldn't even pretend to. But I could tell that the writing was way over the top and tried to give him a sense of how it might (or might not) be understood. Page after page was set in all caps; sentences were punctuated with strings of exclamation points. The vocabulary was archaic and inflated, like something written by an obscure seventeenth-century poet, and elaborately decorated with flourishes of rhyme and alliteration.

"I knew it would be a challenge," I told him one day, "but I'd never imagined anything like *this*!"

Other authors with whom I'd worked—even senior devotees—had generally adopted my suggestions, if only after some discussion. But Aindra was adamant about both what he'd written and how he'd phrased it. No suggested change, no matter how small, went unchallenged; he wanted every detail explained, and argued over most.

Even pronunciation was in dispute. On his request, when he, to my ears, would mispronounce a word as he read aloud, I would correct him. But he rarely accepted the corrections, and the disagreements soon became a competition: he would type the word, and as the computer's dictionary-program voice pronounced it, we'd listen expectantly to hear who had won the round, breaking into laughter when we found out. We soon lost track of the score, but the kirtan guy from the third floor at least held his own against the tenured English professor.

Aindra didn't use a standard *Merriam-Webster* dictionary; he preferred the *Oxford English Dictionary*, a comprehensive scholarly set of twenty volumes tracing the historical development of the language. I would frequently challenge a word's usage; much of the book's language, I felt, would go right over a reader's head, and I had never heard, let alone used, some of the vocabulary. But about the words' definitions, Aindra was rarely mistaken. The meaning he had in mind might not have been the first or even the second listed, but it was always there, somewhere along the line, even if only in a previous century.

I suggested he tone it down. "They'll think you're a crazy man yelling from a soapbox," I warned. But it didn't take long to see the futility of my request. The most I could hope for was for him to leave out some of the caps and exclamation points, simplify some of the sentences, and try to keep the reader in mind. The resulting manuscript retained its blazing intensity, and the content was sure to light fires, as was clearly his intention, but it now also might, I hoped, connect with some readers more easily, allowing more of the ideas to come through.

Aindra was so focused on the book that he didn't want to do anything else. He told me to wake him each morning "no matter what," and at the end of the day, both of us exhausted and his kirtan slot approaching, he would want to go over just one more sentence, one more word—keep working as long as he could—until the very last second, before he sent me down to the temple room for the kirtan (he'd follow "in just a few minutes"). I had never received such a warm welcome as I did each evening when I entered the temple room—my arrival meant that Aindra was on the way. I thought of the ecstasy of the *vraja-vāsīs* awaiting Krishna's imminent return each evening, alerted by the dust of Vrindavan kicked up by the cows on their way home from pasture.

❧ ❧ ❧

Aindra was obviously excited about the book, but he was under no illusion about how it would be received. He knew his style was extravagant and hard to understand; people had said the same about his kirtans. Even though he'd never mentioned ISKCON or any devotees by name, he knew he would get strong reactions both for elaborating on intimate and advanced spiritual matters and for criticizing institutional aspects of the movement. And he knew that publishing the book would put his temple service at risk. When he asked how I thought the institution would respond, I had no doubt: "They'll crucify you."

"You're probably right," he said. "I've already been told that I could lose my slot. But I'm not willing to let that happen. This is my book, the only one I'll ever write. But I won't publish it at the expense of my *sevā*; I won't give up my kirtan. I have the opportunity to print and bind it now, but if I have to, I'll let it sit in a closet, unread, until I'm gone."

When I didn't want payment for my work, he said, "I have something for you," reached up to a shelf, and pulled out a sealed envelope on which he had written, "H.H. Tamal Krishna Goswami," the name of my brother.

Before Tamal Krishna's passing, Aindra said, Maharaja had brought half a dozen personal heaters back from China for the 24-hour-kirtan crew. They could be hung from one's neck and would be perfect for night shifts during Vrindavan's cold, damp winters. Aindra and Tamal Krishna had been somewhat distant after a philosophical disagreement, and as a peace offering Tamal Krishna had brought the heaters, one of which Aindra used as part of a cleansing naturopathic treatment for his gall bladder.

Inside the envelope was a small length of ribbon that in Sri Jagannath Mandir in Puri had wrapped Lord Jagannath's *nābhi-brahma*, "navel," or life force, which remains in the Deity's core even when His body is changed every eight to nineteen years. The identity of the *nābhi-brahma* itself is debated—with theories including it being a *śālagrāma-śilā*, a blue sapphire engraved with a Vishnu *yantra*, a piece of the original Jagannath Deity, a tooth of Lord Buddha, or an actual piece of Krishna's navel—due to it being handled only by blindfolded pujaris, who were also not permitted to touch it directly.

"I wanted to give this to Maharaja, to reciprocate," Aindra said, "but I got it shortly before his departure and never had the chance. Now I am giving it to you instead."

I cradled the *mahā* ribbon in my hand, and for some time—I lost track—we gazed silently into each other's tear-filled eyes. I could only smile my thanks. And when I returned to the States, the ribbon went on our home altar, where we honor it in our worship, remembering Aindra, Tamal Krishna, and Lord Jagannatha.

❦ ❦ ❦

The printing was set in motion, and before long, the press produced two copies of an initial mockup. Radha Madhava brought one to Aindra and, with Aindra's permission, kept one for himself. "Please read it and give me your opinion," Aindra said.

A few weeks later, Radha Madhava returned to Vrindavan. He and Aindra had been speaking about the book on the phone, but now Aindra wanted more detailed feedback. "Did you get to the third chapter?" he asked.

"I'm still on the second one," Radha Madhava said. "I want to go slowly and try to understand every bit."

"The reason I ask is that I have done something in the third chapter that has not been done since Srila Bhaktivinoda Thakur's time. I felt the need, and I think it's time that our Society becomes more aware of these aspects. I would never normally have revealed the secrets of my heart like this, but my Nitai Saci-suta have forced me."

Aindra had included a discussion of *rāgānuga-sādhana*—"when," Bhaktivinoda had written, "one practices devotional service by following the footsteps of the residents of Vrindavan," engaging in loving services to Radha-Krishna. And he had provided vivid descriptions of the spiritual world: a beautiful network of lush gardens on the northern banks of Lalita Kund, with cottages made from wish-fulfilling trees, mosaic paths built from precious jewels, with stopping places to relax and refresh, forming a maze at the center of which was a crystalline love-cottage. Further, he had described some of the services he yearned to perform there for Radha-Krishna, as well as his desired role in Their *līlās*.

Sharing such intimate, advanced matters with other *sādhakas* had not been unheard of in generations of Gaudiya Vaishnavas up to and including Bhaktivinoda Thakur, but had not been prevalent since, and not by Srila Prabhupada or in ISKCON or in such an open forum.

❧ ❧ ❧

Even though Radha Madhava handled most of the business with Thompson Press and Aindra kept his Delhi trips to an absolute minimum, Aindra ended up visiting the press fifteen or twenty times—sometimes staying up to ten hours to explain specific details to the team working on the book's design (but returning to Vrindavan the same night). Each time, he would appear wearing a garland from Radhe-Shyam and bring boxes of *mahā* sweets.

It didn't take long before everyone at the press began to go out of their way to do things with him, curious to see him and hear him speak, and just fond of him, eager to do what he asked and put his ideas into practice. Even when the sixteen-page signatures—page bundles—were printed and ready to bind, and Aindra made further adjustments to the text after editing, Thompson redid the pages at no extra cost, despite Aindra having offered to cover the additional expense. If he found even one small error in grammar or punctuation, or if one arose during editing, he would have the whole signature reprinted. He was as much a perfectionist about the book as he had been with his recordings and was when he was on the altar, dressing and decorating the Deities.

"Who is your book designer?" the press workers asked Radha Madhava, impressed with both Aindra's creativity and his attention to detail.

"*Prabhujī* has done everything himself," he replied. "Every little thing."

Finally, in mid-July, after going back and forth again and again on all the book's details—the editing, cover design, choice of paper, binding, packaging, and other matters—Aindra received a full-color proof of how it would look after production.

"This is what I wanted!" he admired, though there were still a few small changes on which he insisted, even at extra expense.

❧ ❧ ❧

One day a press employee, Benu Agarwal, saw Radha Madhava with his hand in a bead bag entering through the main gate.

"Are you a follower of ISKCON?" she asked.

"Yes," he replied. "And yourself?"

"Yes," she said, "But I am new." She loved coming to Vrindavan, she said, especially to hear Aindra's kirtan. She was a big fan.

"Well," Radha Madhava told her, "Your prayers have been answered. Aindra Prabhu is here right now, sitting in your offices, arranging for publication of his book. Would you like to meet him?"

Hardly believing her good fortune, Benu replied that she would, and so Radha Madhava brought her inside and introduced her to Aindra.

"When I entered the conference room," Benu recalled, "I saw a devotee sitting there chanting on his beads. I saw a great effulgence on his face and a shine in his eyes. I offered obeisances to him. I don't know why I did this; I didn't know anything about the *praṇam* system. I was planning to ask so many questions, as I had so many doubts in my mind, but when I had darshan of him, I forgot everything, all doubts. I was totally immersed in the effulgence of his face."

"What is your name?" Aindra asked. "What do you do here? Do you chant Hare Krishna? How many rounds?"

"I chant only four rounds every day," Benu answered. "I do not seem to have much interest in chanting."

"Who is Krishna to you?" he asked. "How do you see your relationship?"

She didn't know what to say.

"Is Krishna your best friend? Your protector? Your beloved? Who is He to you?"

"Yes," she answered, "He is my best friend."

"That's very important," he told her. "Whenever you chant, you should think, 'I am calling out to my best friend.' If you chant like that, you will get taste for it."

Benu's eyes filled with tears. In just a few minutes, Aindra had brought her to the essence, had helped her realize her relationship with the Lord.

This, Radha Madhava saw, *is preaching*.

"Each one of us has an intimate relationship with Krishna," Aindra told Benu. "We just need to realize it." And the next time he visited Thompson to work on the book, she was there again, this time with two of her friends, whom she had brought to meet him.

❧ ❧ ❧

Whenever Aindra had gone to the press, Radha Madhava had brought him to his home for *prasādam* before returning him to Vrindavan late that night. One cold winter evening, Aindra decided to take a shower before eating. Just before entering the bathroom, however, he got swept up in a conversation about the importance of educated young people following the Vedic lifestyle. He stood for an hour in just a *gāmchā*, with bare feet on the cold floor, asking, "Why don't we wear dhoti and tilak to the office? What are we so shy of? Are we ashamed or what? Why do we want to look and live like *karmīs*?" He hadn't eaten all day, and he was cold and exhausted, but none of that was on his mind. When he was immersed in discussion, he could forget everything else.

Radha Madhava's wife, Manjulali, relished the opportunities to feed Aindra and would prepare elaborate feasts. He was amazed by her preparations. "How did you know I like these Bengali sweets?" he would ask. "Did someone tell you?" He especially liked her stuffed karela, stuffed green peppers, tandoori parathas, and mango pudding. "When I see *prasādam* like this," he told her, "I can just say, 'I'm celebrating Krishna's mercy.' But, whichever way He wants to keep me, I'm happy. I'm happy to starve and I'm happy to take *prasādam* like this. Whatever He wants."

As he ate, he would quiz Manjulali about the ingredients, trying to guess them by taste, and sometimes he would ask for recipes. "When I see your wife running here and there in the kitchen," he told Radha Madhava, "I can imagine how the *gopīs* are so careful and dedicated to making sure everything is right for Krishna."

Fried *arbi*, taro root, was Aindra's favorite. "Radharani loves *arbi*," he told Manjulali.

One evening, he looked her in the eyes and said, "I bless you!"

Manjulali felt her throat choke up with joy.

"I bless you that one day, you will make this very *arbi sabjī* for Srimati Radharani Herself!"

CHAPTER THREE

AINDRA SOMETIMES HELD kirtan at Radha Madhava and Manjulali's and spoke about Krishna, and Radha Madhava organized a program for him at ISKCON Delhi's Sri Sri Radha-Parthasarathi Mandir. On the day of the program, Radha Madhava's mobile phone didn't stop ringing. "Where are you now?" devotees asked. "When will you get here?"

When the car neared the temple, so many people were out in the street to greet Aindra that the vehicle couldn't get through to the parking lot. Like a kirtan rock star, he was met by hundreds of ecstatic devotees singing and dancing in anticipation of his arrival, screaming out his name and doing kirtan with his melodies. And when he'd waded through the throng and begun his kirtan, he was accompanied by several dozen sets of kartals.

The kirtan was uproarious, ending only when Aindra closed his harmonium, prepared to speak, and announced, "I may go a little past the schedule."

"If there is a home away from home," he told the assemblage, "I know for sure this Radha-Parthasarathi Mandir is it. But Sri Vrindavan-dhāma is the real home! Sanatana Goswami says in *Hari Bhakti Vilasa*, 'By the greatest fortune a *jīva* can somehow enter the boundaries of Sri Vrindavan-dhāma. If so, he is strictly instructed never again to leave the boundaries of Vraja-*dhāma*. Only under one condition may he leave: if he goes to spread the glories of the *dhāma* under the order or guidance of his spiritual master. And even then, he should quickly return.' Otherwise, how can we be so foolish to take such a big risk? Just by being in the *dhāma*, we are assured to attain our *sac-cid-ananda svarupa*. Why should we risk leaving it?"

He spoke at length on the *Bhagavad-gita* and then began another kirtan. When he stopped, the devotees cried out, "More! More!" and the program continued into the night.

The kirtan devotees were famished; they had spent the day with Aindra at Thomson Press and then played for hours. But Aindra had not managed to complete his Deities' puja before leaving for Delhi, and he would never eat before Their offering. So, he waited for the other devotees to honor *prasādam* and then until he returned to Vrindavan, well after midnight.

※ ※ ※

The day before Shivaratri, Aindra got a phone call from Radha Madhava. "We were thinking of coming to Vrindavan tomorrow," Radha Madhava said. "Is there anything special we should do?"

"Yes," Aindra replied. "Shiva is a *paraṁ* Vaishnava, and he is easily pleased. So, it's very effective to beg his blessing to help us increase our determination for serving Krishna. You can come with us if you like; we usually go to Shiva's Prachin Mandir in Mathura."

On the way to Mathura, Aindra, Radha Madhava, and Manjulali visited several Shiva temples, making various offerings according to the instructions of each pujari. They returned to Vrindavan in the afternoon and rode over to the Yamuna, where there was a huge celebration.

At ISKCON's big tent on the bank of the river, Aindra spoke to a group of *vraja-vāsīs*. "When Yashoda was trying to bind Krishna," he told them, "all the time her rope was two fingers too short. So, what did she do? She took the help of all of her friends—in her endeavor to bind Krishna. That is *saṅkīrtana*. Krishna was so pleased in seeing Yashoda engage others in His service. That is why He allowed Himself to be tied. That is *saṅkīrtana*—engaging everyone in your pursuit to bind Krishna. The more, the better. Bring as many to help as possible."

"If *saṅkīrtana* is so powerful," someone asked, "why do we bother with *japa*?"

"*Saṅkīrtana* is *rāsa-līlā*," Aindra replied. "*Japa* is *nikuñja-sevā*." It was a distinction he'd often made in comparing the two. "In *rāsa-līlā*, many *gopīs* together celebrate and express their love for Krishna, whereas *nikuñja-sevā* refers to inviting Radha and Krishna to one's own private grove and serving them there.

"So, *saṅkīrtana* is entirely analogous to the cooperative, group service of *rāsa-līlā*, while *japa* is analogous to the quieter, more private services rendered in *nikuñja-sevā*. The two are interdependent. The *rāsa-līlā* increases Krishna's appetite for the privacy of *nikuñja-sevā*, and the *nikuñja-sevā* is what forms the intimate relationship that is celebrated in all the singing and dancing of *rāsa-līlā*.

"In the same way, *saṅkīrtana* and *japa* are interdependent. Without the experience of *saṅkīrtana*, where is the inspiration to go deep into your *japa*? And without deep *japa*, how will there be any sincere *bhāva* in your *saṅkīrtana*?"

For safe keeping while he took his bath in the Yamuna, Aindra draped his Govardhana *śilās* around Radha Madhava's neck. Afterwards, they went to the Gopeswara Mahadev Shiva temple, had darshan and offered puja, and then returned to Krishna-Balaram Mandir in time for Aindra's evening kirtan, following which they spent the night discussing Krishna in Aindra's room. "It was," Radha Madhava later remembered, "the best day of my life."

❦ ❦ ❦

Before Radha Madhava left for a trip to Nepal, he asked Aindra when he should observe Ekadasi there. Aindra checked a Vaishnava calendar and told him the appropriate time the next morning when he should end the Ekadasi by breaking the fast at that geographic location.

"Why is there a specific time for breaking the fast?" Radha Madhava asked.

Aindra spent the next hour discussing the issue. "Most people say that if one does not break Ekadasi on time, one will lose the benefit of having followed the previous seven Ekadasis," he explained. "But I've understood that the more important reason for having a specific time is to help us be very vigilant about our devotional practices so that we can become more careful, particular, and punctual in our services."

Srila Prabhupada had emphasized how much Radharani appreciated careful and attentive service. She would not accept an offering if it was late by even one minute, especially in Vrindavan. "The *mañjarīs* are so absorbed in their service to Radhe-Shyam that they are very punctual and pay great attention to the details," Aindra described. "Once, Radharani sent an offering for Shyam through Tulasi Manjari. The moment Shyam received the love-filled offering made by His Priya, He was extremely delighted. As a token of appreciation for the loving service rendered by Tulasi Manjari, He took a garland of *guñjā-mālā* from His neck and put it around hers.

"When Tulasi Manjari returned, Srimati Radharani was so delighted to see that *guñjā-mālā*. She asked for it and put it on Her own neck. She accepted the *mahā-prasādam* from Her own maidservant because She was so delighted by her attentive service to Shyam."

CHAPTER FOUR

AINDRA WAS PROMISED a chance to make an offering during Srila Prabhupada's disappearance-anniversary temple observance in 2009, and he stayed up the whole night before to prepare his talk. He had not always been invited to speak at the event, and when he had spoken, he'd brought a mood quite different from the often-celebratory tone of others' offerings, addressing the devotees in fiery, emotional terms about the urgent need to redouble their dedication to Srila Prabhupada and their commitment to cultivating personal, loving relationships with Radha-Krishna—a "wake-up call" to Krishna consciousness. "When it was time to preach, to speak strongly," Akincana Krishna commented, "he spoke strongly like nobody else: powerful, with so much shakti, so much purity ... everything was revealed; he spoke the naked truth."

Known for his long talks, this year Aindra was told that he had only ten minutes to speak, and he went over his words again and again, timing himself to make sure he could deliver them in the time allotted. He had written an explanation, supported by references to shastra, of how Prabhupada's approach to *rāgānuga-bhakti*, inherited from Srila Bhaktisiddhanta and Srila Bhaktivinoda Thakur, was legitimate and faithful to the original tradition established by the Six Goswamis of Vrindavan.

Throughout the morning ceremony, Aindra sat next to Gopal, listening to devotees glorify Srila Prabhupada and holding tight to the printout of his offering. But as one speaker after another exceeded their ten-minute limit, it became clear not only that Aindra was being left for last, but also that there wouldn't be time left for him to speak. Eventually the master of ceremonies approached him and said, "We will need you to cut your offering in half."

When Aindra expressed his disappointment, he was told, "It's better than nothing. Be prepared for the possibility that we might not get to you at all."

Aindra stood up and began to walk away.

"Where are you going?" Gopal asked.

"You'll see," he said—and disappeared.

He returned a few minutes later. "Where did you go?" Gopal asked. "What did you do?" He could tell that there was something wrong.

"You'll see," Aindra repeated. "If, after all these years, all they're going to give me is two minutes to speak, I'm gonna give them a piece of my mind."

Gopal knew there was going to be trouble.

When Aindra was finally called up and had taken his place on the speaker's chair—the last devotee to speak—he began, "My observation is that different disciples of Srila Prabhupada represent different aspects of Srila Prabhupada's personality. And I guess I am one of them, so if you'll bear with me ... it takes all kinds, to make a world of Hare Krishna ... I hope that my holy godbrothers will not get too angry with me."

Then he began reading. "To hell with trying to secure a comfortable situation within this temporary world of shadowy afflictions!" he proclaimed. "To hell with hoping for heavenly delights on earth, elevation to *svarga-loka*, or residence on any of the highest planets within this cosmos! To hell with the achievement of mystic perfections!"

He was reading from a draft of his manuscript. He knew that there would be repercussions, but he was driven by his sincere desire to keep ISKCON from straying from Srila Prabhupada's mission to spread Lord Chaitanya's *sankīrtana* movement.

"To hell with conceitedly boasting of our descent from a most venerable disciplic succession of eternally perfect Gaudiya Vaishnava acharyas!

"To hell with our exploiting the prestige of sitting at the feet of such a topmost *rasika* Vaishnava as His Divine Grace A. C. Bhaktivedanta Swami Prabhupada, or any other, for that matter!"

The room fell into awkward silence. Aindra paused and looked up. "This may sound strange to you," he said, "but bear with me please."

"To hell with following from A to Z all the damn rules and regulations of the International Society for Rules and Regulations!

"To hell with trying to become a Hare Krishna clone!

"To hell with toeing the party line!

"To hell with the institutionalism of the institutionalists!

"To hell with religio-institutional corporatocracy!

"To hell with trying to reconcile ourselves to the neoteric drift of a movement's henpecked leadership!

"To hell with being a Hare Krishna yes-man!"

Some of the Society's leaders and senior devotees in the audience were becoming noticeably uncomfortable. But Aindra wasn't finished.

"To hell with our profiling as advanced devotees when we know damn well we're not!" he continued.

"To hell with grappling for socio-religious eminence!

"To hell with the institutional rubberstamping of sampradayic supermen!

"To hell with the 'necessary evil' of (poorly) organized religion…

"I say to hell with the Hindu cash cow!"

One senior devotee stood up and walked out, his face red with anger.

"It's okay," Aindra said. "If you have experience, I think you'll understand what I am talking about."

He continued: "To hell with all our vehemently preaching about preaching about preaching about how we're supposed to preach about preaching about preaching about how we're supposed to preach! What are we 'preachers' supposed to be preach-preachidy-preaching about?"

Another devotee urged the MC to remove Aindra from the stage.

"It's okay," another said. "Just let him finish." But Aindra was barely halfway done.

"To hell with it! Like infatuated children, avidly engrossed in the perpetual pastime of competitively collecting rare and unusual coinage, we accumulate the hundreds and thousands of unqualified neophyte disciples under the pretext of perpetuating the *sampradāya*. I say, to hell with it!

"To hell with, on the plea of concern for others, becoming so blunderingly bogged down with all the petty little problems of the hundreds and thousands of corporeally attached *śiṣya-prāya* 'disciples' that one fails to oneself find the time and space required to complete even the minimum *nāma-bhajana* expected of a new bhakta; what then of achieving the advanced internal devotional realizations needed to become, for the benefit of one's disciples, anything better than a half-baked cookie!"

The MC interrupted to tell Aindra that he had exceeded his time limit.

"It's almost over," Aindra said. Then he dove back in: "To hell with being a pawn on the chessboard of any mortal being's religio-institutional managerialism! To hell with in-house party-spirited pseudo-disciplic partiality."

He followed, "To hell with the fools who conscientiously avoid hearing, chanting, and remembering the Lord's *rāsa-līlā* and other *mādhurya* pastimes with the *gopīs*. They will never attain perfection. If I chance to encounter the likes of such imposter Vaishnavas, I will close my ears to their philosophical absurdities, refuse to see their faces, and scorn the dismal air about their corpse-like material bodies."

The audience sat in stunned silence. No one had ever levelled such a scathing critique at devotees' misapplications of Prabhupada's message, and certainly never on such an occasion.

But Aindra wasn't done.

"To hell with our having distributed billions and trillions of transcendental literatures all over the world in scores of languages to give everyone else a chance to become fully Krishna conscious! I say to hell with it all!"

Someone in the audience called out, "Haribol!"

"Much of the afore-denounced may be wonderful, meritorious or (de)pressingly important on one level or another, but if in the end, after all is said and done, we ourselves, as individuals could not effectively grasp, take to heart, factually realize, and blissfully relish the deepest essential living import of the Gaudiya Vaishnava *siddhānta* (learning to love Vrajendra-nandana Shyam by carefully pursuing the *bhāvas* of the supra-exemplary damsels of Vraja), what would we have really gained from the whole affair? Truly speaking, what would be the sense or significance of any other allegedly laudable undertaking or feat?

"Candidly speaking, charity really begins at home. It's true that the highest realization is to take all risk, to go out of one's way to save the world. That is our mission, for sure. Even so, still higher than that, ultimately, the very highest realization, the profoundest mission, is to save oneself. First make yourself spiritually fit. Doctor, heal thyself! First chant and dance in ecstasy like a madman, then worry about saving the rest of the world."

Aindra had prepared an ending that was meant to explain everything he had said—he had written it all down—but it was too late for that. His talk had been meant as an appeal, an invitation to devotees to give up false prestige and relish Krishna's loving Vraja pastimes, but to many in the assembly, he had simply delivered a relentless condemnation. And its ferocity and vehemence shocked them; all they could hear was an angry "To hell with you."

Aindra participated in the *abhiṣeka* and *ārati*, and when the devotees left for the feast, he went straight to his room.

"Prabhu," Gopal asked, "What are you doing?"

"I was testing the waters for my new book." Aindra replied.

The master of ceremonies came knocking a few minutes later. "The GBC wants to see you," he said. "They don't want you to lead kirtan in Prabhupada's house tonight."

It was the first time in over twenty years that Aindra wouldn't lead the evening kirtan in Srila Prabhupada's quarters on His Divine

Grace's disappearance day, but he went anyway, to hear the other offerings. He was allowed to enter but was almost immediately challenged by the first speaker. "Why was that last speaker [Aindra] allowed to get away with what he said?" the devotee asked. "And why should we have to tolerate him being in our presence now?"

Then one of the temple authorities came in and told him in front of the assembly, "The Krishna-Balaram management requests and requires that you apologize for your speech today. And we would seriously encourage you to make your apology no later than tomorrow morning's *maṅgala-ārati* announcements."

The next morning, Aindra addressed a temple room full of devotees: "I know many of you must have been hurt by the way I spoke yesterday, and I realize that it was not the right way to put it. But I have a Bhaktisiddhanta Sarasvati Thakur way of putting things: I speak very cuttingly. If I have hurt the sentiments of the devotees, I sincerely apologize. If I've upset anybody, if I've said something that is not the truth, I apologize."

Aindra's statement fell well short of the apology the authorities had demanded. "You should simply have said that you were wrong," advised Gopal Krishna Goswami, who at the festival had tried to stop Aindra from ruining his reputation.

"How can I say that?" Aindra asked. "I was *not* wrong. I spoke the truth."

"But you said it so heavily," Maharaja explained. "The GBC will have to ban your book if you print it as it is now. Why don't you edit out the heavy portions?"

"But they are there on purpose," Aindra said. "If you read it, you'll see that what I'm giving in this book will keep people loyal to ISKCON and Srila Prabhupada."

"Well, you've had a chance to apologize," Maharaja told him, "Now you'll have to come in."

At the meeting called to address the issue, some devotees who had previously been Aindra's supporters remained neutral. Others thought he had gone too far. "You've upset a lot of devotees," one told him. "They wonder, 'Why is Aindra saying, "To hell with *maṅgala-ārati*?" I go to *maṅgala-ārati* every day!' "

One devotee appreciated what Aindra had to say—he had listened and had really wanted to hear him out. But by the time Aindra had gotten to his point, the devotee said, he had lost his audience; his presentation had failed. "And that's why we're here today."

Aindra tried to defend himself, but, he was told, he had already said what he'd needed to say. "Now we are here with this group of people and you need to hear what they have to say." Attention turned to not only the book but also Aindra's personal habits, such as why he slept so little, which could "cloud his judgment."

In conclusion, a devotee was appointed to keep an eye on Aindra, to supervise his activities. Aindra had to *actually* apologize to Vrindavan's entire administration—every department. And it was made explicitly clear: if he came out with the book, there would be "consequences."

After the meeting, Kadamba Kanana, now Swami, who had served as chair, came to Aindra's room to speak with him privately. He wasn't coming as an official person, he said, not as a GBC or any kind of management, but as his friend. He said not to worry about the meeting. The book didn't have to come out right away. The authorities would kick him out if he published it. He should wait.

Lokanath Swami had also sought out Aindra to speak with him after the address, but they had met on the *gurukula* stairwell with other devotees present, and he had simply urged Aindra to reconsider what he was saying before printing it in the book, before it was set in stone.

Aindra understood that he had put his position in jeopardy. The evening after the disappearance festival, he had told Radha Madhava, "I did a blunder: I read out a portion from my book even though we had decided that I wouldn't make anything public until the actual release. But maybe Krishna wanted it that way. I can tolerate any personal inconvenience, but by no means can I close my eyes to any deviations or watering down the mission of my guru maharaja or the predecessor acharyas, who sacrificed their very lives so that this most treasured message of Lord Chaitanya reaches everyone in an unadulterated and undiluted manner.

"What wrong did I say? I said that if we have attained so-called everything except pure unalloyed love of Godhead, *kṛṣṇa-premā*, then we haven't attained anything. Doesn't Jesus Christ say the same? 'What does it profit a man if he shall gain the whole world and lose his own soul?'

"Haven't you heard that story of the brahmana and the scorpion? The brahmana tried incessantly to save the scorpion from drowning in the river despite being repeatedly bitten. This world will be what it is. But *sadhu* means living for the benefit of others, no matter what, whether they understand or not, whether they appreciate or not, whether you live or die. 'That great personalities almost always accept voluntary suffering in order to mitigate the suffering of people in general. This is considered the highest method of worshipping the Supreme personality of Godhead, who is present in everyone's heart. [*SB* 8.7.44]'

"Srimati Morarji kept insisting to Srila Prabhupada, 'Why do you want to go to America, Swamiji—to that unknown land with nobody known? You'll die!' But he said, 'No, I must go, I must try. Please help me to serve the order of my spiritual master.' Similarly, I want to make a humble attempt to serve the order of my spiritual master by trying to bring *hari-nāma-saṅkīrtana* to its rightful place of dignity in the forefront of our movement. And I'm asking everyone to kindly help.

"Well, Bhaktivinoda Thakur said that a Vaishnava is one who can turn a disadvantageous situation into an advantageous one. Now let us see how Krishna helps me to turn this seemingly disadvantageous situation into an advantageous one."

Over the next few days, Aindra followed the GBC directive, apologizing to every administrative department and many devotees. His apologies were more straightforward this time, and they were accepted. But it was clear that devotees had been hurt by what he had read. "When you were speaking," one friend told him, "it sounded like you were saying that you were the only pure devotee there."

Only a few expressed appreciation. "Maybe Aindra was in the mood of the brahmanas from the *Kṛṣṇa* book," Bhuvanesvara suggested. "They cursed themselves after their wives recognized Krishna and Balaram when they couldn't. They spoke like Aindra, saying 'to hell with' so many things."

"Thank you for understanding my mood, Bhu," Aindra told Bhuvanesvara when he heard what he had said.

There was talk of banning him from leading kirtan in the temple room for some period of time, and he was called to another disciplinary meeting, during which devotees again criticized a range of his behaviors. "You think you can just get everyone into your room and speak to them about *mañjarī-bhāva*," one said, "but that's not the way it works!"

Eventually he was asked, "What do you think about going on a preaching tour for a year or so?"

Aindra was shocked by the idea. "Why would I ever do that?"

"You may have to."

"You guys accuse me of seeing faults in everyone," Aindra pointed out, "but what are you doing to me? Can you not see the only good thing in me?" As he had written in his book, "After all, bees always delight in finding honey-like good qualities with a view to bring out the best in others."

"Shall we at all dare to see any fault in faulting the faultfinding of the faultfinders?" he had challenged. "Are the pots not calling the kettles black? *Ātmavan manyate jagat*—a thief thinks everyone to be desirous of stealing his ill-gotten gains; a cheat sees the world to be full of cheaters. Kṛṣṇa often allows us to see others' faults just to remind us of the need to fine-tune our own approach to devotional life. We would always do well to remember in this connection that when we point our finger at the faults of others, three fingers conversely indicate our own. This incontrovertibly implies that even (if not especially) religiously ordained administrators who see fit to occasionally employ corrective measures with a view to bring about an individual's or a faction's Kṛṣṇa-conscious cultural conformity should crucially consider it to be thrice their responsibility to address their own shortcomings, their own misconceptions, and their own reform, rather than be obsessed with the reformation of anyone else. Any field of management certainly demands the responsible assessment of the individuals involved—seeing any situation, individual, or faction with one bad eye and one good eye."

"My only good quality is that I do kirtan," Aindra told the disciplinary group. "My only good quality is my dedicated service to the 24-hour kirtan here at Krishna-Balaram Mandir. Why do you want to take that away from me?"

Later, in his room, he confided to Damodarastaka, "I don't want to get kicked out of the temple. It is my guru's ashram. I am attached to my guru and to Radhe-Shyam. This is my *saṅkīrtana* spot—why do they want to take it away? Sometimes I just feel like, 'Damn it, I should just pack my bags and go to Radha Kund to do *bhajana*.' Why should I keep banging my head against the wall here with so much opposition? But I have this kirtan *sevā* given by Srila Prabhupada. That is the only reason I want to stay here."

"What will you do if they kick you out?" Damodarastaka asked.

"I'll just take my harmonium and a begging bowl and sit outside the main gate chanting Hare Krishna."

"Maybe you should just put the book away for now," Kadamba Kanana Swami suggested. "It can be published after you die."

It was not the first time Aindra had considered the possibility. "I thought I would just have to pay a few lakhs of rupees to get this book published," he told Maharaja with a sad laugh. "But it's my life's work. If that's the price I have to pay, I'm willing to pay that too."

"So many devotees have told me that the most-read, the most-popular books are the ones by authors who die," he related to a sympathetic godsister. " 'Banned by the GBC!' " he quoted from an imaginary headline. "Maybe this is Krishna's advertising stunt!"

He even consulted a deck of *Bhagavad-gita* cards to see how the cards would "respond" to the question of what he should do. "What about my book?" he asked. He chanted Srila Prabhupada's *praṇām-mantra* and cut the deck, then chanted the Pancha-Tattva mantra and cut the deck, and then chanted the *mahā-mantra* three times and cut the deck. "I was thinking I'd take the top card, whichever card came out on top," he said, "and that's the one Krishna wanted me to see."

What? he wondered when he saw the first card. "It was a picture of Hanuman," he later described, "and he was ripping open his heart and showing Sita-Rama in his heart. And on it was written *Simplicity*.

"But then I opened the booklet and I was shocked. It quoted Prabhupada's *Gita* purport (13.8–12) that 'Simplicity means that without diplomacy one should be so straightforward that he can disclose the real truth even to an enemy' and that simplicity is the first principle, or the first find, of a Vaishnava and that duplicity and diplomacy are great offenses in the service of the Lord.

"I was amazed. It was a confirmation that in spite of everything, in spite of all repercussions, maybe I was on the right track, that maybe that's what Krishna wanted me to do."

He became even more determined. No matter how many devotees implored him to shelve the book, even for the time being, he would publish—at any cost.

❧ ❧ ❧

Fearing for Aindra losing his service, Gopal kept trying to dissuade him from reading from the book in public. "What is more important for you, prabhu," he asked, "your book or your kirtan?" But Aindra wouldn't restrain himself. "The thing is that if I am gonna read from my book," he told one audience, "it has to be, like, an undercover operation; there are a lot of things in the book that are best kept under wraps for now.... But anyhow, there is need for discussing these things among devotees who are serious about progressing toward the ultimate goal of life. It may not be a discussion for everyone, because maybe not everyone is so serious about advancing toward the ultimate goal of life. Maybe they are just too externally oriented, too superficial in their devotional pursuits, not deep enough about their purpose in life. But Srila Prabhupada said that Krishna consciousness is meant for purposefulness, so therefore I always like to stress that we need to take a close look not only at where we are now but at where we are supposed to be going."

Some months later, Aindra again read aloud from the book, at a program in Radha Madhava's house that was both well attended and recorded. Gopal tried to stop him; he even walked out when Aindra said what he was going to do. But Aindra was adamant. "Gopal says I shouldn't be reading this," he told the devotees in attendance. But he just wouldn't, couldn't, keep his thoughts, or the book, under wraps.

When a property near the Krishna-Balaram Mandir went up for sale, Aindra told Damodarastaka, "If only I had a few *crore* rupees, I would purchase it. Then, if they kick me out, we could have our kirtan ashram there and point a big speaker at Radhe-Shyam so they could hear it."

But when someone offered Aindra a plot of land at a lower price and he was asked if he would consider it, Aindra replied, "No. That is their guru's ashram, and this is my guru's ashram. Even if they kick me out of my guru's ashram, I will stay near it and not go near another's."

❦ ❦ ❦

Aindra's completion of Katyayani-*vrata* that year was more somber than usual. "We went to Katyayani Mandir to complete the *vrata*, like we always did," Ati Sundari remembered. "It was windy, and Aindra kept looking to the other side of the Yamuna. He had a tray with a *mālā* for Shyam in one hand and beads for chanting the Katyayani mantra in the other, with a beautiful lotus flower. Staring at the other side of the Yamuna, he said, 'I wish I could go there and never come back.'

" 'But then you would never see Radhe-Shyam,' I said.

" 'I know,' he replied. 'That's why I never do it. But I wish I could just go live there and chant.'

"I got enthusiastic and said, 'We'll get a boat and bring you *prasādam* from Radhe-Shyam every day!'

" 'No, I can't do that,' he said. 'I can't leave my Radhe-Shyam; I can't leave the kirtan. I live there in the *gurukula* building because I can hear Radhe-Shyam's kirtan. Otherwise I would rather live over there … or in Radha Kund.' "

The censure and threats of exile saddened Aindra. He didn't know what his place would be in Vrindavan. If he could not share his realizations and outlooks with the community, what was the point of living amongst them? He became noticeably more somber and withdrawn. He seemed to friends to be aging more quickly.

He made a brief effort to express his opinions anonymously, using a pseudonym for an article entitled "Religio-Institutional Psy-War":

> WAKE UP, PRABHUS! EVERYONE WAKE UP! Everything is not all right. We have been and are being purposely steered off course. Do not acquiesce to any so-called leader's deviant philosophical misconstructions. We must think with our own minds—not with theirs. Even if the clandestine manipulators of institutional affairs are able to nefariously usurp the external institutional setup, they can neither usurp our souls nor will they ever win our heartfelt camaraderie.
>
> It is time for revolution—a revolution of consciousness. Let the institutional power brokers beware. The increasing

> numbers of we who are onto their antics will have revolution with or without their consent or cooperation. The biggest bubble of *māyā* can doubtlessly be burst by the minutest pinprick of genuine Krishna consciousness. The critical mass of our spark-like grass-roots Krishna consciousness will ultimately prevail and conflagrate their insinuative, billowing cotton-like mayic institutional tyranny.

He concluded the article by calling on devotees to "intelligently fight institutional *māyā* with the most powerful weapon: the Holy Name." How should they use this weapon?

> Form local daily *nāma-saṅkīrtana* cells worldwide. Regularly congregate for prolonged mass *hari-nāma-saṅkīrtana* demonstrations. Start chanting a minimum of one lakh of Holy Names daily. Confront local, regional, and zonal institutional authorities and convince them to do the same—it's either shape up or ship out.

❧ ❧ ❧

Those around Aindra started considering options for what he could do if the temple authorities expelled him, which was looking more and more likely. "Generally," Gopal said, "the administration would ask people to leave for a while and do service elsewhere. So, we discussed different ideas, including shifting the whole operation to Mayapur and starting a 24-hour kirtan there."

Or, since Aindra desired so strongly to share his book, he could go out and sell it himself. If he could go to Mayapur for five days, Gopal thought, why not, say, New York? It was different, of course—New York wasn't the holy *dhāma*—but maybe it would be possible. Just that year, Aindra had been invited to New York for a week of *saṅkīrtana* leading up to and including the June Ratha-yatra, but he hadn't wanted to leave the *dhāma*, even to do kirtan, and had declined. When invited to another festival, he had said, "This is why I don't like to travel: I just think to myself, 'What do I really bring to the table that they can't just do themselves? They should be doing *hari-nāma-saṅkīrtana*. Why aren't they? Why do they have to bring me in to do it for them? And after I go there, what's going to happen when I leave? They still aren't going to do *hari-nāma-saṅkīrtana?*' "

"If you go to North America," Gopal suggested, "you can fire up *nāma-saṅkīrtana* in all the major temples leading up to its Ratha-yatra, and then at the Ratha-yatra you can sell your book." A 24-hour-kirtan festival had already been established in New Vrindavan, inspired by Aindra's example. "You can tour all of North America, and then afterwards, you can come back."

Let's start in Toronto, Gopal thought. He had already organized a kirtan festival there—two 12-hour sessions—for July. His idea was that if he could string together a series of events on the Ratha-yatra tour, coordinating with the youth bus and the Festival of India, beginning with New York and continuing across the U.S. and Canada, Aindra might agree to take part. From there, they could extend the *hari-nāma saṅkīrtana* tour to temple communities and other cities all around the world.

CHAPTER FIVE

AINDRA WASN'T ENTHUSED by Gopal's plans; he didn't want to leave Vrindavan. But even in Vrindavan, he began to question how things were going. He had received a lot of negative reaction to what he had written in his book and spoken in public, he doubted that his efforts to improve ISKCON would ever be welcomed, and he was facing the very real possibility of expulsion from Krishna-Balaram Mandir if he published.

Under what seemed like constant threat and scrutiny from authorities, he found it harder and harder to be at ease on the temple compound, even in his room. His circle of close friends tightened, and sometimes he could find peace and just be himself only outside, in friends' homes, such as at Giridhari and Ati Sundari's, a large house among the flower fields near the Yamuna, made of mud, cow dung, and straw in traditional Vraja style, where one could still experience the old Vraja, with flourishing trees, flowers, and winding creepers, the air filled with the birdsong, not blaring horns—simple village life, far from the strife of temple conflicts.

More than ever, he relished being with friends he could trust and with whom he could speak freely. His last few birthdays were celebrated at Giridhari's by more than a hundred devotees, and Aindra personally served *prasādam*. In both 2009 and 2010, he had spoken about his appreciation—and need—for devotee association and cooperation, especially in kirtan, and about the importance of each individual's unique contribution in devotional service.

"Bhaktisiddhanta Sarasvati Thakur says, and Srila Prabhupada also confirms that every living entity is part and parcel of the pleasure potency of Krishna," he had told assembled devotees in 2009. "Srila Bhaktisiddhanta Sarasvati says that every living entity is a constituent part of Srimati Radharani's loving game plan. We are part of the pleasure potency of Krishna, meant to cooperate, assist, facilitate, in our own little small way, which is also relishable, just like little sprinkles on a cake make the cake more relishable. Some are silver, some are gold, some are green, some are red, some are blue, some are yellow—different colors. Varieties, many varieties.... we have to come together, get off the egocentric platform, and help each other. Because our individual voices are not loud enough—they won't do. Who are we? Small-timers. But if enough of us get together—that's why the acharyas in our line say that the performance of *saṅkīrtana* is the topmost *aṅga* of devotional service ... where hundreds of devotees, or thousands of devotees, come together and cooperate together to loudly petition Lord Chaitanya and Lord Nityananda, Radha and Krishna, for Their special causeless mercy for fallen conditioned souls like us....

"And that's what's really gonna get us there. Krishna is much more impressed with a group effort when He sees that we're surrendering to each other enough, and dependent on each other enough, too; we realize that we're not going to be able to make it on our own. We're not standing up trying to be our own man or woman. We need all the help we can get. I'm the personification of that. I need all the help I can get! And especially the more broken down I become, I'm gonna need more and more help. So, I need all of your help! Spirit soul to spirit soul....

"Anyway, I'm very grateful to all of you for helping. And I pray that Radharani and Krishna and Lord Chaitanya—and my Saci-suta—will recognize you for helping me. Whatever little encouragement, whatever little assistance, but real helping means chanting as loudly as possible in the kirtans, not just sitting there looking pretty. You have to chant loudly! And really cry out to Radharani and Krishna—in the mood of helping each other cry out for Radharani and Krishna."

Breaking into tears as he spoke to the devotees in 2010, he referred to how Mother Yashoda's rope was always two inches too short to bind Krishna in His Damodara pastime because Krishna wanted to see our extra endeavor—"going the extra mile, so to speak."

"But it's interesting," he noted, "that with Mother Yashoda, it wasn't happening. She was collecting ropes and ropes and ropes, and still, again and again and again, Krishna wanted to see the extra endeavor.... But after she became exasperated in her attempt to collect all the ropes and she had collected all the ropes that she had in her own house, what did she do? She got her friends and engaged them in helping her in her attempt to, somehow or other, bind Lord Krishna. And they started bringing ropes and ropes from their houses...."

"So, we can try and try and try and try on our own, but there is something more that Krishna wants to see, and that was exemplified by Mother Yashoda's intelligently engaging her friends in bringing extra ropes and extra ropes, to increase the volume of extra endeavor. That is *saṅkīrtana*. *Saṅkīrtana* means the volume, a louder voice, you can say, to get Krishna's attention with a little help from our friends.

"And that's what it's really all about. It is not an independent show, a one-man show. At least, this is what I am beginning to understand a little more in the course of my endeavor to act as an instrument on behalf of the predecessor acharyas to whatever extent I am able. But I am understanding more and more, and it has a lot to do with the fact that Krishna has mercifully broken my voice down so that I cannot stand on my own anymore. He has forced me into the position of realizing that I need all the help I can get!

"I seriously doubt that I am going to get *kṛṣṇa-premā* without all the help I can get from anyone and everyone I can get it from. And I am praying to all of you, that somehow or other, with all of your kindness and well-wishing and special causeless mercy upon this wretched, fallen soul, that somehow or other I will be able to actually attain the goal of my life of being able to eternally serve Radhe-Shyam in Vraja-*dhāma*. At least I have the audacity to say that this is what I want! ...

"So, we have to help each other. We are all like little mini Mother Yashodas, trying to bind Lord Krishna. And we have to recognize that what we really need is to get together."

"Do not delay—do it today!" he had told devotees in regard to extra endeavor. "And Krishna will reciprocate. In the *Bhagavad-gita* it says that He will reciprocate. Do not think there is not a Krishna checking us out. Krishna is there, checking us out at every moment. *Antaryāmī* never sleeps! He is always checking us out, waiting and waiting and waiting. How many lifetimes do we want to make Him wait?

"Do not make Krishna wait! Do whatever you have to do. Do the needful to go back home and dance with Krishna and play with Krishna face to face and eye to eye in this lifetime. Do not make Krishna wait! He has been waiting long enough; we do not have to make Him wait longer. He wants us to go back home, back to Godhead more than *we* want to go back home, back to Godhead. It is not proper for even the pure devotees to desire to go to Goloka-*dhāma* for their own self-satisfaction. But it *is* proper for them to desire to go to Goloka-*dhāma* because Krishna desires it. Krishna wants us to go back, back home to Godhead. Krishna wants us to enter into the *vraja-līlās*.

"Therefore, it is our responsibility. And what does *responsibility* mean? Ability to respond to Krishna's wishes. If Krishna wishes us to go back home, back to Godhead, we have to respond by doing the needful, going the extra mile, making the extra endeavor, proving to Him that we actually want to be in love with Him. Making Him happy when He sees us." Not only was it crucial for devotees to make the extra endeavor; they had to do it *together*.

And in this spirit, out of deep compassion, at the cost of his own physical health, and despite resistance from temple management and a multitude of obstacles on his path, Aindra continued his indefatigable preaching effort: hours counselling both young and mature devotees—many of whom sought spiritual guidance but had become disenchanted with the institution of ISKCON—to remain in the Society, strengthen their sadhana, deepen their *bhajana*, read all of Srila

Prabhupada's books and then those of his predecessor acharyas, and thereby develop their own personal, loving relationships with the Divine Couple.

He offered himself as an example, not to be imitated, but to establish the principles and show that it was possible, that it could be accomplished in today's world, today's ISKCON. Ultimately, each devotee had to find their own way. "In attempting to openly present my own perspective and personal inspirations as I have done," he wrote, "I intend not that the reader necessarily embrace the details of my particular *aprākṛta-bhāva*, given that each individual soul will seek and ultimately realize a unique angle of loving reciprocation with the Lord according to the individual's natural affinity and personal capacity. Rather, the intent is to encourage one to deepen one's own *bhajana* so as to gain an enhanced internal devotional experience of one's own. It is not that divine revelation is beyond the scope of contemporary feasibility. The Holy Name of Krishna is as real and responsive today as ever. *Ye yatha mam prapadyante tams tathaiva bhajamy aham.* 'As all surrender unto Me, I reward them accordingly.' One should prudently think, 'If it can happen to insignificant Aindra Dasa—if that rascal can do it—anyone can do it! Then what the hell are we waiting for! Let's go for it!' "

※ ※ ※

When on the night of Aindra's birthday in 2010 he was asked about his book being released, it was clear that he understood the possible consequences. There had already been threats and reprimands, and the book hadn't even been published yet. "If it comes out," he replied, "there is no 24-hour kirtan anymore, because Aindra das is kicked out from the temple."

But his position hadn't weakened: he was as determined as ever to broadcast his message about *hari-nāma-saṅkīrtana*, ISKCON, and the whole Krishna consciousness movement—to preach the value of the Holy Name and that *saṅkīrtana* was the panacea for not only individual struggles, but all the ills of Kali-yuga. And to publish the book.

"When I asked Srila Prabhupada [in a dream] if he'd had the chance to go through my book," he said, "he answered, 'We will see when it is published.' So, because he said that to me, I got serious about getting the book edited and what not, and suddenly, miraculously, so many devotees came forward and offered to edit and proofread and do all the work that was needed.... There are so many nice things in the book! I just wish ... I'd like to share it with devotees."

❧ ❧ ❧

The pressure continued to mount, but Aindra was as committed as ever to maintaining the 24-hour kirtan and performing, increasing, his devotional service—and as direct as ever in his preaching. Even his sternest lectures to his kirtan men had always been delivered with love and concern, meant for their benefit, and there had not been any decrease in his care or affection for them. "Even during this period," remembered Akincana Krishna, who lived in the ashram and sat next to Aindra in kirtan for most of that year, "I found his association extremely sweet, with plenty of light-heartedness and humor. It was maybe the sweetest time I had with him, and I felt tons of his love."

Since 1998, Akincana had spent periods of most years in Vrindavan participating in the kirtan, but now Aindra wanted him to stay longer. "Please," he asked affectionately, "make a plan to stay with us, spend some more time with us."

"He was encouraging me," Akincana recalled. " 'Make a plan in your life that you will spend more time with us.' But he was also calling me out in front of everybody—asking me to commit more fully to staying at the ashram. 'Be part of the solution,' he said. 'If you're not part of the solution, you're part of the problem!' "

"I just want a group of men who are ready to live with me here like *gosvāmīs*!" he continued, choking up with emotion as he spoke.

"It was actually devastating," Akincana recalled, "and I think everyone felt absolutely humbled and completely unqualified."

❧ ❧ ❧

Aindra's priorities remained clear. "Three things are more dear to me than life itself," he told Radha Madhava. "First and foremost is any service to my guru, Srila Prabhupada, in his ISKCON movement. Second is my service to the 24-hour-kirtan *maṇḍalī* in Sri Vrindavan-dhāma. And last but not least is my service to Sri Sri Radha-Shyamasundar. These three are more dear than life to me, so it is impossible for me to separate myself from them."

"But still," he said, "if Radharani were to ask me right now, 'Would you like to continue these services or come back home to Me?' I would lovingly grab the second option. I would go."

Radha Madhava urged him to reconsider, but Aindra would not relent. It was not the first time he had expressed to him his desire to join his Lordships. And when Radha Madhava mentioned how Srila Prabhupada had said that his guru maharaja could have stayed longer but left, disappointed with some of his disciples, Aindra replied without hesitation, "I want to leave, too."

"I don't really want to stay in this world anymore," he told Mukunda Datta.

"I want to die in Vrindavan," he told Giridhari and Ati Sundari. "In the hottest heat of the summer, when there is no one around, at the feet of my Nitai Saci-suta, and all alone with no one to bother me by saying, 'Chant Hare Krishna, prabhu.'"

Aindra's pronouncements were worrisome, but he wasn't about to take the matter of his life into his own hands. "One time I had a dream in which I drowned in the Yamuna," he related. "My body went under and was going down the Yamuna, and I came out in my spiritual body and Radhe-Shyam were standing under the tree on the side of the river, smiling at me as I was coming out of the water. So, I was thinking that maybe I should ... that maybe that's how I would leave my body."

He had also read that if a devotee drowned in the Yamuna, they would achieve Goloka-*dhāma*. "But Goloka-*dhāma* is a big place," he pointed out, "and you may not attain the *vraja-līlās* by doing that ... it is not that just by drowning in the Yamuna you are going to attain the highest aspect of the supreme destination. That's not recommended."

There was also the issue of self-ownership. "Besides," he continued, "these bodies are not *our* bodies. We are thinking that they are our bodies, but actually they don't belong to us. So, we have no right to take the body away from whom it actually belongs to." Whatever the decision, it was not his to make.

And finally, there was service. "We want to serve the original feature of Radharani," he said, "and for that we have to cultivate the right *bhāva*—by cultivating the right *bhāva* in the mood of following the *hlādinī-śakti* in order to give pleasure to Krishna. So, why is it that you want to take poison or strangle yourself, or jump in the Yamuna? We have to question if it is really for the pleasure of Krsna. Are we cultivating that mood of supporting or assisting *hlādinī-śakti* Radha's mood of always staying in Vrindavan and never taking a single step out of Vrindavan to be here for Krishna? Because when Krishna needs us, Krishna wants us, and He turns around and we've hung ourselves, then how will it please Krishna? Krishna wants to use us as an instrument in any capacity—whatever it may be, we should be ready to be that for Him! And that means being here for Him when He needs us to be here. If He wants to take us out, then that's it, you know! …

"So, therefore it's better to be a little cool-headed. Don't commit suicide unnecessarily. If Krishna wants you to commit suicide, He'll let you know. Don't speculate. How do you know that He doesn't want to use you for something else in this lifetime to further His mission? Even if it is only to touch the heart of one soul somewhere down the road? If He wants to use you, then hang on, for God's sake. Be prepared to surrender to His will instead of going off the deep end."

❦ ❦ ❦

During Purushottama Masa, around April, Gopal remembered, Aindra went into "a different space." His door, on which Gopal posted a Do Not Disturb notice, was kept locked, and he made himself available to only close friends. "He revved up his chanting even further, and his kirtans were at a whole other level."

"I'm slow with my rounds today," he complained to Martanda one day. "I chanted only 112." In fact, from at least the time of his disappearance-day offering, he had been chanting a minimum of 116.

When a devotee offered to pay for a vehicle to take Aindra to Radha Kund on the last Ekadasi of the month, Aindra accepted, but only on the condition that there would be absolutely no talking on the way, and he selected only a few of the kirtan devotees to come along. "If anyone talks," Gopal warned them, "I'm stopping the car and throwing you right out and you can walk."

At Radha Kund, Aindra bathed, but he remained separate, internal. When they left, he had the driver take them to Shyam Kutir, by Kusum Sarovar, where there was a Govardhana *śilā* with Krishna's foot impression on it. When they arrived, Aindra put his head on the *śilā* and then told a story. "When I first came to Vraja," he began, "Tamal Krishna Maharaja called me one day and said, 'Come with me; Bhagatji [Srila Prabhupada's *vraja-vāsī* friend and assistant] and I are going to Govardhana.'"

"So, they drove out," Gopal related, "and Maharaja arranged that Aindra would receive some Govardhana *śilās* from the hand of Bhagatji at Shyam Kutir. And so, we were at Radha Kund, and he was telling us all this, and I was wondering why. It seemed like he was going back through all the chapters of his life in Vrindavan. It was a very serious, somber mood.

"And then we went back to Vrindavan."

❦ ❦ ❦

On July 13, Vrindavan das went to say goodbye to Aindra before leaving on a preaching tour of Malaysia. Aindra was in his room, chanting. He had recently been getting absorbed in *gaura-līlā*, Vrindavan had noticed, listening to *Caitanya-bhāgavat* every day, something Vrindavan didn't remember him previously doing.

Vrindavan had gone away several times before and always returned, and each time he left, Aindra had made a bit of a joke of it, rubbing his eyes with balled-up fists and making as if he were crying. This time he was very sober. "I know I'm going to miss you," he said. Then he went back to his chanting.

"Chant a lot of rounds," he told Bhuvanesvara that week—"and make sure you die in Vrindavan."

❦ ❦ ❦

On July 15, in Toronto, Gopal was with Akincana Krishna and several other of Aindra's associates for the kirtan festival. The evening before the festival began, he called Aindra in Vrindavan.

When Gopal heard Aindra's voice on the phone, he could tell that something was wrong. "I had never heard him like that," he later recounted. "I had heard that he had locked himself in his room and wasn't engaging with devotees."

"What's going on, prabhu?" Gopal asked. "What's up?"

"You know what's going on," Aindra replied. He sounded down, upset.

There had been an exodus of kirtan devotees, and the team was down to six. "Aindra blamed himself for that," Gopal reflected. "He felt that they had left because they were no longer inspired to follow him. That was really painful for him. And he thought his readings from the book on Srila Prabhupada's disappearance day had upset devotees and created a negative situation."

On top of that, Gopal and Vrindavan, his two main mridanga players and two of his closest confidants, were away. They'd had an arrangement that one of them would always be there—when one traveled, the other remained. But both were gone, and Aindra was feeling alone.

"Listen, prabhu," Gopal said, wanting to reassure him, "we're here in Toronto doing this festival. I'll get some kirtan men from here, and in two weeks I'll be in Vrindavan and I'll bring them back with me. Akincana says, 'Haribol.'"

"You tell him to get his butt back here as soon as possible," Aindra replied.

"Don't worry, prabhu," Gopal assured him. "I'll be back soon."

Preeti had phoned Aindra from Puri. "Prabhu," she had said, "tomorrow Jagannath will come to Gundica and everyone will get the chance to hug him. What should I ask from Jagannath for you?"

After a few seconds, Aindra had replied, "Tell Krishna to come back to Vrindavan soon."

When Preeti returned, she went straight to the temple for kirtan, carrying gifts from Puri. When she gave Aindra a length of rope from Jagannath's cart, he asked, "What benefit will this bestow?"

"The pujari told me it will improve your health."

He grimaced. "What good is that to me?"

She gave him some sacred dust, and he asked, "What is this dust for?"

"It is also for your health."

"This is too much," he protested. "I just want a little bit to eat."

She handed him some Jagannath *prasādam*.

"Is this also for my health?" he asked.

She and other devotees had been concerned about Aindra's well-being, especially since he hardly took care of himself. When she told him about Jagannath Puri and Ratha-yatra, he advised her, "Don't do too much 'Jagannath, Jagannath.' Don't forget Radharani. If you eat something from Krishna's mouth, it is not as beneficial as eating something from Radharani's mouth. Don't forget Srimati Radharani."

She was also concerned that Aindra's health or safety might be compromised by his worship of red *śilās*. When one South Indian brahmana, in Vrindavan to officiate at a wedding, came to Aindra's room to have darshan of Aindra's *śilās*, including his tray of Ugra-Nrsimha *śilās*, he had been alarmed. "These must be put into water immediately," he'd said. "If They are not, there may be danger in your life, there may be fire, and you may die." But Aindra was more focused than ever in his worship and listened silently, unfazed.

After speaking with Preeti, Aindra went up to his room and met with Balaram, a devotee from Nairobi. "As long as you're in Vrindavan," he told him, "please help us by joining the kirtan department."

"But I'm not pure enough to do 24-hour kirtan," Balaram replied.

"How long will you be here?" Aindra asked.

"Three and a half months."

"Don't worry," he said. "In these three and a half months we will mold you into a pure devotee."

Bhagavata Purana came in and joined the conversation around nine, eventually telling Balaram, "It's getting late, and Aindra Prabhu still has *japa* to chant," and Balaram left shortly thereafter.

※ ※ ※

A little before 10:30, two devotees, Rasikendra das and Gopendra das, heard a strange sound—some kind of explosion, like an electrical transformer box blowing up—and looked out from their rooms opposite the *gurukula* building to see what it was.

Rupa Sanatan das and Vraja Rupa das were chanting *japa* on the *gurukula* roof when they also heard a loud noise. "I thought it was an auto rickshaw driving away from the kitchen after a delivery," Rupa Sanatan said later. They looked around and noticed smoke coming from the exhaust pipe above Aindra's back window. Why would Aindra's stove be on in the middle of summer?

The smoke didn't last long, but they came down from the roof to check it out.

Aindra didn't answer his door when they knocked, but that wasn't unusual. And there was a strange smell, but it was also common for Aindra to cook in the middle of the night. Maybe he had burnt an offering. And just recently, when a devotee had offered him a flower from the altar, Aindra had said that he had been having sinus problems and was taking medicine for it but couldn't smell a thing.

They knocked at Martanda's room next door, but there was no response there either. A DO NOT DISTURB sign was posted on Aindra's door, so they decided to give up on their investigation and retired for the night.

After having finished his seven to ten kirtan shift just a few minutes before, Martanda had gone upstairs and found a weird smell in his room. It smelled like gas, so just in case, he tightened the nozzles on his gas bottles before going to Arjuna Krishna das's room for an hour, and then he too went to sleep.

Arjuna Krishna also smelled something, but pollution and odd smells were so common in Vrindavan that he hardly noticed.

❧ ❧ ❧

The next morning, at 6:30, Adi Kesava das, one of the temple pujaris, noticed that Aindra had not come to dress Radha-Shyamasundar. "It was not unusual," he said. "It had happened many times before. So, he sent Rasikendra to Aindra's room to get him.

A few minutes later, Rasikendra returned and said, "He doesn't answer. DO NOT DISTURB is on the door." Then, almost as an afterthought, he said, "Last night we heard some sound from his room and saw smoke."

Adi Kesava rushed up to Aindra's room and banged on the door. "Aindra!" he called. "Aindra!"

Arjuna Krishna, Damodarastaka, and Martanda all came out to see what was going on.

"We have to break down the door," Adi Kesava said, and ran downstairs to get Security. On the way, he met Sanak Sanatana das, who was managing construction.

"Aindra hasn't come to dress Radhe-Shyam," Adi Kesava said, "and he won't answer the door, and people saw smoke coming from his room last night. We have to break down the door—I'm going to get the carpenter."

"He isn't there," Sanak told him. "The workshop is closed."

They ran back upstairs, where Arjuna Krishna was trying to break the door open with chisels.

Sanak found a big iron pipe at the end of the veranda and slammed it into the small trap in the outer door's bottom right corner. Eventually it gave way and opened against the second, inner door. And after more slamming, the inner door yielded just enough for a small person to climb in through the vent.

Adi Kesava crawled into the blackness. "Don't turn on the lights," Sanak cautioned. "Any spark could cause an explosion."

"There was a strong smell of gas," Adi Kesava later reported. "I was calling out his name. A major part of the room, as well as the Deities, was all black, and the front area near the door had been heavily burnt." The foam-and-rubber sound proofing around the door had all melted away.

"I looked to the right at his computer desk, but he wasn't there. I proceeded forward to the altar and looked to the left." There was a copper water pot on the floor under the heavy back window. Heavy as it was, it would not have been enough to break the triple-paned glass.

Adi Kesava found Aindra's body bowed down, as if offering obeisances, at the feet of Lord Nityananda. At first he thought Aindra might still be alive, unconscious from the gas, but when he saw the condition of the body, he knew it was too late. Aindra was gone.

When the others got the door open, they rushed in and helped carry the body out onto the walkway. The upper body, arms, face, and hands were stiff and burnt red. They placed it on a grass mat and covered it with a saffron dhoti, and laid it outside Aindra's room alongside his Deities and tulasi. When devotees heard what had happened, they came and surrounded it, weeping and inconsolable.

The police arrived an hour or so later and took the body to Mathura for a formal autopsy. The death was ruled an accident— leaking gas from Aindra's canister's valve or piping had ignited, and a fireball had swept through the room and depleted the oxygen. With his weakened sense of smell, Aindra would not have noticed the leak, and the reinforced windows and tightly sealed door—and the fire itself—would have prevented his escape. When he hadn't been able to get out, he had taken eternal shelter at the feet of his beloved Lordships Sri Sri Nitai Saci-suta.

The body was released that afternoon, then taken to a ground-floor room outside the temple guesthouse, bathed, wrapped in cloth, placed on a bamboo stretcher, and covered with *mahā* garlands from the Deities. Devotees then carried it in a kirtan procession around the temple, through the streets of Vrindavan, and to the Yamuna. At Keshi Ghat it was submerged in the holy river and, just after 6:30, honored by hundreds of adoring devotees, consumed by the flames of cremation.

⚜ ⚜ ⚜

In October, just three months after Aindra's departure—after years of hard work, with the help of many devotees, and despite efforts to prevent it—*The Heart of Transcendental Book Distribution* was published and distributed around the world.

And today, more than ten years later, as this current volume nears completion, all two thousand copies of *The Heart of Transcendental Book Distribution* have sold out, and, in addition to countless online views and downloads, a second edition is going to print.

Having to choose between the book, which represented his whole heart, and his service to Radha-Shyamasundar and the 24-hour kirtan had been more than Aindra could bear. "Ultimately," one friend commented, "Krishna made the arrangement that he could have both. The book was published, and he got the full *sevā* of eternal 24-hour kirtan and the full *sevā* of Sri Sri Radha-Shyamasundar—in Goloka Vrindavan."

EPILOGUE

GOPAL DAS:
When the news came out that Aindra Prabhu had left his body, the whole world of ISKCON immediately started doing kirtan. Spontaneously. Some devotees went out on *hari-nāma-saṅkīrtana*, some started groups for kirtan, some started twenty-four hours of kirtan in their home temples. In Australia, young devotees just showed up at the temple and started doing kirtan for twenty-four hours. And now 24-hour kirtans have become a standard in ISKCON. He inspired a whole generation who might never have taken up that standard of Krishna consciousness.

As Aindra said, "The *yuga-dharma* will remain the *yuga-dharma*, and whoever decides to pick it up gets the benefit and the blessings. And that cannot be institutionalized or categorized."

The *saṅkīrtana* movement is increasing around the world—people are getting more and more into it—and much of that comes from Aindra....

He didn't see himself as an artist; he saw himself as another brahmachari in ISKCON serving Srila Prabhupada's mission. The main thing about his chanting was the depth and maturity of his *bhāva*. It came from sixteen rounds of *japa*, the four regulative principles, the morning program, and reading, primarily *Śrīmad-Bhāgavatam*.

When we heard his kirtan, we could hear *kṛṣṇa-līlā* coming out of the Holy Name. *Nāma, rūpa, guṇa, līlā*. It was manifesting when he was chanting Hare Krishna. And that's due to the depth of his spiritual *bhajana* and practice. A lot of pure bhakti shakti was manifested through his kirtan.

What Rama Raya is doing is a clear example of Aindra's legacy—the *yuga-dharma*, beginning on the streets of New York City, which Aindra said was his favorite place to preach outside Vrindavan, weathering it every single day for eight years. It's really amazing.

Other *kīrtanīyas* are also part of that legacy. Aindra Prabhu inspired them to do kirtan in *their* way—to be original. "Don't copy me," he said. "Develop your own style, and chant and lead kirtan like that. We don't want 'cookie-cutter' devotees; we want people to be who they are, to be themselves and make their contribution and their offering. When originality manifests itself, it's coming from the heart."

RAMA RAYA DAS:
Unless we're fully self-realized, we are invariably materially attached, which makes us disqualified, or unfit, to truly value the association of a pure devotee when they're present. So, a large part of serving and trying to associate with a departed Vaishnava when they leave is a very powerful process of purification, transformation. One who is sincere in it and wants to continue their Krishna consciousness has to accept the powerful *anārtha-nivṛitti* process that the fire of separation will put them through.

In the case of someone like Aindra—who was so amazing and advanced—practically speaking, the position he attained, the level he was on, was beyond belief to most devotees. Ofttimes, pure devotees are misunderstood, neglected, or even offended. Ultimately, Srila Bhaktisiddhanta Sarasvati Thakur said, this material world is not a fit place for a gentleman. Why? Because someone who is actually a gentle man, a *paramahaṁsa*—they're not meant to be in this world.

Aindra very strongly desired to go back home, back to Godhead, to be with Radha and Krishna, to serve Them eternally. He always recognized the compromised position of having a material body and being in the material world. He wanted to rectify his condition of having "a rotting stool-bag-like body of an Aindra das." "As soon as possible," he would say. "Back home, back to Godhead, *ki jaya*! The sooner, the better *ki jaya*! As soon as possible *ki jaya*!"

We always have to remember that when we are talking about loving devotional service with Krishna, that means reciprocation. As Srila Prabhupada said, in the impersonal philosophy there is no reciprocal relationship, but in the personal philosophy there is.

So Krishna from His side wanted someone like Aindra to come back home to Godhead as soon as possible. We want to have a proper crew here; we want qualified devotees here to conduct the mission of Srila Rupa Goswami, who was established in the material world in order to fulfill the desire of Lord Chaitanya. We wish to have such devotees here. But Krishna wants qualified devotees with Him. So, we can temper our feelings of separation from Aindra by knowing that Krishna is very pleased and satisfied having Aindra with Him at long last....

"I have said it so many times," Aindra told us. "I could shout it so loud that your ears would pop off, and I will keep telling you until the day I die: *Hari-nāma-saṅkīrtana*! We have to place *hari-nāma-saṅkīrtana* back into its rightful place of dignity, in the forefront of this Hare Krishna movement. It's so essential for the proper growth of this movement. Otherwise we get a deformed child; we don't get the desired result."

He would say, "I am just as sinful as anybody—I'm nobody special—but I have the experience of doing ten, twelve, fourteen hours of *saṅkīrtana* a day for years and years. You gain that experience and see what happens to you."

His most powerful and important legacy is for everyone to take up *hari-nāma-saṅkīrtana*. It's not Aindra's idea alone; it's not even Prabhupada's idea alone; it's the conclusion of all the acharyas and Lord Chaitanya Mahaprabhu Himself—this is the way to do it.

So, if we want to remember Aindra, if we hope to gain his

association again and be with him in Nitya Navadwip and Nitya Nikunj, with Radha and Krishna eternally, then while we're in this world we should perform as much *hari-nāma-saṅkīrtana* as possible. It's a very easy thing to understand; we just have to do it. We are not meant to become *jñānīs*, we are not meant to become *yogīs*, and we are certainly not meant to become *karmīs*. We are meant to become *śuddha-prema-nāma bhaktas*....

Vrindavan was very austere back then, and at the same time so sweet. You could really contact the essence of Vrindavan, feel the presence of Radha and Krishna and the eternal associates of the Lord. Aindra was coming out with these recordings, and they were so powerful and went around the world and made so many devotees experience ecstatic symptoms and want to come to Vrindavan.

The revolution of *harināma* was starting; Aindra was rediscovering, excavating Vrindavan's lost glories, its Gaudiya Vaishnava kirtan heritage. Aindra was fulfilling Prabhupada's desire to have 24-hour kirtan manifest in Krishna-Balaram Mandir. And all these wonderful things happened. He was very confident in his discipleship to Srila Prabhupada.

It was a very special time. It was the time of my life, and I thought it would go on forever.

YADAVENDRA DAS:

Every evening in Krishna-Balaram Mandir, Aindra Prabhu performed amazing kirtan. It was magical, and it made a mark on so many people's consciousness. But what did he do during all his other hours—what made that hour so spiritually transformative?

Aindra was passionate in his advocacy of *rāgānugā-bhakti*, spontaneous love of Godhead, and in the need to adopt *rāga-mārg*, spontaneous service to the Lord. He opened this door for me and many others, that if we were serious about making our way to Goloka Vrindavan, we must adopt *rāgānuga-sādhana-bhakti* through *nāma-saṅkīrtana*.

Many devotees have devoted much time and energy to *nāma-saṅkīrtana*, but for Aindra, the heart of *nāma-saṅkīrtana* was *rāgānuga-sādhana*. Some who would like to consider themselves his followers are more focused on his tunes, half-beats, Bangladeshi mridangas, German-reed harmoniums, and other musical elements. But as Aindra said to one fledgling *kīrtanīya*, "You can copy my tunes, but you can't copy my consciousness."

Aindra continues to be a primary inspiration for the *saṅkīrtana* revolution spreading worldwide. But we must draw from his heart as well as his art to experience real change in ours.

AKINCANA KRISHNA DAS:

The first time I saw Aindra Prabhu, my first thought—it struck me so clearly—was, "Oh, now I get what kirtan is supposed to be; it's supposed to be like *that*!" It was on a completely different level. It was just so obvious that this was an incredibly serious person who took this very, very seriously and who had developed his kirtan to a very, very high level of both musical and technical expertise. There was an incredible mood and feeling that he put behind that kirtan. It was really like nothing I'd ever experienced; it left a huge impression on me. I feel like seeing him for those first moments, that's when I entered Vrindavan, that's when I got a little bit of an understanding, "Okay, that's what Vrindavan is really about. It's about people just completely putting their hearts on the line, begging Krishna for some kind of mercy."

He taught me how powerful and ecstatic kirtan can be. I'm super-grateful for that, and I don't think anyone else could have done that for me.

If Aindra were here, I think there would be some aspects of the performance of kirtan today that he would appreciate and some about which he would have very strong commentary. I can't pretend to know exactly what he would say, but definitely any kind of kirtan mixed with ulterior motives—for profit and fame and distinction, for popularity, charging people for kirtans—he would come down on that super, super strong; he was fire and brimstone against it.

"No one ever said that leading kirtan is a cakewalk," he told me. "It's an austerity. It's very difficult to have the necessary purity of purpose, and clout." A good kirtan leader should be a leader, and that's not such a small thing. People look up to you, and that requires having something substantial going for you. You may initially approach it as just an art form and think you have a cool melody or beat, but you really stick with it, doing kirtan and leading kirtan, there's a certain amount of purification comes, and a certain amount of realization: It isn't as easy as just coming up with a good tune; you actually have to gain some spiritual advancement to do it in a profound way.

And we have Aindra Prabhu's example of someone who pushed himself so hard in his Krishna consciousness—some of that must be required to inspire people in kirtan.

Being into kirtan means being a serious devotee—initiation, following the principles, chanting your rounds, reading Prabhupada's books, attending the morning program, and all the stuff we recognize as being fundamental to Krishna consciousness.

DHANURDHARA SWAMI:

No one can deny that the inspiration and potency of Balaram came through Aindra—the potency to attract people to Krishna, to get them to surrender to Krishna, to get them attached to Krishna's Holy Name. When the dust settles, what is left is thousands of people inspired—a spirit of devotion and bhakti that brought people to the lotus feet of Krishna and gave them such intense attraction to the Holy Name. He was able to inspire such a broad range of people who felt Krishna's potency through him—even people coming from different spiritual masters with different views. And I think many of us didn't realize the extent of this until after he left and we saw so many people come forward whose lives were changed. This is the real test and potency of a spiritual personality—that people took up his mood of bhakti.

Among people who come to Vrindavan, or are attracted to Vrindavan, there is often some interest in higher subjects. And more than anybody else, Aindra kept those people within Prabhupada's mission. He had interest in those subjects, but he so vividly demonstrated that the foundation of attaining realizations in that area is dedication to the mission of your spiritual master. Something extraordinary and inspired was coming through him to change so many people's lives—in the mood of Srila Prabhupada.

BHAGAVATA PURANA DAS:

The 24-hour kirtan in Vrindavan is not going to stop. Prabhupada wanted it, and Aindra Prabhu reinforced that desire. And when all of us are long gone from the face of this earth, there will still be people carrying on the *saṅkīrtana* mission, the *yuga-dharma*.

What did I learn from Aindra? I learned humility.

KAUSTUBHA DAS, recounting the first time he saw Aindra, in Vrindavan, 1989, sitting alone in the practically empty temple room one morning after class, chanting and playing harmonium before Sri Sri Radha-Shyamasundar:

He appeared austere. It was cold, and he was wrapped in a ragged wool shawl. His music was unlike anything I had heard before. The melody was stripped bare. A desolate voice accompanied only by a frail harmonium scale, slow and slightly off beat—crawling, barely dragging along. His song was the cry of a dying man. A man in the desert, drying up and desperate, crying for some water—just a small cup—just a drop. It was almost pitiful, but hauntingly beautiful—like nothing I'd heard before. It sounded so remorseful, so humble and completely sincere. It was the first time I heard a man desperately crying out to God.

Spiritual practitioners go through their ups and downs. We struggle to find footing, a place where we can grow. But Aindra's practice was solid and fixed. Year after year, I could always count on him being there, doing what he always did—what he only did—kirtan, kirtan, kirtan. When I would sit on that checkered marble floor, Aindra on my left, Prabhupada's samadhi behind him, Radha-Shyamasundar on my right, the sun going down over the temple courtyard, without fail I would say to myself, "There is absolutely no better spot to be on the face of this Earth than right here, and there is absolutely no better engagement than this, right now." The exquisite melodies. Night after night. Everyone submerged. Those times were so incredibly precious. The beauty, the love—we were sitting in the presence of God.

GOVINDA DAS:
Aindra was always a musician, but it wasn't his musical talent that he was known for. He was known for uttering every single syllable in the Holy Name in so much depth and with so much focus and concentration and so much genuine affection and care for the Holy Name, for Krishna, that it just touched everyone's heart.

He was just so genuine. The relationship that he offered people, it was so real. You could understand that this guy was real; he wasn't faking it. When you saw him sad, he was sad; when he seemed happy, he was happy. He never faked it. That was him.

GIRIRAJ SWAMI:
Aindra Prabhu, just by residing in Vrindavan and doing kirtan with the consciousness he had, was actually purifying the whole world. He was giving shelter to people everywhere, whether they were aware of it or not. Many devotees themselves did not realize until Aindra left how much he meant to them or to the movement or to the planet. He was such a fixture in Vrindavan that one could take him for granted, assume that he would always be there. And he was always there, in the same place, doing the same thing, even looking the same. He seemed to never age. He was such a constant presence in Vrindavan, in the Krishna-Balaram temple, in the 24-hour kirtan, that I for one never imagined what the kirtan or the temple or Vrindavan would be without him, what life would be without him. He was like the oxygen we breathe. It is always there, so we don't think about it. But it gives us life....

We have a lot to learn from Aindra Prabhu. I pray that the feelings his departure has awakened in us, or elicited from us, will continue, that his concern and care for us will be realized in our continued efforts to fulfill that ideal of internally relishing the Holy Name in meditation on Krishna and externally extending the mercy of the Holy Name to others.

RADHANATH SWAMI:
I believe every stone, brick, and pillar of Krishna-Balaram Temple and every tree and particle of sacred dust in Raman Reti is permeated with the sound vibration of Aindra Prabhu's devotion. If we open our hearts we will hear. Aindra Prabhu exported the sweetness of Vrindavan's love throughout the world and we are forever grateful.

AINDRA DAS:
Hari-nāma-saṅkīrtana is ideally loud chanting of the Holy Name for three purposes—to develop love of God, to glorify Him, and for the benefit of others. It is selfless, for celebrating God and to help anyone within earshot. Unfortunately, a semblance or a lesser form of kirtan

is becoming prevalent today. It is materially motivated, or let us say it does not have love of God as the goal. It has mundane motives. Real *saṅkīrtana* is pure, giving, without any holding back. The heart is at the center of real glorification, real kirtan, but it's a science too, handed down by the sages. One should learn this science with full dedication.

There are various kinds of chanting. The lowest kind involves the desire for material gain: people want things in this world and they chant to get them. A little higher is shadow chanting, which is about liberation from the material world. This seems to be a spiritual goal, but for Vaishnavas it's just the beginning, and it is distasteful—it's not about love of God but about wanting to get out of material misery. That's still a material motivation. And then there is the kind of chanting that results in *prema-bhakti*, pure love. This is what our lineage teaches. This is real kirtan.

Lord Chaitanya's movement is meant to give the world *prema-nāma-saṅkīrtana*. This is why Prabhupada came west—to offer the highest benefit, pure love of God, to one and all. We must learn to chant purely, under those who have genuine love, and in this way we can awaken pure devotion, especially for Radha and Krishna. This is what kirtan is really all about.

AINDRA DAS (VARSHANA, 2009):

Please remember, and I beseech you again and again, please remember: Worldwide ISKCON grassroots *nāma-saṅkīrtana* revolution!

Revolution means revolution. It means we have to shed pounds and gallons and gallons of blood to get the job done. We have to turn this movement inside out, upside down—whatever we have to do—but we have to put *nāma-saṅkīrtana* back into its rightful place of dignity in the forefront of our movement. It's absolutely essential for the proper growth of our movement.

Those who have understood this are awake to the need of the hour, and those who have not understood it are still sleeping. It's time to wake up and understand what is the responsibility of every man, woman, and child in this movement—to take seriously that dharma which Lord Chaitanya Himself inaugurated for the deliverance of all the fallen conditioned souls for the rest of this Kali-yuga. There are another 427,000 years left to Kali-yuga. The *yuga-dharma* doesn't change. The next yuga is Satya-yuga, and for them, contemplative, peaceful meditation is where it's at. But in Kali-yuga you've got to get fired up! Every one of you fired up: chanting, dancing—from the heart, like you really mean it, like you really want Lord Chaitanya's mercy so that you can even think, you can even hope, to go back home, back to Godhead in this lifetime.

It's not a joke; it's the real thing. So stand up and do what's right. Do the real thing: perform *nāma-saṅkīrtana* daily for as many hours as possible and you'll get there—I guarantee it. Not that I guarantee it; Lord Chaitanya has guaranteed it. It's the right thing to do: perform *nāma-saṅkīrtana* wherever you go in this world, and help others understand the need to augment the performance of *nāma-saṅkīrtana*, to increase the performance of *nāma-saṅkīrtana*, on a regular daily basis in every major city all over the world....

The soul has to go home, back to Godhead, and the way that's going to happen is that the soul agrees to engage all his psychophysical energies and his whole heart in the performance of *sneha, saṁyuktā hari-nāma-saṅkīrtana*. *Sneha* means with affection; *saṁyuktā* means complete engagement. Full on! Fired up! And back home, back to Godhead in this lifetime. Don't let anyone tell you it can't be done. It *can* be done—by adopting the proper process. And the process, which has been ordained by Sri Chaitanya Mahaprabhu, Lord Nityananda, and all the acharyas in the disciplic succession, is *hari-nāma-saṅkīrtana*. And don't let anyone tell you anything different....

You have to allow every day to be a festival. Then your heart is in the right place. That's what Radhe-Shyam wants for you—every day a festival: chanting, dancing, feasting, and philosophy.... For me, the festival never ends.

ABOUT THE AUTHOR

Kalachandji das (Carl Herzig, PhD) is a professor of English in Davenport, Iowa, where he teaches courses in creative and expository writing, sacred poetry, film, and the *Bhagavad-gita*, and leads service-learning trips to Vrindavan, India. Born and raised in New York City, he was introduced to Krishna consciousness by his brother, Tamal Krishna Goswami, in 1969 and was formally initiated in 2013 by His Holiness Giriraj Swami. He has published numerous articles and works of fiction, nonfiction, and poetry and edited dozens of others, including *I'll Build You a Temple: The Juhu Story* (and all other publications), by Giriraj Swami; *Hiding in Unnatural Happiness*, by Devamrita Swami; *Ocean of Mercy*, by Bhakti Charu Swami; *Reason and Belief, Yoga for the New Millennium*, and *A Hare Krishna at SMU*, by Tamal Krishna Goswami; and *A Transcendental Diary* (*Vol. 5*), by Hari Sauri das. He has served as Director of Writing in Iowa; Testing Coordinator for the University of California-Santa Barbara; Visiting Scholar for Humanities Iowa; reviewer for literary and creative journals; and evaluator for the U.S. Senate Youth Program, the Iowa Humanities Board, and the Illinois Council for the Humanities, and currently serves on the Bhaktivedanta Book Trust's Editing Review Panel. In 2007 Aindra Prabhu brought him to Vrindavan to edit Aindra's book, *The Heart of Transcendental Book Distribution*.